DIVINE

Or

DEMONIAC?

SPIRITUAL MOVEMENTS
AND THE ENEMIES WITHIN

DIVINE

OR

DEMONIAC?

SPIRITUAL MOVEMENTS
AND THE ENEMIES WITHIN

Dhanesvara Das

Shastra-chakshusa Press
2019

Readers interested in the subject matter of this book are invited to comment on our Facebook page: www.facebook.com/DivineOrDemoniac

Please visit the website www.DivineOrDemoniac.com for more details

Quotations from *Bhagavad-gita As It Is*, *Srimad Bhagavatam*, courtesy of Krishna Books, Inc. Quotations of Shrila Prabhupada's letters courtesy of Bhaktivedanta Archives.

Ordering Information:
Quantity sales. Special discounts are available on quantity purchases by corporations, associations, and others. For details, contact through the Facebook page above.

Divine Or Demoniac? Spiritual Movements and the Enemies Within / Dhanesvara Das—1st edition March 2019

ISBN 978-1-7337744-4-4
Library of Congress Control Number: 2019935874

Dedication

To my eternal Divine Master
His Divine Grace A. C. Bhaktivedanta Swami Prabhupada,
by whose grace the Absolute Truth is revealed to the world,

To my *param guru* His Divine Grace Shrila Bhaktisiddhanta,
by whose grace we take courage to preach boldly,
and discern the divine from the demoniac,

And to all of the Lord's devotees who have suffered
at the hands of the demoniac elements,

With the hope that no one will ever again
be victimized in the name of religion

"The truth is propagated in a two-fold way, viz.— positively by the method of direct support, and negatively by the method of opposition. The truth cannot be known by the positive method alone. Propaganda by the method of opposition, more than the presentation of the positive aspect, brings more brilliantly in the world the appearance and glorification of the truth."

– Shrila Bhaktisiddhanta Sarasvati Thakur

Contents

Preface

Some twenty years ago a series of bread crumbs were strewn before me which I followed out of intrigue and curiosity. Gradually the information I picked up bit-by-bit formed a pattern of dots. The dots gradually morphed into a picture, and finally the picture presented a story that wanted to be told.

Wanted is not quite the correct word. Rather I was pressed to tell this story, and not just once, but again and again over those twenty years. Pressed is also not the right word, impelled is much more accurate, the force of which grew to the point where, despite my hesitation, I could no longer say "no."

I write that as a way of saying that I did not intentionally set out to write this book. That is, I did not begin with a conclusion and go looking for supporting evidence. Rather the information coming to me challenged me to question what I "knew," and as I did, I learned that what I "knew" could more accurately be called assumptions. That is, ill-placed, and even, wrong assumptions, in light of the new evidence.

That is the way of all discovery – the willingness to question one's assumptions, and especially in pursuit of a "higher understanding" of life, to question the assumptions we build our lives on. And isn't that what we must do as we strive to reach the ultimate goal of life? Isn't it necessary to overturn every last one of our assumptions until we come face-to-face with *the* Truth – truth with a capital "T"?

1

Yet everyone in this world is very attached to the world they've built around their assumptions. Their assumptions allow themselves to think this world is a nice place where they can live happily, find security, love and enjoyment – especially those who go about it in a religious, or "spiritual" way.

But although assumptions are castles of sand, the enjoyers of this world are very attached to their castles, and vehemently protect them. *Don't touch the sand castles!*

Well, if we won't disturb our own sand castles to dig down to the bedrock of fact and truth, time and tide will inevitably wash the castles away, along with our false assumptions.

However, distinguishing facts from assumptions can be an adventure if we take courage and loosen our grip on what we think we know, and are willing to look at evidence that might challenge, or even contradict our assumptions. Can we survive the journey? Although it might be a bit scary, by continuing we will certainly find the bedrock of Truth where we can become securely established.

In the final analysis the sand castles will assuredly be vanquished, but we have the choice about how it will happen. Which way will we choose? Lost to disillusionment, sadness, confusion and angst? Or intentionally demolished and replaced with permanent structures built on Truth and understanding?

Acknowledgements

I fall again and again at the feet of my eternal master His Divine Grace Shrila A. C. Bhaktivedanta Swami Prabhupada, expressing my unending gratefulness for educating me in the spiritual science, allowing me to see through the eyes of shastra. I pray that by his mercy I might contribute something to his mission.

I fall again and again at the feet of His Divine Grace Shrila Bhaktisiddhanta Sarasvati, my *param guru*, who lends his strength as the Lion Guru, to say what needs to be said as a fit chanter of the kirtan of Hari.

I want to extend great thanks and appreciation to the work of religious scholars and historians Robert Eisenman and the late Hans Joachim Schoeps, who, courageously pursuing truth over acceptance, challenged the establishment consensus to reveal the true identity of the "Jewish-Christians." Their books were the major source material for Part One of this book, and served to put Part 2 in a much broader historical perspective. I also want to thank the late authors Michael Baigent and Richard Leigh, whose books provided the bread crumbs I began following, leading eventually to this work.

I am greatly indebted to my good friend and confidant, Vidura Dasa, who has been of inestimable help in writing this book. He has acted in the role of advisor, editor, counselor and friend. Without the selfless hours he gave of his time, and without his friendship and feedback, this book would be of much poorer quality.

A conversation with my brother, Randall Rousse, set me on this journey. I want to thank him for his friendship, and for introducing me to the *Dead Sea Scroll Deception*. And many thanks to my sister Christine Allyson, for long conversations about all aspects of this book, and her steadfast encouragement.

Dhira Govinda and Saunaka Rsi Prabhus, due to their experience, were very valuable resources regarding child abuse in ISKCON.

Their observations and guidance are gratefully acknowledged. I also want to acknowledge Jitarati and Hansadutta Prabhus for their determination and struggle to keep Shrila Prabhupada's original books in print, and for their helpful knowledge regarding the history of changes to Shrila Prabhupada's books.

Thanks to Jitarati Prabhu, Bhaktin Emily and Sophia Kucherenko and her husband for their financial support. Warm appreciation to Kristina Guley for her artistic cover art, and a special warm thanks are due to my many friends who read the manuscript and offered helpful feedback and encouragement: Hansadutta Dasa, Anuttama Devi Dasi, Bhakti Lata Devi Dasi, Bhaktin Emily, and others who will remain unnamed due to the controversial nature of this book.

Introduction

This book is about freedom. Your freedom, and the freedom of those generations that will succeed you. Specifically, your freedom to live in the way of your choosing, to understand and believe in a reality according to the highest understanding, and the truths connected with it.

There are forces in this world who want to limit your knowledge and understanding. They believe your purpose in this world is to serve *them*. This is not an exaggeration.

Modern man is allowed freedom within certain limits. The fact is that he is so conditioned that he does not, indeed, cannot, recognize his constraints, and indeed, his conditioned nature is such that he is happy to live within them. Like a hamster in a cage content to run in its wheel going nowhere. Like the hamster, he gets up every day and runs in his hamster car to his workplace in the morning, and then again runs home at the end of the day. And for all his trouble he gets some pellets of food and sex with his mate. That he continues to do this for a lifetime, and even trains his children to do the same, is a testimony to the success of the system he functions within. His situation is analogously, but accurately, portrayed in the movie *The Matrix*. If you have not seen it, you should.[1]

Those who have created this system and control you cannot maintain their control without limiting your understanding of reality. They desire to keep you in a cul-de-sac of ignorance regardless of the consequences (karma) you will be subjected to as a result.

In other words, they are happy to let you go to hell (literally) in order to continue their control.

On the other hand, there are those who desire your welfare and who are working to give you the keys to eternal freedom. They are your ever well-wishers.

These two camps exist in a state of eternal conflict, constituting a never-ending clash of civilizations.

Most people are totally unaware of this conflict – especially the fact that they themselves are the booty over which this battle is waged. Consequently they are too often unsuspectingly victimized. We cannot be saved from future karmic tragedy unless we participate in our liberation, but to do so we must understand that there is a battle being waged for our energy and our soul. Understanding that, we must actively engage in the process of emancipation from the dark side.

This is not as easy as it sounds because of the many tricks employed to snare the innocent and unsuspecting. This is an age of deception, and without proper training people are easily misled, just as cattle innocently and unsuspectingly are led through a gate to the slaughterhouse.

Enough euphemism, let's get to the point.

This world is controlled by literal demons who think this world belongs to them, and that your very purpose, and your *only* purpose is to serve them. You do so most unsuspectingly by participating in the economic system that controls this world. By your work, and every time you use their money, you make them richer and continue your own enslavement. Your energy is being usurped while you imagine that you are pursuing a "satisfying career" or some such nonsense. The fact of the matter is that the system they have created for our living is a slaughterhouse for the soul, what to speak of the very destruction of this world.

These forces have controlled this world for millennia, and they maintain that control by immediately suppressing any challenging forces, and ideas, that might undermine their control – especially religious concepts that offer alternative answers to existential questions. The overlords want people smart enough to work, but too dumb to ask any questions about how this world is arranged.

In this book I examine their efforts to usurp the Eternal Religion and transform it into a religion of materialism, devoid of spiritual potency. Our story begins by demonstrating that the Eternal Religion shone brightly in Palestine two thousand years ago. So brightly that tens-of-thousands were following its principles until the demonic Roman powers arrived on the scene. Because of their refusal to be exploited, the Romans destroyed them. I also demonstrate how for a very small, but very important set of people, the same thing is taking place today. My Vaishnava readers are a part of this small, but very important set of people.

The Eternal Religion has manifest again in the West in the form of the Hare Krishna Movement, and again is under attack – this time by insiders who have usurped the mission. The attack is directed at its ideology, followers, and principles of living that free people from slavery, allowing them to use their time in service to, and worship of God. This right way of living is called Sanatana Dharma, or Varnashrama Dharma, but you are not allowed to have it because it conflicts with, and undermines, your ability to be exploited.

Can you awaken to the reality of this world if it is shown to you? Sadly, many will refuse to do so. Overcome by cognitive dissonance they cannot feel their chains, and prefer to see the world as a benign place catering to their happy existence. However, such shirking from the truth only perpetuates their imprisonment.

Self-realization requires that we see beyond false appearances to the reality beneath. But we must be willing to look and learn. And know how to fight back. It is the purpose of this book to make you so aware, and give you the method for achieving victory.

Some Helpful Background Information

Who was the historical Jesus? Many people have searched for the answer to that question, only to be frustrated in their efforts. Professor of Religious Studies at California State University, Long Beach, Robert Eisenman, has given what may be the closest answer that we might ever find. It comes to us somewhat obliquely through Jesus' brother James, for as Eisenman says: "whatever James was, (and he is much more knowable and accessible through the historical record) Jesus, as his closest living heir and predecessor, was as well."

This book offers some insights into both Jesus and James based on the direct evidence of the Dead Sea Scrolls and Nag Hammadi Texts. These scrolls make direct reference to them, their teachings and followers. However, the history presented in the scrolls is dramatically different from traditionally accepted accounts. This should come as no surprise as the direct evidence of the scrolls was only revealed in the early 90s, and quickly followed with a concerted effort by an academic consensus to quash the new revelations.

However, the direct evidence reveals that the religious beliefs and practices of Jesus and James were remarkably similar to that of a modern day "new" (to the West) spiritual movement – the Hare Krishnas. If you are younger than 50 you may never have heard of the Hare Krishnas, who were quite a well-known colorful group of young adults that would chant and dance on city streets everywhere in the 60s and 70s. Their movement was however decimated in the 80s, to the point where they are relatively unknown today.

Having been a follower and practitioner of this religion since the early 70s I was quite intrigued to learn of its similarity with the early Christians. I was likewise intrigued to learn that the demise of the movement of Jesus and James, and the demise of the Hare Krishna Movement had so many parallels. This book offers a comparison of that history. For those unfamiliar with the Hare Krishna Movement and their teachings a bit of background information will aid their appreciation of the comparison.

The Eternal Religion and the Hare Krishna Movement

The Hare Krishna Movement first appeared in the West in 1965, introduced in America by an elderly Indian Swami who desired to share India's rich and ancient spiritual heritage with the world. He was teaching the Eternal Religion, the essence of the Vedas, the world's oldest body of spiritual literature. His name was A. C. Bhaktivedanta Swami, (affectionately called Shrila Prabhupada by his followers) and his spiritual lineage was the "Vaishnava" sect – worshippers of Vishnu, or Krishna, as God. Like Christianity, Vaishnavism is a monotheistic religion.

The Eternal Religion teaches that the Supreme Lord is the father of all living beings, and the fulfillment we seek can be found by

Figure 1 A. C. Bhaktivedanta Swami - Shrila Prabhupada

establishing our relationship with Him. The process of achieving that connection is glorification of, and meditation on, the Lord's names. God has many names, one of which is Krishna, meaning "the most beautiful," another is Rama, meaning "the most powerful," and there are many, many others such as Vishnu, Vamana, Narasimha, etc.

The main prayer and meditation of the Vaishnavas is the Hare Krishna maha-mantra: *Hare Krishna, Hare Krishna, Krishna Krishna, Hare Hare/ Hare Rama, Hare Rama, Rama Rama, Hare Hare.* Just as the Bible exhorts us to glorify the name of God, the Vaishnava devotees would chant this maha-mantra on city streets for hours at a time, and thus became widely known as "the Hare Krishnas," in the 60s and 70s.

The Eternal Religion teaches that all living beings in this world are spiritual beings (spiritual energy) that inhabit bodies of material energy. As spiritual beings we have the same qualities as the Lord – we are persons endowed with intelligence and reasoning ability, and experience emotions such as love, joy, desire, sorrow, etc,. The Supreme Lord has unlimited capacity to experience these qualities whereas we experience them only to a limited degree. For example, we are conscious of our body and feelings, but Krishna is conscious of the feeling and desires of everyone.

This is due to His presence as the Supersoul in the hearts of all living beings. This all-pervading aspect of the Lord corresponds to the Catholic concept of the Holy Spirit.

The Christian worldview is similar to the Vaishnava worldview in that both are replete with an understanding that evil or demonic beings constantly vie with spiritual forces for control of this world and the capture of the many souls within it. The theme of good v. evil, the Sons of Light v. the Sons of Darkness, etc., is played out in both, and is a central thesis of this work.

The driving force of Shrila Prabhupada's movement was his presentation of the essential spiritual wisdom of the Vedas, in his

Figure 2 Hare Krishna devotees happily chanting on city streets in the 60s and 70s

books *Bhagavad-gita As It Is, Srimad Bhagavatam*, and many others. This ancient wisdom explains in detail the spiritual and material energies, and their interaction, and in so doing present the magnificent vista of a spiritual worldview that answers all the existential questions of life, at once satisfying to both the intellect and the heart. The revelation of such powerful spiritual truths, previously absent in any form in the West, gave the rebellious youth a cause to rally around – a revolution of spiritual understanding. Eager to share it with the world they would spend endless hours distributing the transcendental books of Shrila Prabhupada. Translated into more than 75 languages, these transcendental literatures facilitated the spread of the Hare Krishna Movement to more than 100 countries within 20 years.

The Hare Krishna Movement was an American and European phenomenon of the 60s and 70s, attracting thousands of youth to a spiritual path that was far more strict and restrictive than anything they had been raised with. They were willing to accept such a strict regimen as the means of achieving the ultimate goal of spiritual life – full realization of their spiritual nature.

Another aspect of Christianity that corresponds to Vaishnava theology is that of Jesus' role as prophet and spiritual teacher. The Vaishnava equivalent is the self-realized guru, who, having realized God, is in direct contact with God. The bona fide guru is considered the external manifestation of the Lord and his instructions are thus considered as coming directly from God. Shrila Prabhupada is accepted as such a self-realized, bona fide guru by his followers.

As the guru and *Acharya* (one who teaches by example) of the Hare Krishna Movement, Shrila Prabhupada is to his followers what Jesus Christ is to Christians. The reader should not be surprised to observe that the statements of Shrila Prabhupada are accepted by his followers with absolute faith, just as Jesus' words in the Bible are also accepted as absolute.

Another Vaishnava *Acharya* that is quoted extensively herein, and whose words are accepted as scripture, is Shrila Bhaktisiddhanta Sarasvati, Shrila Prabhupada's spiritual master.

About the Book

The book is arranged in three parts – the first regarding the manifestation of the Eternal Religion in first century Palestine, with evidence directly from that time that the Eternal Religion of the Vedas made up the theology and practices of Jesus and his followers. How has it happened that the "teachings of Jesus" no longer reflect those truths? We investigate this question, tracing out not only how, but why, "Christianity" was transmogrified, in the process revealing the actions of the demonic forces and their control of this world, as *the* over-arching characteristic of the present age, up to the present time. Understanding that history will help us identify how the same forces are acting today.

The second part focuses on the manifestation of the Eternal Religion in Twentieth Century America, how Shrila Prabhupada wanted his society to function, and how it was undermined and destroyed from within. History is repeating itself, in that the modern manifestation has also been attacked and decimated, and for exactly the same reasons – the determination of the demonic to eliminate spiritual truths in order to maintain their control.

The third part of the book is a call to start the Hare Krishna Movement again, and how to promote and teach the Eternal Religion and protect the effort from destructive influences. It is a call to arms to challenge the supremacy of the demonic powers, through a Spiritual Revolution based on the chanting of the Hare Krishna maha-mantra.

Who is This Book For?

Those who would best appreciate this book fall into four categories: (1) those who love Jesus but are confused, or alienated, by the actions of the "Church," and "Church leaders," (2) the devotees of Lord Krishna who are bewildered and alienated, or have been abused in the Hare Krishna Movement, and need to reconcile how, what should have been a wonderful experience, turned into such disappointment and disaster, (3) those who know something is wrong with the GBC's ISKCON but can't quite put their finger on it, (4) those who have been red-pilled and want to learn how the demonic elements have used and misused religion for their demonic purposes.

Additionally, I am writing for posterity. This book is my "Dead Sea Scroll" – a warning to posterity of how the manipulation and destruction of the Truth serves the purposes of evil. I have no idea what the world may be like in two or three hundred years. It is possible that the trajectory of the Eternal Religion into the future will be similar to that of the past, and there should be some record of what the Hare Krishna Movement once was, and was meant to be. This book is my effort to create that record. If in the future the Lord's mercy floods the world the true history will be written, of which this book will become a part.

Notes about the Text

Information and notes considered supplementary to the text have been placed as footnotes for the reader's easy reference. Other non-critical notes, such as source and page citations, are relegated to the endnotes.

There are two glossaries – one with Christian terminology, and the other a Sanskrit glossary – at the rear of the book. The reader is encouraged to make use of them as necessary for proper understanding of the text.

The reader will note emphasis frequently added to quotes and blockquotes. *Unless otherwise stated* the added emphasis is mine.

Part One

The Eternal Religion
in First Century Palestine

CHAPTER ONE

The Eternal Religion
in First Century Palestine

In 1945 original documents expressing the beliefs and practices of a spiritual movement were discovered in the Middle East.
Refreshingly original – literally out of a time capsule – ancient
scrolls told of a religion, its beliefs, practices and members. The
scrolls revealed a religion quite unlike any other thought to have
had roots in that region.

Upon deciphering the texts, four major characteristics of the
religion were revealed:[1]

1. Direct, personal and absolute knowledge of the authentic
   truths of existence is accessible to human beings, and the at-
   tainment of such knowledge is the supreme achievement of
   human life. This goal can be further stated as "to know oneself, at the deepest level, is simultaneously to know God: this
   is the secret of *gnosis*....Self-knowledge is knowledge of God;
   the self and divine are identical."[2] Their spiritual process was
   not a rational, proposition-like, logical understanding, but a
   knowing acquired by experience, and more importantly, by
   revelation.

2. "A knowing, by and of an uncreated self, or self-within-the self, a knowledge that leads to freedom."[1] Primary among all the revelatory perceptions was the profound awakening that came with understanding that something within was uncreated. This "uncreated self" was understood by the followers as the divine seed, the spark of knowing: consciousness, intelligence, light. This seed of intellect was understood to be the self-same substance of God. It was man's authentic reality. It was the glory of humankind and the divine alike. There was always a paradoxical cognizance of duality in experiencing this "self-within-a-self." Paradoxical by all rational perception as man clearly was not God, and yet in essential truth, was Godly. This mystery and its understanding were considered their greatest treasure.

3. The third prominent element is their reverence for texts and scriptures that were unaccepted by the orthodox fold of the day. Their experience was rich with poetry and so-called myth, both in story and allegory, and also in ritual enactments. They sought expression of subtle, visionary insights inexpressible by dogmatic affirmation. They held a profusion of "inspired texts" and amplified the creation story considerably beyond the simple idea of Adam and Eve. They held that the spiritual creation, which they aspired to achieve, preceded the material creation.

4. In many of their texts God is a unity of both masculine and feminine, and worshiped as the divine Father and Mother.

Perhaps many Vaishnavas will be surprised to hear such descriptions, as they clearly reflect aspects, almost verbatim, of the Vaishnava *siddhanta*. The parallels would respectively be:

1. An unmistakable reference to the concept of self-realization and God realization being identical and the highest goal of life, with an expression of that realization being beyond book learning, and actualized in one's personal experience.

2. The second characteristic properly expresses an understanding of the Vaishnava concept of spirit, and the duality existing in the aspects of *vibhinamsa* and *svamsa,* respectively the living beings who are part and parcel of the Lord, and the Lord Himself, being qualitatively equal and quantitatively different. This concept comes reasonably close to the understanding of *acintyabedabeda tattva*, the simultaneous oneness and difference of the living being and the Lord.

3. This characteristic corresponds to the Vaishnava reverence of the divine message of the Lord revealed in shastra. The Vedas, written in poetic couplets and meter expound upon many wonderful pastimes of the Lord unacceptable to atheists, and therefore relegated to the category of myth. Their acceptance of "inspired texts" is very much like the Vaishnava perceives his own scriptures. Ritual enactments are a social art form by which sacred lore is communicated within a culture, and are also a regular part of Vaishnava culture. A creation story much more complex than the biblical concept of creation in seven days is not unlike the complex treatment of the subject presented in the *Srimad Bhagavatam.*

4. All Vaishnavas will immediately recognize this as the worship of Sri Sri Radha Krishna, although perhaps not identical in content and understanding.

Who were these people and from where did they derive such understanding? The discovered texts were named *The Nag Hammadi Scrolls* after the place they were serendipitously found by a peasant farmer. The codices consist of 52 sacred texts in 13 books written on papyrus, bound in leather and sealed in an earthen jar. They are the long-lost Gnostic gospels that describe the "early church" and its teachings, which make specific, first-hand references to Jesus and his teachings. We learn about Gnosticism and its early history from the Gnostic Society Library homepage:[4]

Gnosis and *Gnosticism* are still rather arcane terms, though in the last two decades the words have been increasingly encountered in the vocabulary of contemporary society. *Gnosis* derives from Greek, and connotes "knowledge" or the "act of knowing." (On first hearing, it is sometimes confused with another more common term of the same root but opposite sense: *agnostic*, literally "not knowing", a knower of nothing.) The Greek language differentiates between rational, propositional knowledge, and the distinct form of knowing obtained not by reason, but by personal experience or perception. It is this latter knowledge, gained from experience, from an interior spark of comprehension that constitutes *gnosis*.

In the first century of the Christian era this term, *Gnostic,* was used to denote a prominent, even if somewhat heterodox, segment of a diverse new Christian community. Among these early followers of Jesus, it appears that an elite group delineated themselves from the greater household of the Church by claiming not simply a belief in Christ and his message, but a "special witness" or revelatory experience of the divine. It was this experience, this *gnosis,* which – so the Gnostics claimed – set the true follower of Christ apart from his fellows.

Again, Vaishnavas will find the explanation of Gnosis familiar. Their explanation is similar to how we would describe our ability to understand the Absolute Truth: by revelation, not "book learning." As Shrila Prabhupada explains it: "When one attains Krishna consciousness, then everything is revealed to him, as everything is revealed by the sun in the daytime."[5]

Reading further I discovered a surprising number of similarities between the spiritual practices of the Gnostics and Vaishnavas. I also discovered an alarming number of efforts made to diminish the spiritual understanding and the potency of the spiritual practices of the "early church" in these years. There was great contention, and forces vied for dominance against one another. This was not amicable rivalry of both sides striving to achieve the one ultimate truth, but the attempt of each to impose their idea of truth on others. In other words, there was an attempt to establish a reigning dogma and quash the opposition.

The Early Currents of Christianity

Modern scholarship suggests that in the early decades of Christianity when mention of Gnostic Christians first appears, that a variety of views, beliefs, and practices co-existed and vied for dominance in the emerging orthodoxy. The ultimate course Christianity would take was as yet undecided, with Gnosticism being but one of the influences forming that destiny. Some of the others will be mentioned below.

Gnosticism was, at least for some time, near the mainstream of the original Christian church. Their strong influence held sway in the developing church even into the 2nd and 3rd centuries. This is witnessed by the fact that one of the most prominent and influential early Gnostic teachers, Valentinus, had been considered for election as the Bishop of Rome during the mid-second century. Born in Alexandria around 100 A.D. he distinguished himself as an extraordinary teacher and leader in the educated and diverse Alexandrian Christian community. In the middle of his life, around 140 A.D., he traveled from Alexandria to the evolving capital of the Church, and in Rome he had an active, public and influential role. Though a member of some influence in the mid-second century, within less than twenty years of his zenith he was forced from the public eye and branded a heretic.

His treatment reflects the growing influences of the now coalescing establishment of the orthodox Roman Church. It had gathered sufficient political power to turn definitively against Gnosticism by the middle of the second century, and against Valentinus as well. Gnosticism's secret knowledge, revelations, scripture and aestheticism were given increasing suspicion, dereliction, and even revilement. By A.D. 180, Irenaeus, the Bishop of Lyon, was attacking Gnosticism as a heresy, and his polemical work continued with increasing vehemence, as did the other orthodox church Fathers throughout the next two centuries.

According to Owens, orthodox Christianity perceived Gnosticism to be its most dangerous and insidious challenge: a feared opponent that the Patristic heresiologists (church fathers involved in determining heresy and dogma) had maligned under many different names. The Roman Church was profoundly influenced by the struggle against Gnostic ideology in the second and third centuries. To counter and defeat their influence, an orthodox theology was inventively fabricated,[6] which would become established as official church dogma[a] (a device that we will see repeated in years to come). Finally by the end of the fourth century the struggle with Gnosticism as represented in the *Nag Hammadi* texts was eliminated and branded as heresy and anathema to Church teachings. Gnosticisms remaining teachers were exterminated or driven into exile, and its sacred books were sought out and destroyed. Scholars seeking to study Gnosticism in later centuries could do so only obliquely through the denunciations of the early church.[7]

The latter part of this history has of course been recorded and known since the early centuries of the Christian era. The discovery of the *Nag Hammadi* texts and the contrasting light they shed on

---

[a] It is worth a reminder that dogma is defined as a religious doctrine that is proclaimed as true without any scriptural support. It is "true" simply by decree of the ecclesiastical authority, in this case, the Roman Catholic Church.

the machinations of the early Church however, is quite remarkable. They reveal that the emerging orthodoxy rejected what seems to be, by a simple and impartial review, potent spiritual teachings.[8] Replacing them with what? An impotent dogma of little genuine spiritual value, created by spiritually inept empiricists. Posterity owes a great debt to those souls who, in an effort to preserve their sacred teachings, sealed them carefully within an earthen jar. That it was buried in the dry desert of Egypt and discovered in an era of mass communications are clearly the arrangement of the Lord. Otherwise, these texts that shed so much light on the "early church" would never have seen the light of day.

More 1st Century Archeological Finds

An expanding cache of scrolls discovered by a shepherd boy near the Dead Sea and the ruins of the former Qumran community, grew in quick succession as more caves were searched. The significant feature of these *Dead Sea Scrolls*, like the *Nag Hammadi* texts, is that they are original documents, unaffected by interpretations of any orthodoxy or historical consensus. As such they give direct evidence and insight into the early church and the disposition of their times.[9] From the scrolls we learn directly what people of the time knew and accepted as truth, and since the current understanding of Christianity is ostensibly based on this history we have the ability to make a comparative study between the religion of Christianity as it stands today, with the religion of the very first "Christians." Citing any differences we can then look to see the influences that brought us to where we currently stand.

The picture most people have of the Palestinian area two millennia ago comes to us from historians such as Josephus and Pliny, as well as the earliest extant Christian writings from the 2nd century AD. Generally in the Western world it is the understanding of these early church fathers that is promulgated by the Christian churches. It is probably safe to say that very few people have studied the period in detail and knowledge of the time is rudimentary at best. However lacking the understanding of the times may be, it is sufficient for the purposes of the Roman Church, which is to provide a context for the early years of Jesus and his activities.

The generally accepted picture of 1ˢᵗ century Palestine is one of a relatively stable political condition, despite the occupation of the Roman army, with a steady Judaic creed practiced by the inhabitants of the area. Peace prevailed for the most part and the Jewish population found the ways and means to co-exist with their Roman governors. In that environment little of note was taking place save the exceptional dumbfounding of the Temple Rabbis by a precocious youth of just 12 tender years. A mostly quiet and peaceful scene. Or was it?

Professor of Religious Studies, Robert Eisenman, was a key figure in making the Dead Sea Scrolls available to both academia and the general public. As a result of his study of the early Christian era, amplified by his study of the scrolls, he paints a compelling picture of a restless era of fermenting political movements and ideologies. Rather than being at peace with their situation, a local and powerful movement was building, threatening the Roman occupiers. Eisenman portrays the times, recounted by authors Baigent and Leigh in their book *The Dead Sea Scroll Deception,* as follows:

> "This movement has centers in a number of places around Palestine, including Jerusalem. It can exercise considerable influence, can wield considerable power, and can command considerable support. It can dispatch men on tasks of recruitment and fund-raising abroad. It can organize riots and public disturbances. It can plot assassinations, and act to carry them out. It can put forward its own legitimate alternative candidate for the position of the Temple's high priest. It can capture and hold strategically important fortresses such as

Masada. Most significantly of all, it can galvanize the entire population of Judea around it and instigate a full-fledged revolt against Rome – a revolt which leads to a major conflict of seven years duration that necessitates the intervention not of a few detachments, but of an entire Roman army." [10]

What is the identity of the movement that is behind such a significant force? The Essenes, and, as Eisenman explains as he leads us through his painstaking research, the "early Church." However, the range and magnitude of these activities stands in stark contrast to the traditional images of the peaceful Essenes and general notions of the early church. Who then were the Essenes?

The "Peaceful" Essenes

The traditional account of the Essenes comes to us from Roman historians Josephus, Philo and Pliny. It is Pliny who identifies the area of the ruins of Qumran as the home of the Essenes. [11] Josephus, echoed by Philo, gives the generally accepted account of who they were: a monastic order, a sect or sub-sect of Judaism, who were both reclusive and peaceful. They were known to hold all possessions in common and required their members to renounce private property. They are considered to have despised pleasure and wealth. They are presented as being on good terms with the established authorities, even enjoying the special favor of Herod, who is said to have also honored them. [12]

Oxford scholar, Geza Vermes, one of the scholars who had access to the entire corpus of scroll literature, suggests that the term *Essene* is derived from the Aramaic word *assayya* meaning healers. This interpretation of the word fosters the image of medical practitioners. The only problem with this interpretation is that the word "assayya" never appears in the Qumran community's own literature, which is strange. But for that matter though, neither does the word "Essene." We are not lost however, as there are alternatives to this mystery. Eisenman found other important characteristics of the community that were reflected in their nomenclature and their references to themselves.

Let's take the trouble to go through the etymology as it is helpful for our understanding of the community itself, its spiritual practices, and clues to the motives of their future persecution. Bear in mind that while the derivation of these terms may seem speculative, it is necessarily so because of the deliberate obfuscation introduced into the church literature throughout the ages. These perturb Eisenman to no end and he frequently rails against it, which we will quote in the pages to come. His detailed investigation however, provides some genuinely revealing insights into the true history of the times. About the Essenes, he writes:

> If the Qumran community never refer to themselves as 'Essene' or 'assayya', they do employ a number of other Hebrew and Aramaic terms. From these terms, it is clear that the community did not have a single definitive name for themselves. They did, however, have a highly distinctive and unique concept of themselves, and this concept is reflected by a variety of appellations and designations. The concept rests ultimately on the all-important 'Covenant', which entailed a formal oath of obedience, totally and eternally, to the Law of Moses. The authors of the Dead Sea Scrolls would thus refer to themselves, as, for example, 'the Keepers of the Covenant.' As synonyms for Covenant and 'Law,' they would often use the same words that figure so prominently in Taoism – 'way,' 'work' or 'works.' They would speak, for instance of 'the Perfect of the Way,' or 'the Way of Perfect Righteousness' – 'way' meaning 'the work of the Law,' or the 'way in which the Law functions,' 'the way in which the Law works.' Variations of these themes run all through the Dead Sea Scrolls to denote the Qumran community and its members.[13]

Eisenman makes further connections for us in his *Habakkuk Commentary*, where he points out a particularly important variation – the *Osei ha-Torah*, which means "Doers of the Law." This term appears to be the source of the word Essene, since the collective form of *Osei ha-Torah* is *Osim*. The collective community then would have been known as "the *Osim*" (pronounced Oseem). This possibility is verified by an early Christian writer, Epiphanius, who speaks of an allegedly heretical Judaic sect [heretical to so-called Orthodox Judaism] that once occupied an area around the Dead Sea. This sect, he says, were called the *Ossenes*.[14]

The key element that Eisenman here points out is that the Essenes were determined followers of the Covenant or Mosaic Law – the Law of Moses. They were intent not only on doing things right, but doing the right thing, as prescribed by the tenets of their faith. This was a major element of their doctrine, one which Vaishnavas can understand was critical to their spiritual development. Those having but little experience in Vaishnava practices know that the strength of their sadhana (daily spiritual practices) directly influences the quality of their consciousness and their ability to follow their own spiritual principles. Thus, strict following of the spiritual practices and principles form the very foundation from which spiritual strength springs. The strict followers of Shrila Prabhupada could likewise also be considered to be "keepers of the way," "doers of the law," or "followers of the way" should we choose to define his instructions for daily sadhana like that.

Likewise for the Essenes, the numerous references to "the way" indicate that this is an essential part of their doctrine, an important aspect of their manifestation of truth.

Complementing the picture of the Essene community and its widespread influence described above, Professor Black of St. Andrews University, Scotland also informs us that the Essenes were large in number and included many other groups:

...provided we do not define Essenism too narrowly, for instance, by equating it exclusively with the Dead Sea group, but are prepared to understand the term as a general description of this widespread movement of anti-Jerusalem, anti-Pharisaic non-conformity of the period.[15]

There are other groups mentioned in the Scrolls and elsewhere, the profusion of which, and their identity, has baffled scholars. Eisenman, through his detailed study provides us with an understanding that tremendously simplifies what is otherwise almost overwhelmingly complicated, and produces an almost impossible enigma. The key to this puzzle is to understand the connection between the names of groups of 1st century Palestine. He concludes:

> By now it should be clear that these are rather esoteric or poetic variations around the same theme. And terms like: Ebionim, Nozrim, Hassidim, Zaddikim (i.e., Ebionites, Palestinian Christians, Essenes, and Zadokites), turn out to be variations on the same theme, and the various phraseologies the community at Qumran used to *refer to itself*, e.g., 'Sons of light', 'Sons of Truth', . . . 'Ebionim,' 'The Perfect of the Way,' do not all designate different groups, but function as interchangeable metaphors.[16]

His research also clearly demonstrates that the movement that can be known as the "early Church" also manifested itself through other groups generally deemed to be separate – the Zealots for example, as well as the Qumran community, and the Sicarii.

These groups, whether as separate entities, or the same entity under various names, are what constitute the political force spoken of above, thus giving further indication that the Essenes had an extremely large following. Not only were the Essenes a large political force pitted against the Roman establishment, they also had a significant spiritual doctrine that ran counter to what was by then established Judaic practices, and the Jewish establishment of the time. The light of their truth, and the staunch deliberateness of their practices, must have had a significant impact on the social and political currents of the time. For a better understanding of what those currents and countercurrents might have been let's take a closer look at their spiritual understanding and practices and how they contrast with those of the religious and political establishments of their time.

Spiritual Understanding and Practices of the Essenes

In his 1,000 page tome, *James, the Brother of Jesus,* Robert Eisenman draws upon a vast array of early church sources, contemporary secular writings, ancient manuscripts and fragments thereof such as the Nag Hammadi scrolls and the Dead Sea Scrolls, and presents a decided alternative to the establishment view of the development of early Christianity, the differences of which are significant to our analysis and evaluation. He shows that James was the inheritor of the legacy of Jesus, not Peter, and that James was the powerful leader of the growing and influential "early church." Eisenman's efforts have been "to resurrect James from the dustbin of history." But we glean much more from his efforts.

Eisenman's arguments make it clear that James was a strict observer of The Law, a Nazarite (Essene), who was unwilling to compromise his principles with foreigners in general, and with the Roman Empire and their Herodian (family of Herod) puppet kings in particular. If James practiced the principles of the Essene and led the Essene community, we can understand that Jesus did as well, for as Eisenman puts it "whatever James was, (and he is much more knowable and accessible through the historical record) Jesus, as his closest living heir and predecessor, was as well."[17] Eisenman is not alone in his conclusions as many others who study the period without prejudice concur. Even the likes of Frederick the Great wrote that "Jesus was really an Essene; he was imbued with Essene ethics."[18]

These ethics are strikingly similar to the practices of the Vaishnavas, as were the beliefs of the Gnostics depicted above. The Essenes were known to be strict vegetarians and are described as such by the Catholic Bishop Epphanius of Constantia in Cyprus (d 403 AD), who was an authority on Jewish sects. He tells us that the Nazoreans differed from other Jews in that they did not sacrifice animals, nor eat flesh thereof.[19] This is extremely unusual for Jews as animal sacrifice figured prominently in Jewish practice of the time, being the *only* means to atone for ones sins. The practice was therefore extremely prevalent and the need for it great, because animal sacrifice as a religious observance, was also attached to most acts of everyday life; any festivity or misfortune was an occasion of sacrifice, and the rivers of blood ran swift on those occasions. Happy were these priests though – the meat of those sacrifices became their meals, at which point the sacrifice was consummated.[20]

Falsified Scripture and Its Reconstruction

The Essenes were opposed to animal sacrifice because they were of the belief that the Torah had been falsified to such an extent that little remained of the original pure text. Hans Joachim Schoeps writes in *Jewish Christianity: Factional Disputes in the Early Church,* that the Essenes thought that requirements of animal sacrifices had nothing to do with the original teachings. Later, church father Clement of Alexandria confirmed these suspicions: "Sacrifices were invented by men to be a pretext for eating flesh."[21]

The Essenes were also of the opinion that all depictions of God in Hebrew Scriptures were falsified, replacing a loving God with one who was afflicted with all the sins and appetites of the most debauched humans. They believed that it was not the Supreme God whom the Torah is portraying but another, perhaps even a human-formed monster who is fallible, cruel, vindictive, jealous, lives in a tent, thunders, and is hungry for sacrifices. The real God, as envisaged by the Essenes, was kindly and loving.[22] The Essenes thus had to reconstruct their scripture, a lost Torah, which had originally been free of bloodletting and animal sacrifice, with a genial creator God at its center. Jesus, they believed, had come to restore the true law and the original teachings of the Torah that had been suppressed by the sacrificial cult.

There is a good deal of first-hand information to be learned of the Ebionites/Essenes and their history in Schoeps' *Jewish Christianity*. That work draws from the *Kerygmata Petrou* (the preaching of Peter) which Schoeps describes as being "concerned with dialogues between the biblical Peter and Simon (Marcion), and also contains narrative material which apparently represents the remains of an Ebionite historical work with bits of speeches woven in. For [our understanding of] the Ebionite self-consciousness and their particular view of history this 'Ebionite Acts' is of fundamental significance. The texts claim to be documents deriving from the physical descendants of Jewish Christians belonging to the original church in Jerusalem."[23] As such, these texts offer a window directly into those times, the Jewish Christians and their practices, which will be especially significant to Vaishnavas as they learn how closely Vaishnava beliefs and practices are mirrored.

Beliefs and Practices of the Essenes

It is sufficient for our purposes to simply list the practices of the Essenes learned from this history, without going into the detail that accompanies their presentation by Schoeps. The spiritual practices of the Ebionites/Essenes included the following:[b]

1. Celibacy was advocated and practiced by some. James, brother of Jesus and leader of the community after Jesus, was a life-long celibate (naisthika-brahmacari) but the practice of monogamy

was the general rule. They condemned divorce and promoted early marriage among youth to prevent immorality.[24]

2. The practice of early morning bathing rituals, washing before/after eating, before prayer, and bathing after defecation. A morning immersion-bath was a principle and not to be avoided. According to *Tosefta Yadaim*, the "morning bathers" say to the Pharisees, "We bring this charge against you, that you pronounce the name of God in the morning without bathing." Some rejected the custom of these morning bathers as going too far. But these purificatory rites were so important to the Ebionites that they declare that all who neglected them were duped by the devil (Rec. 6.11 f.).[25]

3. Evidence indicates that they may have practiced some method of *harinam sankirtan*. The New Testament contains many references to the holy names of God, and church members calling on, or praising the name of the Lord, although those specific names curiously go unmentioned. In many cases "the name" indicates God the Father, especially in events prior to Paul's establishment of Christianity and the deification of Jesus.

For example, in Acts 9:14 referring to Paul: "and here he hath authority from the chief priests to bind *all that call on thy name*" or Acts 9.21, which states: "Is not this he that destroyed *them which called on this name* in Jerusalem, and came hither

---

[b] This long list derives mostly from Schoeps. In his presenting of the material in this book he begins by trying to understand the Ebionites from their own perspective. He asks and answers: How did the Ebionites themselves view their past? The pertinent material is provided by those parts of Recognitions 1 which we have attributed to the Ebionite "Acts of the Apostles," a writing to which Epiphanius witnessed (Pan. 30.6.9; 16.7) but which, unfortunately, is no longer extant. In any event, these portions are older than the Jewish Christian parts of the *Pseudo-Clementines* which have been called the *Kerygmata Petrou*. p. 38.

for that intent, that he might bring them bound unto the chief priests?" or "Our Father which art in heaven, *hallowed be thy name*," Matt. 18:20 or "Blessed is he that cometh *in the name of the Lord*; Hosanna in the highest." Matt. 21:9 or "baptizing them *in the name of the Father*" Matt. 28.19 or "Father, *glorify thy name*." There are many more such references.

4. The Essenes used water baptism as an *unrepeatable* rite for initiation, symbolizing spiritual rebirth, transforming a first-birth derived from material lust. This initiation rite was accompanied by invoking the name of Jesus.[c]

5. They practiced water purification as atonement as established by Jesus, abandoning the Jewish custom of requiring the blood sacrifice of animals for cleansing of sins.[26]

6. They took great pains to preserve their scripture, even with a view of countering *future* heresies. We may reasonably suspect that this was their motivation in preserving their teachings and history in sealed jars, and placing them in the Dead Sea caves. Jesus renewed the original doctrine (bona fide Mosaic Law) by removing false pericopes (false passages) from the Torah, such as those requiring blood sacrifice, those that depicted a false god replacing the kind and loving, all-good, true God above all others, and verses that disparaged the previous prophets. The Jewish Christians saw Jesus as a true prophet and representative of Moses, whose will they sought to follow explicitly.[27]

7. The Essenes held a concept of disciplic succession of *Acharyas*. They considered the prophets to be representatives of God – akin to the concept of spiritual master. Noah, Abraham, Moses, and Jesus, are in the narrowest sense the contracting parties

[c] Schoeps, p. 104-6. Vaishnava practice also allows for only one initiation. Also: The initiation and the installation of the Deity, in fact every part of sacrifice in this age is accomplished by *the chanting of the Lord's holy names*.

of the divine covenant. The truth of each earlier messenger is taken up into the proclamation of the one who follows.[d]

8. They practiced voluntary seclusion, avoidance of world-ly-minded people, and detachment from the world and worldly things. They avoided association with non-believers as much as the Vaishnava is recommended to avoid material-istic association. They would in fact bathe if they chanced to even touch such a person, much like the smarta brahmanas of India.[e]

9. They advocated simple living, to the extent that some did not maintain a fixed household.[f]

10. They kept all things in common, as common property from God the Father, and provided for each other according to their individual needs.[g]

---

[d] Schoeps, p. 139. Large gaps in disciplic succession are explained by Shrila Prabhupada in his books. For example in a letter to Dayananda 68-04-12: "In a similar way, we find in the *Bhagavad-gita* that the Gita was taught to the sungod, some millions of years ago, but Krishna has mentioned only three names in this parampara system—namely, Vivasvan, Manu, and Iksvaku; and so these gaps do not hamper from understanding the parampara system. We have to pick up the prominent *Acharya*, and follow from him."

[e] Schoeps, p. 132. Avoiding materialistic persons is also a Vaishnava principle. "Devotees actually serious about advancing in spiritual life should give up the company of non-devotees and always keep company with devotees. . . Therefore devotees who are determined to perform *tapasya* (penances and austerities) to realize the self, and who are determined to become advanced in spiritual consciousness, must give up the company of atheistic non-devotees." Purport SB 7.5.37 And: "The term *sanga-varjita* is very significant. One should disassociate himself from persons who are against Krishna. Not only are the atheistic persons against Krishna, but also those who are attracted to fruitive activities and mental speculation." Purport *Bhagavad-gita* 11.55

11. Essenes held meat-eating (including fish) as contrary to nature and were thus strict vegetarians, nor did they drink wine or any other inebriating substance, and some to the extent that they would not even cultivate grapes.[28]
12. They ate only the pure food of the community at a communal meal and not any other food, especially that offered to idols worshiped in the many other temples (taken to mean demi-gods, or others).[h]
13. They took severe vows to strictly observe their principles and carried them out. Hippolytus writes of this: "If, however, anyone would attempt to torture men of this description with the aim of inducing them to speak evil of the Law, or eat that which is sacrificed to an idol, he will not affect his purpose,

---

[f] Schoeps p. 101; Shrila Prabhupada encouraged his followers to live simply saving time for self-realization: "Another feature of the devotee is nirihaya, simple living. Niriha means "gentle," "meek" or "simple." A devotee should not live very gorgeously and imitate a materialistic person. Plain living and high thinking are recommended for a devotee. He should accept only so much as he needs to keep the material body fit for the execution of devotional service." Purport SB 4.22.24

[g] Schoeps, p. 101; In the days when most Hare Krishna devotees lived in an ashrama this principle was practiced. I refer to this concept in my book Spiritual Economics. This principle was many times illustrated by Shrila Prabhupada as follows: "Advesva sarva-bhutanam maitrau karuna eva ca, nirmamaù. Nirmama means without claiming any personal proprietorship or any nepotism. Nirmama. Everything belongs to Krishna. That is the fact. Krishna says bhoktaram yajna-tapasam sarva-loka-maheshvaram. He is the proprietor. God is actually proprietor of everything. Why shall I shall claim "This is mine"? Nothing belongs to me. Everything belongs to Krishna." Bhagavad-gita 12.13-14 Bombay, May 12, 1974

[h] Eisenman, James, p. 835; Shrila Prabhupada's followers are likewise enjoined to avoid foodstuffs not offered specifically to Krishna. "The three

for these submit to death and endure any torture rather than violate their consciences."[29]

14. Another extremely important part of their vows was to swear to transmit the teachings exactly as he had received them without even the smallest change. In this way they attempted to maintain the purity of their understanding.[i] New teachers received the *Kerygmata Petrou* from the hand of the bishop after taking a solemn oath to transmit them only to approved men of the same character and to other candidates for the teaching office under the same conditions.[30]

15. They rejected the ancient Israeli monarchy, preferring a theocracy guided by pure priests. This is similar to the concepts of varnashrama dharma where the priests give guidance to the kings. For the Ebionites the monarchy was so suspect that the biblical sources concerned with its institution were branded as false. According to *Recognitions* 3.52, the monarchy was not part of the original content of the law, apparently because of the wars conducted by them. In *Recognitions* 1.38 the kings

transcendental qualifications – cleanliness, austerity and mercy – are the qualifications of the twice-born and the demigods. Those who are not situated in the quality of goodness cannot accept these three principles of spiritual culture. For the Krishna consciousness movement, therefore, there are three sinful activities which are prohibited – namely illicit sex, intoxication, and eating food other than the prasada offered to Krishna. These three prohibitions are based on the principles of austerity, cleanliness and mercy." SB 3.16.22. And: "Generally the goddess Kali is offered food containing meat and fish, and therefore Kashyapa Muni strictly forbade his wife to take the remnants of such food. Actually a Vaishnava is not allowed to take any food offered to the demigods. A Vaishnava is always fixed in accepting prasada offered to Lord Vishnu." SB 6.18.49

[i] Eisenman, *James*, p. 835; Unauthorized changes to scriptures are strictly forbidden. This activity is causing great turmoil amongst the followers of Shrila Prabhupada. We will discuss this topic in Part 2.

were placed in a different category from those favorably depicted during the period of peace. There also, the ancient Israelite kings are called "tyrants rather than kings."[31]

16. The Essenes were absolutely convinced that the then current Pentateuch was falsified, stating in the *Kerygmata Petrou*: "Everything which is said or described concerning God is false" (Hom. 2.40). They held the existence of a Supreme God Who was served by a creator-god, and saw themselves as servants of the Absolute God. .[32] Again, this is similar if not identical to the Vaishnava understanding of the Supreme God Vishnu who is served by Brahma, the secondary creator (demigod).

17. The Ebionites accepted as fact that the devil was the then (1st century) lord of this world, but that the Christ would have lordship of the earth in an age to come.[33]

18. They are depicted as being almost fanatical followers of the reconstructed Judaic Law as a practice or demonstration of their faith. They went far beyond the common practices of the Jews (i.e., being strict vegetarians in contrast to just following kosher laws). This was in contrast to the establishment Jews (Pharisees) who had compromised many of their principles in order to coexist with, and accommodate the occupying Roman forces, earning for themselves the pejorative "seekers after smooth things." The liberties taken by the Pharisees were greatly offensive to the Essenes, and they were therefore considered spiritually unqualified although they held the positions of orthodoxy at the Temple in Jerusalem.[34]

19. Regarding Jesus they denied him divinity, accepting him as a natural-conceived-and-born man. Nonetheless, they honored him as a true prophet, meaning one who comes in disciplic succession to establish the true law. It was Jesus who established the doctrine of false pericopes, struck them from the Pentateuch, replacing them with bona fide spiritual principles.[35]

While this list is mostly derived from Schoeps, it is supported and confirmed, in the main, by Eisenman as well. These practices apply to those designated as either Essenes or Ebionites, which as Eisenman explains are most likely different branches of Jewish Christians. In all likelihood they are one and the same, especially on a philosophical, if not political, basis.

As I have mentioned, many of the points listed above reflect Vaishnava practices and beliefs quite well. This is especially true for those who participated in ISKCON during Shrila Prabhupada's manifest presence. Presently ISKCON is almost devoid of the type of ashrama-life that was required at that time, in which simple living and communal ownership were a substantial part of what it meant to be a devotee.

I encourage the Vaishnava reader to focus on the similarities between the Vaishnavas and Ebionites and not the differences. The rules of cleanliness, praising the names of the Lord, and the principles of no eating of meat, no intoxicants, no illicit sexual relations, avoiding contact with materialistic people, etc. are all practices the Essenes and Vaishnava have in common. As Vaishnavas know so well, following of these principles is extremely difficult without spiritual strength obtained through daily worship and spiritual sadhana. Beyond their practices, they also held conception of the self as a spiritual being, quite distinct from the body, again almost identical to the Vaishnava conception.

Essene Understanding of Spirit Soul

Additional examples of the spiritual understanding of the Essenes comes to us from Josephus as he recounts the exhortations of Eleazar ben Yair, the leader of the remaining 975 Zealots at Masada – the last holdout of the Palestinian population that shared the Essene understanding – which had all but been eradicated or driven to Syria and Egypt by the Roman army during the siege of

Jerusalem from 66 to 73. Masada, an almost impregnable fortress located high on a flat hilltop, had been completely cut off from support for almost two years, and the Roman army was now prepared for the assault that would be the final act of war, extinguishing the revolt that began in Jerusalem almost seven years earlier. The community members knew it was to be their last night together. The next day the men would be killed, the women defiled, and the children taken away as slaves. Faced with such unbearable humiliations, Eleazar argued that they should prefer to die at the hands of each other rather than be slaughtered by the Romans. His persuasive appeal reveals their understanding of a spiritual reality that lives beyond the material body, which is our emphasis here, the question of suicide left aside. The story was recounted to Josephus who entered the fortress with the Roman troops finding a mere three survivors, a woman and her two children, who hid themselves to avoid that tragic end:

> The words of our ancestors and of the gods, supported by the actions and spirits of our forefathers, have constantly impressed on us that life is the calamity for man, not death. Death gives freedom to our souls and lets them depart to their own pure home where they will know nothing of any calamity; but while they are confined within a mortal body and share its miseries, in strict truth they are dead.
>
> For association of the divine with the mortal is most improper. Certainly the soul can do a great deal when imprisoned in the body; it makes the body its own organ of sense, moving it invisibly and impelling it in its actions further than mortal nature can reach. But when, freed from the weight that drags it down to earth and is hung about it, the soul returns to its own place, then in truth it partakes of a blessed power and an utterly unfettered strength, remaining as invisible to human

eyes as God Himself. Not even while it is in the body can it be viewed; it enters undetected and departs unseen, having itself one imperishable nature, but causing a change in the body; for whatever the soul touches lives and blossoms, whatever it deserts withers and dies: such is the superabundance it has of immortality.[j]

Who Were Those "Jews"?

We see that the Essenes had a well-developed understanding of the spirit soul as completely distinct from the body. Likewise their understanding of a loving God, their vegetarian practices and strict adherence to following spiritual disciplines, shows them to be a group endowed with highly potent spiritual understanding. It should not be too surprising to learn from Josephus that the Jews spring from the same source as the Vaishnavas – the Indian

Figure 3 The Nearly Impregnable Masada Fortress

philosophers. He tells us in *Apion*, Book 1, verse 22:

> For Clearchus, who was the scholar of Aristotle, says that 'Aristotle his master related what follows of a Jew,' and sets down Aristotle's own discourse with him. The account is this, as written down by him: 'Now, for a great part of what this Jew said, it would be too long to recite it; but what includes in it both wonder and philosophy it may not be amiss to discourse of. I shall herein seem to thee to relate wonders, and what will even resemble dreams themselves. For this cause it will be the best way to follow the rule which requires us first to give an account of the man, and of what nation he was, that so we may not contradict our master's directions.

> 'This man then was by birth a Jew. . . *these Jews are derived from the Indian philosophers; they are named by the Indians Calami,* and by the Syrians Judaei, and took their name [Jews] from the country they inhabit, which is called Judea.'

Dr. S. Radhakrishnan offers confirmation of this heritage in his book *Pracya Mattu Paschatya Sanskriti,* "that the Greeks asserted that the Jews were Indians whom the Syrians called Judea, the Sanskrit synonym of which is Yadava or yaudheya, and the Indians called them Kalanis, [sic] meaning orthodox followers of scripture."[36] The characteristic of strictly following scriptural injunctions is a noted similarity, and would seem to be a requirement of anybody to be identified as a Jew.

The likelihood of a Vedic connection becomes even greater when we learn that Jesus is said to have worn "a line in the middle of his head in the manner of the Nazoreans," implying that the Nazoreans (i.e., Jewish Christians) did as well.[37] It is Vaishnava practice to mark the body with sacred clay, including the forehead,

---

[j] Josephus, The Jewish Wars, Book VII, Chapter 8, Section vii; the translation used is that of G.A. Williamson, The Jewish War, p.387

as a temple of God with signs called *Vishnu tilak,* as seen on the forehead of Shrila Prabhupada on page 9. The Bible indicates (Rev. 14.1) that the "144,000 elect" will also bear the name of God on their foreheads.

Where did It All Go?

Despite the similarities between the Jewish Christians and Vaishnavism, these concepts have not been carried forward into either normative Jewish or Christian understanding or practice of the present day. They have been dropped by the wayside somewhere, for some reason. The startling and substantial differences beg the question of how Christianity got here from there. Why were the spiritual practices of yore, which the modern Vaishnavas know by experience to be spiritually potent, abandoned?

In the last two millennia an untold number of personages and events have influenced the story of Christianity, and we shall look at the most significant. However, the background story that fully explain the influences affecting Christianity take us back even further in time – some four millennia prior to the time of Jesus. A seminal historical event of that time, retold in the great history of India, the *Mahabharata,* marks the beginning of this age of Kali and defines its subsequent history. That event was the invasion of the earth and its subjugation by demonic forces. We will continue from there in the next chapter.

Note: Given the almost total similarity presented above of the principles and practices between those whom Schoeps calls the Ebionites/Essenes/Jewish-Christians and the Vaishnavas, and given the confirmation of Dr. Radhakrishnan, to emphasize their factual nature *as understood by modern Vaishnavas,* henceforth I will refer to this group as the *Jewish Vaishnavas,* rather than Ebionites,

ETERNAL RELIGION IN PALESTINE | 43

Essenes, Nazoreans, Sicarii, early church, primitive church or any of their other appellations. As far as I am aware (although I cannot be considered a scholar of these times) this is the first time they are identified as such, but I do not think it is a stretch of perception to apply such a label. My intention in using this name is to continually recall the major theme of this book – the challenges of establishing the Eternal Religion in this degraded age of Kali.

CHAPTER TWO

Conquest of the Earth

The wolf in sheep's clothing now goes about whispering in our ear that evil is nothing but a misunderstanding of good and an effective instrument of progress. We think that the world of darkness has thus been abolished for good and all and nobody realizes what a poisoning this is of man's soul. C.G. Jung

During the previous age, the Dvapara-yuga, people followed the Laws of Dharma and lived happily on the earth. The great history of the earth, told in India's epic *Mahabharata,* recounts the unhappy events brought about by invasion of the "fallen angels":

Thenceforth living for hundreds and thousands of years, and bent upon the vows of the Law, men were wholly free from worries and diseases. The kshatriya kings once more governed the entire earth, with her ocean borders, mountains, wilderness, and woods. And while the baronage reigned over this earth in accordance with the Law, all the social orders, headed by the brahmanas, found unlimited joy. Casting off such vices as spring from lust and anger, the kings protected their subjects, using their staff according to the Law. As the kshatriyas were law-abiding, and sacrifice was performed according to scriptural injunction, Indra rained sweet rain at the right time and place, prospering the people.

Thus this ocean-girt earth was filled with long-living population. The kings offered up grand sacrifices for which ample stipends were given. The brahmanas studied the Vedas with their branches and Upanishads. The brahmanas rendered their services to all as sacrifice and not for personal gain. The farmers plowed the earth with bullocks, did not put cows to yoke, and let the lean cows live. Men did not milk cows whose calves were suckling, and merchants did not sell their wares with false weights. People did their lawful chores looking to the Law, devoted to the Law. The people devoted themselves to their tasks, and thus the Law was in no way diminished in that age. The cows and women gave birth in time; trees stood in fruit and bloom in all seasons. And thus the entire earth became filled with many creatures.

In this flourishing world of men, the Asuras [demons] were born in the land of kings, having been defeated in battle by the demigods, and falling from the heavenly realm, they took birth here on earth. Wanting to be gods on earth, the prideful demons were born from men and from all manner of creatures that live on earth, from cows, horses, asses, camels, and buffalo, from beasts of prey, elephants, and deer. And when they were born and went on being born, the wide Earth could no longer support the terrible burden.

Now some of them were born as kings, filled with great strength. Powerful, insolent, bearing many shapes, they swarmed over the earth, crushing their enemies. They oppressed the brahmanas, the kings, the farmers, even the serfs, and many other creatures were oppressed with their power. Sowing fear and slaughtering all the races of creation, they roamed all over earth by the hundreds of thousands, menacing everywhere the great seers in their hermitages, impious, drunk with power, callous in behavior.

When she was thus tyrannized by the grand asuras, who were bloated with power and strength, Earth personified came to Lord Brahma as a supplicant. Neither the wind, nor the elephants, nor the mountains, were able to support the Earth so forcefully overrun by the danavas. Earth, sagging under her burden and brutalized with fear, sought refuge with the grandfather of all beings. Surrounded by worthy demigods, brahmanas, and seers, she approached Lord Brahma, the creator of the world, his praises being sung by joyous Gandharvas and Apsaras, musicians of the heavenly realms.

Seeking refuge, Earth spoke to him in the presence of all the Guardians of the Worlds. But Earth's business had long before been known to Brahma, the unborn, who dwells on high. For how could he, creator of the universe, fail to know entirely what is lodged in the minds of the demigods and asuras?"[1]

The peaceful and bountiful conditions described are the previous age, Dvapara-yuga, thousands of years ago, and that pleasant atmosphere continued almost until the close of that age, at which time the demonic *Asuras* invaded the earth. Vaishnavas will recognize the story as the prologue to the advent of Lord Krishna Who appeared on the earth at that time, to rescue the earth from her plight, while also performing His transcendental pastimes.

The *daityas*, descendants of Diti, and the *danavas*, descendants of Danu[a], are of the race of the demons, and this story depicts their arrival on the earth after having been expelled from the planets of heaven. Due to the great disturbances, Lord Krishna killed many demons who had assumed the forms of animals, such as *Bakasura*, the stork demon, and *Aghasura*, the snake demon, during His childhood pastimes. Those who had been born into the ruling class, the godless *kshatriyas*, were mostly killed in the great battle at

Kurukshetra. Aside from these, there remained on earth many other godless kings who had abandoned the godly Vedic culture and fled greater India in fear of Parasurama, as he waged his campaign of regicide.[b] These godless *kshatriyas* established themselves as the ruling order of Greece, Europe and the Middle East.[2]

This is not without sanction for each season has its purpose, and during *Kali-yuga* the earth is given to the ungodly for their use. Gradually the demonic class have increased their control and influence and for a very long time have dominated the entire earth, as Shrila Prabhupada explains: "At the present, especially on this planet earth, the influence of Lord Brahma has decreased considerably, and the representatives of Hiranyakasipu – the *rakshasas* and demons – have taken charge. Therefore there is no protection of brahminical culture and cows, which are the basic prerequisites for all kinds of good fortune. This age is very dangerous because society is being managed by demons and *rakshasas*."[3]

Shrila Prabhupada first mentioned this in a lecture in New York in 1966, and repeated it several times in his writing:

> *Rakshasas* are man-eaters, more than tigers. For their self-satisfaction they can eat even their own sons. *Rakshasas*. No shame. 'My sense gratification should be satisfied. Never mind. You go to hell.' So this is the age. . . This is going on. *You can know this world is now managed by the rakshasas.*
>
> *Rakshasas, they are prepared to sacrifice everything* for fulfilling their whimsical nonsense. [4]

---

[a] *Srimad Bhagavatam* 6.18.12–13. Also: "Diti and Aditi are two sisters. The sons of Aditi are called Adityas, and the sons of Diti are called Daityas. All the Adityas are devotees of the Lord, and all the Daityas are atheistic." *Bhagavad-gita* 10.30

[b] Parasurama is a partial incarnation of the Supreme Lord who killed many generations of wayward kings who had deviated from Dharma.

On Shrila Prabhupada's authority we take it as a given that the *rakshasas* are indeed controlling this world. Very well then, how would we recognize them today? Although the leaders of the world all appear as nicely dressed gentlemen, looks mean nothing, as Shrila Prabhupada explains:

> One cannot judge whether a person is a devata, an *asura* or a *rakshasa* by seeing him, but a sane man can understand this by the activities such a person performs. A general description is given in the Padma Purana: a devotee of Lord Vishnu is a demigod, whereas an *asura* or Yaksha is just the opposite. Thus one can judge who is a devata, who is a *rakshasa* and who is an *asura* by how they conduct their activities.[5]

In Sanskrit this is called *phalena paricyate* – judging by the result. Or in Christendom, "you shall know a tree by its fruits."

To say that this account of our modern world stands in stark contrast to what most people believe would be a significant understatement. The notion that *rakshasas* control society is as disconcerting as it is unsuspected by the general public. But by the horrors we see going on in the world today we can understand that it is a fact, and one that has tremendous impact on the lives of everyone and the future of the earth. To truly understand what is going on we must look behind the surface, behind the form, and discern the truth based on the activities of the personalities involved. Understanding the influence of the demonic element within the sphere of religion is the subject matter of this book, therefore understanding who they are is our point of departure.

The Demonic Nature

Since it is not by external appearances, such as clothing, or conveyances, etc. that the nature of a person is known, but by their qualities and activities, we must know the qualities and character of the demonic. In the sixteenth chapter of the *Bhagavad-gita* Sri Krishna explains that there are two types of beings in this world – the divine and the demoniac – and He fully explains the demonic nature:

> Arrogance, pride, anger, conceit, harshness and ignorance – these qualities belong to those of demonic nature. The demoniac, who are lost to themselves and who have no intelligence, engage in unbeneficial, horrible works meant to destroy the world. Taking shelter of insatiable lust, pride and false prestige, and being thus illusioned, they are sworn to unclean work, attracted by the impermanent. They believe that to gratify the senses unto the end of life is the prime necessity of human civilization. Thus there is no end to their anxiety. Being bound by hundreds and thousands of desires, by lust and anger, they secure money by illegal means for sense gratification.
>
> The demoniac person thinks: 'So much wealth do I have today, and I will gain more according to my schemes. So much is mine now, and it will increase in the future, more and more. He is my enemy, and I have killed him; and my other enemy will also be killed. I am the lord of everything, I am the enjoyer, I am perfect, powerful and happy. I am the richest man, surrounded by aristocratic relatives. There is none so powerful and happy as I am. I shall perform sacrifices, I shall give some charity, and thus I shall rejoice.' In this way, such persons are deluded by ignorance.[6]

Are They Real?

It is not uncommon for people to feel that such descriptions of demonic personalities are exaggerations, folklore, or ancient myth. In fact, much effort has been made to bring people to this conclusion through the manipulation of public opinion.[c] Modern literature does not constitute conclusive proof for the Vaishnava however. Our standard for discerning fact from fiction is the bona fide scriptures, and not soothing words that lull us into a state of false security. The Vedic literature teaches us that those demonic characters are very real, both in history and in modern society.

About the *rakshasas*, we learn from Shrila Prabhupada's commentaries that they are extremely intelligent as a class, and because they are very good organizers and offer strong leadership, they have little difficulty establishing themselves as the leaders in the world – many of the politicians and business leaders of the present day are said to be psychopaths, the modern language for *rakshasa*.[d] Moreover, raksasas possess another extraordinary ability: they can change their form to appear differently than they actually are.

Throughout the Vedic literatures we find many examples of raksasas who change their shape in order to beguile others. In Lord Ramachandra's pastimes, the *rakshasa* Marica assumed the form of a golden deer to lure Rama away from Sita's side. In Krishna's pastimes the witch Putana was a great *raksasi* who knew the art of changing her form. She appeared in Vrindavana as a beautiful woman, but when she was killed her original hideous form was

---

[c] Manipulation of literature, particularly scripture is covered in detail in later chapters. As an example of social indoctrination I cite here an article entitled *The Language Police* in *The Atlantic Monthly*, March 2003. Professor of Education Diane Ravitch reproduces there a list of words that have been banned from use by writers of textbooks and tests for K-12 students. Included in the list are God, hell, devil, dogma, fanatic, insane, and Satan among dozens of others. Obviously if children are not to read, and hence discuss God, hell, the devil or Satan they will have little or no understanding of these ideas, or use of them to understand their world—especially if their parents don't take them to church, or otherwise provide any spiritual education. Such ignorance opens these individuals to exploitation at the expense of untold karma.

revealed. Similarly, Carvaka was a *rakshasa* who was a close friend of Duryodhana who changed his form to that of a brahmana to condemn Yudhisthira as an enemy of the people.

This may be fine as far as distant history goes, but what about today? Is there any evidence that these shape-shifting, human-eating creatures still prowl the earth? Well, in fact there is. A quick internet search of "shape-shifters," or "humanoid reptilians," or related words will bring hundreds of thousands of references. These will refer to mysterious beings who, although not human, appear to be so, having the ability to change their appearance from something resembling a reptile, having a lizard-like tongue and eyes, to that of ordinary looking humans. Zulu historian *Credo Mutwa*, says that his people have known about reptilian presence on the earth for many hundreds of years. These beings are said to be a cross between an intelligent reptilian form of life and human beings.[e] Moreover, there is evidence from Mutwa and others that these beings have actually been controlling the earth for thousands of years. And as you may have guessed, they are said to eat the flesh and drink the blood of humans who are ritually sacrificed. There are by now, many people who have revealed their personal experiences of witnessing such shape-shifting. The description of these reptilian shape-shifters is identical in most details to the Vedic description of the raksasas, and they may even be exactly the same.

The reaction to such news is often stunned disbelief, even among those who otherwise accept the Vedic worldview. Apparently testimony of such a present-day reality disturbs the pleasant world in which we seek false shelter. And although we may feel more comfortable with our heads in the sand, such a reaction plays well into the hands of those demons. In any case, even for those who

---

[d] I make this connection between the *rakshasas* and psychopaths, and detail the nature of psychopaths in my book *Spiritual Economics*. Please look there for detailed information.

are reluctant to accept the Vedic version of history, there is corrob-
orating information in the modern era for those with the courage
to accept it.

See for example *The Biggest Secret* by David Icke where he cites a
number of people who tell of their first-hand accounts of witnessing shape-shifting humans, especially politicians: Cathy O'Brien
in her book *Trance Formation of America*, Hunter S. Thompson in
his book *Fear and Loathing in Las Vegas*, Alex Christopher in his
book *Pandora's Box*, Credo Mutwa in *The Reptilian Agenda*.[7]

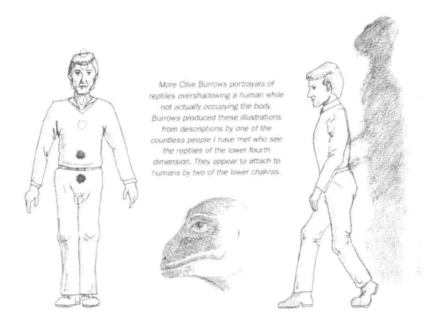

More Clive Burrows portrayals of
reptiles overshadowing a human while
not actually occupying the body.
Burrows produced these illustrations
from descriptions by one of the
countless people I have met who see
the reptiles of the lower fourth
dimension. They appear to attach to
humans by two of the lower chakras.

Figure 4 Illustration of demonic control from The Biggest Secret, *p. 204*

[e] There are many such highly-intelligent other-than-human life forms
described in the Vedic literatures. The Yaksas, for example, although demons
have mystic powers with which they bewildered Dhruva when he fought
with them. The Nagas are a race of intelligent serpents also endowed with
intelligence and even mystical abilities. Apparently they can also adopt
different forms since Arjuna married a Naga King's daughter and had a son by
her, just as Bhima had a son by the raksasi Hidimbi.

Besides their individual presence they apparently also have the ability to influence humans by different psychic methods. While not occupying the body they attach to humans by two lower chakras, and thereby have dominating influence over them.

Atheistic Controllers and Their Modus Operandi

As noted above, the godless *kshatriyas* have established themselves as the ruling order, and with rare exceptions have controlled the entire world for millennia. One thing that clearly stands out when reviewing their history is war and conquest. The very earliest of these cultures were warlike, conquering and destroying their enemies and profiting from the booty of war.

The warlike activities of these early Western people included not only their human populations, but the host of their gods as well. The Hittites would go to war only when their supreme God TESHUB ("The Stormer") gave the word. He apparently gave his order often as the Hittites are said to have expanded their kingdom to imperial proportions. [8]

This was taking place thousands of years ago, a time when there was still contact between humans and the beings of the higher realms. Those beings, having powers vastly superior to humans were regarded as gods, and were worshiped as such. Later, as *Kali-yuga* progressed, they stopped visitations to earth.

The Hittites expanded as far south as Canaan which they treated as a neutral zone, apparently not considering it as part of their kingdom. The Egyptians were of a different inclination however and sought to bring Canaan under their rule by repeated warfare, and eventually succeeded. Their manner of warfare was decidedly demonic as they attest in their inscriptions. Thothmes III, the pharaoh who was victorious over the Canaanite kings describes his destruction of the conquered with apparent pride: "Now his majesty went north, plundering towns and laying encampments waste." And of a vanquished king this pharaoh wrote: "I desolated his towns, set fire to his encampments, made mounds of them; their resettlement can never take place. All the people I captured, I made prisoners; their countless cattle I carried off, and their goods as well. I took away every resource of life; I cut down their grain and felled all their groves and all their pleasant trees. I totally destroyed it." And he then notes that it was all done on the command of his god Amon-Ra.[9]

Recalling the description of the demonic nature from the *Bhagavad-gita*, we see it manifest in these accounts, both on the part of the earthly kings as well as their gods. This manner of killing and destruction – domination, exploitation and control – can be understood as the hallmark of the demonic *rakshasas*. We discern their presence by such activities, which stands in sharp contrast to that of the upholders of dharma, the *kshatriya* kings of Bharata. Glancing through the pages of history, from these early ages to the succession of emperors of Rome and even beyond that to the popes of the Roman Catholic Church and the Islamic kings, we witness a restless fury for domination and control. These rulers, one after another, conquered and were conquered, as often by their own relatives as by enemy rulers, as they wrestled for the crown and its powers.

As *Kali-yuga* has progressed the rulers have abused the citizens to such an extent that monarchies have been abolished everywhere only to be replaced by men whose qualities are even more degraded. [10]

Observance of Atheism in Modern Western Culture

In seeking to establish themselves as the supreme enjoyer the *rakshasas* not only conquered who they could but, out of envy of the Supreme Lord, forever engage in activities of propaganda meant to disparage any idea of religion. In past ages, the demons

Venu, Hiranyakasipu, and Kamsa, each one typical of the *rakshasa* host, stopped the sacrificial fires, and the chanting of Vedic hymns. In later times followers of the Eternal Religion were simply killed. In our modern day however people are more aware and the suppression of religion is done in more subtle, but very effective, ways. Mainly through teaching and promoting irreligion and atheistic propaganda.

This pressure is felt by sensitive observers within society and many books detailing the attack of atheism on modern culture have been published. Huston Smith, professor emeritus at University of California, Berkeley, wrote about the influence of atheistic propaganda in all sectors of society. In his book *Why Religion Matters* he details the omnipresent atheistic propaganda that emanates from: the halls of science that unquestioningly support the flawed and failed atheistic-based ideologies of Darwinism and the Big Bang; from "higher education" in which an implicit atheistic orientation operates in the disguise of "value neutral" objectivity; from the media wherein "liberal" atheistic values are presented without question, yet theism is made to appear as a silly superstition of an earlier, unsophisticated day; and within laws in America, diminishing the protection of the first amendment in support of citizens' practice of religion.[11]

This creeping atheistic influence especially has penetrated university education for several generations. William Buckley, Jr. upon his graduation from Yale University (1950) stunned the Eastern Establishment with an acerbic review of religious instruction and (its lack of) influence at the prestigious university. In *God and Man at Yale*, he took the university to task for, at best, benign neglect of religious instruction, despite the fact that the university began its life, as did all of the early New England schools, as a seminary. He details an overriding academic "tolerance" of theism felt by students in many of the university's social sciences including economics, sociology, history and government. Particularly acute was his exposure of atheistic influences within the Department of Religion, where Religious Professor Goodenough described himself to his students as "80% atheist and 20% agnostic"! "No wonder," says Buckley, "that the preponderant influence of a scholar of his persuasion is to drive his students away from religion, the subject he 'teaches.'"

Atheistic influence has become extreme in the modern liberal universities and culture where religious belief is now openly ridiculed, while homosexuality is flaunted as a positive virtue. Now let's look at atheistic influences *within* religion.

Atheism in the Disguise of Religion

An essay entitled *Putana* written by Shrila Bhaktisiddhanta Swami, published in *The Harmonist,* January 1932, focuses on the atheistic elements active in this world and their efforts to suppress the appearance of Truth.[12] He describes these elements as Kamsas and Putanas – demons present in Krishna's earthly Lila – and uses them as icons for their descendants in succeeding generations. As noted above such agents actively control the world, although they keep themselves hidden and disguised. Shrila Bhaktisiddhanta tears off the disguise exposing them, alerting us to their presence and activities:

> Sri Krishna manifests His eternal birth the pure cognitive essence of the serving soul who is located above all mundane limitations. *King Kamsa is the typical aggressive empiricist, ever on the lookout for the appearance of the truth for the purpose of suppressing Him before He has time to develop.* This is no exaggeration of the real connotation of the consistent empiric position. *The materialist has a natural repugnance for the transcendent.* He is disposed to link that faith in the incomprehensible is the parent of dogmatism and hypocrisy in

the disguise of religion. He is also equally under the delusion that there is no real dividing line between the material and the spiritual, and is strengthened in his delusion by the interpretation of scriptures by persons who are like-minded with himself. This includes all the lexicographic interpreters.

Their lexicographical interpretation is upheld by Kamsa as the real scientific explanation of the scriptures, and is perfectly in keeping with his dread of, and aversion for, the transcendental.. *These lexicographical interpreters* [editors] *are employed by Kamsa in putting down the first suspected appearance of any genuine faith in the transcendental.* King Kamsa knows very well that if the faith in the transcendental is once allowed to grow it is sure to upset all his empiric prospects.

There is historical ground for such misgivings. Accordingly if the empiric domination [materialism] is to be preserved intact it would be necessary not to lose a moment to put down the transcendental heresy the instant it threatens to make its appearance in earnest. King Kamsa, acting on this traditional fear is never slow to take the scientific precaution of deputing empiric teachers of the scriptures, backed by the resources of dictionary and grammar and all empiric subtleties to put down, by the show of specious arguments based on hypothetical principles, the true interpretation of the eternal religion revealed by the scriptures.

Kamsa is strongly persuaded that faith in the transcendental can be effectively put down by empiricism if prompt and decisive measures are adopted at the very outset. He attributes the failure of atheism in the past to the neglect of the adoption of such measures before the theistic fallacy has had time to spread among the fanatical masses.

But Kamsa is found to count without his host. When Krishna is born He is found to be able to upset all sinister designs against those who are apprised by Himself of His advent, the apparently causeless faith displayed by persons irrespective of age, sex and condition may confound all rabid empiricist who are on principle adverse to the Absolute Truth Whose appearance is utterly incompatible with the domination of empiricism.

But no adverse efforts of the empiricists, whose rule seems till then to be perfectly well-established over the minds of the deluded souls of this world, can dissuade any person from exclusively following the Truth when He actually manifests His birth in the pure cognitive essence of the soul.

Putana is the slayer of all infants. The baby, when he or she comes out of the mother's womb, falls at once into the hands of the pseudo-teachers of religion. These teachers are successful in forestalling the attempts of the good preceptor whose help is never sought by the atheists of this world at the baptisms of their babies. This is ensured by the arrangements of all established churches of the world. They have been successful only in supplying watchful Putanas for effecting the spiritual destruction of persons from the moment of their birth with the cooperation of their worldly parents. *No human contrivance can prevent these Putanas from obtaining possession of the pulpits. This is due to the general prevalence of atheistic disposition in the people of this world.*

The church that has the best chance of survival in this damned world is that of atheism under the convenient guise of theism. The churches have always proved the staunchest upholders of the grossest form of worldliness from which even the worst of non-ecclesiastical criminals are found to recoil.

It is not from any deliberate opposition to the ordained clergy that these observations are made. The original purpose of the established churches of the world may not always be objectionable. *But no stable religious arrangement for instructing the masses has yet been successful.* The Supreme Lord Sri Caitanya Mahaprabhu, in pursuance of the teachings of the scriptures enjoins all absence of conventionalism for the teachers of the eternal religion. It does not follow that the mechanical adoption of the unconventional life by any person will make him a fit teacher of religion. Regulation is necessary for controlling the inherent worldliness of conditional souls.

But no mechanical regulation has any value, even for such a purpose. The bona fide teacher of religion is neither any product of nor the favorer of, any mechanical system. In his hands no system has likewise, the chance of degenerating into a lifeless arrangement. The mere pursuit of fixed doctrines and fixed liturgies cannot hold a person to the true spirit of doctrine or liturgy.

The idea of an organized church in an intelligible form, indeed, marks the close of the living spiritual movement. The great ecclesiastical establishments are the dikes and the dams to retain the current that cannot be held by any such contrivances. They, [the great ecclesiastical institutions] indeed, indicate a desire on the part of the masses to exploit a spiritual movement for their own purpose. *They also unmistakably indicate the end of the absolute and unconventional guidance of the bona fide spiritual teacher.* The people of this world understand preventive systems, although they have no idea at all of the un-prevented positive eternal life. Neither can there be any earthy contrivance for the permanent preservation of the life eternal on this mundane plane on the popular scale.

Those are, therefore, greatly mistaken who are disposed to look forward to the amelioration of the worldly state in any worldly sense from the worldly success of any really spiritual movement. *It is these worldly expectants who become the patrons of the mischievous race of the pseudo-teachers of religion, the Putanas, whose congenial function is to stifle the theistic disposition at the very moment of its suspected appearance.* But the real theistic disposition can never be stifled by the efforts of those Putanas. *The Putanas have power only over the atheist.* It is a thankless but salutary task which they perform for the benefit of their willing victims.

But as soon as theistic disposition proper makes its appearance in the pure cognitive essence, of the awakened soul, the Putanas are decisively silenced at the very earliest stage of their encounter with newborn Krishna. The would-be slayer is herself slain. This is the reward of the negative services that the Putanas unwittingly render to the cause of theism by strangling all hypocritical demonstrations against their own hypocrisy.

But Putana does not at all like to receive her reward in only form which involves the total destruction of her wrong personality. King Kamsa also does not like to lose the services of the most trusted of his agents. The effective silencing of the whole race of pseudo-teachers of religion is the first clear indication of the appearance of the Absolute on the mundane plane. *The bona fide teacher of the Absolute, heralds the Advent of Krishna by his uncompromising campaign against the pseudo-teachers of religion.*

As with all of his writing, Shrila Bhaktisiddhanta's analysis cuts through the illusory and materialistic externals such as institution, position and dress, that so enamor us ordinary folk, and directly shines a brilliant light exposing the actions of the demonic, offering his uncompromising observation that "the church that has the best chance of survival in this damned world, is that of atheism under the convenient disguise of theism!"

Atheism under the convenient disguise of theism! Yes! Where best, and most effectively, to hide the antithesis than in what is supposed to be the thesis? Like a map that has been altered it cannot be effective, simple people have no idea how they are being misled away from God rather than toward Him.

No other vehicle can do so much for the destruction of the spiritual beliefs and sentiments as when the tender creeper of devotion is crushed by agents of Kali appearing in the disguise of the spiritual preceptors. History offers many notorious examples. And that, of course, is how so many people around the world have justifiably come to condemn the religious ideal as the perpetrator of so much evil throughout Western history. Under the influence of *tamo-guna*, so-called religion has become the home of irreligion and what is irreligion is foolishly taken as religion. Sinful acts perpetrated in the name of religion have so insulted people's sense of decency that they have come to believe that true peace can only be attained in the absence of religion! Such ideas have become immensely popular, reflected in John Lennon's song *Imagine:* "imagine there's no heaven . . . and no religion too . . . you may say I'm a dreamer . . . but I'm not the only one; perhaps someday you'll join us, and the world will live as one."

'Religious Atheism' Established in Kali Yuga

The atheistic influences are explained further in Shrila Prabhupada's writing. For example in the Fifth Canto of the *Srimad Bhagavatam*, (5.6.9 Purport) Shrila Prabhupada comments:

> The people in this age are described as *mandah sumanda-matayo,* generally they have no spiritual culture, and therefore they are very fallen. Due to this, they will accept any religious system. Due to their misfortune they forget the Vedic

principles. Following non-Vedic principles in this age, they think themselves the Supreme Lord and thus spread the cult of atheism all over the world.

And in another place Shrila Prabhupada makes it clear that much that goes on under the disguise of religion in Kali is actually atheism:

Foolish *Mayavadis* say that worshiping demigods is as good as worshiping the Supreme Personality of Godhead, but that is not a fact. This philosophy misleads people to atheism. One who has no idea what God actually is thinks that any form he imagines or any rascal he accepts can be God. This acceptance of cheap gods or incarnations of God is actually atheism. It is to be concluded, therefore, that those who worship demigods or self-proclaimed incarnations of God are all atheists. Chaitanya-charitamrta, Adi 10.11 Purport

With these warnings and the guidance from our *Acharyas* we should be alert for such manifestations of irreligion. But do we recognize it? Do we even look for it? How would we recognize and understand such contemptuous parody of truth, disguised to the eye of the uninitiated and inexperienced? We take it on the strength of Shrila Bhaktisiddhanta's eminent stature as a Vaishnava *Acharya* that such conclusions are both valid and undeniable, and there must be some manifestation of which he writes. Beginning from the threshold of his good advice we now embark on a journey examining the historical record for indications of such activity.

It is my intention to show herein that such evidence exists and willingly exposes itself to those who will look for it. For what purpose? To reconstruct the map to Transcendence that has been, and is, being altered, so that those who are able to discern the truth may properly direct their own path and guide others to their destination of the Absolute. In this book we are going to journey to the past, both distant and near, and we shall see how the Kamsas of Kali attempt to put down the truth as before it has time to develop.

What Will We Believe?

As explained by Shrila Bhaktisiddhanta, the necessary requirement by which the Kamsas and Putanas achieve their success is the willingness of the masses to accept their atheistic propaganda as true. Naturally we ask how they can be successful with such lies. Why are people not able to discern truth from lies? The answer is that their understanding and acceptance of what is true depends entirely upon the purity of their consciousness. Those with pure consciousness will feel something amiss when faced with falsity. Those with a crooked heart will hear what pleases them, and on this basis, accept it as true. Benjamin Franklin noted that it is impossible to cheat an honest man – he is immunized by his righteousness. Conversely, con artists are most successful when soliciting the help of people to engage in dishonest schemes. Using the victim's willingness to reap unearned rewards by cheating someone else, the con swindles them in such a way that they have no recourse to legal authorities, since the entire endeavor was illegal to begin with.

These same principles apply in the area of religious belief. The cheating business can go on only because of the atheistic tendencies of the masses, by which they would "cheat" religion, making it the tool of their own pleasure seeking efforts. Truth is revealed to the pure souls who are free from the cheating impulse, and who hear *submissively*, giving up false understanding for the Truth. If the hearer maintains an attitude of superior understanding, he offers no fertile field in which truth can be sown. Rather than surrendering to the truth he rejects it because he does not perceive in it what he wants to hear. In this way the crooked hearts reject truth, and purchases falsity.

It is my position that the words of Vyasadeva, Shrila Bhaktisiddhanta and Shrila Prabhupada are not written allegorically, but are factually true: that there are demonic personalities that control the earth at this time, and they are staunchly opposed to any manifestation of the Absolute Truth. Their efforts to suppress the truth by any means fair and foul is a given and can be observed if one simply examines the evidence and judges by the result.

This chapter is an introduction to the historical fact that the demonic have long been using religion as a cover for their nefarious activities. This background information – the invasion and control of the earth by demoniac powers – lays the foundation that will help us see through the veil of illusion that has covered the activities of the churches for millennia, helping us to understand what has actually been going on in the name of religion, and giving it a bad name.

We shall now return to first century Palestine to learn how the demonic elements dealt with the Jewish Vaishnavas.

CHAPTER THREE

Jesus and James

The Kamsas of the 1st century certainly did employ the services of many Putanas to diminish the effect of the appearance of the Truth. As Shrila Bhaktisiddhanta warns us, they did not lose one moment in their efforts. Not only did they employ lexicographical interpreters, or word jugglers, but at that time they had license to use hit men who carried out their savage attacks with impunity and the full support and blessings of governing officials. We will explore the many methods used to destroy and confuse the truth about persons and events in this early Western era, but before we do we must complete the background picture by introducing in some detail the main figures of this era – Jesus, and his brother, the factual protagonist of this history – James. The roles of both provide an exceptional contrast to the story that you have likely heard, and reveal the determined efforts of the Kamsas to destroy the truths of this history.

Attempts to know the facts of the historical Jesus, apart from the deified Christ of faith, have remained elusive over the past century and a half, though many religious historians have tried to sort it out. Both Eisenman and Schoeps detail how within the canonical literature there has been deliberate omission and obfuscation of information, personalities are merged into one, activities of a single individual parsed to several others, with some events entirely neglected or told from a particularly biased point of view.[1]

Eisenman expresses his exasperation with all of this in his opening remarks to *James*:

> Unfortunately, *the facts themselves are shrouded in mystery and overwhelmed by a veneer of retrospective theology and polemics* that frustrates any attempt to get at the real events underlying them. . . Questions not only emerge concerning Jesus' existence itself, at least as far as the character so confidently portrayed in Scripture, but also regarding the appropriateness of the teaching attributed to him. . . Where the man 'Jesus' is concerned we have mainly the remains of Hellenistic romance and mythologizing to go on, often with a clear polemicizing or dissembling intent . . . Where the Gospels are concerned, whatever can be said with any certainty about Jesus is largely presented in the framework of supernatural story-telling.[2]

Schoeps also takes the establishment academics to task for deliberately looking in the wrong places and at the wrong things, and making interpretations according to their way of seeing the world instead of seeing it in its own time:

> The New Testament exegetes [those who studies and interprets texts, especially religious writings] pursue with great ingenuity a task *which is suspect* and in reality futile. In spite of 150 years of modern critical research, they have seldom correctly perceived the weak role played by Judaism in the ancient world and the slight significance the object of their study had for its contemporaries. For the most part, they look back at Christian beginnings from a point of view *derived from a later period and thus read into the earlier situation standards which are actually foreign to it.*"[3]

Jesus in His Times

Who was Jesus then? From Paul we learn only two *facts* regarding the historical Jesus. 1) He was crucified at some unspecified date, and 2) he had a number of brothers, one of whom was James.[4] Our recourse to know Jesus is to understand him not by who he is said to be, but rather by what he *did*. And for that history we turn to Schoeps.

To understand Jesus *in his times* let's go back to 1st century Palestine. As we noted in our opening remarks about the Jewish Vaishnavas, 1st century Palestine was a hotbed of political activity. Roman forces had occupied the area since before 60 B.C. with significant resistance. There were local skirmishes and guerilla attacks, and sometimes full-scale warfare carried out by members of the Zealots, *Sicarii* (translated as "assassins") and others.

To the north, Galilee was ruled by Arabian puppet-kings (dynasty of Herod Antipas: the Herodian kings) who maintained their power through force. But the southern area of Judea, which was both the spiritual and secular capital of the Jewish Vaishnavas, as described in *Holy Blood, Holy Grail*, was

> subject to direct Roman rule, administered by a Roman procurator based at Caesarea. The Roman regime was brutal and autocratic. When it assumed direct control of Judea, more than three thousand rebels were summarily crucified [a punishment reserved exclusively for political crimes]. The temple was plundered and defiled. Heavy taxation was imposed. Torture was frequently employed and many of the populace committed suicide. This state of affairs was not improved by Pontius Pilate, who presided as procurator from A.D. 26 to 36. In contrast to the biblical portraits of him, existing records indicate that Pilate was a cruel and corrupt man who not only perpetuated, but intensified the abuses of his predecessor.[5]

Figure 5 First Century Palestine

What kept this period in turmoil was the apocalyptic-eschatological perspective [eschatological: of or relating to or dealing with or regarding the ultimate destiny of mankind and the world] that the Jewish Vaishnavas held – that these atrocities would be revenged in a final battle of the Sons of Light, led by the Messiah and the Heavenly Host, against the Sons of Darkness.[6] They were of the opinion that the forces of evil, *Rasha* in Hebrew (interesting similarity to *rakshasa*, the Sanskrit word for demonic beings), or the Devil, had control of the earth, but would be defeated, after which, there would be a 1,000 year period during which the Archangel of Christ would rule the earth. They believed that battle was imminent.

At the time, the priesthood and the throne were governed by two parallel lines of Messiahs – one presiding over spiritual affairs descending from the family (tribe) of Levi – and another presiding over secular affairs through the lineage of David. At the core of the Jewish Vaishnava movement lay *the question of dynastic legitimacy of both the ruling house and the priesthood*. They considered both the puppet-king Herod and his wicked Temple Priest Ananas (installed by the Romans), as illegitimate, and sought to remove them both, and then to install legitimate heirs to both the priesthood and throne. Of the two, the greater concern was for the priesthood – and an *authentic* spiritual leadership.[7] Jesus was the one person that could fulfill the role of *both* Messiahs placing him in a paramount position, and made him the enemy of both the political and ecclesiastical establishments.

Jesus, the Messiah

In our times the word Messiah has taken on connotations of divine or savior and this is not without reason. The Greek word for Messiah is Christ, or Christos, and both terms simply meant "the anointed one,"[a] as it was the custom to install kings in a ceremony in which they were anointed with oil. David, when he was anointed king became a "Messiah" or a "Christ," as was every subsequent Jewish king. Of course, the Vedic understanding of king is *kshatriya*, whose prerogatives derived solely from his being a qualified representative of God properly leading the people through progressive spiritual and social development. Thus the divine right of kings, and the divine import of the word Messiah. In preparing for his demonstration of assuming his rightful position as the Messiah, and King of Judea, Jesus was also anointed, indicating the assumption of his rightful heritage.

Was he a Messiah whose purpose was the overthrow of the occupation, or a Messiah whose purpose it was to bring spiritual salvation? A military commander Jesus was not. At least that intention had not manifest before he was crucified. He had at that point assumed no militant leadership thus the frustrating prophecy that a ruler of the house of David would once again rise to lead the people to freedom from the yoke of the Romans.[b]

But as mentioned, the more important aspect of prophetic fulfillment was a Messiah who, being accepted as a bona fide prophet, would fulfill the Law. What was of greatest importance for them was that the "eternal Law" given to Adam at the time of the

---

[a] Christos is derived from Krista, or Krishna; Following is a conversation between Father Emmanuel, a Benedictine Monk and Shrila Prabhupada, 22Jun74: Father Emmanuel: Yes, Christ, Krista, Kristos, who is Christ by oil. Anointed. Christos, Christ, means anointed. It's the same word. It's the same form. Christo and Kristos in Greek is the same word, anointed. Prabhupada: Oh, I see. This Christo is a version of the word 'Krishna.'

[b] A uniquely different version of Josephus written in "Old Russian" was discovered in Russia in 1261. It portrays a Jesus who is described as human being (i.e., not divine), a political revolutionary and as a "king who did not reign." It should be noted that like the Gospels the works of Josephus have also been edited to various degrees. Cited in *Holy Blood, Holy Grail* p. 377

Creation and renewed by Moses, would again be renewed to eternal validity. That was another prophecy that Jesus was expected to fulfill.

Jesus appears to be what we would call an *Acharya* for the Jewish Vaishnavas, and was said by Shrila Prabhupada on several occasions to be a *shaktyavesh avatar*.[8] As such he would have been qualified to discern the Truth and reestablish the principles of religion, and as required by the Pseudo-Clementines: "absolute knowledge requiring no external mediation marks the True Prophet and exalts him above all men."[9]

So significant is this concept of Jesus as the person who was qualified to understand the falsifications of their scripture, the Torah (Old Testament), replacing them with proper understanding and restore it as a bona fide and potent scripture, that Schoeps covers it repeatedly – no less than six times! His development of the Ebionite perception of Jesus and the Law has so many parallels for us today that I believe it worthwhile to quote him extensively. ISKCON observers will find that much, if not most, of what follows in this quote can be directly applied to the changes made to their sacred scriptures, and whatever may not directly apply will otherwise bear a strong parallel to recent events:

> The eternal law was inscribed by God's hand on the world at the Creation as the first teaching delivered to mankind. It was known to Adam and revealed anew to Moses. The scribes and Pharisees, originally the legitimate incumbents of the seat of Moses... *betrayed their calling by allowing it* [the Law] *to become increasingly obscured through errors,* [and by their negligence threw] *away the key of the Kingdom which had been entrusted to them, the key which opens the gate to eternal life, and so made access impossible for those who wanted to enter.*

For this reason Jesus arose from the "seat of Moses" and restored "that which was hidden from times immemorial" to the worthy through his proclamation.[c] *The standard for the proclamation of Jesus is the distinction between what is genuine and what is false in the Law. For the Ebionites, therefore, to believe in Jesus means to be instructed by him concerning the Law and to obtain the "knowledge of the secrets,"* i.e., "the more secret understanding of the Law," of which Christ is the sole expositor.

The real Ebionite accomplishment consisted therefore, in the attempt to reform the Jewish Law, and in their internalization of the Old Testament Law. *On the one hand they wanted to purge it of falsifications, and on the other hand, they wanted to renew both the letter and the spirit of the Law, with the clear intention of expressing the will of God as the ultimate purpose behind the scriptures.* This treatment of the Law was based on the assumption that some passages in the Torah were not as original as others and were in fact later falsifications. False pericopes were contained in the genuine "tradition of Moses" because God's will was consigned to oblivion by means of evil instruction, erroneous interpretation, and many other causes. Thus, it was charged, *the forefathers were responsible for the fact that the revelation had not been transmitted without falsification;* because the Law had been lost, the revelation had become burdened in later editions with additions that were contrary to God's will.[10]

The commission of Jesus to reestablish the principles of religion is not disharmonious with the Vedic siddhanta. Shrila Prabhupada supports the notion that select persons can do this: "[Lord Krishna]

---

[c] "Seat of Moses" refers to the office of teaching the oral tradition in the succession which goes back to Moses.

descends to reclaim the fallen souls and to reestablish codes of religion which are directly enacted by Him. Except for God, no one can establish the principles of religion. *Either He or a suitable person empowered by Him can dictate the codes of religion.*"[11]

One other significant point must now be added: what Jesus was doing was not merely reinterpreting parts of the Law, but also discarding them outright. In the context of the times this was shocking, for he was breaking another Jewish law of denying the fundamental teachings of Judaism. This carries with it the heavy price of prohibiting any part in eternal life to those who reject the heavenly origin of the Torah, i.e., the Torah *as a whole.*[12] In other words, one cannot pick and choose what to accept from the Torah. It must be accepted in its *entirety.* But understanding that the Torah had been falsified, and having realized the actual principles of religion, Jesus was qualified to make the necessary changes.

In the person of Jesus we have a challenge to the entire Jewish establishment of his day. His rejection of significant sections of the Torah and their replacement with other passages meant "to fulfill the Law" was in no doubt a great challenge to the falsity that had covered the Truth in that era. Jesus was qualified and empowered by the Lord for this task. He is said to have passed through India, studying at Jagannath's temple in Puri, and there to have castigated the brahmanas for their exclusivity and ill-treatment of the *sudras.* Other evidence places him as far as Tibet where chronicles still extant describe his staying and teaching there.

In his position as Prophet (*Acharya*) he was acting to re-establish the principles of religion. He demanded that his followers strictly adhere to the Law,[13] and from the evidence presented in the first chapter we may surmise that following such a strict regimen resulted in genuine spiritual potency. This made him a target of the establishment Jews, and a possible bid for the throne of Judea made him a target of the Roman political powers.

James the Righteous One

According to Eisenman "James is not only the key to unlocking a whole series of obfuscations in the history of the early church, he is also the missing link between the Judaism of his day, however this is defined, and Christianity."[14] James is thus a pivotal character in the entire story, and one whom we must not overlook.

> The disciples said to Jesus: 'We know that you will depart from us. Who is he who shall be our leader?' Jesus said to them: 'In the place where you are, go to James the Righteous One, for whose sake Heaven and Earth came into existence.'[d]

James was thus not only the brother of Jesus,[15] but was declared by Jesus as his successor as the 'Head' or 'Bishop' of the 'Jerusalem Church' and thus the whole of the Jewish Vaishnavas.[16] His stature as a spiritual leader was without question and he was renowned for his purity and extreme penance. Schoeps provides this understanding of James:

> As far as we can tell, James the brother of Jesus, by disposition a mediator, was the guarantee of the church's unity; with his death the era of schisms began. The second and third generations idealized the person of James the Righteous and projected their own ideal upon this universally revered figure

---

[d] Gospel of Thomas, 12, *Nag Hammadi Codices;* his appointment as successor of Jesus is also confirmed in *Recognitions* of the *Pseudo-Clementines*, which tell us: "The Assembly of the Lord, which was constituted in Jerusalem, was most plentifully multiplied and grew, being governed with the most Righteous ordinances by James," (Recognitions of Clement 1.43); and again by Epiphanius of Caesarea (260–340 CE), Archbishop under Constantine, in his *Ecclesiastical History,* 2nd Book, 1st chapter (2.23): "James, who was surnamed the Just by the Forefathers on account of his superlative virtue, was the first to have been elected to the Office of Bishop of the Jerusalem Church".

in order to invest him with full authority as their champion. The Jewish Christian legends, reported by Hegesippus and preserved by Eusebius in his Ecclesiastical History (2.23.6), made him a vegetarian, a teetotaler, and an ascetic, in accordance with their own style of life; they claimed that he prayed so long in the temple for the forgiveness of the sins of his people that his knees became calloused like those of a camel. Because of extreme intercession he seems to have been honored as a Paraclete [intercessor, or advocate] and to have received the honorary title *ho dikaios* (the Righteous) *kaioblias*.[e]

The theologian Jerome (4th C) wrote of James: "This same Josephus records the tradition that this James was of so great Holiness and reputation among the people that the destruction of Jerusalem was believed to have occurred on account of his death;" and in a commentary on Galatians 1:19: "so holy was James that the people zealously tried to touch the fringes of his garment."

James is said to wear only linen, and to have never worn wool or any clothing originating from animals. Interestingly he wears the clothing that was the prerogative of the temple priests, thus giving us some indication of what can only be understood as a legitimate birth rite to attend to Temple functions.

---

[e] Schoeps, p. 20. In his notes of this quote Schoeps writes: "The obscure word *oblias* was probably badly coined by Hegesippus to represent shaliach ("apostle"). The later Ebionites probably distinguished James from all other apostles by calling him "the righteous apostle" and giving him precedence over the others." It is interesting that the schisms began after James' death, and not after the death of Jesus. As we have seen, Jesus authorizes James to be the head of his church upon his departure, which James governs for some 30 years before his death. He can be understood by his deeds and passing as a genuine *Acharya* in their line, in that we understand that chaos prevails in the mission upon the departure of the *Acharya*.

As the heir to Jesus' mission, Bishop James stood at the head of the church's hierarchy. According to the Letter of Peter which introduces the Clementines, he ordained some 72 teachers, issuing letters of accreditation indicating who had been approved and was "fit and faithful for the preaching of the word of Christ." Holding the highest office and teaching authority he would require even Peter and the other apostles to submit annual reports of their preaching activity.[17]

The foregoing acknowledges James as also being an *Acharya* of the Jewish Vaishnavas. It was he who would approve of every preacher's understanding and discourse, and it was he who provided the litmus test of authoritative teachings. From Homilies we learn:

> Our lord and prophet, who has sent us, declared to us that the Evil One, having disputed with him for forty days, but failing to prevail against him, *promised that he would send apostles from among his subjects to deceive them.* Therefore, above all, *remember to shun any apostle, teacher or prophet who does not accurately compare his teaching with James*...and this, even if he comes to you with recommendations. [18]

Where the Nag Hammadi texts have first and second person accounts of James, the Dead Sea Scrolls do not refer to him by name. However, they repeatedly refer to a Teacher of Righteousness. Eisenman demonstrates through twenty pages of painstaking detail the similarities between this teacher and James, concluding them to be one and the same.[f] Such was the high position he commanded

---

[f] Eisenman, *The Dead Sea Scrolls and the First Christians*, p. 332–351.

There is some conjecture that the Teacher of Righteousness is not mentioned by name as an attempt to minimize hostilities with the established powers. In a similar way, two other major figures associated with the established powers are identified only by their activities rather than by name.

in that culture that James was considered holy from his mother's womb.[19] As the leader of the church in Jerusalem, James thus represents a faction of Jews who, like the Qumran community, are "zealous for the Law." These would include the Zealots, Sacarii, Ebionites, Zadokites, and the like as explained above who were known as determined to follow the Law in exacting measure.

The faction he leads is understandably hostile towards the Pharisee priesthood and the Temple High Priest Ananas, who, although without qualification, were appointed by Herod, and betrayed their nation and religion by concluding an accord with the Roman administration and its Herodian puppet-kings. The Temple priest at this time is the brother-in-law of Herod, who being a "seeker of smooth things" transgressed the Law by, among other things, allowing "unclean" foreigners into the Temple, and accepting gifts from foreigners. So intense was the hostility generated that James arrogates to himself the priestly functions which Ananas has compromised. On at least one occasion he dons the miter of the high priest and enters the inner sanctum of the temple, the Holy of Holies, and conducts the rituals himself.[20] Eisenman describes him in this episode as a sort of "opposition priest" who will dutifully and properly carry out the prescribed temple functions, even where Ananas and his staff abuse their position and continually violate temple protocols kowtowing to the rulers.

The Qumran documents describe James as having two adversaries, who although unnamed, are identified by their activities. One is referred to as the "Wicked Priest" and understood to be the High Priest Ananas who is responsible for James' death. The other a "treacherous," "self-willed, often rebellious and argumentative individual with the Movement," also referred to in Qumran writings as "the Liar," "Man of Lying/Pourer out of Lying," who "speaks derogatorily about the Law in the midst of the whole congregation," "leads many astray"/"tires out many with a worthless service" – the very opposite of the Righteous Teacher's proper "justifying" activity of "making many righteous" by showing a "zeal for the Law."[21]

This adversary within the Movement provides no end of grief for James, who he takes to task several times for his errant ways. We will deal with this individual in detail in the next chapter.

Not only is James the spiritual leader, but as leader of the Jewish Vaishnavas (comprising the Zealots, Sacarii, Essenes, Ebionites, Nazoreans, etc.,) he also sits squarely in the center of the "opposition alliance" involved in and precipitating the uprising against the Roman occupation. James thus occupies the most significant seat in leading what was a significant Movement that had an extensive following in early Palestine.[22]

The Death of James

James, like Jesus, died at the hands of the established powers of the time. Jesus by the political powers, James some 30 years later, by the ecclesiastical. Hegesippus tells us that the Scribes and Pharisees decide to do away with James in order to effect some control over the people – so that the people "will be frightened and not believe him." They would proclaim that "even the Righteous one has gone astray," and justify their actions by invoking a quote from the Old Testament, Isaiah 3:10. Isaiah (many of whose prophecies were not fulfilled) had prophesied the death of the "Righteous One," so in murdering James, they would fulfill Isaiah's prophecy.

Eusebius goes on to describe the death of James in the following manner:

> So they went up and threw down the Righteous One. They said to each other "let us stone James the Righteous," and began to stone him, [but] in spite of his fall he was still alive ... While they pelted him with stones . . . [a member of a particular priestly family] called out: "Stop! What are you doing!?" Then

one of them took the club which he used to beat clothes, and brought it down on the head of the Righteous one. Such was his martyrdom.[23]

As it turns out, Eisenman considers James to be an extremely pivotal character in understanding not only the events of the time, but what became known as Christianity as well. Why? Because there is so little direct information about Jesus. However, the profuse information about James allows us to understand Jesus and his Movement, for, Eisenman's study reveals that "who and whatever James was, so was Jesus."[24] As James was the leader of the Jewish Vaishnavas, we understand that Jesus was as well. They were the most important personalities, for they were the *Acharyas*, and leaders of the Jewish Vaishnavas. And because of the threat they represented to the establishment, they were both murdered.

James' killing was so egregious that it precipitated a revolt. The whole of Judea rose up to avenge his death, wherein Ananas is quickly killed as a pro-Roman collaborator. This riot turns into a full-blown rebellion and as it gains momentum emperor Vespasian leads Rome's forces. The pitched battle requires Rome to bring in tens-of-thousands of troops. Apparently they decided to rid themselves once and for all of the troubles endemic there, resulting in a full-scale war lasting seven years. Jerusalem is sacked and the Temple destroyed in 70 A.D. The war culminates with the fall of the Masada fortress in 74 A.D. In the process it is decreed that no Jews could enter Jerusalem, and thus many Jews fled to the hinterlands of Palestine, Egypt and other parts of Africa.[g] Many of the Jewish Vaishnavas paying heed to the prophecy of the destruction of the Temple, fled into Syria prior to the revolt and invasion.

---

[g] One of my friends, Ashrama Swami, was born in West Africa, Nigeria. After leaving home and becoming a Hare Krishna devotee, he returned to tell his family and friends about Krishna Consciousness. When telling the elders

We have now covered who James and Jesus were, their activities, and their roles as *Acharyas* and leaders. Understanding this, and their Movement portrayed in the first chapter, we again ask, "what happened?" Eisenman makes it clear that

> "the historical James [and thus Jesus] is almost diametrically opposed to the Jesus of Scripture and our ordinary understanding of him . . . *The situation is for the most part just the opposite of what most people think it is or consider to be true.*" [25]

As we shall see, that has been the work of Kamsas and Putanas, after they saw the light of Truth shining brightly in first-century Palestine. How "Christianity" got here from there will provide information that helps us better understand how ISKCON got here – effectively eliminated in America and Western Europe – from there – its heyday in Shrila Prabhupada's presence.

---

about Radha and Krishna he was told that They were well-known, and had been known there for many, many generations, as were many other aspects of Vaishnava philosophy.

CHAPTER FOUR

The Enemy, Liar and Sower of False Things

Acarya James had one adversary who was a constant problem. He was "a self-willed, often rebellious, argumentative individual within the Movement" who "leads many astray" and "tires out many with a worthless service." Who was this person? Why was he a problem? Our introduction to "the Enemy" of the early church begins with the first known interaction between him and James – at the Temple in Jerusalem.

> The High Priest sent priests to ask the leaders of the Assembly in Jerusalem, led by James, if they would enter into debates on the Temple steps with the Orthodox Priesthood. The invitation is accepted, and preliminary debates ensue between the apostles on one hand, and Caiaphas and the other High Priests on the other. In the midst of this, James "the Bishop" went up to the Temple . . . with the whole church. Therefore standing on an elevation so that he might be seen by all the people, James begins his discourse, continuing for seven days.

When James is about to win over "all the people," an Enemy entered the Temple with a few other men and started arguing with James. However, when he [the Enemy] was about to be overcome in debate by James, he [the Enemy] began to create a great commotion, so that matters that were being correctly and calmly explained could not be either properly examined, nor understood and believed. At that point, he raised an outcry over the weakness and foolishness of the Priests, reproached them and crying out, "Why do you delay? Why do you not immediately seize all those who are with him?" then he rose, and was first to seize a firebrand from the altar, and began beating people with it. The rest of the priests, when they saw him, then followed his example. In the panic-stricken flight that ensued, many were beaten.

Much blood poured from those that had been killed. Now the Enemy cast James down from the top of the stairs, but since he fell as if he were dead, he was not hit a second time.[1]

This account is taken from the *Recognitions* in the *Pseudo-Clementines*.[2] The Pseudo-Clementines are part of a genre of literature characteristic of the Hellenistic world generally, called pseudepigrapha – meaning books written under a false pen name, which do not represent the genuine reports of the person named. In this case "Clementine" purported to be a possible traveling companion of Peter, or Titus Flavius Clemens, who are perhaps one and the same person, who is, in any case pseudo, or unknown.[3]

Both Eisenman and Schoeps place high value on this literature because the *Pseudo-Clementines* contain much valuable information of the true history. Eisenman writes, "Fortunate, indeed we are to have the *Pseudo-Clementines*. Though these are generally held in contempt by scholars of an orthodox mindset, they contain traces of events that are of the most inestimable value for sorting out the history of early Christianity." Indeed.

James' injuries are less than fatal, but his legs are broken in the fall. Spirited away to Jericho he recovers after some time. This attack spurs a retreat of some five thousand followers to the safety of Jericho, away from Jerusalem, for the time being.

> The Enemy then, in front of the Priests, promised the High Priest Caiaphas that he would kill all those believing in Jesus. He set out for Damascus to go as one carrying letters from them, so that wherever he went, those that did not believe would help him destroy those who did. He wanted to go there first, because he thought that Peter had gone there.[4]

As he proceeds to his destination however, he suddenly falls off of his horse bewildered by a blinding flash. Then in a "vision" revealed to him, and him alone, he claims to see the risen Jesus who challenges him: "Saul, Saul, why do you persecute me?" in this well-known scene The "Enemy" is revealed as Saulus, a persecutor of "Christians," who later becomes Paul – the supposed disciple of Jesus.

These beginning events give some insight into the character who is Paul. Beginning as he does with an attempt on the life of the leader of the Jewish Vaishnavas, and threats to kill the rest, anyone with intelligence must wonder about his motives. Of course, nobody's future is forever dictated by their past, and all of us have the right to mend our evil ways and take up a spiritual life. The question as regards Paul is *did* he have a change of heart, or rather, did he simply feign one in order to better carry out another agenda? Is he a case of "atheism in the convenient disguise of theism" or was he the genuine article he purports to be?

The answers will be found in his attitudes and activities—*phalena parichyate*—you shall know them by their fruits. Concerning Paul, and given the factual history of the Jewish Vaishnavas and their leaders Jesus and James, we have the ability to understand what those fruits actually were. We shall solidly establish here that Paul is not any follower of Jesus, but an infiltrator, and determined enemy, who seeks to destroy and pervert everything about Jesus, the Jewish Vaishnavas and their teachings. Further it is Paul that establishes the very foundation of a false religion based on Jesus. A religion that serves the purposes of the Kamsas of his time. Understanding the truth of Paul provides a crucial warning of what we might expect from the Kamsas of our time.

Who was Paul?

Like so many characters from that era, Paul is seen in different ways in the texts available to us. In the canonical texts the history has been written in such a way to make Paul the protagonist, and anyone who is against Paul, even if it's the apostles themselves, are pictured in a derogatory light.[5] The Gospels are representative of Paul's perspective, and the Biblical version of Christianity is regarded as Pauline. For example, fourteen of the twenty-one "Letters" of the New Testament are Paul's, and they often take an autobiographical tone, emphasizing his perspective. Interestingly, his perspective is one that is both submissive to, and accommodating of, Roman power, rather than in opposition to that power as were the Jewish Vaishnavas. The author of the Gospel Luke, a physician friend of Paul's of the same name, was perhaps not coincidentally, the author of Acts of the Apostles. Acts also favors Paul's perspective, with little to say about the other apostles, and all the while casting him in a generally flattering light.

Other sources for Paul's biography are scattered in various unexpected places, such as the "Damascus Document," an Arabic manuscript preserved by an unlikely chain of circumstances. He also figures most prominently in the Qumran literature, although not identified by name, save for a margin note identifying him as The Enemy, who is repeatedly castigated therein for his malicious work. This Enemy is also clearly identified for us by Schoeps as

Paul in the *Kerygmata Petrou*: "Their old enemy, here appears under the pseudonym 'Simon.' This 'Simon who is also Paul' (*Simon qui et Paulus*) is for them 'a certain deceiver,' 'the enemy,' and a 'false apostle' who taught 'apostasy from Moses' and proclaimed a false gospel. As the true apostle, Peter opposes him in a debate which exposes him." [6]

Schoeps continues:

> Of more decisive importance, however, is the claim of the original apostles that there was no other gospel than the one which Jesus' disciples had learned from Jesus himself. One could see that Paul was a false apostle simply by the fact that he did not teach and expound the discourses of Christ; *his thought was the very opposite of Jesus' teaching*. This is stated in *Recognitions* 2.55: 'Whoever does not learn the law from teachers but instead regards himself as a teacher and scorns the instruction of the disciples of Jesus is bound to involve himself in absurdities against God.' For this reason Peter, whose apostolic office was founded upon the Lord's promise (Matt. 16:17 f.), also attacked Paul and exposed him in this debate as the *antikeimenos*, the great adversary. Since Paul was viewed at least by the descendants of the early Judaists as 'the adversary,' and as the *echthros* ("enemy"), indeed, even as the Antichrist (Rec. 3.61), it is probable that he was so regarded by the early Judaists themselves. [7]

This clearly establishes that the Jewish Vaishnavas considered Paul to be "The Enemy" identified at the beginning of the chapter, and more as well.

These events raise some questions, the answers to which, bring some interesting and insightful backgrounds to the character of the "Enemy." One might ask why this person is so ready to begin chasing after the faithful. What is his motive? What is it that is driving him to do this? Is he just an ordinary citizen with a personal vendetta? If so why would the High Priest provide him with "letters" (i.e., a writ carrying with it legal authority for arrest)? If not, then on whose behalf is he working? And most intriguing of all, why does this hunter of "believers" have such a turnabout that he wants to become one of them, or is this behavior a disguise for another agenda, and what might that be?

But this account has taken us a little ahead of our story. Let's back up to the events on the road to 'Damascus' and look at it in some more detail, following them through some of the Paul's "formative" years as a novitiate with the Jewish Vaishnavas.

Looking at the life of Paul

Eisenman raises the point of how unusual it would be for Saul as a relatively young man to have established sufficient authority in Jerusalem to independently take on such a project. How could he do so? It is much more reasonable that instead of taking up this task on his own volition, he is carrying out the bidding of other established authorities such as the High Priest who issues Saul's writ. But why would he be acting on behalf of the Priest?

Looking at every event of the time under his detective's glass, Eisenman finds much evidence that links Saul's Roman citizenship, with highly placed personages in the Roman government, accoutrements that are both rare for the place and time. His citizenship is a known fact as he avails himself of its advantages at several pivotal moments. Moreover, he is also observed to be quite comfortable in speaking, and his dealings with highly placed Roman officials, even including Nero's own household members,[a] for example—a behavior that belies something deeper than the formal

---

[a] Phillippians 4:22 gives reference to Paul's having one of his closest associates in the person of one Epaphroditus, who is likely both Nero's secretary

relationships, if not animosity, that would otherwise be expected from a true Essene.

Later, in an unguarded moment Paul speaks of his "kinsman Herodian."[8] This is most interesting, and the use of the term kinsman is not likely to be just an offhanded remark. As it turns out Herod Antipas, for services rendered the Roman cause, was granted citizenship along with his heirs in perpetuity. Paul's given name, Saul, at times, Saulus, is the same as a member of the Herodian family,[9] and one suspects that he may in fact be that Saul who is related to Herod. Evidence links the two, for example, Herod's Saul was known to enjoy the same favorite haunts as Paul liked. There is other evidence for Paul's Herodian connections and Roman citizenship as well, the details of which take us too far afield from our story and the interested reader is referred to the source material.[10] Eisenman's conclusion arrived at after twenty pages of investigation, and cross-referencing dozens of minutiae, concludes they are one and the same man. In the main, it is these Roman connections that offer the best explanation of all of the relationships and behaviors of Paul as regards the Roman establishment and figures.

Paul's relationship with the High Priest and other government officials would certainly explain why he was tasked with the job of ferreting out the Jewish Vaishnavas, who were seen as a threat to both the political and ecclesiastical Establishment. It would also explain why he was given the authority to arrest them, and his enthusiasm for the job as well.

---

and Josephus' publisher. Paul refers to his as his "comrade-in-arms", and "my brother, co-worker, and fellow soldier". There is also apocryphal correspondence between Paul and Seneca, Nero's Chief Minister, as well as between Paul and Seneca's brother Gallio (Acts 18:12-17). See Eisenman, *Paul as Herodian*, p. 244-5 in *The Dead Sea Scrolls and the First Christians*.

Recognitions tells us who was the instigator and authority of the posse: Saul "received a commission from Caiaphas, the High Priest...that he should arrest all who believed in Jesus, and should go to Damascus with his letters, and that there also, employing the help of unbelievers, *he should make havoc among the faithful*, and that he was hastening to Damascus chiefly on this account."[11] It appears then that the invitation to debate was a ruse designed by Caiaphas and Saul to ambush and kill the leader of the Movement, James, and with that now done (so they thought), proceeding to take care of the others. So we have established probable cause for Saul's actions based on politically motivation and familial connections, and on whose account this action is taking place.

One of the results of his "vision" of the risen Jesus is that Saul is struck blind, the other is that by this visionary miracle he presents himself as a totally changed man—converted from a persecutor of the Jewish Vaishnavas to a believer like them. Now understanding the Truth, he asks to be taken to their community and be allowed to join them as one of the faithful. Novitiates are required to complete three years of training . . . at Qumran.

This asks a lot of any rational person. First of all Paul is a known killer of the Jewish Vaishnavas. Secondly, his supposed "vision," blindness and change of heart are phenomena to which only Saul can attest. Nonetheless, we are asked to accept these attestations blindly, convinced as it were, of these miracles wrought by the grace of Jesus. The nature of such a request challenges the true believer's acceptance of Jesus' potency. *Can* Jesus do such things? The innocent believer is inclined to accept that his Lord can indeed do such things. But *did* Jesus do such things? In the scenario created, while the scoffer can or will be challenged as an unbeliever, lacking faith in the Lord, the unquestioning believer may well be taken for a fool. *The final truth of these matters must therefore be based on Saul's actions.*

Saul, who remains blind for three days is somehow accepted into the community. There is an adage that it is better to have an enemy insides one's camp than outside. This view is apparently not shared across the board however, and many of the community have strong reservations about accepting him, and even after years the hostility never dissipates. And then another miracle takes place. Saul is "cured" of his blindness, ministered by the prayers and laying-on-of-hands of one of the faithful, after only three days. Praise the Lord! This man is privileged to receive all sorts of blessings and miracles!

Saul's 'Training'

A 3-year training-probationary period was required prior to being admitted as a full-fledged member of the Essene community. Saul, now "renewed" by baptismal initiation as Paul, relates the tutelage completing his novitiate in his letter to Galatians, Chapter One. By some accounts he is now as much a fanatic as he previously was, only now to his new cause. Actually, he turns out to be something of a loose cannon, or lightning rod, for trouble. After his probationary period he goes about giving witness to Jesus and the miracles he had experienced, and this testimony from a former persecutor is sufficient to convince some to follow him as disciples.

But his preaching is causing trouble and rumors of his assassination are heard. Fleeing town with his companions in the dead of night he goes to Jerusalem to join the disciples there. However, they won't yet accept him, some being afraid of him, not believing in his change of heart. He is thus obliged to repeatedly prove himself by his earnest preaching, and eventually counts Barnabas and others among his supporters. Still, threats of his murder are again heard. Finally, for his own safety, or perhaps more likely to free themselves of this troublesome case, the church leaders send him to Taurus, in present day Turkey, the city of his birth.

Authors Baigent and Leigh suggest that this assignment was tantamount to exile.[12] The community in Jerusalem being preoccupied almost entirely with the events at home is little concerned with the rest of the world. If by fluke he manages to do something there, well and good. If he meets some other unfortunate end, why, what can be done; and he won't be unduly missed.

Paul has three trips abroad covering fourteen years of his preaching career. After Tarsus he preaches in Antioch, the place where his followers are the first people to be called "Christians." It wasn't long afterward that the area is bristling with dispute over the content of Paul's message. Representatives of the church travel there, and unable to convince Paul and Barnabas of the necessity of strictly following the Law, they are ordered back to Jerusalem. In the assembly of the elders Paul makes his case, and then, surprisingly, or perhaps not, Biblical Acts from there on out defers to Barnabas' and Paul's opinions, becomes their apologist, and exalts the "signs and wonders worked through them."

For the unschooled nothing may seem amiss here. But for those who understand the ideology of the early church as represented by James this is alarming! Baigent and Leigh comment on this: "by careful consideration of the implications of non-sequiturs in extant texts as well as glaring omissions, Eisenman clearly presents the working method of Acts and the Gospels as nothing more than deliberate obfuscation and rewriting of early church history in order to downplay the parts played by Jesus' brothers (especially James) and to try to justify Paul's doctrines with those really held by the Jerusalem Community."[13] The activities of the Putanas now begin to show.

Paul's Self-Arrogated Special Position

Jesus and James, as the leaders of the early church, had established and maintained its teachings and standards. The early church was established on their authority, and the faithful were those who followed their teachings. Now here comes Paul, who, while doing what is necessary to remain associated with them, attempts to establish his own authority, and thereby introduce an understanding that is diametrically opposed to the church he fashions himself to represent!

For our entry into the nature of Paul we must begin with that which demonstrates his attempts to establish himself as a true and authoritative representative of Jesus. But Paul was a late-comer, someone who appeared on the scene *after* Jesus had been gone for at least three years. He never even met Jesus. Nonetheless, and despite his reproachful introduction to the Jewish Vaishnava community, after only a brief time, and on the flimsiest of credentials, he presents himself as a peer, if not superior by dint of vision, to the original apostles, a member of a very select group chosen by Jesus himself to present his teachings. How does he do this? Schoeps answers:

> Over against the principle of belonging personally to the narrowest circle of Jesus' associates, as enunciated by the primitive church, Paul set the principle of the new post-messianic period, *according to which apostleship no longer depended upon association with Jesus according to the flesh* but only upon the fact of being a witness of the Resurrection. And this must have meant for him a special calling, a sending and commission by the risen Christ directed especially to him. That is, he believed himself commissioned to proclaim the gospel to the Gentiles. *By God's will he was called to be 'an apostle of Jesus Christ,'* as stated in the introductions to most of his epistles, having the office of the 'servant of Christ,' who is a tool in God's hands. To his opponents in Galatia *he retorted that his apostleship was independent of men* since it had originated in a separate revelation of Christ which was imparted only to him.

His apostleship did not derive from human authorization ("not from men nor through a man") but was uniquely derived from the commission of Jesus Christ and his divine Father.[14]

From the above it is easily and repeatedly seen that Paul's promotion to the post of apostle is entirely self-arrogated. Recall that his "vision" of the "risen" Jesus is his own unverifiable, and dubious, testimony, and it is on this basis that he makes his claim. Moreover, it is a claim that has no precedent within the church he purports to be a member of. Nor is his claim, or its basis, recognized by the authorities of that church.

In fact, the Apostles unconditionally rejected Paul's claims. In *Homilies* 17, Peter flatly asserts that Paul *could not* have seen the risen Christ. Furthermore, the principle had already been established – only eyewitnesses of the earthly Jesus could be considered Apostles.[15] The Jerusalem church had maintained a rigorous limitation of the apostolic office to the Circle of the Twelve, and a thirteenth apostle was as unthinkable as a thirteenth month in the year. The "visions" and "revelations of the Lord" to which Paul pointed constitute no claim to any objective truth. Indeed, in *Clementine* Peter reviles them as manifestations of an evil demon or a lying spirit,[16] and he rages against them as a basis for any authority:

How then can one be qualified for the teaching office by means of instruction received in a vision? And if you protest, 'It is possible,' then why did the Master spend a whole year with us who were awake? How are we to believe you when you say that he has really appeared to you? And how can he really have appeared to you, since you think precisely the opposite of his teaching? If, however, by means of one hour's instruction you have become an apostle, then also proclaim his discourses and expound them, love his apostles, do not quarrel with me, for I was with him. You have opposed me, a firm rock, the bedrock foundation of the church. If you were not my adversary, you would not slander me and revile my preaching, so that I am not believed when I declare that which I received directly from the mouth of the Lord himself, as if I were a condemned man and you were the one who was highly extolled. When you call me *kategnosmenos*, you indict God, who revealed Christ to me; you attack him who praised me as blessed on account of this revelation. But if you do in fact want to work for the Truth, then first learn from us what we have learned from Jesus, and become as a disciple of the Truth our co-worker.[b]

It must now be clear that Peter is Paul's most vehement adversary. Schoeps finishes the subject by reiterating the rejection of Paul's visions and his claims to any position of authority, as well as his gospel that diverges so significantly from that of the apostles quoting *Homilies* 2:17: "it is said that he [Simon/Paul] "came with the pretense of proclaiming the Truth in the name of our Lord, but was actually sowing error."

Paul Exclusively Holds the 'Correct' Understanding

In another remarkable display of self-arrogated authority Paul will claim *sole exclusivity in understanding the teachings of Jesus.* He attributes to himself a virtue widely acknowledged and attributed to James—that of being holy from his mother's womb—and asserts on this, again self-established, claim[17], that God had especially

---

[b] Schoeps, p. 52-53. Note that the accounts given in the *Pseudo-Clementines* (*Homilies* and *Recognitions*) are understood to be fictional dialogues, reconstructions as to what the characters would likely have been thought to have said. Epiphanius is an important witness in support of the view that the original Clementine writings, now no longer extant, are to be associated with the Ebionites. See also Schoeps, p. 15-17.

chosen him and "revealed His son to him" and how the Gospel as he taught it "among the Gentiles" was the result of a direct "revelation of Jesus Christ" and how if anyone preached a Gospel contrary to the one he has preached – even an "angel in heaven" – "he is to be accursed."[18] We know by now however what the Apostles would have thought of this arrogant claim. It is not to the Apostles that he speaks however, but to the innocent and naïve.

Paul's Alternative Gospel

We saw above that Peter rejected not only Paul's visions but also his deviant gospel. Just as his claim to apostleship ran counter to that of the tradition of the early church, so did his claims about the person of Jesus and his teachings. There are at least three items in his preaching that must have enraged the disciples, because they are such egregious deviations. The first regarded his neglect of the Law, the second his introduction of the idea of Jesus' blood sacrifice for atonement of sin, and the third, the divinity of Jesus.

As we have endeavored to make clear, the Jewish Vaishnavas sought to follow the true Mosaic Law reestablished by the prophet Jesus. They were fastidiously attentive to the Law, and demonstrated the fact by doing intentional good works. But along comes Paul and his supposed vision, saying in Jesus' name that it isn't necessary to do works of any kind, nor worry about following the Law. He declares that there was a new covenant declared by Jesus by which everything was already taken care of, and *all* that was necessary was faith—and not faith in reality—but faith in a fantasy. His gospel, purported to be the teachings of Jesus, and by extension to embody an understanding of him, was almost diametrically opposed to what James, and the remainder of the Jewish Vaishnavas, including Jesus, stood for.[19] A result that is not accidental.

We return again to Schoeps for insights into Paul's understanding of the Law. In the closing paragraph to the chapter entitled *The Content of the Message of the Ebionite Christ*, he reiterates the Ebionite understanding, and Paul's misunderstanding, deliberate or otherwise, of the same:

> In concluding this chapter we must again emphasize that for the later Ebionites the real point of Christ's message was the reformation of the Mosaic Law. They were convinced that they were judging the Law on the basis of Jesus himself; they saw in his life and teaching the real fulfillment of the Mosaic Law. What was of divine origin, he confirmed; what was not, he annulled. The knowledge of this, the 'mystery of the Scriptures, 'as transmitted by Jesus, the Christ, to the apostle Peter and through him to the Ebionite congregations, while 'Simon, who is also Paul,' was reproached by them for having tried 'to learn from the law what the law did not know.'

Trying "to learn from the law what the law did not know" is a euphemism for misunderstanding, misinterpreting, or deliberately altering the Law. We suggest that Paul, now clearly identified as an agent of Kamsas of the time, was deliberately altering it for the purpose of misleading the innocent down a false and impotent, spiritual path. His technique is to introduce half-truths, a method that confuses many people. It's a baited hook. Sensing some inherent truth and accepting it, they also accept the falsity, not being able to make the distinction.

Paul seemingly derives his theology from the original Book of Habakkuk, a text of Old Testament Apocrypha. There we find the exhortation that "the upright man will live by his faithfulness."[20] This idea is expanded upon in the Habakkuk Commentary, found among the Dead Sea Scrolls:

> But the righteous shall live by his faith. Interpreted, *this*

concerns all those who observe the Law in the House of Judah, *whom God will deliver* from the House of Judgment because of their suffering and because of their faith in the Teacher of Righteousness. [21]

We see that in this passage that the emphasis is on *how to live*: having faith in the Teacher of Righteousness *those who observe the Law* will be delivered by God. This, as understood in conjunction with the many passages from the *Pseudo-Clementines*, is the doctrine of the Jewish Vaishnavas. It can be restated as: *those who are Righteous*, because they have proper faith, *will live the Law*; or as: *the way they live* is *an expression of their faith* in the Law, and faith in the results accrued by such works.

But Paul takes the passage and reorients the emphasis: instead of works he emphasizes faith, although that is not the actual spirit of the passage. Paul thus takes the truth of *living* by faith, and makes it a half-truth of living, presumably in any manner, as long as one *has faith*. In doing so, he creates confusion for everyone, and we presume that this is his objective.

This idea of "faith not works" being the salvation of man has opened the door to much foolishness. I have been told by one "Christian" that after receiving Jesus as my personal savior – simply by saying so many words – I would then be free to do any sinful act, having been forever redeemed from all sin by the atonement of Jesus. This was exactly the idea so roundly criticized by Shrila Prabhupada that the Christians were using Jesus as a door mat on which to repeatedly wipe their sins.

So much for Paul's creation of the theology of "grace not works." Let us now turn to his other major alteration of the Jewish Christian doctrine, that of Jesus' blood sacrifice as atonement for sin.

The Sacrificial Cult of Paul

Paul reiterates throughout the Gospels that he is "building" a community where both Greeks and Jews can live in harmony,[22] insisting that Jesus is the precious "Cornerstone" with the Prophets and Apostles being "the Foundation" and the members "the building." [23] From our perspective two millennia later it would seem a noble effort. It was not, however, viewed in such a flattering light by his contemporaries, for the early church determinedly rejects wholesale Paul's ideas of building any community calling it "a City of Blood" – "The Spouter of Lying" "led many astray to build a Worthless City upon blood and erect an Assembly on Lying, and for the sake of his [own] Glory, tiring out many with a Worthless Service, instructing them in works of Lying, *so that their works will count for nothing.*"[24]

This reaction comes from the early church regarding several of Paul's newly created doctrines: the New Covenant where the Messianic Christ, now God incarnate as a redeemer, shedding his blood as a remission for the sins of mankind. There are also the putative statements of the Last Supper where Jesus asks his disciples to eat of his flesh and drink of his blood as a sacrifice of the New Covenant.[25] Paul mandates this dogma *establishing it on a threat:* that those who partake of the Communion without seeing it as the body of the Lord, eats and drinks Judgment to himself."[26] The Roman church later formally defined this doctrine in 1215,[27] and it became official dogma only in 1564. Under the name "Transubstantiation" the bread and wine of the Mass must be literally perceived as the very body and blood of Jesus transfigured, which they are then asked to eat at Communion!

The very idea of anything to do with eating blood was abhorrent to the Jewish Vaishnavas who were strict vegetarians long before Jesus arrived on the scene,[c] and they looked to him to remove the false pericopes of the Torah that required animal sacrifice. In their view, they had been freed from the sacrificial worship established with Josiah's reform[d] – not through the universally efficacious sacrifice of the "Son of God," as Paul led people to believe— but rather through the cleansing water of baptism whereby Jesus extinguished the fire of the sacrificial cult, relieving the act of atonement, once and for all, of all of the foul connotations of blood.

"The notion of blood and consuming it is one that exercises those responsible for the literature at Qumran to no small degree" writes Eisenman, and he connects the Qumran allusions to the "City of Blood," etc., with Paul's "Communion with the Blood of

---

[c] Judas Maccabee, Jewish independence leader, and his followers as precursors of latter day Zealots, were all strict vegetarians dating back to 165 BC.

[d] "According to Ebionite belief, Moses received a Pentateuch [first 5 books of the Bible] different from their present one; the latter, written a thousand years after Moses, has been falsified. Approximately five hundred years after Moses' death it was rediscovered in the Temple (Josiah's reform, Deuteronomy); after another five hundred years it perished in the flames (under Nebuchadnezzar), then was written down again (Priestly Code, under Ezra), with the result that in successive drafts it became more and more falsified. In any event, we may regard it as certain that the Ebionite theory of false pericopes did not come out of the blue but derived from ancient recollections that the extant version of the Torah was not identical with the Sinai version but had been distorted by additions and alterations. The Ebionites were as justified in maintaining that the Sinai legislation was originally non-cultic [without animal sacrifice] and that it was the post-Deuteronomy Priestly Code which introduced the many sacrificial commandments into the Torah for the first time, wrongly giving Jewish religion a cultic [sacrificial] character." Schoeps, p. 83-4.
"We may say that Jewish Christian antagonism toward the law of sacrifice is directly descended from statements of the prophets on this subject. The statements of the prophets. . . can only be understood when one remembers that the standardization of the sacrificial cult is the product of later Israelite history; it occurred, at the earliest, in the era of Manasseh (698—643 B.C.). Consequently, the Mosaic origin of the cultic laws is a fiction, or, to employ Ebionite terms, the product of false pericopes. Schoeps, p. 118

Christ" and the "New Covenant in my blood, which was poured out for you." [28] On these points Eisenman comments:

> One can well imagine how, in particular, this [Paul's New Covenant] would have infuriated those of a Qumran perspective . . . Paul knows full well what he is doing. Again, as we have pointed out *ad nauseam – but it cannot be repeated too often –* on almost all these issues Paul is systematically allegorizing and turning the Qumran positions back against them. He is doing the same to James. That Paul groups his positions regarding 'dining in an idol-temple' and 'Communion with the blood of Christ' under the heading of 'loving God' or 'Piety' would have only infuriated groups like Qumran even more.[29]

There are a many additional references to these themes, but suffice it to say that these main doctrines of Paul were an abhorrent to the Essene community, and Eisenman may be consulted further for additional details.[30] Nor did Paul disregard the teachings and example of those before him just on these issues, but for all practical purposes on every single doctrine the Jewish Vaishnavas followed.

So, Who is This Paul?

The New Testament of the Bible is often referred to by scholars as "Pauline Christianity" as it presents Paul's point of view, with hardly a word from the supposed "Savior" Jesus. Indeed, it was Paul that coined the phrase "Christianity" and laid the foundations for a "religion" out of his own imagination that is almost completely contrary to those he is supposedly following, and in whose name he was supposedly acting. In fact, he was not a follower, but a determined enemy of Jesus, James, the Jewish Vaishnavas, and the Eternal Religion. His history is one of creating incessant confusion and conflict, earning him the negative appellations of "the Liar," "the Enemy," "the false apostle," "he who leads others astray," etc.

Paul's character is revealed both in his own letters, as well as in the Book of Acts, to include his insubordination, jealousy, incessant bragging and vindictiveness. He denigrates the authority of those he calls "leaders," "pillars," "Arch-apostles," and displays an unwillingness to follow their views. This man is not at all a saint, although he has been promoted as such by political powers for political purposes (apparently "fake news" is not original to the 21st century).

Paul is a Herodian, an agent of the Roman forces, who, judging by the results, infiltrated the Jewish Vaishnava group for the purpose of destroying from within everything it stood for and taught, while at the same time laying a foundation for a competing "religion" that serves the purposes of the controlling secular powers. Paul is the poster child for "atheism in the convenient disguise of theism." There is much, much more evidence of Paul's efforts to undermine the Jewish Vaishnavas and Eternal Religion not included here to minimize the size of this book. The interested reader is referred to the works of Schoeps and Eisenman.

Paul's deviations demonstrate just how far the Kamsas and Putanas were willing to go to destroy the Eternal Religion in the first century, and how far they will be willing to go when the Eternal Religion next makes its appearance in the West in the 20th century. Next we will see how the Putanas continue with the destruction from where Paul leaves off.

Putanas, Scribes & Exegetes

Shrila Bhaktisiddhanta Maharaja alerts us that "lexicographical interpreters are employed by Kamsa in putting down the first suspected appearance of any genuine faith in the transcendental. King Kamsa knows very well that if the faith in the transcendental is once allowed to grow it is sure to upset all his empiric prospects."

"Lexicographical interpreters" is perhaps a difficult, but wonderful, metaphor referring to those who interpret the bona fide scripture according to their atheistic mindset. They re-write it as something resembling the original Truth, but devoid of any potency to conduct the Truth. Shrila Prabhupada called them "word jugglers." Through the ages they have gone by other names such as Scribes (in Europe and the Middle East 1000 - 3000 years ago), and in our modern day as Exegetes – those who study and explain scriptural passages – also known as academics, or even scholars. But we lump them all together as Putanas – the agents of the atheistic controllers who sow falsity in place of Truth, and who seek out any appearance of the Truth for the purpose of killing it.

The review of history in this chapter offers lessons in the destruction of truth and the creation of false doctrines that keep people in ignorance. It is the task of the scribes to "fine tune" the dogma to establish falsity as superior to Truth. The Exegetes are also tasked with maintaining the then well-established position of ignorance, deriding any subsequent discoverers of the Truth as "deviants," ridiculing them, and surrounding them with a wall of shame and derision to keep them separated from the masses.

The interpretations of the Putanas are given the highest credence by the establishment powers who laud their credentials and social standing, and herald their understanding. Their role is to make interpretations of scriptures based on specious arguments using a high-sounding specialist vocabulary, and all manners of hypothetical possibilities – and outright lies – to mislead the general mass of people.

The word jugglers have a number of tools in their bag of tricks for creating misunderstanding. Among them are:

1. substituting words or assigning words with different meanings in place of an original word, as is done in translation or interpretation,
2. changing doctrines, replacing the Truth with outright lies, or dogma, and then compelling acquiescence by threats of physical harm and eternal damnation,
3. the use of Half-truths, fooling the gullible to accept a half-lie,
4. destroying, omitting, hiding, or otherwise removing genuine knowledge from circulation,
5. ridicule and harassment of those who uncover and declare the Truth, causing the foolish to avoid such persons and their ideas, and
6. reinterpretation of events and ideas from an earlier era in the context of the modern era,

7. accusing purveyors of Truth of that which they themselves are guilty,

8. Silence. This is reserved for the most ominous threats, which they ignore all around. And finally,

9. a very effective method used often throughout history – silencing truth with the sword.

The lessons of history offer keen insights in understanding our own mission to spread the Truth and to protect Shrila Prabhupada's legacy for posterity. But we must learn this lesson well, since the Kamsas repeatedly use these same tools that have proven so effective in the past to bewilder the innocent, the foolish and the naïve.

To fully understand the efforts of the Putanas we must remember their goal of suppressing the Truth before it has time to develop. Today we are all witness to the information war in the print, broadcast and online media going on before us. A war in which our thoughts and opinion are the object of conquest. Public perception and belief is important because the few cannot control the many without their acquiescence.

Control by the Sword to Control by Belief

We can understand by their conquering, controlling, and exploitative activities that the Romans were the leading *rakshasas* of their day. They extended their territories by conquest and dominated the entire Western world, desiring to be the lords of all. They loathed the Jewish Vaishnavas because of their defiance and refusal to submit to them.[a] The Romans were the ones who,

---

[a] This *Rakshasa* attitude of control or kill is displayed by Hiranyakasipu toward his very own son Prahlada: "Just as uncontrolled senses are the enemies of all yogis engaged in advancing in spiritual life, this Prahlada, who appears to be a friend, is an enemy because I cannot control him. Therefore this enemy, whether eating, sitting or sleeping, must be killed by all means." SB 7.5.38

through their local agents, or by their agents' own initiative, put Jesus to the cross, sent Paul as an agent within the church, thereby wreaking havoc in its name, plotted the death of James, sacked the Temple and Jerusalem, and eventually exterminated or drove out of Palestine all of the Jewish Vaishnavas. Whatever survived, was what they allowed to survive.

After the fall of the Temple, the Judaism of the Establishment Rabbis was the only tradition the Romans were willing to tolerate, because of their accommodating attitude towards foreign rule. "The same was to hold true for the form of Christianity we can refer to as 'Pauline,' which was equally submissive or accommodating to Roman power . . ." Eisenman tells us, continuing,

> The development of this genre of 'Overseas' Christianity was actually concurrent and parallel to the development of Rabbinic Judaism – if something of its mirror image. Both were not only willing to live with Roman power, *they owed their continued existence to its sponsorship. . .* the power and brutality of Rome was operating to both drive out and to declare heretical what is now called Jewish Christianity, 'Essenism' or 'Ebionitism.'[1]

Not only were the Jewish Vaishnavas driven out, but their Truths were replaced with "a largely hellenized, other-worldly mystery cult. . . This surgery was necessary if Christianity in the form we know it was to survive, since **certain doctrines represented by James, and probably dating back to his Messianic predecessor 'Jesus,'** *were distinctly opposed to those ultimately considered to be Christian.*"[2] That is, the Truths held by the Jewish Vaishnavas were a considerable threat to Pauline Christianity and had to be eliminated.

This assessment by Eisenman is as striking as it is, by now, expected. Striking in that Eisenman has understood and reported the

relationship of these two "religions" with the Establishment powers of Rome. If Rome sponsored them, it did so for some purpose.
We identify that purpose as a tool for the control of the masses
by suppressing the Truth that manifest in the movement of Jesus
and James, a Truth that gave its followers freedom in behavior
based on deep spiritual understanding. Its replacement by Pauline
Christianity was to keep the population subservient to Rome, and
ignorant of spiritual Truth – yet provide them with an outlet for
religious sentiments and mysticism, for which they were naturally
inclined.

As we add up the evidence regarding Paul – his travels, his connection with the Romans, and the development of his ideology –
an intentional design begins to reveal itself. Two-thirds of Paul's
twenty year ministry was spent "overseas" mainly to and throughout Greece. In contradistinction to the early church, his main effort was in converting Gentiles (i.e., Greeks), not Jews, to *his* new
religion: "Christianity."[b] Further the earliest existing Gospels are
written in Greek, not only with a distinctive Pauline orientation,
but simultaneously with a blatant disregard of the historical Jesus,
James, the other Apostles, and anything of the perspective of the
Jewish Vaishnavas. This combination reveals a possible blueprint
designed to portray an idealized, even mythical, reality to those
persons who would have had little opportunity to verify Paul's
claims.

---

[b] Real religious principles are enacted by the Supreme Personality of Godhead.
SB 6.3.19; and, Shrila Prabhupada in conversation with a Benedictine Monk:
"To practice bhakti-yoga means to become free from designations like
"Hindu," "Muslim," "Christian," this or that, and simply to serve God. We
have created Christian, Hindu, and Muhammadan religions, but when we
come to a religion without designations, in which we don't think we are
Hindus or Christians or Muhammadans, then we can speak of pure religion, or
bhakti." From *Science of Self Realization*.

If Paul intended to sow a false representation of the early church, which area would offer the most fertile field? Palestine where the Jewish Vaishnavas were well known and likely the majority of the population? Or a distant land where people would know little of Jesus or his teachings? Had Paul attempted to pursue his preaching in Palestine he would have been laughed at or killed. His portrayal of events in Palestine, as Eisenman has shown, as well as the Gospels written after his own creed, are almost entirely a fiction. But by and large his audience, ignorant of the facts as they were, and having no means by which to verify what was presented to them, accepted Paul's version of the teachings of Jesus, and his "miraculous redemption" of all sinners. Anywhere but Palestine is thus preferential for Paul's, and Rome's, purposes.

The conquest of Jerusalem by the sword was a seven-year task that exacted harsh tolls. Undoubtedly the Romans had many casualties. Unrest and uprisings also demand a regular expenditure of effort and blood when the sword is the main tool of coercion. How else then, to develop a control mechanism that requires little of one's own blood but provides for the willing forfeiture of others' when necessary? Certainly the unflagging conviction of the Jewish Vaishnavas was not lost on the occupying forces. The Jewish Vaishnavas could withstand any amount of torment, even at a tender age, rather than defile their conscience.[3]

Could not this rock-solid allegiance be garnered and used by the Kamsas themselves? Why should the unseen God of these believers be the only enjoyer of such willing sacrifice? Hiranyakasipu was similarly bedeviled by his son's determined devotion to some supposed and unseen God other than himself. After all, the demons' opinion is "are we not gods who deserve such supplication? Don't we deserve that place of worship? And if we can't take the place of God, then at least we must be the sole intercessors to His access." How? Control men by controlling their beliefs! A man's

commitment to his religious beliefs is far stronger and more inde-
fatigable than his allegiance to any other cause. What is wanted
then is the successful creation and development of a religious belief
system that subordinates the believer to the will of the ruling elite
(and conveniently acts as a powerful tool to bury any manifestation of the Truth). And it is the development of this new "religion"
that becomes the keystone in the battle for the Truth. It was with
the creation and development of the Christian Church that the
*rakshasa*s enter in the disguise of "leaders of the faithful" – leading
them astray that is.

The development of both Rabbinic Judaism and Christianity
have been significant to the West, but Rabbinic Judaism is outside of our scope and we leave it aside. It is Pauline or Hellenic
Christianity that will be our focus. Our interest lies in the history
and the development of the Christian dogma, it's scripture, and
interpretation, and the more recent archeological finds that shed
light on this early time. Our story focuses on the machinations of
the Putanas, scribes and exegetes.

Development of the Pauline Doctrine and the Canonical Bible

Pauline Christianity was the antithesis of what Jesus and James
stood for, supporting as it did the purpose and ambitions of the
powerbrokers that developed it. Its development begins of course
with Paul, who, as we have seen by his activities, words, and invented philosophy, provided the Putanas with sufficient material
to flesh out the creation of the Christian religion, complete with
sacred mystery, promise of heavenly reward and threats of eternal
damnation. Paul was exceedingly clever and articulate. He knew
full well what he was up to, as Eisenman respectfully acknowledges
writing "in Paul we are dealing with one of the most able rhetori-
cians (read: word-juggling, lexicographical interpreters) Western
culture ever produced."[4]

Pauline Christianity is built around doctrines that eventually became established in the Bible and canonized at the Council of Nicaea in 325 A.D., later ratified at the Council of Hippo in 393. It was at these councils that the authorized books of the church's New Testament were established, and what was left out is probably more important than what was included. The orthodoxy developed in the 2nd century established much of the church dogma through Polemics written in support of the Pauline doctrines, and largely in opposition to the Truths of the Gnostics and Manicheans. Further we must remember that Guttenberg was yet more than a thousand years away, and the creeds were *hand-copied,* one by one. Did these scribes adhere to the principle of respecting these texts as sacred and not changing *anything,* as did the "keepers of the Law," or did they have another agenda? [c] The veils of the past are parted for us by the scholarship of the past two centuries, allowing us to review the textual, literary and historical veracity of the Bible – all important lessons for us on the consequences of starting down the slippery slope of scriptural "editing."

By the time the Gospels were first penned the Jewish Vaishnavas had been decimated and/or driven from Palestine. Typical dates given for their creation is *after* the destruction of the Temple, AD 70, but perhaps as late as AD 110. Who wrote them then? It's often news to most people, even those raised as Christians that the books of the New Testament – those of Matthew, Mark, Luke and John – were not likely written by men of those names; *or even by those who were the contemporaries of Jesus.* Eisenman tells us that "they are still representative of a genre of literature characteristic of the Second Temple Period and the Hellenistic world generally, called

---

[c] "So in the parampara system in that disciplic succession, you will find no change. The original word is there. That is the thing. They are not foolish to manufacture something new." Shrila Prabhupada Lecture 3Jun76.

pseudopigrapha – meaning books written under a false pen-name – and do not represent the genuine reports of a man called Matthew, a man called Mark and a man called Luke, whoever these men might have been."[d]

The earliest of the Gospels is generally considered to be Mark's. Not one of the original apostles, he is thought to have been a companion of Paul, and, according to Clement of Alexandria, wrote his gospel in Rome for a Hellenistic-Roman audience. The observed Roman connections would necessarily impart a pro-Roman bias to the work, and preclude a Jesus who was in any way anti-Roman. His writing, not surprisingly, bears an unmistakable Pauline viewpoint.

Besides the usual redactions, editing and censorship, there is another peculiar irregularity with the Gospel of Mark that introduces the deceptive polemics of the Patriarchs. A "missing" fragment of Mark's gospel, found by Professor Morton Smith in 1958 in a Jerusalem monastery, appears to have been deliberately left out, or even suppressed, by one of the church Patriarchs, Clement of Alexandria. One Theodore wrote to Clement to complain of the interpretation of Mark by a Gnostic sect, the Carpocratians, who, according to their own understanding, not surprisingly arrive at a conclusion far afield from that of the Patriarchs. It may well be that the Carpocratians had misinterpreted the tract of the Gospel, but the exchange of letters is more telling.[e] Theodore consequently

---

[d] James, p. 57; That may not be as troubling as it sounds though, since "for the ancients authorship was a much broader concept than it is today. In their time a man could be called the 'author' of a work if he was the authority behind it, even though he did not write it. Stated in *Introduction to the Books of the New Testament,* The New American Bible, p. xxxiv

[e] The episode in question refers to the possible interpretation of Jesus' raising of Lazarus as a homosexual affair, as the Carpocratians, like their modern day counterpart Bagawan Rajneesh, were said to advocate a path to transcendence

attacked their interpretation, reporting it to Clement, to which Clement wrote the following missive:

> You did well in silencing the teachings of the Carpocratians.
> . . Such [men] are to be opposed in all ways and altogether.
> For, even if they should say something true, one who loves
> the truth should not, even so, agree with them. **For not all
> true [things] are the truth** [?!], nor should that truth which
> [merely] seems true according to human opinions be preferred
> to the true truth, that according to the faith.[5]

This is the tell-tale signature of polemicist, advocating a denial of any even obvious truths that stem from his ideological adversaries – what to speak of disparaging them and their motives. In other words if these Gnostics speak the truth Theodore is admonished to deny it, and even lie, if that will help to defeat them! This would appear to be from Paul's "winning at all costs" strategy. Yet, he goes on, encouraging more lies and deceit, that:

> one must never give way, nor, when they put forward their
> falsifications, should one concede that the secret Gospel is by
> Mark, **but should even deny it on oath.** For 'not all true
> [things] are to be said to all men.'

---

via total satiation of the senses. Were the accusations true then a responsible reply would warrant censorship. Others however have interpreted this event concerning Lazarus as a mystery initiation rite into an esoteric understanding of spirit, with the interpretation of sexual impropriety being given by Clement to throw him off the real scent, i.e., spiritual truths that were rejected from "Christian" teachings. This reputation attributed to the Carpocratians may therefore have been false allegations or a deliberate and false character assassination of this Gnostic sect. In any case, the instructions of Clement go beyond the correction of faulty doctrine to the point of cult-like mindless adherence to a particular train of orthodox thought and blind following of the Patriarchs. See Part 2, Chapter Ten for ISKCON parallels.

The author of the gospel of Luke is generally considered to be another friend of Paul's, who also had no first-hand experience of the events in Palestine. His gospel is dated somewhere around AD 80. Luke was a Greek doctor, an educated man, and he is supposed to have composed his work for a high-ranking Roman official at Caesarea, the Roman capital of Palestine. These connections again favor the Romans, against the attitudes of the xenophobic Jewish Vaishnavas. Luke is also the supposed author of Acts of the Apostles, which are considered to be the "second half" of the gospel. As Paul's friend we expect, not disappointedly, sympathetic support of Paul's "theology."

With regard to the Gospel according to John, how much of the gospel is actually from "John" is impossible to know. But how much of *any* of the original Gospels remain with us today we do know: **None.** All of the original works have all been "lost in time," and the earliest extant editions date from the fourth century, all in Greek. In fact, of the nearly 5,000 Christian writings that have survived till today, none predate the fourth century. Perhaps it took 300 years to get the story straight? That matters little now, two millennia later.

With the exception of Paul writing his own letters, the other authors are those who *did not* have first-hand witness to the events they describe – events that had taken place 40 to 80 years *prior*. How likely is it that what they portray is accurate or even true? Did the events described actually take place at all, and are the words and teachings ascribed to Jesus factual? The dogma of course is that the Bible is the "inspired" word of God, and as such it must therefore be inerrant, and cannot be impugned. But the fact of the matter is that the inerrant Gospels impugn each other! And not just once or twice, but dozens of times.

Despite the facts, an army of Putanas have been mustered to defend the integrity of "scripture" as it stands, by whatever means, and very often the best means has been silence. The contradictions that arise are conveniently overlooked by the parish priest and scholars alike, and only those few religious historians or scholars who delve deeply into analysis of the texts will discover the contradictions. If they happen to raise a cry of alarm they are overshadowed by a scholarly consensus who point out the "patently obvious" misunderstanding. [f]

Biblical Redactions

So much for the creation of the Bible. Let us now turn to the alterations of its doctrines, however true or false it may have been to begin with. If we ask when scriptural alteration began, we can say as early as the second century, the same era in which it was written, with documented evidence from that era in support of this claim. The changes introduced to the early church scriptures were in fact met with much alarm and consternation, similar to that produced

---

[f] This is elaborated on many times over by both Schoeps and Eisenman who have both put forward a thesis that lies outside the acceptable limits of the debate. For example, Schoeps writes of his suggestion on p. 43 that the events of martyrdom attributed to Stephen, were actually events that happened to James. The polemic reaction must have been intense as he responds: "This central section of Stephen's speech, which is doctrinally totally unique both in the New Testament and in the literature of the ancient church, has, as far as I know, only a single parallel in terms of content, viz., this passage of the Recognitions which we have attributed to the Ebionite "Acts." *This gives pause for thought!* In my book **I proposed an explanation for this which I will not repeat** since **all theologians immediately see red** *when the historicity of the alleged Hellenistic deacon Stephen is questioned.* In any case, we have in the speech of the Ebionite "Acts," whether it was delivered by James, Peter, or someone else, a counterpart to Stephen's speech in Acts 7. **I regard it as a dereliction of duty on the part of the exegetes when they pass by this unique parallel without showing any interest in it.**
Later (p. 45) he declares a polemic victory over this issue, his confirmation

by the changes to Shrila Prabhupada's books. Celsus, an Epicurean philosopher of the second century writes: "Certain Christians, like men who are overcome by the fumes of wine and care not in the least what they say, alter the original text of the Gospels so that they admit of various and almost indefinite readings."

This word-juggling of the ancients is confirmed by the works of modern scholars who have access to a wide variety of ancient texts. Dr. F. H. Scrivener points to second century shenanigans in his *Introduction to the Criticism of the New Testament,*[6] writing: "In the second century we have seen too many instances of attempts to tamper with the text of Scripture, some merely injudicious, others positively dishonest." He goes on to state that although it sounds paradoxical "the worst corruptions to which the New Testament has ever been subjected, *originated within 100 years after it was composed.*"

The multitude of differences that appear in Christian scripture are not easy to catalogue, what to speak of understanding their origins. As it happens in all times (and is likewise happening with ISKCON), soon there were many factions holding to various conceptions of understanding: their proxy of the Truth. They wrote to establish and promote their own positions, and all the while criticizing the changes made or rejected by others. It wasn't long before we witness how *those who introduced the heresies themselves* adopt the age-old tactic of accusing others of that which they themselves are guilty.[g] The "church fathers" had themselves

---

issuing not from any modern scholars, but from the Gnostics themselves! He writes: "Moreover, an Apocalypse of James has turned up among the Gnostic writings discovered at Nag Hammadi which has induced its editor, A. Bohlig, to declare that 'the traditions concerning James and Stephen belong together.' *This means that, despite all my opponents, my view is the correct one!*"

Make note that Schoeps writes in 1961; Eisenman subsequently does unravel much of this decades later in *James.*

become heresiologists, accusing those who deviate from their own deviancies as deviants, as we saw with Clement above.

Similarly, Patrician Origen was commissioned by the church in the third century, to answer the allegations of Celsus written in the second century, and in doing so he acknowledges that there: "are some who corrupt the Gospel histories, and who introduce heresies opposed to the meaning of the doctrine of Jesus." Of course he does not admit that the person whom he is pointing his finger at is the now established orthodoxy. Rather he would convince the reader that it is the very keepers of the Truth who deviate.

Further, Origen's reply also verifies that this wholesale corruption of the scriptures did in fact take place as early as the second century when Celsus originally leveled his charges against the Church. And what was it that Celsus charged? That the Christian scriptures *"admit of various and almost indefinite readings* [because] *the original text of the Gospels* has been altered *to coincide and substantiate the doctrines of the Gentile converts in an attempt to prove their tenets of belief."* That is, the doctrines had been arranged to support Paul's religion – his newfound "Christianity" – and specifically *to favor the understanding of his converts* as opposed to that of the actual followers of Jesus, the Jewish Vaishnavas. This is the establishment of "spiritual truth" by increasing political weight. It oddly gives a greater emphasis and importance to the opinions of new converts over the opinions of the older, more experienced and knowledgeable contemporaries of their *Acharyas* Jesus or James.

---

g Paul: "But what I do, that I will do, that I may cut off occasion from them that desire an occasion; that wherein they glory, they may be found even as we."

The Scribes

Very few people were literate in the first century and those capable with letters were often the hirelings of the establishment. They were employed to write its version of the truth. Josephus was one, who, although previously a Palestinian revolutionary, capitulated to the Romans and took up their cause in order to save his skin. Eusebius was another. They were both younger contemporaries of Paul, and they were both beholden to the powers of Rome. The victors write history, and as victors do, they commonly give little if any voice to those they subjugate. That is one reason why we find emphasis given to Paul and his perspective in the New Testament, in opposition to Jesus and every one of the Apostles. Beyond that there were the changes introduced by individual scribes who often took matters into their own hands, as it were.

Those who copied scriptures often altered the original words and meaning in accordance with their own beliefs. St. Jerome confirms this for us: "*They write down not what they find* but what they think is the meaning; and while they attempt to rectify the errors of others, they merely expose their own."[h] Thus, each copy was edited to clarify the beliefs of the copyist, or perhaps his employers.

And Eusebius adds to this his own experience:

> Therefore they have laid their hands boldly upon the Divine Scriptures, alleging that they have corrected them.[i] For if anyone will collect their respective copies, and compare them one with another, he will find that they differ greatly. . . And many of these can be obtained, because their disciples have assiduously written the corrections, as they call them,[8] that is

---

[h] Jerome, Epist. lxxi.5; compare this of course to the many quotes from Shrila Prabhupada on not inventing anything and by strictly following the *parampara*, maintaining the connection to The Truth.

the corruptions, of each of them. . . For you can compare those prepared by them at an earlier date with those which they corrupted later, and you will find them widely different. But however daring this offense is, it is not likely that they themselves are ignorant. For either they do not believe that the Divine Scriptures were spoken by the Holy Spirit, and thus are unbelievers, or else they think themselves wiser than the Holy Spirit, and in that case what else are they than demoniacs? [sic]

It is astounding to realize that despite dozens of undisputed statements exactly like these by many scholars, these revelations remain tightly sealed behind the high walls of the church and academia, the majority of Christian followers ignorant of any such machinations, complacent with what is given them. Such is the nature of childhood training that what is once learned in innocence is rarely questioned in maturity. Where is their discernment? Cheated by their own crooked intentions to use religion in the service of their senses it never enters their minds. Christians continue to maintain their faith in the Bible as the inspired word of God despite so much evidence of corruption, and the so-called ministers make no attempt to educate their charges in the Truth, continuing to feed them on the poisoned cakes of falsified doctrine.

Avoidance and Neglect: The Weapon of Silence

Those who control the propaganda efforts of the Establishment are generally in a position to choose what they respond to and how. Where they feel on safe ground and able to defeat their adversaries they will enjoin the battle. When they feel themselves outgunned however, their best response is often a conspiracy of silence. In

---

i ISKCON observers will note similar claims by BBT editors.

the case of keeping people in ignorance it is much easier if they are not taught doctrines that belie the wrangling of the church, as the vast majority will never look far enough on their own, or give credence to challenges to what has already been accepted as truth.

Schoeps writes, referring to the "early church," that "the synagogue [Rabbinic Judaism]. . . pursued the still more effective tactic of steadfastly ignoring its opponents. The weapon chosen by the Pharisaic (sic) rabbinate was extreme and hence effective. The vanquished not only died out but were buried under a blanket of silence. Hence the surprise provided us by the Dead Sea Scrolls."[9]

Changes to Support Falsified Doctrine

As mentioned earlier, many changes in biblical texts were made later as the doctrines of the church were developing. Examples are legion, but I would like to offer just one as a demonstration. I will use for this example the central doctrine of the Trinity – God in three aspects of the Father, the Son and the Holy Spirit. This was not a doctrine of the original texts but was later added to the Bible in an attempt to establish proof from the "divinely inspired word of God." Our proof of the falsity of this assertion lies not in polemical debate, but with historical artifacts: copies of the ancient texts themselves.

Testament to the Trinity is found in 1 John 5:7 where the King James Bible states it as: "For there are *three that bear record in heaven, the Father, the Word, and the Holy Ghost: and these three are one.*" But in Biblical translations, such as the New American Standard Bible, derived from older biblical manuscripts, this verse is entirely without any support for the doctrine of the Trinity, stating merely: "And it is the Spirit who bears witness, because the Spirit is the truth."

Regarding the validity of the verse 1 John 5:7, the *Adam Clarke Commentary* states that: "It is likely this verse is not genuine. *It is wanting*[missing] *in every manuscript of this letter written before the invention of printing, one excepted,* the Codex Montfortii, in Trinity College, Dublin; the others which omit this verse amount to one hundred and twelve. . . *It is wanting also in all the ancient Greek fathers; and in most even of the Latin."* But while missing in all of these it now appears in the majority of Bibles, but still not all.[10] Plainly, it was added at a later date to substantiate the doctrine.

The divinity of Jesus did not take root everywhere, nor all at once. Jesus' humanity persisted in the understanding of many, especially the descendants of the Jewish Vaishnavas, Ebionites and Gnostics. One of their descendants was Arias, a presbyter of Alexandria, who participated in the discussions at the Council of Nicaea in AD 325. The temperament of compromise at the proceedings was effectively demonstrated when Arias, upon advocating the supremacy of a single omnipotent God Who was not to be humiliated in the flesh (therefore by necessity excluding the crucified Jesus from any divinity) was summarily punched in the face and ejected from the proceedings. The doctrine of the Trinity and the deification of Jesus the Christ was then decided by a vote and ensconced as Catholic dogma although there was never any theological basis to support this "conclusive truth" of Catholicism.

It is further suggested by some that in the competition for converts, the one-upmanship of gods was a requirement. In today's terms, Jesus' divinity was a marketing ploy. To be able to hold his own against already established creeds, any new god had to be at least comparable to the others, because why switch if "my (demi) god is better than your (demi)god?" In promoting Jesus he could thus could be no less than a "god," but would preferably be "God." By vote it was made so, and Jesus was thus raised to the status of Godhead.[11] This is also the likely source of the many miracles attributed to Jesus. Suffice it to say that the doctrine is fiction, supported by nothing other than fiction, yet it is promoted by the Kamsas and accepted as truth by their willing victims.

The Church of the State

Emperor Constantine was instrumental in creating not only the Catholic Church but also the Roman Catholic Empire. He convened the Council of Nicaea bringing together the many disparate groups for the purpose of developing a Catholic (meaning "universal") doctrine sufficiently acceptable to bind everyone together in one "faith." Of course by the Vedic understanding this is ridiculous on its face, as real religion can only be established by God.[j] Because the purpose of real religion is the realization of the eternal Truth it can never be a democratic affair. This gives us a clue as to how spiritually potent the combined efforts of the Council would be. However, a pure and spiritually potent understanding of the Truth was not their objective.

The objective of the Council was to create doctrinal consensus. Thus within a year of having concluded the canon of the New Testament any writings that contradicted the new orthodoxy were collected and destroyed – even if (or perhaps especially if) they were from the original followers of Jesus – who would now be considered pagans. This, after Diocletian had undertaken to destroy all "Christian" writings in 303 AD, resulted in the virtual elimination of any texts predating the 4th century. Constantine further facilitated the coalescence of an orthodoxy by commissioning new copies of the Christian writings deleting any conflicting material as heresy – which were in fact the Truths of the Jewish Vaishnavas.

As with the efforts to establish the divinity of Jesus, the new Catholic doctrine was adjusted to win numbers by accommodating,

---

[j] Real religious principles are enacted by the Supreme Personality of Godhead. SB 6.3.19. and "The Bhagavatam does not mention that the Hindu religion is first class or the Christian religion is first class or the Mohammedan religion is first class or some other religion is first class. The Bhagavatam says that that religion is first class which helps one advance his devotional service and love

and then co-opting, the demigod cults. For example, the Sun god was a very popular deity, and emperor Constantine numbered among his devotees. The sun cult reserved his day, Sunday, for his worship, whereas the Jewish Vaishnavas observed the Jewish Sabbath on Saturday, the 7th day. To ease the entrance of sun worshippers into the Catholic fold, the day of religious observance was moved to Sunday. Likewise the birth of Jesus was formerly celebrated on January 6th, but to accommodate the transition of sun cult members, it was changed to December 25th, the festival of the birth of the sun, after which the days begin to grow longer. There were many other such compromises and adjustments made to blur the lines between religions and culturally ease the transition from one to the other. All in all the new religion was construed as a hybrid designed to accommodate as many competing parties as possible.

Having birthed the Catholic Church, Constantine also sought to give it Imperial proportions. Interestingly it was his mother Helena who is credited with at least suggesting the idea that control by religious doctrine is a much easier method of managing people than by the sword. Taken with this idea Constantine approached Pope Sylvester with the offer to make Catholicism the official religion of the Roman Empire, on two conditions: (1) that the pope would be both the temporal and spiritual ruler, and (2) that he be allowed to name the next pope. Sylvester agreed, and overnight it was decreed that every Roman citizen must accept the Roman Catholic Faith, or be put to death. Most, at least ostensibly, agreed to this very persuasive proposal.

---

of God. That's all. This is the definition of a first-class religion. We do not analyze that one religion is first class or that another religion is last class. In the same verse, the Bhagavatam says that real religion must be *ahaituki* and *apratihata*: without selfish motivation and without any impediment."

Eradication of the Eternal Religion

The power in Rome came to dominate the Western world, making and breaking kings. All the while the Kamsas pursued their efforts to extinguish any manifestation of the Truth wherever it existed, leading them to the Manicheans, where for centuries embers of Gnostic Truth still glowed. Considered a fusion of Gnosticism with elements of Zoroastrianism (which is also replete with spiritual Truths deriving from Vedic theology) and the Mithraic traditions, they emphasized vegetarianism, celibacy and aestheticism. Mani, the founder, espoused an understanding of the soul, the doctrine of reincarnation, and the battle for the soul between the Forces of Light and Darkness. They also thought that Yahweh, the God of the Old Testament was Satan himself, and like the Jewish Vaishnavas, that the book of Moses had been largely falsified.[12] The Manicheans, long-established in France, later became known as the Cathars. Despite their restrictive practices, but undoubtedly because of the Truths they taught, the Cathars attracted converts from the Roman Church at an alarming rate.

Unsuccessful in subjugating the Cathars to Catholic dogma through ecclesiastical efforts, Pope Innocent III had the Cathars declared heretics. Beginning in 1209 they were hunted down and exterminated in the Albigensian Crusade, completed thirty-five years later with some one million souls tortured and slaughtered. It should be noted that it was for the discovery of Cathars that the Inquisition was first created.[13] One of the ways of separating "true Christians" from the Cathars was to require suspects to eat meat! The Cathars of course, would rather be burned at the stake.

These examples illustrate efforts by the Roman church to destroy any remnant of the Truth in the Western world. This, along with their demonic character reveals the popes as genuine *Rakshasas*. They eventually garnered both secular and political power through all of Europe. The Bible even refers to the church itself as the *"synagogue of Satan,"* [k] and in a letter to Pope Leo X on September 6th, 1520, Martin Luther wrote of the Christianity of his day that the church, *"...has become the most licentious den of thieves, the most shameless of all brothels, the kingdom of sin, death, and hell. It is so bad that even Antichrist himself, if he should come, could think of nothing to add to its wickedness."*[14]

Here Martin Luther is merely confirming a prediction made by Paul. How would Paul have known that the Prince of Darkness would be worshiped as God in the church identified as that of Christ? However it was, he correctly predicted the demonic intentions of these *rakshasas* to be worshipped as God when he wrote that the demonic *". . . opposes and exalts himself above all that is called God or that is worshiped, so that he sits as God in the temple of God, showing himself that he is God."* (2 Thomas 2:4 NKJ) And in apparent disdain for the foolish people who follow them blindly, he again boldly announces this deception, implicating the Putanas as well: "For *such men are false apostles, deceitful workers, fashioning themselves into apostles of Christ.* And no marvel; for *even Satan fashioneth himself into an angel of light.* It is no great thing therefore if his ministers also fashion themselves as ministers of righteousness, *whose end shall be according to their works."* (II Cor. 11:13-15)

Thus we have the successful completion of atheism in the convenient disguise of religion as explained by Shrila Bhaktisiddhanta. This form of control lasted until another development that brought a more complete control, after which the iron fist of the church was allowed to be broken by Luther and others. That control continues

---

[k] He that hath an ear, let him hear what the Spirit saith unto the churches; . . . I know thy works, and tribulation, and poverty, (but thou art rich) and I know the blasphemy of them which say they are Jews, and are not, but are the synagogue of Satan. Rev 2:7-9. Revelation 3:9 Behold, I will make those of the assembly of Satan who claim to be Jews and are not, but are lying. . .

to exist today almost entirely unobserved. It is so complete and has such an insidious interference with the genuine practice of religion that in our modern day people are allowed to have "religious freedom," but only within limits that cannot challenge the control of our demonic overlords. I refer to the control of state-issued money.

Having learned some historical lessons of how an earlier manifestation of the Truth was dealt with, we now move into the modern day to observe the methods of the Putanas to maintain this artifice. Scribes now occupy the most respectable posts under the title of *academics* and *exegetes*.

Controlling the Limits of the Debate

The *rakshasa* Kamsas who now control the world have made sure that since the trend of the world was to become educated, that the people have been given a suitable version of history. Those who are familiar with, and accept as factual, the Vedic version of history (from the *Srimad Bhagavatam* and other Vedic literature such as the Puranas and Mahabharata), recognize the version of history taught in the schools of the dominant culture as extremely revisionist. However, the perspective of the dominant culture is that the history presented in the Vedas and practically all other indigenous cultures, is condescendingly referred to as "myth," and history prior to the arrival of the *rakshasas* and their domination of the planet (i.e., before 5,000 years ago) is considered "pre-history." Attempts made to establish the validity of anything prior to this are met with derision and ostracism, particularly within the academic community.

Limits are placed around what is acceptable for debate and what isn't. Scholars who stay within those limits achieve the respect of other academics and advance in their careers regardless of how ridiculous their theses may become.[1] Those who disregard these limits do so at the peril of their academic survival.

Michael Cremo and Richard Thompson (Drutakarma Dasa and Sadaputa Dasa), in their seminal work *Forbidden Archeology*, have labeled this phenomenon as a "knowledge filter." Since their work was intended to compete in an academic environment they have politely limited their criticism and have avoided speaking too directly in this regard. Shrila Bhaktisiddhanta however, sought no such acknowledgment and spoke freely, referring to these minions of "Kamsas as Putanas," demons who would attempt to slay the Lord whenever He makes His appearance as Truth. Kamsas and Putanas are very real elements in the world today, not story-book creations of Vedic lore, and their existence must be taken seriously in order to properly defend the Truths they actively seek to destroy.

Drutakarma and Sadaputa are not alone in their evaluation of the consequences of speaking out of turn. In the Introduction to his *Bloodline of the Holy Grail,* a book that definitely pushes the boundaries of accepted thought, author Lawrence Gardner explains that conformity alone is valued:

> . . . above all such considerations there is a further requirement: the requirement to toe the party line while paying homage to the demigods of power. This prerequisite has nothing to do with obeying the law or with behaving properly – it relies totally on not rocking the boat, and on withholding opinions that do not conform. Those who break ranks are declared heretics, meddlers and troublemakers, and as such are deemed

---

[1] For example, the current explanation for **all** human behavior is relegated to programming in our genes, and an entire field of study, Sociobiology, has developed around this *unproven theory*. Scholars in this field continue to advance their ideas that within our genes lies the key to human behavior. Well, for those who cannot accept an understanding of spirit soul, what else, however ridiculous, is there?

socially unfit by their governing establishment. Perceived social fitness is consequently attained by submitting to indoctrination, and forsaking personal individuality in order to preserve the administrative status quo. By any standard of reckoning this can hardly be described as a democratic way of life.[15]

The efforts to control the limits of debate extend well into the field of religious history and that story, central to the thesis of this work, cannot be better portrayed than the effort required to bring the Dead Sea Scrolls, and their unbiased interpretation, to light. Eisenman is the key figure in that drama.

Discovery and Sequestering of the Dead Sea Scrolls

Discovered after two thousand years, parchment scrolls pre-served by the dry desert offered revelations extremely at odds with what was thought to have be so soundly established – seemingly once-and-for-all. The scrolls, authorities unto themselves, offered first-hand evidence of Jesus' own community and teachings, at odds with that offered in the New Testament, thus calling into question the authority of the Roman church and its version of his-tory. What was to be done? Why, a new round of obfuscation, of course! The method of choice? Silence, accomplished by seques-tering the evidence.

These "Dead Sea Scrolls," although discovered in 1949, were effectively withheld from the academic community and general public for more than forty years. The International Team of mostly Catholic scholars who were given a monopoly to study the scrolls held them in abeyance, publishing and revealing so little of their contents that it became an international academic scandal of the highest order. Despite the International Team's efforts, unfettered access was finally achieved in 1991 through the sustained efforts of others, amid the furious protestations of the former.

With the use of computer technology Professor Ben-Zion Wacholder of Hebrew Union College, had broken the monopoly on the scrolls, reconstructing them from a concordance published in the 1950's. The reconstruction was thought to be 80% accurate. Then, later that year, in large part due to the sustained efforts of Robert Eisenman, the Huntington Library in California opened the flood gates by offering complete photographic sets of the original scrolls to any interested scholar.[16]

Prior to their release, Eisenman vehemently criticized the lack of free debate concerning the Dead Sea Scrolls and their contents. In *The Dead Sea Scrolls Deception* authors Baigent and Leigh detail the entire story of how a cadre of scholars sought to control, not only the release of the scroll material, but even their interpretation. Their book is set in motion by Eisenman's revelations of a controlling "consensus" in his earlier books. In his Introduction to *The Dead Sea Scrolls and the First Christians* Eisenman details the efforts of this Establishment consensus regarding the Scroll contents. You can feel his frustration in this quote:

> . . . the editing and interpretation of the Scrolls had been controlled by a tightknit and secretive group of scholars, all indebted to each other and all having the same basic perspective; it was impossible to have free and open debate in this field. . . In fact, so effective was the dead hand of these scholarly cabals that the field of the Dead Sea Scroll Studies was virtually moribund from the 1950's to the mid-1980s. . . . *Maccabbees, Zadokites, Christians and Qumran* [Eisenman's book] also called attention to the preconceptions . . . which either accidentally or otherwise tended to obscure the links of the tradition represented at Qumran to early Christianity in Palestine. . . It was this consensus, followed blindly as it were by its proponents and their students – who seemed hardly to read the manuscripts for themselves or, if they did, missed their thrust.[17]

On the basis of all of the foregoing I suggest that they did not miss the thrust at all, but deliberately avoided it so that they would not have to report it, thus calling attention to it. This cabal constitutes the Putanas that Shrila Bhaktisiddhanta describes, and their purpose is obviously to restrict any access to the Truth when it makes an appearance.

Now that the Scroll material has been released the efforts of controlling any understanding of it are ongoing. Continuing in the Introduction following the above Eisenman writes:

> Since the publication of all the remaining unpublished materials and attenuant (sic) works, and their translation in many languages, this consensus, aided and abetted now by persons within Israeli official circles, has in the aftermath of the initial blush of excitement over the new freedom engendered by open access, begun to reconstitute and reassert itself, now backed by all the new people brought into the continuing process of preparing "official editions." In fact, adherence to the consensus view or its variation was a *sine qua non* for being invited to participate in this process. This, in turn, once again highlighted the control exercised by those previously charged with editing the unpublished texts over the parameters and direction of debate in a field where there is still *no really free* exchange of ideas. (emphasis in original)

This statement by Eisenman reveals the continuing effort to control the thinking of the masses, directing them into a cul-de-sac of ignorance. I personally witnessed this during the time that I was writing these chapters. Prominent displays of a half dozen or more new books about the Dead Sea Scrolls appeared in the major booksellers. Examining them I found them to be exactly as Eisenmen describes – all variations on the same consensus view supporting the history of the first century as described, and already well-known, in Biblical stories. In other words, there is nothing to see here folks, just move along.

There is unlimited material that can be added to this chapter demonstrating what we hope has already been sufficiently made clear – ample historical evidence certifies the truth given to us by Shrila Bhaktisiddhanta:

> King Kamsa is never slow to take the scientific precaution of deputing empiric teachers of the scriptures, backed by the resources of dictionary and grammar and all empiric subtleties to put down, by the show of specious arguments based on hypothetical principles, the true interpretation of the eternal religion revealed by the scriptures.

We must not, for even a moment, think that such machinations are a thing of the past and that we needn't be concerned with the preservation of the Truth. Indeed, the followers of Shrila Prabhupada must carefully act to preserve the Truths he has given us lest his transcendental movement be likewise transformed into a mundane religion with little spiritual potency. *Schoeps offers this warning, to which the sincere followers of the Eternal Religion in the twentieth century should pay heed:*

> **"Those contemporary with events do not know what the future holds. To Paul's opponents it would likely have seemed improbable if someone had told them that Paul and his gospel would be victorious and conquer the world, while they themselves would be left behind and even be branded as heretics a mere few generations later."**[18]

CHAPTER SIX

Caesar's Messiah and the Creation of the Roman Church

Although I had finished writing the previous chapters by 2004, I put this book on hold as I traveled around the world for the next 10 years. Imagine my surprise when in 2012 I came across a book that completely supported my thesis that Christianity was a creation of the Roman powers for the purpose of maintaining political control. – that book is *Caesar's Messiah: The Roman Conspiracy to Invent Jesus*.

Author Joseph Atwill was a seminary student in his youth, but after pursuing other work returned in 1995 to a decade long study of the Bible, the Dead Sea Scrolls and other first century literature. His knowledge of the facts of first century history revealed inconsistencies within the biblical story that caused him to be suspicious of the Bible story as it was presented. He wrote:

What contributed most to my skepticism was that at the exact time when the followers of Jesus were purportedly organizing themselves into a religion that urged its members to "turn the other cheek" and to "give to Caesar what is Caesar's," another Judean sect was waging a religious war against the Romans. This sect, the Sicarii, also believed in the coming of a Messiah, but not one advocating peace. They sought a Messiah who would lead them militarily. It seemed implausible that two diametrically opposite forms of messianic Judaism would have emerged from Judea at the same time.

Atwill questioned how other anomalies and background evidence of the Palestinian sect curiously and repeatedly pointed to Rome as the birthplace of Christianity, instead of Palestine where Jesus lived and taught. For example, Christianity's structures of authority, its sacraments, its college of bishops, the title of the head of the religion – the Supreme Pontiff – were all based on Roman, not Judaic, traditions. He questioned how Rome, the center of persecution of the "Christians," was chosen as Christianity's headquarters. He questioned how a Judean cult eventually became the state religion of the Roman Empire with a Roman worldview that saw itself as ordained by God to spread throughout the world when that was not at all the original purpose of the Judean cult. He questioned why so many members of a Roman imperial family are recorded as being among the first Christians, martyrs, saints, as well as the pope that succeeded Peter! He further questioned why Jesus' travels and activities in Palestine exactly match those of the military campaign of Titus Flavius against the Jewish Vaishnavas during the 7-year war, and how it was that Titus Flavius fulfilled all of Jesus' doomsday prophecies. And he questioned how the Flavian Emperor's family created so much of the literature that provides documentation for the religion, how they were responsible for its oldest known cemetery, and how it happened that they housed individuals named in the New Testament within their imperial court. One or two of these may be chalked up to coincidence, but so many altogether?

He gives a striking analogy to these anomalies regarding Christianity's purported origins: imagine a cult established by Polish Jews during World War II that set up its headquarters in Berlin and encouraged its members to pay taxes to the Third Reich!

Sorting out the above and many more anomalies, parallels and "coincidences," Atwill concluded that the Flavians created Christianity to serve as a theological barrier to prevent messianic Judaism from again erupting against the empire.

Atwill confirms this in a most interesting way. He details how the story of Jesus' ministry told in the Gospels could have been constructed as a "prophetic" (after the fact) satire of Titus Flavius' military campaign through Judea, using parallels to show that it was the activities of Titus that Christians unwittingly worship, making him thus the real "Christ."[a] And because Christianity came from them, the Flavians would naturally have been highly honored as counting among the first Christians.

Atwill's book provides many details to explain his thesis that the Caesar's created Christianity, but there are several points that are of more interest to us and support our thesis. One is his explanation of how the Roman state employed religious belief as a way bringing the masses in line with the will of the state. Another is his discussion of the destruction of the "fourth philosophy" with the fall of the Masada fortress.

---

[a] It was the policy of the Caesar's to allow those they had conquered to continue their normal religious worship, however, they were required to place the image of the Caesar on their altar. This was something that the Jewish Vaishnava's refused to do. Indeed, if tortured none, not even the children, would call the Caesar "Lord."

Using Religious Belief as a Political Tool

As early as 63 B.C. Cicero advocated that the state should use theology in managing the citizens, urging them (the citizens) to adopt the beliefs most appropriate for the empire. It should be no surprise therefore to learn that the Caesars did attempt to control Judaism. From Julius Caesar on, the Roman emperor claimed personal authority over the religion and selected its high priests, that is, the Pharisees, who had capitulated and compromised their principles to cooperate with Rome. Rome micromanaged the Temple to the extent of even determining when its priests could wear their holy vestments, and they appointed all the high priests recorded within the New Testament from a restricted circle of families who were allied to Rome. By selecting the individual who would determine any issue of "Jewish customs" the Caesars were managing Jewish theology for the interests of their empire.

The Jewish Vaishnavas, as determined as they were to strictly follow the Law, would have been extremely unhappy with this. However, due to political support of the Romans, the Pharisees became the establishment party, and the Jewish Vaishnavas the opposition party. The Romans were therefore controlling the establishment Jews, but not the Jewish Vaishnavas, whom they were intent on bringing under their control. Their approach was to send Saul to infiltrate the group and create havoc within, and to preach a false gospel in their name. Then using Paul's "preaching" as a foundation, they created a pacifist Christianity that served the purposes of Rome.

To conclude the matter as *already settled,* the Jesus created by the Romans in the New Testament had *already* fulfilled the Messianic prophecy, and rather than taking up arms against the Romans the Messiah instructed everyone to give to Caesar what was Caesar's.

Therefore there was no reason for anyone who accepted Jesus as the Messiah to continue to challenge Rome.

Other than the Dead Sea Scrolls and the Nag Hammadi Texts, all of the written works that survived the first century (Josephus, etc.) had a pro-Roman perspective in which the holiness of political subservience is emphasized. It is not unreasonable to assume that this was all that was allowed to survive, because, after all, it is the victors that write the history. Further it was taught that since God had given the Romans their power, it was against God's will to resist them – a motif that we shall see repeated in the next appearance of the Eternal Religion two millennia later. Paul and Josephus both promoted the idea that the Romans were God's servants and that God inflicts punishment *only* upon evil-doers.

From Josephus we have:

> Indeed what can it be that hath stirred up an army of the Romans against our nation? Is it not the impiety of the inhabitants? Whence did our servitude commence? Was it not derived from the seditions that were among our forefathers?[1]

And from Paul's *Romans* we have:

> Let every person be subject to the governing authorities; for there is no authority except from God, and those authorities that exist have been instituted by God. Therefore whoever resists authority resists what God has appointed and those who resist will bring judgment upon themselves. For rulers are not a terror to good conduct, but to bad. [...] For the same reason you also pay taxes, for the authorities are God's servants, busy with this very thing. Pay to all what is due to them – taxes to whom taxes are due, revenue to whom revenue is due, respect to whom respect is due, honor to whom honor is due.[2]

Conquest of the Eternal Religion

Josephus writes that the fall of Masada brought an end to what he described as the "fourth philosophy." This is understood as a synonym for the messianic movement of the Sicarii or Zealots. Josephus also records that Judas' descendant "Eleazar" was in charge of the Sicarii at Masada in 73 CE when the "fourth philosophy" was finally destroyed.

What was the fourth philosophy? It is more than the messianic movement of the Sicarii, but Josephus avoids mentioning it by name, perhaps not to call attention to it. But remember from chapter one, Eleazar's exhortation to the people at Masada that we are not the body? The remnants of the Sicarii at Masada were all that was left of the Jewish Vaishnavas in Palestine, and the seven years' war ended with the fall of Masada. Therefore Josephus' statement that the "fourth philosophy" ended with the fall of Masada indicates that the fourth philosophy was the Eternal Religion. Because it was a formidable foe its defeat was an accomplishment worthy of mention by the empire's official historian.

Why was the Eternal Religion a problem for them? Because its followers wanted to live according to their own ways, according to the principles of the Eternal Religion, the Law, refusing to subordinate themselves to the ways of the demonic ruling powers. Rome did not face such formidable resistance anywhere else in their vast empire. Remember, the demonic think that they own everyone, and that everyone should serve them. In those days this meant not only paying taxes, but allowing oneself, and one's countrymen, to be used as property, without protest. With the end of the "fourth philosophy," Josephus is making the point that a "Christianity" that did not challenge the status quo was the ideological victor.

That may have been a premature estimation because even though there was a massive exodus from Jerusalem after the war there continued to be intermittent resistance in the area, so much so that another major rebellion was launched in 132 CE. Finally, in 135, Emperor Hadrian expelled all Jews from Judaea, making Jerusalem a Roman city, and renaming it Aelia Capitolina.

The Eternal Religion and the Druze of Israel

By the mid-second century CE the Jewish Vaishnavas were largely destroyed and scattered. Many fled the area of Judea both before and after the Jerusalem War – some south to Egypt and others north to Jericho, and even beyond to Syria. Thus although the Eternal Religion remained in the general area its practitioners kept their heads low.

To avoid persecution some in Israel continued to practice their faith in an underground manner to avoid calling attention to themselves, and do so even to this very day. These people are identified as the Druze, or more specifically as they call themselves, the *Muwahidoon*, a word that translates exactly to "followers of the Eternal Religion." Although considered by establishment scholars to be unorthodox followers of Islam, this conclusion may have been projected by the Muwahidoon themselves as a cover to avoid further persecution. Evidence of this is that they developed a philosophy of social interaction called *taquiyya*, meaning that one should perform duties externally according to the national milieu, while internally remembering their identity as a member of the Muwahidoon.

This connection was discovered by Dhira Govinda Dasa (David Wolf) when preaching and distributing Shrila Prabhupada's books in Israel. Meeting with the Druze and discussing together their beliefs and practices, both were stunned to find such greatly similar, and in some cases identical, precepts. Certain Druze rabbis were convinced of the connection between the Druze and Vaishnavism by the fact that the original language of their scriptures was Sanskrit, and that incarnations such as Buddha and Krishna are described therein. On several occasions Dhira Govinda and his companions met the late Sheik Tarif Amin, the former world spiritual leader of the Druze. The Sheik expressed genuine appreciation that hundreds of Druze households were placing sets of the *Srimad*

Bhagavatam in their homes. Sheik Amin even stated that he wanted the Druze people to work with the Hare Krishna movement "as one race." [3]

There is even more evidence linking the Druze with India, or at least the East. Jethro, Moses' father-in-law, was a member of the Kenites, a tribe from the East, with roots perhaps stemming from India, and he is, to this day, the major preceptor of the Druze. Interaction between Jethro and Moses suggests that Moses, at least in some capacity, was Jethro's disciple. This hypothesis conforms to the theory of some scholars of the Kenite origins of the Hebrew religion, revealing the Vedas as the possible source of the Judaic religious tradition. These connections also further confirm the connections made between the Vaishnavas and Jews in chapter one.

Just as the Druze continued to follow their spiritual principles in an underground manner, other adherents continued to do so under various appellations, with a mixture of understanding and beliefs, well into the Middle Ages. These included the Arians, the Manicheans, the Gnostics, Cathars, etc., who were hunted and destroyed in the Albigensian crusade. An estimated one million were tortured and killed in the crusade, while up to 50 million perished at the hands of the papacy from the Middle Ages through the early Reformation Era.[4]

Given the evidence presented, we are convinced that Christianity was created by the Roman powers as a tool of political control, the transcendental teachings of Jewish Vaishnavas being destroyed and replaced with a dogma whose main objective was subservience to the state. After endeavoring to eradicate the Eternal Religion for centuries, they thought it was finished once and for all, but did not realize that its origin – India – was intact and would spawn a world-wide comeback of the Eternal Religion, many years into the future.

Part Two

The Eternal Religion in
Twentieth Century America

Foreword to Part 2

In Part 1 of this book we have examined the methods practiced by Kamsas and Putanas to deal with the appearance of the Eternal Religion in the West, which included:

- Kill the *Acharyas*
- Infiltrate their movement, then in their name
- Create and spread false teachings
- At a certain point declare war on the faithful, and kill every one of them
- Stamp out any remaining evidence of the original understanding by destroying, and later altering, every last copy of the original teachings
- Create a false and spiritually impotent philosophy and religion in the name of the *Acharya*, all the while extolling its true fidelity to his teachings
- Use this religion to promote sentimental, "religious" concepts that direct people to remain subservient to the state
- Base this "religion" on a newly created false scripture written by mundane men specifically for the purpose of misleading people about the goal of life, then unendingly claim it is the "inspired word of God"
- Establish the mechanisms by which to centralize control of the followers, allowing a select few to control their beliefs, and thereby their actions

- Convert as many people as possible to this new religion by any means possible, including threatening their life, and thus bring them under control.
- Kill everyone that will not comply
- Ferret out all remaining followers of the Eternal Religion by a 'religious crusade,' reducing their numbers through means of torture and death, making an example of them to discourage others
- By these means become the ruling elite of society for the next millennia

Suppressing Him Before He has Time to Develop

Fast forward two millennia into the future. The Kamsas and Putanas didn't just go away. They are as real today as they were when Sri Krishna advented to relieve the earth's burden. They were not all vanquished at Kurukshetra, and over time they have reconstituted their numbers, taking control of the world by means of political machinations and death. Although they now dress in suits and appear as gentlemen they are anything but, and they control the world with the same ruthlessness that has always been their trademark.

In the mid-20th century Lord Chaitanya's mercy manifests under the leadership of His Divine Grace A. C. Bhaktivedanta Swami Prabhupada, and gains a foothold in almost every country of the world. What are the methods of the Kamsas and Putanas in dealing with the new manifestation of the Eternal Religion?

As we shall demonstrate in this section they have, by and large, been the same as they were earlier, with some modification for time and circumstances. It is my contention that the above history has been, and will continue to be, repeated in some modified version. Aided by an understanding of their methods gained from the foregoing chapters we are in position to connect the dots and understand what has happened (and is happening) to the next manifestation of the Eternal Religion. Looking at the bigger picture will allow us to understand the factual nature of the problem, as well as the solution.

While my Vaishnava readers likely have detachment from the events of two millennia past, that will not likely be the case as we discuss the modern manifestation of the Eternal Religion in the form of the Hare Krishna Movement. Because of our involvement in the mission, and attachment to various personalities, and because of our limited perception and experience, and sometimes downright denial, we may find the present discussion much more difficult to accept as factual. We want the world to be as benign as we have imagined it to be, but the reality is ugly even if we cannot see its terrible form right in front of us. In the modern age all of the horror is hidden behind a wall, or a veneer, of respectability and decorum. Out of sight is out of mind for most of us, and it is impossible to fight an enemy that you cannot see – or will not recognize.

Therefore, one must learn to see through the eyes of scripture – *shastra chakshusa* – to recognize what is not immediately apparent, and look through the façade to the reality. Then one knows where and who to fight.

Our situation is similar to Dhruva Maharaja's fight with the Yaksas described in the fourth canto of the *Srimad Bhagavatam*. Being overpowered by Dhruva they employed illusions to bewilder him, but by taking shelter of the Lord the illusions immediately dissipated:

> The demon Yakshas are by nature very heinous, and by their demoniac power of illusion they can create many strange phenomena to frighten one who is less intelligent.

When the great sages heard that Dhruva Maharaja was overpowered by the illusory mystic tricks of the demons, they immediately assembled to offer him auspicious encouragement. All the sages said: Dear Dhruva, may the Supreme Personality of Godhead kill all your threatening enemies. The holy name of the Lord is as powerful as the Lord Himself. Therefore, simply by chanting and hearing the holy name of the Lord, many men can be fully protected from fierce death without difficulty. Thus a devotee is saved.

When Dhruva Maharaja heard the encouraging words of the great sages, he performed the *achamana* by touching water and then took up an arrow made by Lord Narayana and fixed it upon his bow. As soon as Dhruva Maharaja joined the arrow to his bow, the illusion created by the Yakshas was immediately vanquished.

There is a struggle continually being fought for the future of this planet between the forces of light and darkness. The Eternal Religion living in the hearts of the Lord's devotees is the light of this world, and the most formidable obstacle the demoniac face. They will do everything they can to destroy it, and have already done so much. But sadly, their dirty work is mostly unrecognized since most prefer to live in a world of happy illusion, as if this world is some wonderful place where anyone can find real happiness.

It's time to wake up to reality. Here's your red pill. Take it by continuing to turn the pages.

The Supreme Lord is the most powerful of all. Just as He empowered Dhruva and the Pandavas to be victorious over darkness, He can empower any of us who willingly surrender to Him allowing ourselves to be used as His instrument.

CHAPTER ONE

The Rise of Sri Chaitanya's Sankirtan Movement

The Absolute Truth is not anything limited or partial, neither can it be divided. It is not dependent on any condition excepting itself. It is always one and the same. Listening to or chanting of it is always and necessarily beneficial being the natural function of the soul. Shrila Bhaktisiddhanta Sarasvati

Advent of the Eternal Religion in 20ᵗʰ C America

The Supreme Lord's incarnated as the Golden Avatar, Sri Chaitanya Mahaprabhu, 500 years ago in what is now West Bengal, India. He inaugurated the *yuga dharma*, or religion for the Age of Kali, the congregational chanting of the holy names of the Lord.

Through His principle associates He taught the Eternal Religion, incorporating His own mood and the ultimate form of love, that of Sri Sri Radha and Krishna. Although this love is very rarely

145

achieved, Lord Chaitanya gave the benediction that this pure love would one day flood the entire world and carry away with it all but the most envious persons. He predicted that this would be accomplished by his *senepati bhakta*, the great devotee general.

That great devotee was none other than His Divine Grace A. C. Bhaktivedanta Swami Prabhupada, the founder-*Acharya* of the Hare Krishna Movement. He accomplished an amazing feat, unparalleled in all of the history of the world – single-handedly spreading the Eternal Religion over the entire globe in just twelve short years, installing it complete and with it its own culture.

He was the first jet-age swami who used every technological advantage he could to distribute his message far and wide. He did not create anything new, nor cater to people's base desires as many so-called spiritual leaders do. What he brought to the world was the Eternal Religion, the Vaishnava spiritual practices. He insisted that his followers strictly follow what he termed, the four principles of freedom: no meat eating, no intoxication, no illicit sex, and no gambling. Yet despite these prohibitions of activities that were the very order of the day in the "liberated" 60s, his movement grew quickly, attracting the youth who were looking for a genuine alternative to a culture steeped in materialism, selfishness and hypocrisy.

He attributed his strictness as one of the reasons of his success. When asked by a Catholic priest how he was able to attract so many youth away from their native religion he responded that it was because they (the Catholics) did not follow their own precepts. He challenged the priest that the Bible says "thou shalt not kill", but daily they are guilty of killing so many animals without even a twinge of conscience.

Shrila Prabhupada's success mirrored that of the 13th century Cathars of France who experienced tremendous growth in their ranks despite similar austerities they required of their followers:

no eating of meat, no intoxicants, no illicit sex, and prolonged and austere worship practices. Their growth was so alarming (and apparently threatening) to the Roman Powers that a crusade was enjoined against them, and an inquisition ferreted them out. The Cathars were obviously giving the people something of significant value that was lacking in their experience with the Roman church.

Likewise Shrila Prabhupada's movement was growing exponentially. Besides the strict prohibitions, he offered his followers the opportunity to taste the nectar of devotion that is the concomitant factor of every genuine religious process, and he gave the taste for which they would always be anxious to achieve. His devotees hadn't need to wait until death to experience the truth of their religious activity – they experienced it immediately – an incomparable joy that was reflected in their bright smiling faces. It was an irresistible attraction to many a forlorn youth, who sought some meaning for their lives.

Shrila Prabhupada didn't simply offer the dried cakes of religious dogma. He challenged his followers with an intellectually stimulating theology and a personal spiritual world view sufficient to satisfy the most inquiring and discriminating minds. And even more enticing, he showed by his own personal example how each and every one of his followers could achieve self-realization in this very life. His was a sterling example of what could be achieved on the spiritual strength of *bhakti-yoga*. Purity is the force he would say. At last, in a culture that was exploiting and cheating its members at every turn, here was someone who was their genuine well-wisher, giving them not just a religious process, but the very highest conception of God that could be found anywhere! Under his capable shelter the Movement grew to include thousands on every continent. The devotees, in their authentic Vaishnava dress, and blissful street-chanting, became a modern phenomenon.

These dedicated devotees worked incessantly to fulfill the desire of their spiritual master to spread Krishna Consciousness in every town and village. They blissfully distributed his books by the millions, distributed sanctified foodstuffs to additional millions, and with joy spent hours instructing any inquisitive person about the philosophy of Krishna Consciousness. They did this selflessly, with no remuneration, and even at times at considerable expense to themselves. In every country, rich or poor, at peace and in strife, these thousands of eager soldiers of the Sankirtan army are fit to be counted amongst the greatest souls of this world. They have done immeasurable good for the world by giving the gift of the Absolute Truth, without discrimination.

As Shrila Prabhupada's society grew he guided it as a loving father, constantly traveling to personally visit centers all around the world. The recordings of his conversations and lectures during his visits give testament to the loving guidance that he offered to all of his disciples. The wayward he would lovingly correct, or perhaps severely chastise if it were called for. But it was an extremely rare circumstance under which he would reject anyone from his society, and it practically never happened. He would always encourage everyone in some way to serve the Supreme Lord. He would fan the spark of devotion, and his attendance to their efforts would cause the fire of devotion to flame. Encouraged and empowered by his faith in them, his disciples demonstrated the amazing results that could only be generated by love. Just twelve short years of such encouragement resulted in a significant social movement with a presence in every major city across the globe, even if sometimes forced underground, as in some Communist countries.

Shrila Prabhupada never deviated from his own high standard. His personal moral standard went far beyond that expected by anyone. As the *Acharya* he demonstrated the ideal behavior of a devotee by his own personal example. The main preoccupations of material society: eating, sleeping, mating and defending, were practically absent in him. He slept so little that some thought he slept not at all, using the quiet hours of the night to do his translations and writing. He was completely regulated in his habits of eating and activity despite traveling the globe almost incessantly. Wherever he would arrive he would simply adjust his schedule to the local time and continue as if he had always been there. In terms of a residence he had none, yet he had one everywhere, at each stop moving into one single room with all of his worldly possessions in two suitcases. Sex life, he taught, was the shackles of the material energy, and he showed himself to be completely free of any inclination for it.

He was completely honest both in word and finance. Nor was there any vice that he was given to in private while making a public display of renunciation. He explained that for one experiencing a higher taste there is no such thing as renunciation from the mundane pleasures of this world – they were simply unwanted. He was quite obviously enjoying such a higher taste.

Prabhupada made time for everyone who approached him. Whether it was visitors who, pressed by their own schedule and without regard to his, demanded to see him, or any of his disciples who wrote to him, he would make time to give *darshan* and to reply to every letter. His secretaries write how they frequently became frustrated in their attempts to provide him with time for rest and recovery from the grueling demands of international travel, as he would make himself available to anyone who approached him.

He was the embodiment of kindness, mercy, compassion, caring, proper guidance, encouragement and support. Simply put, he was a saint of the highest order. He was the very personification of Krishna Consciousness and his example held out to each of his followers the promise that the process he had given them, while difficult, was the crucible that could transform them into saints.

Nobody else in their lives had expected so much from any of them, nor helped them understand their natural constitutional position as a spiritual being, much less shown how to realize that truth. Always encouraging, he purchased their hearts with his love.

Shrila Prabhupada's purity and the high standards that he set for his followers, although often beyond their reach, were the very attributes that convinced many that what he offered was real. God is not cheap he repeatedly said. And if anybody knew what God was, it was Shrila Prabhupada. Nobody else in the modern world spoke with such authority and knowledge on this subject as he did. He spoke not on his own authority about a God that he had conjured up, but on the authority of the Vedas and confirmed by his own realization. He was the next *Acharya* – the eminently qualified person to deliver the message in a way suitable to the understanding of the people of his time – which he did in a wonderful manner through his Bhaktivedanta purports. Understanding the power of *sadhana bhakti* he was able to promise that, however difficult it might be, if we held to his instructions, chanting the prescribed mantras every day, following the four principles of freedom, and attending morning *sadhana*, then we were guaranteed to return to the spiritual world after this life. But if we tried to cheat Krishna we would find that He is more clever, and we would only wind up cheating ourselves.

By his grace he put that topmost objective within our reach – every one of us – who would keep our end of the bargain. He set the mark, with his standard becoming the target for our lives. There were individual failures among his thousands of disciples, but standards remained constant, protecting the potency of the process, as well as the transcendental results. The standards of purity and honesty were the most visible indicators of the health and success of the Movement. Tampering with the standards would indicate a cheating process of religion – *kaitavah dharma* – false religious activities that are rejected from the *Srimad Bhagavatam*.

Shrila Prabhupada planted the seeds of Krishna Consciousness in the capital of atheism, Moscow, and established Lord Jagannatha's Rathayatra in almost every major city of the world. His crowning successes were grand Rathayatra parades in London and down Fifth Avenue in New York City, what he called "the most important street in the most important city in the world." These public Rathayatra festivals were an invasion of the transcendent into the dark world of ignorance, and served notice to one and all that the Eternal Religion had arrived. Besides establishing the Eternal Religion in the land of the *mlecchas*, he brought the living example of it back to his own country in the form of his followers, and with their help established large temple complexes from which he could now educate his countrymen who had become hopelessly confused about the Eternal Religious principles. Such is the manifestation of the Eternal Religion in the 20th century, not only in the West, but throughout the entire world.

The Creation of ISKCON

Shrila Prabhupada's mission grew slowly at first. By incorporating as ISKCON - the International Society for Krishna Consciousness – in New York, in July 1966, when there was but one center – Shrila Prabhupada demonstrated his intention of taking it worldwide. In quick succession came temples in San Francisco, and Montreal.

ISKCON centers began popping up everywhere like exploding popcorn – all over the world during the seventies. Young men and women joined in droves. From ISKCON's incorporation at a single lone center in New York in 1966, to 34 centers by 1970, to more than 100 temples and farms by the time of Shrila Prabhupada's departure from this world in 1977.

With the famous Beatle George Harrison's help, the London devotees recorded the best-selling single "Hare Krishna." Selling over 70,000 copies the first day of its release, and making it to the top of the charts, everyone in Europe had heard the maha-mantra, and about the mission it represented. By doing *Harinam* on Sunset Strip in Hollywood each week the devotees attracted the attention of Hollywood producers who placed them in more than a dozen movies, some prominently. Shrila Prabhupada's massive book distribution campaign, and his challenge that the numbers doubled each year, became millions of points of light in an otherwise spiritually dark world. Seriously engaged in fighting a war against Maya, the devotees wasted no time. So many were doing day-long *harinam* in different locations in major cities that they appeared to be everywhere, and by their distribution of books in every major airport, Hare Krishna became known even to the business class. "Hare Krishna" was a household word throughout the U.S. and Europe in the 1970's. It was a tsunami creating a countercurrent that was sweeping away the youth of the world into a serious spiritual counterculture. Shrila Prabhupada remarked that if we continued like we were doing for just another 25 years Krishna Consciousness would be the only religion in the world.

ISKCON's Invasion of Ravana's Kingdom

Of course this did not go unnoticed by the Kamsas and Putanas of this world. Recall Shrila Bhaktisiddhanta's admonition: *King Kamsa is ever on the lookout for the appearance of the Truth for the purpose of suppressing Him before He has time to develop. This is no exaggeration of the real connotation of the consistent empiric position.*

And Shrila Prabhupada was all too aware of this. In a conversation with Siddha-svarupa Das in 1976, ISKCON's heyday, Shrila Prabhupada clearly anticipates a strong reaction from the established order:

So this movement should be pushed very vigorously. And so far, we have become successful. And enemies will be always, as soon as there is something good. That is the way of material world. Even Krishna had enemies, what to speak of us. So many enemies, but He was powerful; He killed all them. Nobody could kill Him, but there was attempt to kill Him from the very beginning of His birth. He had so many enemies. As soon as Kamsa heard that his sister is now newly married, but as soon as there was some foretelling, 'Ah, you are taking care of your sister so nicely. The eighth child of this sister will kill you.' 'Oh, where is your child? Where is pregnancy?' Nothing. He became angry. 'So why wait for eighth child? Kill my sister'. . .

So we are instructing: no intoxication. So those who are flourishing by selling cigarettes and wine and liquor, they do not... 'Immediately kill him.' Oh, yes, in this way they are thinking: 'If the movement goes and becomes very strong, then our business will be lost. Kill him.' So naturally they will be enemies. The same thing, the Kamsa saw that 'This my sister, now she is married. So although it will take some long time, but here is the cause.' So they are thinking like that. No meat-eating, then all slaughterhouses will be closed: 'They are enemy.' Although there is no such symptom that slaughterhouse is going to be closed, but they'll think like that. They'll think like that, the same way.

We have forbidden: no illicit sex, no intoxication, no meat-eating, no gambling. The whole Western world living on these four pillars. Just see our position. And the same conscious way, everyone is thinking, 'If this movement goes on, then how all these nightclubs will go on? How all breweries will go on? How all slaughterhouse will go on, cigarette factories will go on?' This is all foolish. So you cannot expect that we will get more, many friends. That is not possible, because *the world is full of Kamsas, demons. So we have to struggle. . .it is very dangerous to the modern way of life.* They're feeling the pulse. Now everywhere we are meeting obstacles.

In India also, they will want to crush down this movement. So this will be up to Him. Krishna or Krishna's movement, the same thing. And Krishna was attempted to be killed by Kamsa class of men and his company, the demons. *So it will be there; it is already there. Don't be disappointed, because that is the meaning that it is successful.* Krishna's favor is there, because Krishna and Krishna's movement is not different, identical. So as Krishna was attempted to be killed, many, many years before He appeared. . . *So there may be attempt like that.* And Lord Jesus Christ was killed. **So they may kill me also.**"

Siddha-svarupa: I don't think that is possible.

Prabhupada: No, I mean to say, I am not so important man. *But it is the, this is the* way *of the law.* If we become weak by factioning, then that is not good. We must be strong and...But you should not expect that this movement will be accepted. In India the so-called yogis, Rama Krishna Mission – they are also being afraid of us. There are so many... *But if we remain sincere, even we are feeble, new-born, nobody can kill us. That is a fact.* Just like Krishna when He was three months old, attempt was made by Putana to kill Him, but the Putana was killed. A big demon, gigantic, her dead body was six miles long, and she is killed by a small child, sucking breast and sucking life. That is Krishna. . .

Similarly our movement, it may appear just like other movement, but because the movement is giving Krishna, that means it is as good as Krishna. This is the example. *Ajnaya hana* (follow the order). **It is actually Krishna. So long it adheres to the principle. If we begin to think 'I'll enjoy, I'll** *be accepted' it then becomes ordinary movement.* A man, he's guru, so long he gives the real knowledge of Krishna. And the same man, he's ordinary man, as soon as he cannot give. Same thing, just like a stone doll, when it is worshiped according to the regulative principles – Krishna. And the same doll, kept in the sculptor's showroom, it is stone. *So if we keep our movement pure, then you are as strong as Krishna. And as soon as you deviate from it, immediately, ordinary. This is the secret. Now it is up to us, how to keep it pure. Then no enemy can kill us. Nobody can kill you. That purity is wanted, then it will continue...Follow the rules and regulations, worship the Deity, and chant Hare Krishna mantra, then you will remain as strong as Krishna.* [1]

The prescription is there: if the devotees remain strong and keep to the principles given by Shrila Prabhupada, it is as good as Krishna—unlimitedly strong. If however there is deviation, then potency is lost and it becomes an ordinary movement, meaning having no spiritual potency.

Today, with 40 years of hindsight, and having witnessed what has transpired within his movement after Shrila Prabhupada made that statement, we can say with certainty that the purity and the spiritual strength have not been upheld. Even less than a decade after Shrila Prabhupada's departure from this world his mission was decimated and hardly a shadow of its former brilliance. By that time more than 80 percent of his initiated followers had abandoned direct participation in the mission, many of the farms in America were sold or simply abandoned, and many of the temples having more deities than devotees were in serious financial trouble. ISKCON's decline was as breathtaking as its ascent. ISKCON in the 21st century is nothing like what it was in the 20th. Although currently having apparent success in Russia and India, many of the remaining direct disciples of His Divine Grace share the opinion that "this is not the transcendental ISKCON that I joined." Many that had a genuine transcendental experience in the 1970s find today that it is conspicuous by its absence, while those that weren't there have no idea what they are missing. Of course the transcendental experience is immediately available to those who do follow strictly, but by and large the transcendental spiritual potency of the mission appears to be lost.

What happened? Our analysis and answer to that question is presented in this section of the book.

CHAPTER TWO

Shrila Prabhupada – Social Reformer and Change Agent

A chanter of the kirtan of Hari is necessarily the un-compromising enemy of worldliness and hypocrisy. As chanter of the kirtan of Hari it is his constant function to dispel all misconception by the preaching of the truth in the most unambiguous form without any respect of person, place or time. That form has to be adopted which is least likely to be misunderstood. Shrila Bhaktisiddhanta Sarasvati

Some 55 years ago or so, when I was a young teenager, and almost 10 years before I had ever heard the words Hare Krishna, I chanced upon a television movie that foreshadowed Shrila Prabhupada and his Hare Krishna Movement. In the movie, a typical couple of the late 60s, who indulged in all of the "normal vices" of that time, such as smoking and drinking, were experiencing a difficult relationship. They decided to take a trip to Brazil in hopes that being together in a relaxed setting might help them salvage their marriage.

They had a wonderful time, seeing all the sights, took a guided tour through the rainforest, returning home refreshed and with the love of their marriage restored. As a living reminder of this wonderful experience they brought home a colorful Toucan as a pet. It was a very transformative experience for both of them. To their great surprise and relief, they both gave up their nasty ways of bickering with each other, and they lost all interest in smoking and drinking. Somehow or other they had become genuinely happy and loving people.

Bewildered by this miraculous transformation, they tried to determine the cause, and realized that they had picked up a virus from their pet bird – a virus that made them happy! They wanted to share this great blessing with everyone and brainstormed how they could spread the virus in the quickest possible way. Going wherever there were crowds of people they would repeatedly cough. They went to sporting events, into subway trains, crowded elevators, and tourist attractions to infect everyone with the "happy virus."

Their efforts were wonderfully successful and people everywhere were quickly becoming happy. Being self-satisfied they all gave up drinking and smoking, and other degraded behaviors. Everyone became kind and helpful to others, and the entire society was quickly being transformed.

Captains of the sin industries however, were alarmed at the unexplainable sudden drop in sales and profits, and they met to address the great threat to their businesses. Somehow they were able to determine that the cause was the "happy virus" and colluded to wipe it out. The movie had a sad ending. The businessmen were successful in isolating and eliminating the happiness virus, and people returned to their previous unhappy ways, restoring profits of sin.

I'm sure the experienced Vaishnava reader will see the strong parallels between this Hollywood movie and the wonderful adventure we lived in the early days of the Hare Krishna Movement. The question remains however, if the Hare Krishna Movement can be restored to its former glory, and again infect society with the "happy virus" of Krishna Consciousness.

Is it possible that the alternative ways of living that Shrila Prabhupada promoted explain all of the attacks on his mission? To understand this, let's first recall that the goal of the Kamsas is empiric domination, from Shrila Bhaktisiddhanta Sarasvati's Putana:

> . . .if the empiric domination is to be preserved intact it would be necessary not to lose a moment to put down the transcendental heresy the instant it threatens to make its appearance in earnest.

Just to make it is absolutely clear, *empiric domination* means control and exploitation of the masses of people, primarily though the mechanism of state-issued money.

The Forced Establishment of *Ugra-Karma* Society

It required an enormous, centuries-long effort to replace the more-or-less sattvic medieval subsistence economy with *ugra-karma* industrialized, money-economy. To give some appreciation of the scope and nature of this endeavor, and the determined effort necessary to effect this change, I quote at length from my book *Spiritual Economics*:

> Under the influence of *sattva-guna* material wealth was shared [in subsistence economies directly tied to the land], but under *rajo-guna,* personal profit and gain come into play, along with the concept of individual private ownership. Indeed, the entire concept of "I and mine" changes dramatically. The change of consciousness from *sattva* to *rajas* brought with it dramatic

changes in relationships between people and the manner in which they handled their economic affairs. This shift did not occur spontaneously on the part of the people, but was imposed on them by the ruling classes with the use of force.

In one sense the idea of controlling the people did not change, but the locus of power was shifted. The ruling classes of the early modern times determined to create a culture of dependence with themselves replacing the popes as the dispensers of favor; those favors now being decided by money. It was necessary therefore to make the populace dependent on money alone, and for that their sustenance from the land, and mutual dependence, had to be abolished. The desired social transformation would turn the independent commoner into a dependent of *disinterested* others (owners of industry or government). It would force the common people to compete with each other to obtain such favors as the right to *survive*—paid employment being the only means of sustenance available. To achieve this, the former social customs of shared ownership, mutual aid, and the commons had to be destroyed. It mattered not what was lost in the process. More important was that society be transformed into the concept that the ruling classes wanted. It was a concept that was to chiefly benefit the ruling class at the expense of everyone else.

These changes in the social structure were accomplished, as they typically are in *Kali-yuga*, by force. From the 16th century and continuing into the 20th century, land has been confiscated by state authorities, forcing people into a dependent lifestyle. In England from the 16th through 19th centuries a series of "enclosure laws" were enacted to eliminate the use of village lands and the commons. Of course the commoners resisted the loss of their prerogatives with petitions, threats, foot dragging, the theft of new landmarks and surveys, covert thefts and arson. By law, the commoners had previously been entitled to the produce of the soil. Their cattle also had a right to the grass. The soil itself, the land, was not owned by the commoners, but the use of it was. That use, what the law called *profit a prendre*, was a common right that ensured the survival of peasants whose social relations were structured by access to land, common agriculture and shared use-rights, and they did not want to surrender any of these rights. This contest of wills was decided by force over the course of three centuries. . .

In the history cited above, and continuing on into the present day, the shift in social organization brought with it a change in the social contract, and with it political forces became arrayed against the common man. No longer were a people protected by their betters against common external threats and enemies. Class distinctions were now based on wealth and the control of wealth, with the owners of wealth occupying, influencing and engaging governmental forces on their behalf, organized against the common man. With enclosure, the rulers of society had devised a method that would free them from all responsibility to those who labored on their land, or in their factories. In feudal society the lord was responsible to see to the maintenance and protection of those in his charge, however meager it might have been. They were a source of expense to him, and he wanted to be free of it. They determined to reorganize society in a manner that would bring them all of the benefits with none of the expense. They reorganized the kingdom into the state, and for that they wanted to create a situation in which everyone was dependent on them through an impersonal mechanism such as a wage job. The developments of the nation state, exclusive title to property, industry, and a paper money economy gave them the means to do so.[1]

The effort to create a work force for industrial enterprises did not stop there. It has continued everywhere throughout the world, destroying indigenous cultures and forcing people off of the land by concentrating land ownership in very few hands. In the late nineteenth century for example, 80 percent of Ireland was owned by 616 absentee landlords, and 1.5% of the Russians owned an amazing 25% of that vast country. Even today in Brazil less than 3% of the population own two-thirds of the country's arable land, and two-thirds of England is owned by a mere 0.3% of the population.

For the entire 20th century it was actually the policy of the US Department of Agriculture to drive small farmers *off* of the land. "Get big (incorporate) or get out" was their policy. By their efforts more than 2,000 farms a week, for an entire 50 years, went under or were sold, and the percentage of people living on the land plummeted from 50% to 3%.[2] The Communists under Stalin accomplished the same thing, but with much more brutality, at an estimated cost of 50-60 million lives.[3] In 1989 two-thirds of all violent conflicts in the world involved the efforts of indigenous peoples to maintain their independent way of life on the land, free from the encroachment of Western culture.[3] There are hundreds of examples from history, some of which are provided in my Spiritual Economics book and website.[4] This continues up to the present day.[a]

The money powers are extremely careful not to lose this advantage, and anywhere a threat appears they immediately act to

---

[a] See for example, magazines such as Cultural Survival Quarterly, reporting that many of the wars in the world are indigenous people fighting to maintain their culture and way of living on the land; See also *The Globalization of Poverty and the New World Order*, by Michel Chossudovsky; other examples are given in my book Spiritual Economics.

remove it. This is one of the main tasks of intelligence agencies – maintaining the status quo.

Shrila Prabhupada Challenges the Demonic Culture

Anyone who has read Shrila Prabhupada's books knows that he railed against every aspect of this system: he condemned paper money as worthless, he condemned universities as slaughterhouses, degrading people to the level of dogs (job-seekers) that go begging for a master. He condemned modern society as an animal society, and its entire populace for being nothing more than dogs, hogs, camels and asses. And he rightly, and repeatedly. emphasized that real wealth was land, cows, and actual goods that people can use. Time and again he challenged modern "civilization" as demonic:

Atreya Rshi: Would God sanction activities in the factory, technological, scientific world?

Prabhupada: No, *there is no sanction. These are all sinful activities. . . You have created all these things. God has not sanctioned.* God has not sanctioned for running on a factory. *Therefore as soon as you run on a factory, you simply commit sinful activities.* In the *Bhagavad-gita* we don't find any such sanction that you run on a factory, a slaughterhouse or the brothel and this business and brewery no such sanction. But you have done at your whims. 24May74 Rome

And here, these verses of Rsabhadeva, He says warning. He's warning, He's speaking to His sons, but we can take the lesson. He says, *nayam deho deha-bhajam nrloke kastan kaman arhate vid-bhujam ye* [SB 5.5.1]. *Kaman* means the necessities of life. You can get your necessities of life very easily. By tilling the field, you get grains. And if there is cow, you get milk. That's all. That is sufficient. *But the leaders are making plan that if they are satisfied with their farming work, little grains and milk, then who will work in the factory?* Therefore they are taxing so that you cannot live even simple life - this is the position. *Even if you desire, the modern leaders will not allow you. They'll force you to work like dogs and hogs and asses.* Lecture 8Sep73 Stockholm

Vedic culture is meant for the whole world. *So you produce your own food grains, not for making money but just for feeding yourself* and the animals, cows… And then you become peaceful, no anxiety for your maintenance. And then cultivate this spiritual knowledge the same way. . . *Don't be dependent on anyone else. Become self-independent. And don't be after money. Simply produce your bare necessities of life.* Keep yourself fit, strong. And chant Hare Krishna, read book. Then you'll grow strong. Is there any difficulty? Lecture 5Oct75 Mauritius

So similarly, in villages, everyone, if he has got some land, he can live simply without any gorgeous building. What is the use? Just have a cottage and have garden. You'll live very peacefully…Produce your own food, live peacefully, fresh vegetable, fresh grains, fresh milk. . . Offer to the Deity. Eat sufficiently. What is the use of going outside? Simple life and chant Hare Krishna. . . What is this rascal civilization, whole day "Where is money? Where is money? Where is money? Where is money? Where is money?" Everyone. Busy means "Where is money? Where is money?" Just like the hog, he is busy: "What time…? Where is stool? Where is stool? Where is stool? Where is stool? *That is not civilization.* First of all be engaged yourself. Set the example and they will join. Lecture 28Oct75 Nairobi

Everywhere he went – Rome, Nairobi, Mauritius, Detroit, Stockholm, etc., year after year, in his lectures, morning walks and his letters, Shrila Prabhupada repeatedly condemned the modern way of life as a sinful, soul-killing civilization that simply exploits people, encouraging them to live in ways that will take them to hell.

But Vaishnavas are not like that. They have compassion for all of the fallen conditioned souls. Lord Chaitanya instructed "*para upakra*," do good to others, as Shrila Prabhupada instructed us:

> You have created this animal civilization. Now they are coming out as naked animals. This is the result. Now you have to reform them. That reformation is Krishna consciousness. So you have to make an example, what is actually human life. Then others will see. You cannot stop them. But some of them, those who are intelligent, they will see, "Yes, here is life." As they are coming to nakedness, they will come to this, our mode of life. So you have to become an ideal society. *You live locally, and be self-sufficient. They will see that it is possible to live locally without movement, and still highly cultured men, self-sufficient.* That is required. So you have to set up real human society in a small scale so people will see, "Yes." Lecture 28May74 Rome

Any example of local, self-sufficient living without money, without cars, without oil, would be a huge threat to the demons and their ability to control society, and they are not about to let that happen. I was told by one who would know, that even my own humble efforts at self-sufficiency in a Ukrainian village would not be allowed.

Bhaktivedanta Swami Must be Stopped!

Do not, for one minute, think that Shrila Prabhupada's preaching was not seen as a great threat by the powers-that-be, especially as he encouraged his followers to get farms and live directly from the land without the use of money. He gave the youth of the 60s and 70s the revolution they were looking for, and this is why the Krishna Consciousness Movement exploded in those years.

Shrila Prabhupada understood that the government would not like his ideas:

> Prabhupada: I think this farm organization will not be liked by the government.
>
> Hari-sauri: Because of the self-sufficiency? Once they know that we can live independently, they won't like it.
>
> Madhavananda: They don't like it already. They are attacking in New Vrindaban, publicity saying that this is just a hippie farm and this and that. They don't like.... *It is the state. They see that we are living independently of the entire society. They don't like that. They want everyone to be following their way of society.*
>
> Prabhupada: Why not our way of life? If you want to enforce your way of life, *why not I enforce my way of life? Then where is my independence* [freedom]? You cannot enforce your way of life. . . That is the difficulty. The government is *rakshasa*. Conversation 14Jun76 Detroit

And in his quite famous Stockholm lectures Shrila Prabhupada predicted their reaction:

> But still, we have to refrain from such unnecessary hard labor. *It may be that government may take action against me because I'm speaking something revolutionary.* [chuckles] Yes. But that is the fact. *Why you should work?* God has made provision for the birds, beast, animals, ants, and if I'm devotee of God, He'll not give me food? You will have all your necessities of life, but you remain fixed up in your determination in Krishna consciousness. Lecture – 8Sep73 Stockholm

Indeed. They will take action, not only against him personally, but against his entire effort to change the world.

This cannot be allowed!
Bhaktivedanta Swami must be stopped!

CHAPTER THREE

The Infiltration of ISKCON

The chanter of the kirtan of Hari is not to be confounded with the malicious critics and censors of this world. It is malice and vanity which lead worldly people to find fault with their neighbor and to attempt to impose by falsehood and cunning their un-truth on their victims. Such critics and their victims are likely to misunderstand for opposite reasons the opposition offered by the preacher of the truth to both for the purpose of doing real good to them. Shrila Bhaktisiddhanta

Everyone Gets Infiltrated

When Shrila Prabhupada was with us ISKCON was a very different society than it is today. To be considered a devotee you were expected to leave your entire life behind, including your possessions, and move into the ashrama with almost nothing. This extreme sacrifice was an unofficial test that separated the serious from the merely curious. Those who didn't do so, but continued associating with devotees were called 'fringies,' an expression of mild derision.

167

ISKCON in those days was on a war footing – we were in a war against Maya – and as soldiers in Shrila Prabhupada's army we were determined and convinced that we would win that war. After all we were flooding the land with Lord Chaitanya's mercy to fulfill the prophecy. By 1977 it appeared that we were making serious progress. We were having a tremendous impact all over America and Europe, to the point that "Hare Krishna" had become a household word.

The 60s and 70s was a time of revolutionary fervor and efforts to change the status quo. Hare Krishna was but one among many – the anti-war movement, the women's liberation movement, the Black Panthers movement, the Weather Underground, Earth First!, Students for a Democratic Society, and more. The youth of the day were not content to find accommodation in a world that didn't work for the majority of people. They wanted change. The Hare Krishna's also wanted to change the world, and Shrila Prabhupada taught us that the only effective way to do so was to raise people's consciousness, his books and the maha-mantra being the best way to accomplish that. We had complete faith in his words.

The Black Panthers wanted change, but they had different weapons – rifles. Blacks were being beaten and shot by police, and they wanted and end to this unjustified violence. The determining factor in forming the Panthers was the police beating of Oakland California residents as they held a candlelight protest demanding a stoplight at a dangerous intersection.

Under the leadership of Huey Newton, they formed Panther Patrols to intercede and stop the Oakland police from randomly beating and shooting black men on the street. Although they carried rifles – legal until the law changed in 1968 – they didn't need to use them. It was enough to show that they knew their rights and were prepared to shoot back if necessary. Under Newton, the Black Panthers exercised very strict discipline. Alcohol, drugs, womanizing and illegal weapons were strictly forbidden at meetings and protests. Men, women and children flocked to join the Panthers, who organized classes in literacy, Black History, revolutionary theory and firearms training – in addition to their famous children's breakfasts and other food distribution programs. As dozens of chapters sprang up and membership swelled into the thousands the Oakland police and FBI infiltrated the Panthers with the intention of dismantling it.

Infiltration is the Norm, not the Exception

Government powers want stability, and they attempt to control any group that would upset it. Infiltration is an age-old tactic of warfare. Almost every group is infiltrated for the purpose of learning firsthand what is being planned, as well as to attempt to control it from within. However, most people, not being politically motivated, have no understanding how widespread it is. The following article informs us about infiltration of movements that might possibly have any political influence in the 60s:

> Almost every movement in modern history has been infiltrated by police and others using many of the same tactics we are now seeing in Occupy [movement in 2012 NY city].
>
> Virtually every movement has been the target of police surveillance *and disruption activities*. The most famous surveillance program was the FBI's COINTELPRO which, according to COINTELPRO Documents,[1] targeted the women's rights, Civil Rights, anti-war and peace movements, the New Left, socialists, communists and independence movement for Puerto Rico, among others. Among the groups infiltrated were the Southern Christian Leadership Conference, the NAACP, Congress for Racial Equality, the

American Indian Movement, Students for a Democratic Society, the National Lawyers Guild, the Black Panthers and Weather Underground. Significant leaders from Albert Einstein to Dr. Martin Luther King, Jr., who are both memorialized in Washington, were monitored. The rule in the United States is to be infiltrated; the exception is not to be.

The Church Committee[2] documented a history of use of the FBI for purposes of political repression. They described infiltration efforts going back to World War I, including the 1920s, when agents were charged with rounding up "anarchists and revolutionaries" for deportation. The Church Committee found infiltration efforts growing from *1936 through 1976*, with COINTELPRO as the major program. While these domestic political spying and disruption programs were supposed to stop in 1976, in fact they have continued. As reported in "The Price of Dissent," Federal Magistrate Joan Lefkow found in 1991, the record "shows that despite regulations, orders and consent decrees prohibiting such activities, the FBI had continued to collect information concerning only the exercise of free speech."

How many agents or infiltrators can we expect to see inside a movement? One of the most notorious "police riots" was the 1968 Democratic Party Convention. Independent journalist Yasha Levine writes:[3] 'During the 1968 protests of the Democratic National Convention in Chicago, which drew about 10,000 protesters and was brutally crushed by the police, *1 out of 6 protesters was a federal undercover agent.* That's right, 1/6th of the total protesting population was made up of spooks drawn from various federal agencies. That's roughly 1,600 people! The stat came from an Army document obtained by CBS News in 1978, a full decade after the protest took place. According to CBS, the infiltrators were not passive observers, monitoring and relaying information to central command, but *were involved in violent confrontations* with the police.' [All emphasis in original.][4]

Did you catch that? The *rule is to be infiltrated*, and our Hare Krishna movement was/is no exception to that rule, because as our numbers grew we were very much a threat to the status quo, as we quoted Shrila Prabhupada above. Indeed, *our stated intentions were to change the world!* We also wanted to reform modern society, albeit not by violent means, but through a revolution of consciousness, a difference that likely was of little significance to the agencies as the end result would totally change the way of life they were working to preserve.

Every country engages in such activities and the Soviet Union was no exception. There was a division of the KGB called the Fifth Chief Directorate whose purpose was to "protect the ideological purity of the Soviet Union." Their mandate was to infiltrate *every* organization and to control it from within. While those in the lower ranks of the organization are busy pursuing the stated goals of the organization, the infiltrators were subtly altering the direction of the effort. Such infiltration has been widely documented and written about.[5]

Evidence of Infiltration in ISKCON

There are many examples of ISKCON's infiltration, and we'll begin with a case from Los Angeles in the 70's. A number of men who fancied themselves as *kshatriyas* would go to a local gun range for target practice, and over time became friendly with the range manager. One morning the manager called one of those devotees telling him that he was taking his family and leaving the country, because the FBI had been pressuring him to infiltrate ISKCON and he didn't want to be their snitch. "Beware that others will be infiltrating you," he warned.[a]

In another instance, one of ISKCON's leaders confided in me that he became close with someone connected with high level intelligence services who revealed to him the names of *numerous* individuals in ISKCON connected with intelligence agencies. He told me how he watched with amazement to see how those agents were moved to different zones for various purposes and he could clearly see how the society was being manipulated. As much as I pleaded with him he would not divulge even one name, saying that doing so would put both of our lives in danger.

Another godbrother told me of a Polish devotee recounting a first-hand experience of ISKCON's infiltration. Back in the 1980's a young man started coming around one of the Polish temples, very enthusiastic to chant, wear *tilak*, attend *arotika and* classes, etc. In due course of time the newcomer revealed that he was a government agent sent to investigate ISKCON Poland from the inside. He also revealed that the CIA was also active there and that they also had a man on the inside (in Poland).

While on my first trip to Russia I met one of the first Russian devotees, Vrindavana Das, who endured several years in a Soviet prison as a prisoner of conscience. He told me that while in confinement, he was told by the KGB that ISKCON had been infiltrated by the KGB – from America no less (New York specifically) – in the early seventies.

Tapapunja Dasa also confirmed infiltration by the intelligence agencies. He learned while in prison that the American FBI or CIA, had infiltrated our movement – all the way to the GBC.

Interesting. Can we trust what these people say? After all, the "intelligence" agents are professional liars. Well, this is confirmed

---

[a] Told to me personally by one member of the kshatriya group

by even more people.

So Much More

Another devotee who was the secretary of one ISKCON *sannyasi* back in the 80s told me he saw numerous passports of that *sannyasi* from different countries – one of which showed him as a woman. There were other anomalies or curious characteristics about that *sannyasi* that were very out of place, such as banks deposit books showing large amounts of money on deposit. I confronted that same *sannyasi* much later when he was a GBC member and ISKCON guru, about the infiltration of ISKCON. In reply to my challenges that we have to find out the infiltrators and remove them, he simply giggled and said "What are you going to do?" which I took to mean "What can be done about that?" But it could have been a challenge: "what are *you personally* going to do?" I was flabbergasted! Here he was, essentially agreeing that infiltration was going on (he did not object or disagree), and giving the impression that nothing could be done, and certainly that he was not going to do anything!

A Russian devotee related to me that he was told by a devotee from Soviet times, how the KGB had infiltrated a number of religious groups. One day they got a new bhakta. He was very enthusiastic and learned quickly, and had superb intellectual ability. One day other devotees asked him what other temples he had visited. The boy drew an exact map of the places where they had been, something that would have been quite unusual for a very new man, making some suspicious of him. It was only years later that they learned the truth, and surprisingly from another new bhakta who had been a former Christian. The new "Christian" bhakta recognized that "devotee" in old photos. He said that that same man had joined their Christian sect too and was a very impressive member there initially, but he created a lot of division that damaged their group.

We would be totally naive to think that many intelligence agencies have not infiltrated our movement, and in many places. Are all of their efforts the same as the Fifth Chief Directorate? Well, consider again what these agencies want. We can get a hint from their well-known infiltration of anti-war, and Black Power groups in America in the 1960s. The Western agencies' objectives are very much like the KGB's idea of protecting the Soviet ideological purity – and that would be to maintain the status quo. The establishment powers work very hard to mold society to their ways and purposes. They don't want anyone rocking the boat – and want to prevent the boat from rocking at all – to the point where we find suspicious and untimely deaths of rock singers whose lyrics and popularity challenge the establishment. John Lennon and Bob Marley are two that quickly come to mind. The establishment acts quickly before anything can even begin to get out of hand.

Directly from the KGB

A number of years ago I visited Pridnestrovie, a breakaway republic of Moldova. When the Soviet Union was breaking up the people there voted to stay aligned with Russia and reject their affiliation with the host country. A local Russian general backed up their efforts resulting in a small war with several thousand deaths.

In the end they maintained their independence, but tanks remain on the streets and soldiers everywhere carry automatic weapons.

The person directly in charge of their intelligence operations had been coming to the temple and taking an interest in Krishna consciousness, making no effort to hide who he was. Upon meeting him I was invited to speak at his school for revolutionaries, and instructed them to carry out a spiritual revolution instead of a violent one.

My KGB friend was trained by the Soviets and knows all the tricks of the spook trade. In conversation with him, I explained my efforts to establish a community demonstrating the gift economy of Spiritual Economics. After listening intently he immediately asked me how I was going to protect my efforts, which bewildered me. He explained that the powers-that-be will not like that I am trying to establish an alternative spiritual and economic culture. He said "first they will try to destroy you from the inside by infiltrating your group. If that is not successful they will then make all kinds of bad propaganda against you so that you will lose the support of the local people, causing the effort to fail. And, failing with that, they will then destroy you physically." The Branch Davidians of Waco Texas came to mind with that statement. He explained that everybody gets infiltrated and this is how the entire world is controlled.

In that regard we should not forget the very early days of ISKCON when Shrila Prabhupada brought his American devotees to India, and the rumors were heard that the American Vaishnavas were CIA agents. However, those agents were not there to spy on India, but were likely planted with the intention of controlling ISKCON from within, and preventing their control of society.

The powers-that-be no longer openly oppose us as they did in ISKCON's early days. It is much easier to work from the inside, and after gaining confidence and a position of authority, then do things that derail the group's efforts. There have been too many stupid, inept, incompetent (or should we say conniving and dastardly?) things that were done to be explained simply by incompetence.

Doing something that will result in a court case for example, such as allowing minors to live in our temples against the wishes of their parents. This happened in America resulting in a huge lawsuit that cost millions of dollars, but somehow or other the same stupidity was repeated in Russia decades later. Or engaging in illegally acquiring properties that are later lost after long and costly lawsuits that siphon off money and consume time that could go toward preaching (I know of at least two instances of such fool-ishness); or individuals who sold properties and ran off with all the money. It could have happened by an infiltrator rising to a position of leadership and then "falling down" thereby discouraging followers who had faith in them. Or deliberately and knowingly placing pedophiles in charge of gurukulas, perpetrating physical and sexual abuse on the children, destroying their faith, and the faith of the adults who came to know of such horrors.[6]

There was a campaign by *sannyasis* of discouraging women in the early-to-mid-70s in America causing many to leave out of disgust and taking their husbands/boyfriends with them. Since the 90s there has been a feminist backlash due to those earlier efforts to disturb the women. The so-called Vaishnava feminists are directly challenging Shrila Prabhupada's statements regarding women, and dismissing his comments and instructions as being old-fashioned and irrelevant for our modern times. Are these "devotee feminists" actually devotees? Or perhaps the infiltrators were using this issue to challenge Shrila Prabhupada's absolute authority?

There are so many instances of not doing things that should have been done, or doing them untimely, doing things that shouldn't have been done, etc. It is easy to destroy any group from within. Shrila Prabhupada himself said that our Movement could only be destroyed from within – not from the outside, and it certainly has been destroyed by the very leaders who were meant to protect it, discouraging thousands who left the movement they once cherished with a broken-heart.

Infiltration for deviant purposes is described in the Bhagavatam itself: Kali in the dress of a king to bewilder the innocent while harming Dharma the bull; Indra who disguised himself as a *sannyasi* to steal the sacrificial horse from Pritu's sacrificial arena (since that time many men have adopted the dress of a *sannyasi* for false pretenses), and the snake-bird Taksaka who disguised himself as a brahmana to get close to Pariksit in order to bite him, and Ravana disguising himself as a mendicant. So we should not be surprised that such things go on – and we would be foolish to think that they do not!

Shrila Prabhupada so often used the expression – *phalena paricyate* – judge by the result, and wrote in the *Srimad Bhagavatam*:

> One cannot judge whether a person is a devata, an *asura* or a *Rakshasa* by seeing him, but a sane man can understand this by the activities such a person performs. . . one can judge who is a devata, who is a *Rakshasha* and who is an *asura* by how they conduct their activities. *Srimad Bhagavatam* 7.1.9 and Purport

Our movement has suffered so many setbacks from things done on the inside. If somebody actually wanted to destroy what Shrila Prabhupada began they couldn't have been more successful than what our "leaders" have done. Judging by the result we must conclude that indeed Shrila Prabhupada's mission has been infiltrated to the highest ranks and they are misdirecting it into a cul-de-sac of spiritual ignorance. And be forewarned! It will continue unabated! We must give up our sentimental notions and wake up to the realities of this world. We must judge from our head as well as our hearts, and not follow 'leaders' superficially based on position or title alone, but develop discriminating intelligence to see who is serving Shrila Prabhupada's mission and who is undermining it.

There is no question that the agents of Kali, the *kali-chelas* have infiltrated ISKCON. Nor was there any doubt in Shrila Prabhupada's mind as he wrote of it himself:

> *There are many jealous people in the dress of Vaishnavas in this Krishna consciousness movement, and they should be completely neglected.* Madhya Lila 1.218 Purport

> *There are so-called disciples who become submissive to a spiritual master most artificially, with an ulterior motive. They also cannot*

understand what Krishna consciousness or devotional service is.
Srimad Bhagavatam 3.32.40

Before we look at what has been done by the so-called leaders however, we will must think carefully about what a devotee actually is, and the difference between a devotee and a non-devotee.

Hint: it is more than just appearance.

CHAPTER FOUR

Who is a Devotee?

After the time of Sri Caitanya Mahaprabhu, those faithful to Him kept apart from non-devotees, to avoid contamination. Seeing this, the personality of Kali sent his representatives in disguise to pollute the Vaishnava sampradaya. Posing as Vaishnavas, they spread their wicked doctrines, and appeared so intelligent and devoted that only pure devotees could detect their real identity. Most devotees – not only the most neophyte – were enchanted by their tricks. In this way Kali's agents expertly introduced karma, jnana, and anyabhilasa in the Vaishnava sampradaya and caused shuddha-bhakti to vanish from the world.[1]

Form v. Substance

The very idea that there are imposter devotees within our ISKCON society gives rise to incredulity. When Shrila Prabhupada makes such a declaration we are left to wonder who they might be, and how we can judge who is bona fide and who is an imposter. The *prakrita bhaktas*, or neophyte devotees, do not have the ability for such discrimination. Such bhaktas are more or less conditioned souls, who, by their nature, are preoccupied with form because

179

having little understanding of Krishna Consciousness and spiritual truth, form is all they have by which to judge. When referring to "form" herein we mean any or all aspects of form, including: appearance, position, title, behavior and words.

The second-class devotee, or *madhyama*, is qualified to understand the difference between the advanced devotee, innocent persons, and the envious. Making such discrimination he seeks the association of the advanced devotees, preaches to the innocent, and avoids the envious. The *madhyama* can understand who is a devotee and who is not:

> An intermediate devotee can identify the non-devotee or motivated devotee. The motivated devotee or the non-devotee are on the material platform, and they are called *prakrita*. The intermediate devotee does not mix with such materialistic people. Madhya 16.72

Neophyte devotees would do well to take the help of their counsel (as *sadhus*) to understand who is actually a qualified devotee. But the nature of a neophyte is that he does not consider himself as such, and thus comes to his own conclusions. They will typically, and innocently, follow official leaders because they have position and title, and thus are considered "advanced devotees." However, a brief examination of the history of ISKCON quickly destroys that supposition.

Shrila Bhaktisiddhanta Sarasvati explains that external features can never reveal who is an actual Vaishnava. Knowing that we must be careful not to leap to conclusions:

> One of the most familiar tenets of Vaishnavism acquaints us with the significant fact that it is impossible to know a Vaishnava except by the mercy of the latter. If the external marks and the regular performance of the rituals recommended by the Scriptures could make one a Vaishnava then the process

could, indeed, be handed down from father to son intact. But one person may scrupulously perform all these affairs and continue to be a non-Vaishnava, while another may omit, them wholesale and yet be a genuine Vaishnava. It is never possible to find out the Vaishnava by the external marks.[2]

Fortunately our scriptures offer many examples to teach us to look beyond external form to the actual substance of a genuine devotee. Typically what we find is that those who have actual substance *do not* display any special form, position, or title, as these material designations have nothing whatsoever to do with spiritual qualification. Let's take a look at the lessons that shastra offers us in this regard.

Devotees Who Have Substance but Not Form

Jada Bharata

A wonderful example of a person with spiritual substance but without external form is Jada Bharata. In a previous life he was the famed Bharat Maharaja, and was such a great personality that the entire earth is named after him as Bharatvarsha. In that life he perfectly performed devotional service advancing to the platform of bhava, just one step away from total liberation, prema, but he died accidentally while thinking of a deer, and was obliged to take the form of a deer in his next life. Subsequently, in his next human birth as Jada Bharat, he was determined not to be deviated from the goal of spiritual perfection:

> Due to his being especially gifted with the Lord's mercy, Bharata Maharaja could remember the incidents of his past life. Although he received the body of a brahmana, he was still very much afraid of his relatives and friends who were not devotees. He was always very cautious of such association because he feared that he would again fall down. Consequently

he manifested himself before the public eye as a madman – dull, blind and deaf – so that others would not try to talk to him. In this way he saved himself from bad association. Within he was always thinking of the lotus feet of the Lord and chanting the Lord's glories, which save one from the bondage of fruitive action. In this way he saved himself from the onslaught of non-devotee associates.

Jada Bharata behaved before his father like a fool so that his father would know that he was unfit for instruction and would abandon the attempt to instruct him further.

After the father died, the nine stepbrothers of Jada Bharata considered him dull and brainless, and abandoned the father's attempt to give Jada Bharata a complete education. The stepbrothers of Jada Bharata were learned in the three Vedas – the *Rg Veda, Sama Veda and Yajur Veda* – which very much encourage fruitive activity. *However, the nine brothers were not at all spiritually enlightened in devotional service to the Lord. Consequently they could not understand the highly exalted position of Jada Bharata.* SB 5.9.3-8

Jada Bharata, although practically self-realized, *does not show any* of the features of a person who typically might be thought of as being spiritually elevated. It is important to note that Jada Bharata's own brothers, although learned in the Vedas, could not recognize his qualification. This is *due to their lack of spiritual qualification.*

Later, the *Srimad Bhagavatam* refers to many such great personalities who wander the earth in disguise:

I offer my respectful obeisances unto the great personalities, whether they walk on the earth's surface as children, young boys, *avadhutas* or great brahmanas. Even if they are hidden under different disguises, I offer my respects to all of them. By their mercy, may there be good fortune in the royal dynasties that are always offending them. SB 5.13.23

Utkala – Son of Dhruva Maharaja

Jada Bharata is not the only great soul who behaved as a fool to escape becoming implicated in material life. Utkala, the eldest son of Dhruva Maharaja, did also:

> When Maharaja Dhruva departed for the forest, his son, Utkala, did not desire to accept the opulent throne of his father, which was meant for the ruler of all the lands of this planet. . . He was situated in transcendental bliss, and he continued always in that blissful existence, which expanded more and more. This was possible for him by continual practice of *bhakti-yoga*, which is compared to fire because it burns away all dirty, material things. He was always situated in his constitutional position of self-realization, and he could not see anything else but the Supreme Lord and himself engaged in discharging devotional service.

> Utkala appeared to the less intelligent persons on the road to be foolish, blind, dumb, deaf and mad, although actually he was not so. He remained like fire covered with ashes, without blazing flames. For this reason the ministers and all the elderly members of the family thought Utkala to be without intelligence and, in fact, mad. Thus his younger brother Vatsara became king of the world. SB 4.13.6-11

Ramananda Raya

In Ramananda Raya we have a very different example of one who appears not dull, but very materialistic, although a highly advanced devotee. Generally people holding high offices of power, and who dress opulently, are considered *vishayees*, materialistic persons, but this was not the case with Ramananda Raya. About him Shrila Prabhupada writes:

> "Sarvabhauma Bhatacarya informed Lord Caitanya Mahaprabhu that Ramananda Raya, although belonging to the *sudra* class, was a highly responsible government officer. As far as spiritual advancement is concerned, materialists, politicians and *sudra*s are generally disqualified. Sarvabhauma Bhatacarya therefore requested that Lord Caitanya Mahaprabhu not neglect Ramananda Raya, who was highly advanced spiritually although he was born a *sudra* and a materialist, and was engaged in government service. He was certainly not a *sannyasi* in saffron cloth, yet he was in the transcendental position of a *paramahamsa* householder. Before becoming Caitanya Mahaprabhu's disciple, Sarvabhauma Bhattacarya considered Ramananda Raya an ordinary vishayee. *However, when the Bhattacarya was actually enlightened in Vaishnava philosophy, he could understand the exalted transcendental position of Sri Ramananda Raya.* Madhya 7.63 purport

Shrila Prabhupada states that Ramananda Raya did not *appear* as an advanced spiritual personality to Sarvabhauma. Indeed, he seemed to be quite the opposite:

> Sarvabhauma Bhattacarya continued, "Ramananda Raya is a fit person to associate with You; no other devotee can compare with him in knowledge of the transcendental mellows. He is most exalted, and if You talk with him, You will see how glorious he is. *I could not realize when I first spoke with Ramananda Raya that his topics and endeavors were all transcendentally uncommon. I made fun of him simply because he was a Vaishnava. By Your mercy I can now understand the truth about Ramananda Raya.*" Madhya 7.64-67

Again we point out that Sarvabhauma could not properly recognize the exalted status of Ramananda *until after he was purified and enlightened by Lord Chaitanya*. As the saying goes "it takes one to know one." The exalted devotees presented here, who have substance – but not the apparent form – can only be recognized by those who are similarly qualified. Indeed, the brahmanas who had accompanied Ramananda Raya to the river were bewildered by the behavior of Lord Chaitanya:

> The brahmanas thought, "We can see that this *sannyasi* has a luster like the effulgence of Brahman, but how is it He is crying upon embracing a *sudra*, a member of the fourth caste in the social order? This Ramananda Raya is the Governor of Madras, a highly learned and grave person, a maha-pandita, but upon touching this *sannyasi* he has become restless like a madman." Cc. Madhya 8.26-28

These brahmanas are examples of those who had form (of proper brahmanas) but not the required substance (*adhikar*) to understand the exalted position of Ramananda Raya, whereas Lord Chaitanya did.

From these examples we understand that there will always be conflicting opinions amongst devotees as to the proper understanding of things, each judging from their own understanding, whether it be *kanishta*, *madhyama* or *uttama*. *Kanishta*s cannot recognize an *uttama*, do not defer to them, but instead adhere to their own limited understanding, and for this reason we should not expect that there will ever be unity of agreement amongst all devotees.

There are a few other examples we will briefly mention:

Lord Chaitanya - before accepting sannyasa

Although He was/is God Himself, and although He was encouraging everyone to take up the chanting of the holy names of Krishna, still, because He did not have the form of a so-called advanced spiritualist, those without qualification ridiculed Him. Therefore Lord Chaitanya decided to accept the sannyasa order so the fallen souls would at least respect Him as a *sannyasi*. (See Cc., Adi-lila, 7.29-40)

Lord Shiva

Although considered as the greatest Vaishnava, Lord Shiva's father-in-law, Daksha, could not see past Shiva's external features to recognize his spiritually elevated nature. Thus when Lord Shiva did not receive him as he expected Daksha strongly rebuked him, which became the path to his own destruction. (See S.B. Canto 4, chapter 2)

The Cowherd Girls of Vraj

Simple village girls with no formal education, madly in love with Krishna, despite their thinking that He is simply a village cowherd boy, are the most exalted devotees in all existence. They have no position, no titles, no external form to suggest that they are big, big exalted devotees. Yet they are. And they demonstrate that by continually thinking about how to serve and please their Krishna. Their *adhikar* is so complete that Krishna, God Himself, is captivated and conquered by their loving devotion. (See for example KRISHNA Book, Chaps. 30-35)

There Are Many More

There are many more examples shastra offers to instruct us in how not to be bewildered by form, but look beyond that to determine the substance, or *adhikary* of a devotee. How many can you think of? In this category of substance without the external appearance of an advanced devotee, we suggest the following (not an exhaustive compilation):

- Haridasa Thakur
- Pundarika Vidyanidhi
- Bilvamangala Thakur
- Gaurakisor Das Babaji
- Kolavecha Sridhar
- Prahlada Maharaja
- Vrit*asura*

None of these exalted personalities had any official title, institutional position, nor even any social position. Pundarika Vidyanidhi appeared to be a vishayee, and Vrit*asura* appeared circumstantially to be a demon. But they were wonderful servants of the Lord who, being fully satisfied with the Lord's service, neither needed, nor desired, the acknowledgement of others.

Now let's look at the corollary situation – those who display form, but have no substance.

Form Without Substance

Materialistic persons are naturally bewildered by form. That is the very definition of being materialistic – those who are concerned with the material aspects of life – form, position, title, etc. This group includes the *kanishta/prakrita bhaktas*. Being bewildered by form they project their own understanding onto others. In Sanskrit this is called *atmavan manyate jagat* – everyone thinks of others according to his own position. The Bhagavatam and Chaitanya-charitamrita also provide us with many examples of such devotees, some of whom we have commented on above, namely Daksha, the brothers of Utkala, and the brahmanas accompanying Ramananda Raya. There are numerous others. Thinking over the lessons offered in Shrila Prabhupada's books, who comes to mind for you? Here are a few:

Kali

Once, when Maharaja Pariksit was on his way to conquer the world, he saw the master of *Kali-yuga*, who was lower than a *sudra*, disdisguised as a king and hurting the legs of a cow and bull. The King at once caught hold of him to deal sufficient punishment. SB 1.16.4

Kali had disguised himself as a king in order to carry out his dirty deeds. When innocent persons observed his activity in harming the bull Dharma they would assume that since this person is dressed as a king he must be a king, and he must be administering proper punishment to a wrong-doer. Pariksit on the other hand, having *adhikar* of a king, was not bewildered and immediately understood that Kali was a wrong-doer. Although Kali showed himself to have the form of a king, he did not have the qualification of a king, but a qualified king could understand this based on his activities, not on his dress.

Putana

Putana Rakshasi's heart was fierce and cruel, but she looked like a very affectionate mother. Thus she resembled a sharp sword in a soft sheath. Although seeing her within the room, Yashoda and Rohini, overwhelmed by her beauty, did not stop her, but remained silent because she treated the child like a mother. Lord Sri Krishna however, as the all-pervading Supersoul, understood that Putana was a witch who was expert in killing small children, and that she had come to kill Him. Thus Putana took upon her lap He who was to be her own annihilation, just as an unintelligent person places a sleeping snake on his lap, thinking the snake to be a rope. SB 10.6.9-8.

Mothers Yasoda and Rohini, being simple village women were bewildered by the form of Putana as a beautiful woman, and could not understand the actual nature and intention of the witch, although Sri Krishna could do so, even as an infant. Of course Krishna in the form of an infant is no different than Krishna in His eternal form as a blooming youth. As the omniscient Supreme Personality, and the Supersoul of everyone, He could understand Putana's intention. Putana had adopted the form of a beautiful woman to bewilder the inhabitants of Vraj, but she could not bewilder child Krishna.

Paundraka

Paundraka was emboldened by the flattery of childish men, who told him, 'You are Vasudeva, the Supreme Lord and master of the universe, who have now descended to the earth.' Thus he imagined himself to be the infallible Personality of Godhead. Thus slow-witted King Paundraka sent a messenger to the inscrutable Lord Krishna at Dvaraka. Paundraka was acting just like an unintelligent child whom other children are pretending is a king. [On Paundraka's behalf, the messenger said:] 'I am the one and only Lord Vasudeva, and there is no other. It is I who have descended to this world to show mercy to the living beings. Therefore give up Your false name. O Satvata, give up my personal symbols, which out of foolishness You now carry, and come to me for shelter. If You do not, then You must give me battle.'

Lord Krishna saw that Paundraka was carrying the Lord's own insignia, such as the conchshell, disc, sword and club, and also an imitation Sharnga bow and Srivatsa mark. He wore a mock Kaustubha gem, was decorated with a garland of forest flowers and was dressed in upper and lower garments of fine yellow silk. His banner bore the image of Garuda, and he wore a valuable crown and gleaming, shark-shaped earrings. Lord Hari laughed heartily when He saw how the King had dressed up in exact imitation of His own appearance, just like an actor on a stage. SB 10.66.2–15.

Paundraka obtained a benediction from Lord Shiva that would allow him to imitate the dress of Lord Krishna. He foolishly thought that by adopting the dress of Vishnu he would actually be Vishnu, to the point of challenging the actual Vishnu, Krishna. Indeed, he did in fact bewilder foolish people, who have no substance, into believing that he was Vishnu, but he could not bewilder Krishna.

The Ongoing Conflict Between *Prakrita* and *Uttama* Bhaktas

Due to their overestimation of themselves, it is not uncommon to find the *prakrita bhaktas* offending the actual devotees who have substance, but not the expected form. Because of their form, title, position, etc., the *prakrita bhaktas* think of themselves as being superior to those who lack such visible accoutrements. Thus bewildered, they criticize and reject those without such insignia. If they have position or rank, they expect certain behavior on the part of others, such as deference, or inordinate respect, and when that is not forthcoming become offended to the point of offending others.

Some of these examples (Utkala and his brothers, Shiva and Daksa, Ramananda and Sarvabhauma, etc.) exemplify the perennial conflict between the neophyte or *prakrita bhaktas* and the *uttama* bhaktas. We also observed this conflict earlier in this book between the Pharisees and the Jewish Vaishnavas.

This is also true in our day, and we see such conflicts played out on Facebook and other social discussion forums. This being the case we can confidently say that this work will have many detractors, including those of rank and title, who, lacking adequate discernment, will accuse us of aparadha. This conflict is ever-present because there are always *kanishta*s and *prakrita bhaktas*.

Daksa

As one of the progenitors, Daksha was a powerful and exalted personality, whom we learn about in the fourth canto of the *Srimad Bhagavatam*:

> When Daksha, the leader of the *Prajapatis*, entered the assembly of the demigods and sages, his personal bodily luster was as bright as the effulgence of the sun, and all the assembled personalities became insignificant in his presence. Influenced by his personal bodily luster, all the fire-gods and other participants, with the exceptions of Lord Brahma and Lord Shiva, gave up their own sitting places and stood in respect for Daksha. Before taking his seat, however, Daksha was very much offended to see Lord Shiva sitting and not showing him any respect. At that time, Daksha became greatly angry, and, his eyes glowing, he began to speak very strongly against Lord Shiva. SB 4.2.5-8

Due to Lord Shiva's being his son-in-law Daksa considered himself in a superior position and expected appropriate respect from Shiva. That expectation was based on bodily considerations however. Spiritually speaking Lord Shiva is in a superior position as a guna-avatar, but this was overlooked by Daksha due to his over-estimation of his material qualities and relationship. Daksa thus offended Lord Shiva resulting in a great tragedy wherein Daksa's daughter voluntarily gave up her body due to its connection with her offensive father, and Daksha lost his head.

Keepers of Sri Mandir, Lord Jagannath's Residence

It was the custom in Lord Chaitanya's time that the *mlecchas* (non-Hindus, or non-devotees) were not allowed to enter the temple of Lord Jagannath in Puri. Those in charge of the temple have positions of authority, but by their actions show that they cannot discriminate between who is a bona fide devotee and who is not. The namAcharya Thakur Haridas, for example, was forbidden to enter the temple due to his being raised in a Muslim family.

This mentality continues to this very day. Some of ISKCON's members, even though Indian by birth, are refused entry into Sri Mandir because of their association with other members of ISKCON who are overwhelmingly from outside of India, and thus considered *mlecchas*.

Despite what the temple authorities thought, Lord Chaitanya understood the truth:

> Sri Caitanya Mahaprabhu requested Haridasa Thakura, 'Remain here and chant the Hare Krishna maha-mantra. I shall personally come here to meet you daily.' Sri Caitanya Mahaprabhu promised to come daily to see Shrila Haridasa Thakura, and this indicates that Shrila Haridasa Thakura was so advanced in spiritual life that, although considered unfit to enter the temple, he was being personally visited by the Lord every day. Cc. Madhya 11.191-195

Mystics, Swamis and Popes

We can also find unlimited examples of bewilderment of form v. substance outside of Vaishnavism – so many bogus yogis, saints and swindlers, who cut the profile of mystics with long hair and beard, and flowing robes. They easily bewilder other materialistic persons who are impressed with form, but the limited extent of their spiritual realization is revealed in their empty aphorisms and attachment to sense gratification.

This is true even in traditional religions, and the Catholic Popes are a perfect example. It is taught that the Pope is the Vicar of Christ, and is infallible in his proclamations. In Vaishnava terms, the pope is considered the guru of the Catholics. The bona fide guru however must be in contact with the Supersoul, but this connection is not achieved simply by occupying an institutional position with title of pope, swami or guru.

The debauched history of the Catholic Popes is well document-ed, and we have recounted some their unsavory behavior earli-er. Although they have the form of spiritual leaders, they haven't the substance, which we can understand by their actions – *phale-na parichyate*. When Shrila Prabhupada met with French Cardinal Jean Danielou, this highly-placed representative of the church could not begin to understand that meat-eating was an abomina-ble practice that impeded spiritual progress.

There are more examples within Shrila Prabhupada's books of those who have form but lack substance. Perhaps you can identify some since there are many. In our own time, we can add the many *sannyasi* gurus who have taken a post for which they were not qualified, only to later fall from that exalted position.

It is clear from these examples that external form is meaningless in denoting who is an actual Vaishnava. The neophyte devotees unfortunately, having no other basis for discrimination, cannot identify the truly great devotees. Indeed, referring to the epigraph from the periodical *Sajana Tosani*, sometimes only the most pure devotees can understand the actual truth. We can only understand to the extent of our own qualification. As we make progress in devotional service and our *adhikar* increases, we are better able to recognize what is what and who is who, our illusions having been dispelled by the torchlight of knowledge and realization.

We must therefore be very careful in who we dismiss or crit-icize, and who we exalt as being "advanced." We should not be surprised that, over time, as our own qualification increases, our perspectives change dramatically.

Using the Form of a *Sadhu* to Introduce Irreligion

When there is a problem an intelligent person will naturally look for the cause in order to remove it to solve the problem. Since so many of ISKCON's problems stem from the upper echelons of the society we are required to look there. And if we are going follow Shrila Prabhupada's admonition to neglect jealous persons in the dress of a Vaishnava, we are required to identify them. Kundali Prabhu has correctly written that they do not infiltrate ISKCON to be the potwashers, the implication being they achieve positions of authority. We cannot be so fearful of aparadha that we abandon discrimination and become victimized by these jealous persons.

The *Srimad Bhagavatam* offers us a very good lesson of this in the history of Lord Indra's stealing the sacrificial horse from Maharaja Prithu, described in the 4th canto, 19th chapter of the *Srimad Bhagavatam*.

There we learn how the King of Heaven stole the horse from the sacrificial arena of King Prithu, the ruler of the earth. Previously Indra had been the only person to perform 100 horse sacrifices, and he was envious that Prithu Maharaja would soon equal his accomplishment:

> When King Indra was taking away the horse, he dressed himself to appear as a liberated person. Actually this dress was a form of cheating, for it falsely created an impression of religion. When Indra went into outer space in this way, the great sage Atri saw him and understood the whole situation.

Here we have a person who adopted the form of a spiritually advanced personality for the purpose of performing irreligious acts. Shrila Prabhupada comments:

> The word *pakhanda* used in this verse is sometimes pronounced *pasanda*. Both of these words indicate an imposter who presents himself as a very religious person but in actuality is sinful. Indra took up the saffron-colored dress as a way of cheating others. This saffron dress has been misused by many imposters who present themselves as liberated persons or incarnations of

God. In this way people are cheated. As we have mentioned many times, the conditioned soul has a tendency to cheat; therefore this quality is also visible in a person like King Indra. . . Cheating *sannyasis* and yogis have existed since the time of Prithu Maharaja's sacrifice. This cheating was very foolishly introduced by King Indra. *Srimad Bhagavatam* 4.19.12

We note that it was a spiritually qualified person – the great sage Atri – who was able to identify the cheating behavior of Indra, upon which he informed a qualified authority to take action:

When the son of King Prithu, Vijitashva, was informed by Atri of King Indra's trick, he immediately became very angry and followed Indra to kill him.

King Indra was fraudulently dressed as a *sannyasi*, having knotted his hair on his head and smeared ashes all over his body. Upon seeing such dress, Vijitashva considered Indra a religious man and pious *sannyasi*. Therefore he did not release his arrows. When Atri Muni saw that the son of King Prithu did not kill Indra but returned deceived by him, Atri Muni again instructed him to kill the heavenly King.

Bewildered by Indra's disguise Vijitashva desisted from killing the wrong-doer. But Atri Muni was not deceived and again instructed him to administer punishment. When Indra felt his life threatened by Vijitashva he gave up both the horse and his false dress, and the horse was successfully returned to the sacrificial arena. However, Indra persisted, again adopting the disguise of a saintly person:

Indra, being the King of heaven and very powerful, took the horse a second time. This was observed by Atri who again pointed this out to Vijitashva who took chase. But, as in the first instance, after seeing that Indra was wearing the dress of a *sannyasi*, he chose not to kill him.

When the great sage Atri again instructed Vijitashva he became very angry and placed an arrow on his bow. Upon seeing this, King Indra immediately abandoned the false dress of a *sannyasi* and, giving up the horse, made himself invisible. Then the great hero Vijitashva again returned to the sacrificial arena with the horse. Since that time, certain men with a poor fund of knowledge have adopted the dress of a false *sannyasi*. It was King Indra who introduced this. Whatever different forms Indra assumed as a mendicant because of his desire to seize the horse were symbols of atheistic philosophy.

Shrila Prabhupada comments:

> . . . There are many different types of *sannyasis*. . . All of them were introduced under some meaningless circumstances, and those who have a poor fund of knowledge accept these false *sannyasis* and their pretenses, although they are not bona fide guides to spiritual advancement. . . such *sannyasis* are *pakhandis* [atheists]. . .

> These so-called *sannyasis* are very much appreciated by sinful men because they are all godless atheists and very expert in putting forward arguments and reasons to support their case. We must know, however, that *they are only passing as adherents of religion and are not so in fact.* Unfortunately, bewildered persons accept them as religious, and being attracted to them, they spoil their life.

Who are the Infiltrators?

We now come to the crucial point of this discussion, which is to examine the actions of those who may have been, or who are now, the infiltrators of ISKCON.

The almost unlimited malfeasance and blunders that have created havoc in the mission, and destroyed the spiritual lives of many devotees, obliges responsible devotees to carefully examine the history of ISKCON in order to identify wrongdoing and take corrective action. This is pointed out by both shastra and Shrila Prabhupada:

> A person who knows things as they are and still does not bear witness becomes involved in sinful activities. CC Madhya 5.90

> One who tolerates mischievous activity, he is also culprit. If you are mischievous, you are criminal. But if you tolerate mischievous activities that is also criminal. Conversation 3May73

This foregoing discussion of "who is a devotee" is presented to help the reader avoid becoming bewildered by external symbols such as dress and title as we examine ISKCON's troubled history in order to identify those "devotees" who have done so much damage to the mission. We acknowledge that this is a tricky landscape to negotiate. On one hand shastra advises that Vaishnavas patiently overlook the faults of others, knowing that in time all misgivings will be rectified, and also to approach superiors submissively. However, these instructions are not meant to be a shield for irresponsibility and malfeasance, although some ISKCON authorities wrongly use them in that way.ᵃ Both Kali and Indra attempted to use a false dress to cover their criminal actions, but alert, discriminating devotees were able to recognize, and thwart, the wrongdoing.

On the other hand, Shrila Prabhupada himself informs us of materialistic devotees within our midst, and warned us to discriminate with whom we associate:

> There are *many* jealous people in the dress of Vaishnavas in this Krishna consciousness movement, and *they should be completely neglected. There is no need to serve a jealous person who is in the dress of a Vaishnava.* Purport Madhya 1.218

The harmful, foolish and passionate cannot be devotees of the Lord, *however they may advertise themselves as devotees by outward dress.* Purport SB 1.2.19

The resolution of this dilemma is given in the episode of Bali Maharaja, which illustrates the proper rejection of spiritual authorities who mislead their followers. When Bali's spiritual master, Sukracarya, instructed him not to fulfil his promise to the dwarf brahmana, Lord Vamanadeva, whom Sukracarya had earlier identified as Lord Vishnu, Bali found himself in a dilemma. Shrila Prabhupada comments:

Shrila Visvanatha Cakravarti Thakura remarks that Bali Maharaja remained silent at a critical point. How could he disobey the instruction of Sukracarya, his spiritual master? It is the duty of such a sober personality as Bali Maharaja to abide by the orders of his spiritual master immediately, as his spiritual master had advised. But Bali Maharaja also considered that Sukracarya was *no longer to be accepted as a spiritual master, for he had deviated from the duty of a spiritual master. . .* Under the circumstances Bali thought that there would be no fault if he disobeyed the order of his spiritual master. He deliberated on this point – should he refuse to accept the advice of his spiritual master, or should he independently do everything to please the Supreme Personality of Godhead? He took some time. After deliberating on this point, he decided that Lord Vishnu should be pleased in all circumstances, even at the risk of ignoring the guru's advice to the contrary.

Anyone who is supposed to be a guru but who goes against the principle of visnu-bhakti cannot be accepted as guru. If one has falsely accepted such a guru, one should reject him. Srimad Bhagavatam 8.20.1 Purport

Statements by our *Acharyas* and Shrila Prabhupada, and on the evidence of the previous chapter, make it clear that Kali send his agents to confuse devotees and thwart the Sankirtan Movement. How do we distinguish them from the sincere and earnest souls – especially if they might be our institutional authorities? How exactly can one tell who is a serious devotee and who is an imposter? Shrila Prabhupada answered that question many times: *phalena parichyate* – judge by the result – and that is just what we shall do. This is important for all of us, as our progressive development in Krishna consciousness requires us to recognize, and reject, the association of such pretenders.

We will be looking at ISKCON's history to learn how unqualified persons have undermined Shrila Prabhupada's mission, but before we do we need to consider exactly what ISKCON is, in terms of both form and substance, to further prepare ourselves with a solid basis for judging by results.

A Word of Caution

In the coming chapters I shall be discussing what has been done to limit, interfere with, and destroy Shrila Prabhupada's mission and identify the responsible parties. In a few cases we will name names, in other examples names are self-evident. In other cases groups of devotees are identified – the Board of Education, or the GBC body, for example. Of course it is extremely important to avoid criticizing devotees of the Lord, and we caution the reader to always bear that in mind. But like Atri Muni, we are going to identify irresponsible parties, or wrongdoers. Shrila Bhaktivinode informs us that *doing so with the correct motive is not aparadha*:

> If, *without* a good intention, one discusses faults arising by chance within a Vaishnava, one makes the offence of criticizing a Vaishnava. The main point is that if one makes

false accusations about a Vaishnava or discusses his previous faults, one make offences to the holy name.

However, deliberation on the faults of others *with* the right motive is not considered criticism as per the scriptures. The right motives are of three kinds: If the deliberation is done on someone's sinful or faulty activities with the motive of benefitting the person concerned, that kind of deliberation is auspicious. If deliberation on other's faults is to protect the interests of human society in general, then that kind of deliberation is counted amongst auspicious activities done for the benefit of everyone. And, if the discussion is done for one's own welfare, then that is also virtuous, and not faulty.

If the disciple prayerfully inquires from the spiritual master about the identity of true Vaishnavas, the guru may point out persons who are dressed as Vaishnavas but are not following the Vaishnava principles and describe them as '*avaishnavas*.' This action on the part of the guru is for the benefit of the disciple, because if the disciple associates with such pretenders his spiritual life is spoiled, and for the benefit of the whole world, because when the pretenders are identified, the sanctity of pure Vaishnava dharma is protected. The bona fide guru does not do so because of envy or malice towards any individual, but acts for the benefit of everyone. Thus it is not '*sadhu-ninda*' (criticism of devotees) or '*vaishnava-aparadha*' (offense to the devotees) to instruct others to reject the association of those impostors who have taken shelter of the exalted position of Vaishnavas but are engaged in performing activities against the Vedic scriptures.[3]

Although we are pointing out wrong-doers, we will be very careful to avoid offenses, and will not curse them, call ill names, or otherwise express criticism. The reader is urged to do likewise.

Shrila Prabhupada advises that we do not avoid pointing out wrong-doers simply to be polite: "by calling a thief a thief, he will feel insulted, does it mean that I shall say that 'You are very honest?' A thief shall be called thief." [4]

CHAPTER FIVE

What is ISKCON?

Falsehood is resorted to only by those who are enamored of the enjoyments of this world. As everybody wants to secure the lion's share of a stock of enjoyment whose amount is limited by its very nature it gives rise to a struggle inspired by malice. Falsehood is used as a convenient method worthy of the cause for securing fame and wealth by deceiving others preventing them from knowing that they have been gained at their expense. Shrila Bhaktisiddhanta

The question "what is ISKCON?" is not rhetorical. It is observed almost everywhere that devotees speak of ISKCON in various ways. Sometimes they refer to the institution, sometimes reference is made as if ISKCON were a person, sometimes devotees may refer to the local president, or the GBC, as ISKCON. Very often devotees make reference to their own history and experiences within the group time spent "in ISKCON."

Because it is very common that ISKCON is referred to in these many ways, and because the meaning of ISKCON is extremely important in the present discussion, we must examine the concept of ISKCON and understand what it is, and as importantly, what it is not.

Just as one must discriminate between form and substance for devotees, consideration can also be made between the form and substance of ISKCON.

The Corporate Form

Shrila Prabhupada incorporated his society as ISKCON - the International Society for Krishna Consciousness – in July of 1966. Incorporation gave Shrila Prabhupada's fledgling society a name and his followers a shared identity. It also provided a means of standardizing and teaching the lessons and practices he wanted his students to follow. With it he also made a formal declaration of the purposes of his society, and importantly, provided the basis for formal recognition of Krishna Consciousness as a bona fide religion.

The corporation is one way of defining ISKCON: it is a legal entity recognized by the government and courts of law. Every corporation is controlled by real persons who typically make use of and control the corporation, ostensibly, as defined in its bylaws.

Corporations are legal contractual agreements around which people establish relationships, say as employer and employee. Corporations pervade our lives – restaurants, schools, businesses, and even governments are corporations where relationships are defined in legal agreements, as well as their methods of operation.

In all such examples we relate to corporations as something real, but it is sometimes helpful to remember that they are legal fictions – creations of men that have no substance in fact. You cannot touch or hold a corporation, or see it. Even if you see a building that has the name of Google on it for example, you do not see the corporation, but merely a place where people gather and perform activities *in the name of* Google. Neither can you see or touch your English, American or German government, although it has buildings and representatives who act in the name of the government. Corporations are simply agreements between people that define their principles of action, the objectives of their common activities and their relationships with each other.

The same is true for the *corporation* of ISKCON. ISKCON is defined as a group of principles and values that inspire and define human action, around which various parties have agreed to lend their energies and cooperate together to perform various tasks.

ISKCON's Substance

To make this clear, let's look at the seven objectives stated in the original ISKCON corporate filing:

The purposes for which the corporation is organized are:

(a) To systematically propagate spiritual knowledge to society at large and to educate all peoples in the techniques of spiritual life in order to check the imbalance of values in life and to achieve real unity and peace in the world.

(b) To propagate a consciousness of Krishna as it is revealed in the Bhagawat Gita and Srimad Bhagawatam [sic].

(c) To bring the members of the Society together with each other and nearer to Krishna, the prime entity, and thus to

---

[a] For example, Bhakti Charu Swami has written on Facebook: "There are so many ways one can attack ISKCON. The worst of all is to attack ISKCON by criticizing its leaders. We should be very, very careful not to criticize the leaders of ISKCON. We should not find faults in those who are in leadership positions." However, one should not throw out his intelligence and turn a blind eye to wrongdoing. Discrimination is always required.
But immediately after this BCS challenges his own statement writing correctly: "Leaders are open to criticism if they are not made accountable to the people. Shrila Prabhupada also taught us to not to accept anything on blind-faith etc." And "unfortunately ISKCON's leaders are not held accountable, despite so much protest against wrongdoing."

develop the idea, within the members, and humanity, at largo, that each soul is part and parcel of the quality of Godhead (Krishna).

(d) To teach and encourage the Samkirtan [sic] movement congregational chanting of the holy name of God as revealed in the teachings of Lord Sri Chaitanya Mahaprabhu.

(e) To erect for the members, and for society at large, a holy place of transcendental pastimes, dedicated to the personality of Krishna.

(f) To bring the members closer together for the purpose of teaching a simpler and more natural way of life.

(g) With a view towards achieving the aforementioned purposes, to publish and distribute periodicals, magazines, books and other writings.

Every devotee knows that these are the activities and pursuits that Shrila Prabhupada, as the founder and *Acharya* of ISKCON, engaged his followers in. Worshiping Krishna in His deity form, printing and distributing books, preaching the principles of Krishna Consciousness to the public, doing *Harinam* Sankirtan, etc. It is these activities and objectives that are the actual *substance* of ISKCON, an organization having the *form* of a legal entity. *It is important not to confuse, or conflate, the substance with the form*, because in doing so we easily lose sight of what ISKCON is meant to be.

That being said, many people do confuse the substance and form of many organizations. Government is probably the most common example where an individual politician's wrong, or even illegal, behavior is equated with the concept of the government itself being wrong. The Constitution and Bill of Rights are the substance of the U.S. government, but as politicians increasingly ignore those principles the citizens rightly become cynical about what the United States is, or has become. The *laws which are the substance of the government* are meant to guide the behavior of government employees and elected officials, but if they deviate, the government fails its purpose, and those *who placed their faith in the substance* are cheated. When the deviations are too egregious revolutions occur. Bear in mind that although some put their faith in the substance *of what government is supposed to be*, others place their faith *in the form alone*, which gives rise to unrooted nationalism and blind flag-waving allegiance to government authorities, even if they want to send innocent boys to fight their distant wars.

It is often, even typically, the case, in many corporations and institutions, that *those who have official positions do* conflate the form with the substance. Because they have control they begin to think that *they are the organization and whatever they do in the name of the organization is justified*. A common example is a police officer telling someone "*I am the law*" while he is breaking it. It is not uncommon that the leaders deviate from the substance of the organization without being conscious of the fact. Examples are legion.

Failure of Substance, but Success of the Form

The same holds true for the organization of ISKCON. If the legal representatives of the form (the GBC) do not adhere to the stated principles (the substance), the mission is put in jeopardy. If deviations continue, at some point the substance is lost and thus the mission is lost. Shrila Prabhupada explained that this is what happened with his spiritual master's mission, the Gaudiya Math.

Devotees who joined *attracted by the substance of Shrila Prabhupada's teachings* can recognize deviations, and become disappointed and disheartened. When the deviations are too great they will leave the organization (the form), although they may continue their dedication to the substance by personal sadhana.

There are others however, who come to ISKCON *attracted by the form.* Focused on the form, these devotees may never learn the substance, and thus *cannot be aware of discrepancies* between form and substance, and will continue to remain involved regardless of how great the deviations become. Thus, *the mission may fail its purpose, even though there are apparent symbols of success in terms of temples and numbers of members.*

Indeed, we find that many of the members who joined ISKCON early on, *before* there was any, or little, form (those who created the form by opening the first temples), are much more conscious of, and vocal about, the deviations of the leadership, than many others who came later when there was significant form in terms of temples. It is telling that, except for an extremely small number, *all* of these early devotees have left the form of ISKCON as of the time of this writing.

Shrila Prabhupada recognized this at the very beginning of the legal ISKCON. One of Shrila Prabhupada's first disciples, Achyutananda Dasa, was present when Shrila Prabhupada received the incorporation papers. He chronicles the event: "Beaming like a father over his newborn son, Swamiji said, 'This International Society for Krishna Consciousness, ISKCON, is a great tool that we can use to spread our Hare Krishna chanting. If it is not helpful we can dissolve it. So we must be very careful.'"[1]

Indeed. Now let's look further into the form of ISKCON.

Establishing His Assistants

In just a few years after incorporating ISKCON there were 34 centers across Europe and the Americas and Shrila Prabhupada needed help to manage the growing organization. Thus on July 28, 1970, he established the Governing Body Commission (GBC) and named various disciples to it, who were to function as his official representatives. He did so with a document titled "Direction of Management," (DOM)[c] reproduced in part here:

As we have increased our volume of activities, now I think a Governing Body Commission (hereinafter referred to as the GBC) should be established. I am getting old, 75 years old, therefore at any time I may be out of the scene, therefore I think it is necessary to give instruction to my disciples how they shall manage the whole institution. They are already managing individual centers represented by one president, one secretary and one treasurer, and in my opinion they are doing nice. But we want still more improvement in the standard of Temple management, propaganda for Krishna Consciousness, distribution of books and literatures, opening of new centers and educating devotees to the right standard. Therefore, I have decided to adopt the following principles and I hope my beloved disciples will kindly accept them.

There was a meeting in San Francisco during the Rathayatra festival 1970 and many presidents of the centers were present. In that meeting it was resolved that an ad hoc committee be set up to form the constitution which is taken into consideration. My duty was to first appoint twelve (12) persons to my free choice amongst my disciples. . .

These personalities are now considered as my direct representatives. While I am living they will act as my zonal secretaries and *after my demise they will be known as Executors.*

As was stipulated by the ad hoc committee, the function of the GBC will be as follows with particulars:

---

[c] The entire document "Direction of Management" can be found on the Vedabase under the heading Legal Documents.

PARTICULARS OF THE GOVERNING BODY COMMISSION

The purpose of the Governing Body Commission is to act as the instrument for the execution of the Will of His Divine Grace. And further,

1. The GBC oversees all operations and management of ISKCON, **as it receives direction from Shrila Prabhupada and His Divine Grace has the final approval in all matters**.

2. His Divine Grace will select the initial 12 members of the GBC. In the succeeding years the GBC will be elected by a vote of all Temple presidents who will vote for 8 from a ballot of all Temple presidents, which may also include any secretary who is in charge of a Temple. Those 8 with the greatest number of votes will be members for the next term of GBC. Shrila Prabhupada will choose to retain four commissioners. In the event of Shrila Prabhupada's absence, the retiring members will decide which four will remain.

3. The commissioners will serve for a period of 3 years, and they may be re-elected at the end of this period.

4. The chairman is elected by the GBC for each meeting. He has no veto power, but in event of a vote tie, his vote will decide. The same will apply for votes cast by mail between regular meetings.

5. Throughout the year, each of the commissioners will stay with His Divine Grace for one month at a time and *keep the other commissioners informed of His Divine Grace's instructions.*

6. *The primary objective of the GBC is to organize the opening of new Temples and to maintain the established Temples.*

7. Advice will be given by the GBC in cases of real property purchases, which will be in the name of ISKCON, INC.

(Trucks or other vehicles will be purchased in the name of the local president).

8. Removal of a Temple president by the GBC requires support by the local Temple members.

9. The GBC has no jurisdiction in the publication of manuscripts, which will be handled by a separate committee; profits to be returned to Shrila Prabhupada."

So far my books are concerned, I am setting up a different body of management known as the BHAKTIVEDANTA BOOK TRUST. The trustees of this body are also members of the GBC, *but their function is not dependent on the GBC.*

ISKCON Press was created for the exclusive publication of my books and literatures and should be continued in that way.

A.C. Bhaktivedanta Swami (all emphasis added)

We see that in this document Shrila Prabhupada adds to both the form and substance of ISKCON by establishing in writing persons who will act as his representatives. Establishing representatives and their relationships with other members adds to the form, while defining the scope and nature of their activities adds to the substance (the principles, faith in what can be expected of, and from, the representatives of His Divine Grace).

It is important to note that this important document was never revealed to the devotees by the leadership. It remained hidden from the rank and file devotees until the GBC submitted it in the Long Island legal case as evidence of their control of ISKCON temples. However, the judge rejected it because the corporate papers of ISKCON New York (Long Island) make no reference to the GBC. Subsequently the GBC made sure all ISKCON temple corporate documents stipulated control by the GBC, giving them legal control over all temple properties – against the arrangement of Shrila Prabhupada that each temple remain independent.

In establishing the GBC and naming his most senior disciples as members, Shrila Prabhupada wanted them to assist him *by doing what he was doing*: travel to the various centers, see that the devotees are attending mangala arotika, chanting their rounds, studying his books and learning the philosophy, following the principles, adjudicate any problems, and whenever possible, to open new centers. It was not his intention to create a hierarchy of management and unnecessary bureaucracy. As shall be seen below, bureaucracy was an anathema to Shrila Prabhupada. Rather, he intended for each temple to be independently managed by the local authorities, thus ISKCON was meant to be a federation of independent temples with the GBC (form of ISKCON) as overseers to see that all activities conform to the stated principles (substance is upheld).

Form and Substance Conflated

Very quickly however, their title and authority went to the heads of the GBC and almost immediately they began to misuse their authority to manage the mission as they saw fit, even independently of Shrila Prabhupada. One could say that *they thought that they were ISKCON and could do with it as they pleased.* When word of this reached Shrila Prabhupada he was extremely angry, and he disbanded the GBC, sending notice of such to all temple presidents:

72-04-08

MEMO TO ALL ISKCON TEMPLE PRESIDENTS:

My Dear ___

Please accept my blessings. I beg to inform you that recently some of the Governing Body Commission members held a meeting at New York on 25th through 28th March, 1972, and they have sent me a big big minutes, duplicated, for my consideration and approval, but in the meantime they have decided some appointments without consulting me. One of the items which struck me very much is as follows:

"Atreya Rsi das was selected to be the Secretary for GBC and receive all correspondence including monthly reports." I never appointed Atreya Rsi member of the GBC, and I do not know how he can be appointed Secretary to GBC without my sanction. "He was also appointed to be on the Management Committee with Karandhara for the purpose of supervising ISKCON business and implementing the decisions reached by GBC." This has very much disturbed me.

Sriman Atreya Rsi das may be very expert, but without my say he has been given so much power and this has upset my brain.

I also understand that immediate actions are going to take place even prior to my permission, and that, also, "without divulging to the devotees(!)"

I do not follow exactly what is the motive of the so-called GBC meeting, therefore I have sent the telegram which you will find attached herewith, and I have received the replies as well.

Under these circumstances, I AUTHORIZE YOU TO DISREGARD FOR THE TIME BEING ANY DECISION FROM THE GBC MEN UNTIL MY FURTHER INSTRUCTION.

You manage your affairs peacefully and independently, and try to improve the spiritual atmosphere of the centers more carefully.

I shall be very glad to know the names of your assistants such as Secretary, Treasurer and Accountant. Finally, I beg to repeat that ALL GBC ORDERS ARE SUSPENDED HEREWITH

BY ME UNTIL FURTHER NOTICE.

You may reply me at ISKCON Tokyo. Hoping this meets you in very good health and advanced spiritual mood.

Your ever well-wisher,

A.C. Bhaktivedanta Swami (all emphasis in original)

Thus Shrila Prabhupada indicated that the authority of the GBC was limited to acting *as his agents* to develop the concept of ISKCON *as he defined it*, and not as they thought they might do with it, especially independently of his authority.

In a letters to Hansadutta and Satsvarupa just several days later, Shrila Prabhupada corrected their faulty behavior emphasizing that there was to be no centralization: "*From now on, the temples will operate independently* and try to improve their spiritual life more carefully, so there is no more need for such financial arrangement of centralization, as you have proposed." 10 April, 1972

Unfortunately, the lesson was not learned, and later in that very same year Shrila Prabhupada again had to stop the GBC *from acting independently of his desires in centralizing the management and creating bureaucracy*. In a now quite famous letter to Karandhara, December 1972, Shrila Prabhupada admonished the GBC and made it explicitly clear how ISKCON was to function:

> Regarding your points about taxation, corporate status, etc., I have heard from Jayatirtha you want to make big plan for centralization of management, taxes, monies, corporate status, bookkeeping, credit, like that. **I do not at all approve of such plan. Do not centralize anything. Each temple must remain independent and self-sufficient. That was my plan from the very beginning, why you are thinking otherwise? Once before you wanted to do something centralizing with your GBC meeting, and if I did not**

interfere the whole thing would have been killed. Do not think in this way of big corporation, big credits, centralization -- these are all nonsense proposals. Only thing I wanted was that books printing and distribution should be centralized, therefore I appointed you and Bali Mardan to do it. **Otherwise, management, everything, should be done locally by local men.** Accounts must be kept, things must be in order and lawfully done, *but that should be each temple's concern, not yours.*

Krishna Consciousness Movement is for training men to be independently thoughtful and competent in all types of departments of knowledge and action, not for making bureaucracy. Once there is bureaucracy the whole thing will be spoiled. There must be always individual striving and work and responsibility, competitive spirit, *not that one shall dominate and distribute benefits to the others and they do nothing but beg from you and you provide. No.* Never mind there may be botheration to register each centre, take tax certificate each, become separate corporations in each state. That will train men how to do these things, and they shall develop reliability and responsibility, that is the point. I am little observing now, especially in your country, that our men are losing their enthusiasm for spreading on our programmes of Krishna Consciousness movement. **Otherwise, why so many letters of problems are coming, dissatisfied? That is not a very good sign.** *The whole problem is they are not following the regulative principles, that I can detect. Without this, enthusiasm will be lacking. Even mechanically following, and if he gets gradually understanding from the class, he will come to the point of spontaneous enthusiasm. This spontaneous loving devotional service is not so easy matter, but if one simply sticks strictly to the* *rules and regulations, like rising early, chanting 16 rounds, chanting gayatri, keeping always clean -- then his enthusiasm will grow more and more, and if there is also patience and determination, one day he will come to the platform of spontaneous devotion, then his life will be perfect.* All of this I have told you in Nectar of Devotion.

So I do not think the leaders are themselves following, nor they are seeing the others are following strictly. That must be rectified at once. **Each centre remains independent**, that's all right, but the president and other officers must themselves follow and see the others are following the regulative principles carefully, and giving them good instruction so they may understand nicely why this tapasya is necessary. And GBC and *Sannyasis will travel and see the officers are doing this, and if they observe anything lowering of the standard, they must reform and advise, or if there is some discrepancy I shall remove it.* Of course, if new men are coming, they may not be expected immediately to take to our regulative principles cent per cent. Therefore we should not be so anxious to induce them to live in the temple. Anyone who lives in the temple must agree to follow the rules and regulations without fail. So if some new man moves in with us he may become discouraged if he is forced in this way. Therefore let them live outside and become gradually convinced in the class why they should accept some austerity, then they will live with us out of their own accord and follow nicely everything. It is very difficult to give up very quickly so many bad habits as you have got in your country, so educate them gradually, first with chanting, *and do not be so much anxious to count up so many numbers of new devotees,* if such devotees go away later being too early forced. **I want to see a few sincere devotees, not many false devotees or pretenders.**

So my point is that the regulative principles must be followed by everyone. Otherwise their enthusiasm dwindles and they again think of sex and become restless, and so many problems are there. There is some symptom of missing the point. *The point is to be engaged in doing something for Krishna, never mind what is that job, but being so* engaged *in doing something very much satisfying to the devotee that he remains always enthusiastic. He will automatically follow the regulative principles because they are part of his occupational duty -- by applying them practically as his occupational duty, he realizes the happy result of regulative principles.* So the future of this Krishna Consciousness movement is very bright, so long the managers remain vigilant that 16 rounds are being chanted by everyone without fail, that they are all rising before four morning, attending mangal arati -- our leaders shall be careful not to kill the spirit of enthusiastic service, which is individual and spontaneous and voluntary. They should try always to generate some atmosphere of fresh challenge to the devotees, so that they will agree enthusiastically to rise and meet it. That is the art of management: to draw out spontaneous loving spirit of sacrificing some energy for Krishna. But where are so many expert managers? All of us should become expert managers and preachers. We should not be very much after comforts and become complacent or self-contented. There must be always some tapasya, strictly observing the regulative principles -- *Krishna Consciousness movement must be always a challenge, a great achievement to be gained by voluntary desire to do it, and that will keep it healthy.* So you big managers now try to train up more and more some competent preachers and managers like yourselves. **Forget this centralizing and bureaucracy.** Letter to: Karandhara 22Dec72 (all emphasis added)

We can understand from this letter 1) more about the substance of ISKCON that Shrila Prabhupada wanted established, and 2) that Shrila Prabhupada detected that the GBC were not fulfilling the functions given to them by Shrila Prabhupada, and were attempting to manage ISKCON according to their own manufactured ideas, greatly upsetting Shrila Prabhupada. From this we can understand that the GBC were equating form (their title, position) with substance, leading them to think that they could do what they wanted independently of Shrila Prabhupada, and not in accordance with the guidelines he established.

This has proven to be *permanently* the case, unfortunately.

The Ultimate Managers or Ultimate Authority?

As the highest authority of ISKCON Shrila Prabhupada was final arbiter (decision maker). His decisions on all matters were the final word. In Shrila Prabhupada's Last Will and Testament he wrote that the GBC would be the Ultimate Managing Authority for the entire society, just as Shrila Prabhupada was during his manifest presence. There is nothing wrong with that. However, again this title (form) has been misinterpreted by the GBC, taking this phrase to mean that they are both the "Ultimate Managers," and the "Ultimate Authority." Thus they think they can do with ISKCON as they see fit (creating substance), while disregarding Shrila Prabhupada's earlier statements of what ISKCON is meant to be – *forgetting that their authority stems from him even to this day*. They interpret their title to mean they are equal to Shrila Prabhupada himself, even stating that whatever they say is as if Shrila Prabhupada himself had said it. And beyond that, through this idea of being the "ultimate authority" they attempt to create siddhanta (spiritual principles), contradicting long-established Gaudiya Siddhanta. Thus many of their 'laws' are simply dogma. The most glaring example of this is their idea that all gurus connected with ISKCON must be subordinate to their control, ignoring the fact that the bona fide guru *must be* a transcendental autocrat.

Becoming Shrila Prabhupada

Further confusion between form and substance on the part of the GBC is reflected in a pivotal document on Shrila Prabhupada's relationship with ISKCON. It was written by Ravindra Svarupa Dasa, and as stated in the introduction, signed-off by the entire GBC body. It is titled "Shrila Prabhupada – Founder/*Acharya* of ISKCON" and is noted to be a "GBC Foundational Document." Ravindra Svarupa explains its purpose in the introduction: "I was assigned the task of writing a foundational document for ISKCON devotees on the import of Shrila Prabhupada's position as Founder-*Acharya*."

However, the document is not so much about Shrila Prabhupada as it is an attempt to make the GBC synonymous with Shrila Prabhupada, and by extension, convey to the GBC the full authority of the Founder-*Achaya*.

Using flowery language Ravindra confounds the institution as a person, or persons, which it can never be, and imparts qualities to it that an institution can never have:

> "Prabhupada founded a new organization that, as a whole and in its every part, would embody and develop that realization—a realization that manifests itself as an unwavering, indefatigable commitment to deliver pure love of God to suffering humanity everywhere. The *institution* that would be able to act on this commitment with united force over large spans of space and time needs a unique form."

Ostensibly every *member* of ISKCON should ideally *embody* and develop said principles, but because it is not a person *an institution can never do so.* However, this flowery language leads the reader to think that it can be so, as if every manifestation of ISKCON any-where, has in fact achieved, or will achieve, that desired outcome. He then goes on to equate the institution ISKCON with another aspect of its form – the GBC – declaring that "ISKCON" (which we take here to mean all of the *members* of the society) must foster "an intense loyalty common to [both] ISKCON [the institution] and the GBC."

Regardless of how much the GBC or their representatives may try to convince anyone that the GBC body is the equivalent of Shrila Prabhupada, the fact of the matter is that the GBC, nei-ther individually nor collectively, are NOT ISKCON, and nei-ther are they Shrila Prabhupada. Their authority is derived *from* Shrila Prabhupada, *and they have no authority independent of* Shrila Prabhupada. The *position* of GBC *can only ever be but a part of the form* of ISKCON, while individual GBC *are members of ISKCON,* and as such are also duty bound to conform to the substance of ISKCON – the principles and practices established by Shrila Prabhupada. To the degree that they, or any devotee, deviates from those principles they no longer represent ISKCON.

The actual substance of ISKCON – what ISKCON is – is Shrila Prabhupada's teachings (presented in his books and lectures), and the principles that he embodied. This can be gleaned from the particulars of the corporation presented above, and Shrila Prabhupada's own statements.

Shrila Prabhupada succinctly summed up the substance of ISKCON when Yamuna Devi Dasi approached Shrila Prabhupada to relieve her angst: "Shrila Prabhupada, some of the leaders are saying that we have lost your mercy because we left ISKCON, and without your mercy, there is no meaning to our lives." To which Shrila Prabhupada retorted **"ISKCON is where you are chanting the Holy Names of Krishna. That is ISKCON."**[2]

I'll repeat this again for emphasis: **the actual substance of ISKCON – what ISKCON is – is the teachings of Shrila Prabhupada (presented in his books and lectures), and the principles that he embodied.** That is what draws all of the members of the society together. *If they understand the substance* they are very capable of seeing when the form and the substance are at odds, while unfortunately the GBC, bewildered by thinking themselves to be the substance, seem unable to make this distinction. Thus the GBC, thinking that they are ISKCON and can do as they please with it, have been responsible for driving hundreds and thousands of devotees from the society by undoing what they are supposed to be protecting.

CHAPTER SIX

Extinguishing the Torchlight of Knowledge

I was born in the darkest ignorance, and my spiritual master opened my eyes with the torch of knowledge. I offer my respectful obeisances unto him.

This prayer, offered by many Vaishnavas each day, pays tribute to the grace bestowed upon them by our ever well-wisher and *Acharya*, Shrila Prabhupada. He appeared on the scene at the very dawn of worldwide communication, and immediately put to use modern technology, developed specifically (in my opinion) to facilitate the spread of his transcendental message of the Absolute Truth. He, and his followers, have used every bit of technology to take the message of the Godhead to every town and village throughout the world.

Perhaps it was Shrila Prabhupada's appearance as an old and apparently harmless man that allowed him to get a step ahead of the

Kamsas and Putanas, since in an amazingly short period of time he produced a wonderful and complete library of transcendental literature and established the Eternal Religion all over the earth. That his books did not sell well in the shops but were distributed directly to individual persons would prove to be a blessing, as this caused the transcendental seeds to be cast far and wide, lying in wait to fructify at the most opportune time. There are many stories of devotees who tell how a book had sat on their shelf, or in their closet for years, or even decades, before they picked it up and read with interest, suddenly finding the answers to questions they had long been asking.

Shrila Prabhupada knew very well the transcendental nature of his books and the influence they could have, because, as he stated several times, it was Krishna that actually wrote his books – he simply dictated as Krishna spoke to him. Therefore he was adamant that the transcendental message be preserved exactly as it had been written.

No Changes

Many of Shrila Prabhupada's ardent followers, such as Rupanuga Prabhu and Govinda Dasi, who spent a great deal of time with Shrila Prabhupada, tell how he repeatedly stressed that nothing in his books should be changed, warning that by doing so "everything will be lost." Yet on a number of occasions to his great displeasure, Shrila Prabhupada found changes to his books. This excerpt, from a room conversation June 22, 1977, is titled "Rascal Editors." It informs us of changes being made to his books even while Shrila Prabhupada was with us:

Prabhupada: That... Find this verse, munayah *sadhu* pristo 'ham... [SB 1.2.5].

Tamala Krishna: Munayah *sadhu* pristo 'ham. . . munayah-O sages; *sadhu*-this is relevant; pristah-questioned...

Shrila Prabhupada : *Sadhu? Sadhu* means 'devotee,' not 'this is relevant.'

Prabhupada: The nonsense, they are... They are correcting my trans... Rascal. Who has done this? Munayah is addressing all these munis. *Sadhu* means they are very pure. These rascals becomes Sanskrit scholar and do everything nonsense.

Tamala Krishna: Translation: "O sages..."

Prabhupada: Now here is "O sages," and the word meaning is "of the munis." Just see. Such a rascal Sanskrit scholar. Here it is addressed, sambodhana, and they make it—"munayah—of the munis." It is very risky to give them editorial [discretion]. Little learning is dangerous. Immediately they become very big scholars, high salaried, and write all nonsense. No, they cannot be reliable. They can do more harm. . . How they can be relied on?

Yasoda-nandana: Sometimes they appeal that 'We can make better English,' so they change like that, just like *in the case of Isopanisad. There are over a hundred changes.* So where is the need? Your words are sufficient. The potency is there. When they change, it is something else. . . What is it going to be in five years? It's going to be a different book. . .

Prabhupada: You write one letter that 'Why you have made so many changes?' And whom to write? Who will care? All rascals are there. Write to Satsvarupa that 'This is the position. They are doing anything and everything at their whim.' **The next printing should be again to the original way**. So write them immediately that **'The rascal editors, they are doing havoc,'** and they are being maintained by Ramesvara and party. . . So you bring this to Satsvarupa. **They cannot change anything**. So **on the whole, *these dangerous things*** are going on.

A Vaishnava standard for dealing with the writing of *Acharyas* is called *arsa-prayoga* – *preserving the truth* – meaning *nothing* is allowed to be changed. Even apparent mistakes would not be changed. In this way the *Acharyas* are honored. Shrila Prabhupada, again and again in lectures, letters and his books, emphasized that nothing should be changed. Here are just of few of such statements:

> Nothing should be changed except for grammar or spelling mistakes: **"I want two editings only, just to see if there is any grammatical or spelling mistake."** Letter to Satsvarupa, Feb 15, 1970.

> **Be careful not to change anything but present it exactly as it is. This is how we receive *Bhagavad-gita* through the disciplic succession as stated in the Fourth Chapter.** Letter to Frederico, Oct 24, 1974

> **This transcendental writing does not depend on material education. It depends on the spiritual realization.** You'll find, therefore, **in the comments of** *Bhagavatam* **by different** *Acharyas*, **even there are some discrepancies, they are accepted as** *asat-patha*. **It should remain as it is.** Lecture *Srimad Bhagavatam* 7.5.23-24 — Vrndavana, 31 Mar 76

> **You have done a great mistake by changing the front picture and it will hamper the sale. In future you don't do any changes without asking me first.** Letter to Bhargava (regarding printing of Bengali *Gitar-gan*), May 29, 1976

> You may title this book, *Teachings of Lord Kapila*, but it must be subtitled, *The Son of Devahuti*. That will remain, **do not try to change it. . . . Do not try to change anything without my permission.** Letter to Radhavallabha, Aug 26, 1976

There are many more quotes like these, but this sampling is enough to make the point very clear: Shrila Prabhupada was adamant that nothing in his books should be changed – *not the size, not the cover, not the pictures, and certainly not the text*. And of course Shrila Prabhupada especially emphasized such things to those who were assisting him with his books, seemingly to no avail, since the changes continued while he was with us, and accelerated after his departure.

Putanas, Scribes and Exegetes

As we have quoted from Shrila Bhaktisiddhanta, the Kamsas and Putanas are diligent to thwart the manifestation of the transcendent as soon as it makes its appearance in this world, whether that appearance be in form, in sound or print.

In the first century the Roman powers put an end to the spread of transcendental knowledge by killing the spiritual leaders as well as *all* of their followers, and physically destroying every piece of written teachings they could find. Save for the Dead Sea Scrolls and Nag Hammadi Texts (and whatever else may be in the crypts of the Roman church) nothing remains of the teachings of the Eternal Religion from the first century.

Due to the one-to-one distribution of Shrila Prabhupada's books, and infinite electronic replication, eliminating the teachings is a much more difficult task. And since we have been granted freedom of religion it is no longer acceptable to kill the followers. Since millions of books have already been spread across the world, another method had to be used by the Kamsas to thwart the spread of the pure transcendental teachings.

Kamsa is very patient and operates on a long time frame. He carefully plans his moves, and steadily works his plan. He will find a way to eradicate the pure teachings regardless of the time required. The Christian writings were edited and re-edited over the course of centuries, to the point where very little of the Truth remained. That method that worked so well in the past is being employed again. Given that Shrila Prabhupada's books are *not* held sacred by those who are charged with protecting them, over the course of several generations his books will likely be changed to the point that they are completely bereft of transcendental potency – especially after Shrila Prabhupada's immediate disciples are no longer present to challenge the Putanas. However, the mischief began almost immediately.

Posthumous Changes

Just a few short years after Shrila Prabhupada's leaving this world Jayadvaita Swami, the then chief editor of the BBT, had the audacity to "improve" Shrila Prabhupada's 1972 Macmillan Gita. At least that is his claim.

Jayadvaita Swami said that he petitioned the GBC for permission and explained his rationale to them. However, when another editor, Dravida Dasa, searched the GBC resolutions from 1979-1983 he could find no reference to the *Bhagavad-gita As It Is*, nor any proposal of changing it. I also searched for, and also failed to find, any such reference. However that may be, it is something of a moot point since Shrila Prabhupada established the Book Trust as a separate legal entity, with its own Trustees, *independent of the GBC*. Thus it would be the BBT Trustees that Jayadvaita should have appealed to, not the GBC who legally have no say in the matter. But neither is there any record of the BBT Trustees authorizing Jayadvaita to edit Shrila Prabhupada's *Bhagavad-gita As It Is*.

Higher level approval or not, Jayadvaita pushed ahead and made almost 5,000 changes! The adulterated *Bhagavad-gita*, published in 1983, was then made, and continues to be, the BBT's *official version* of the book, setting off a continuous firestorm of protest from rank and file devotees around the world. The BBT Trustees and the GBC circled their wagons to vigorously defend their changes. They offer various arguments to justify their actions, none of which are actually pertinent since first of all it is not Jayadvaita's book to change, secondly Shrila Prabhupada gave numerous, adamant instructions not to change *anything*, and thirdly such editing has completely ignored the standards of posthumous editing.

The 1983 edition of Shrila Prabhupada's *"Bhagavad-gita As It Is"* should better be titled *Bhagavad-gita As It Isn't* given the thousands of changes. Shrila Prabhupada's *KRSNA* Book has dozens and dozens of changes. Lengthy sections have been omitted from *Perfect Questions, Perfect Answers*. And as noted above, more than one hundred changes were made to the *Sri Isopanisad* while Shrila Prabhupada was with us. Indeed, the changes have been so constant that **every book now produced by the BBT/BBTI is assumed to be adulterated** – *including translations into other languages*, since the policy of the BBTI is that all translations must be made from the edited 1983 edition, *not* Shrila Prabhupada's original 1972 Macmillan edition.

Sincere disciples and followers have written hundreds and thousands of lengthy complaints, exposés and diatribes protesting these changes, to which the so-called Book "Trust" turns a deaf ear.

Ramesvara Dasa, the former head manager of the BBT has written and spoken about these changes. Here are some pertinent excerpts:

> I've had many experiences with Prabhupada literally drilling me, pounding it into my head that you're never allowed to change anything in his books. He trained me so intensely on this point. *Even when the changes make sense* [to Ramesvara] *he wouldn't let me change.* Just to train me.

In a rebuttal to the BBT publication to justify their actions, "Responsible Publishing" (RP) Ramesvara stated:

> The RP publication has either a significant misleading or a significant historical inaccuracy. There are [web]sites which

claim to list more than 5,000 changes. Certainly there were thousands of changes. The RP paper states that every change to the translations was reviewed and approved by the trustees, leading ISKCON devotees, the GBC, etc. Later the RP cites or implies in its endorsements that all the changes were approved. **Of course,** *no one other than the editors ever saw, back in 1981 or 1982, ALL the changes.*

As for the changes to the translations, ultimately there was a five member GBC/BBT committee charged with the approval, including Satsvarupa, Hridayananda, Bhagavan, Harikesa and myself. For myself, *I have always admitted that my great failure as a trustee was not carefully reading every proposed change,* and instead, relying on the endorsement of Hridayananda and Satsvarupa – along with Jayadvaita.

I only reviewed examples of changes that seemed to be excellent – such as the paper itself includes. I know that in talking years ago with others on that committee that *they also admitted performing only a cursory review of the proposed changes,* being similarly impressed with the dramatic, obvious and excellent samples of proposed changes in a summary paper that we reviewed.

No one back then did their job or acted with full responsibility for what they were endorsing. I assure you that no one on that Committee ever even asked to see all the changes, and we would have been astounded to have learned in 1981 or 1982 that there were thousands, maybe more than 5,000 changes. **I lazily assumed that the work done on manuscripts as close to the original as possible was the only thing that mattered.** *I failed to consider all the other Prabhupada instructions, the ramifications for making changes if they didn't ultimately change the meaning; the effect of* *changes that in some cases loses the flavor of the Gita* we had been studying for 10 years, **and most importantly, that breaks the etiquette of changing a Sampradaya Acarya's books after His disappearance and opens the "change door" for possible future other changes over the decades and centuries to come.**

The RP paper implies that the changes were carefully reviewed and approved throughout the leadership of the BBT, GBC and ISKCON. *I am certain that by interviewing all the leaders of that time, we would find most guilty of the same mistake that I made.*

It is true to state that the leaders of ISKCON at the time endorsed the changes. However, **it is overtly misleading to state or suggest that the leaders actually performed a careful review.** And getting back to the fact that there are thousands of changes, **no leader, including the BBT trustees, was ever shown every single change. No one! That is the sad historical fact...**[1]

There can be no confusion about Shrila Prabhupada's instructions, yet Ramesvara was the person in charge of the BBT and it was he who allowed the changed books to be printed, disobeying Shrila Prabhupada as much as Jayadvaita by approving the changes. But regardless of his statements, we have Shrila Prabhupada's own statements – the statements of, not just the author, but our guru and *Acharya*, not to change his books.

Many, many devotees share a grave concern about future changes. As for myself, I am convinced by the information presented in this book that the Kamsas and Putanas of this world have in fact commandeered ISKCON with the intention of destroying the spiritual potency of Shrila Prabhupada's books and mission over time. I say this based on the simple method of *phalena parichyate*:

judging by the result. Since even rank and file devotees are mortified by their actions, responsible and dedicated trustees would never have acted as they have. *The lack of action on their part is nothing short of criminal negligence and malfeasance.* But not only do they continue to allow Jayadvaita's *Bhagavad-gita As It Isn't* to be presented as if it were Shrila Prabhupada's, **it remains GBC policy to *insist* that every ISKCON temple sell *only* the changed books.** Some temples will not even allow Shrila Prabhupada's original book on the property! The only obvious conclusion that can be drawn is that the entire GBC body and BBTI Directors are working in concert to diminish the transcendental light of Shrila Prabhupada's teachings, and their blind followers having thrown away all discrimination, simply do as their told.

Shrila Prabhupada's Books – Authentic or Not?

One ploy of the BBTI is to make the book appear to be the original when in fact it is not, which is what happens when the Bhaktivedanta Book Trust logo is present. Trust is the key word. Devotees trust in that symbol despite the fact that the GBC/BBTI have abused that trust for decades. Shrila Prabhupada set up his BBT as a separate legal entity from the GBC, appointing several of his trusted disciples as trustees. Their job was to protect the Trust, which unfortunately they have failed to do. Changes continue to be made with each new printing – all in the name of correcting the mistakes – but as we shall see this is nothing but a cheap excuse to introduce unnecessary and unwarranted changes.

Another excuse is that the changes are made to make the books more acceptable to academics, but in fact scholars consider them illegitimate because the BBTI has not met the standards for posthumous editing.

It is essential that any and all posthumous editions be dated and numbered, and that the editor (editors) names be prominently displayed on the cover and/or title page, and the changes must be noted, perhaps with footnotes, explaining the why the change was made. This is the accepted procedure which also clearly delineates what was printed during an author's lifetime, and the changes that were made after his demise. Abuse of this standard has led one academic, while referring to the *Bhagavad-gita As It Is*, to quip: "Which *Bhagavad-gita*? You have almost a dozen different versions!"

Who are these Kamsas and Putanas putting out the light of Truth? The identity of the actual infiltrators is very difficult, if not impossible to know. The most solid thing we have to go on are the results after so many decades, and the results tell us that Shrila Prabhupada's movement is being destroyed from within. I know Dravida and most of the GBC personally, and although I've had little experience with most of them, they *appear to be* sincere devotees who want to do the right thing. However, the many significant things that are going wrong tell us that not everyone is a sincere and loyal servant.

As if all of this were not enough, later actions by the corporation (not Trust) BBT International, Inc., (BBTI), have demonstrated their intent to remove Shrila Prabhupada from the picture altogether, as documented just below. We are forced to wonder what exactly they are doing, as has always been the case since there is no transparency! And this is all going on by the unified action and approval of those in charge of ISKCON and the BBTI.

Copyright and "worker for hire"

The data page of the 1972 Macmillan edition of Bhagavad-gita As It Is it clearly states: "Copyright ©1972 by His Divine Grace A.C. Bhaktivedanta Swami Prabhupada." But in 1995 the BBTI submitted a revised registration to the Copyright Office for a book titled "*Bhagavad-gita As It Is – The Great Classics of India*," listing *Bhagavad-gita As It Is* as the *previous* title, and **the author as The**

Bhaktivedanta Book Trust! The application further indicates that any contribution to the book was "Work Made for Hire." A copy of the application can be found on our website www. DivineOrDemoniac.com.

The application states:

- Author's nationality as: USA.
- Contribution to the work: Not anonymous, Not pseudonymous.
- **Year in which creation of this work was completed: 1985**
- **Date and Nation of first publication of this particular work: March 6 1985. U.S.A. and England** [1985!? and England?!].

Shrila Prabhupada was not an American national, and the Bhagavad-gita As It Is was completed in 1972 – not 1985. But **the BBTI claims that Shrila Prabhupada was hired by the BBT to write the *Bhagavad-gita!* His name is not shown as the copyright holder, nor even as the author. This is preposterous! This is blatant theft!**

Clearly those who have taken such actions cannot be anything but atheists, regardless of how they pose themselves, who don't believe they will be held accountable for their actions after this life. Without a doubt those making these changes, or going along with them, cannot by any consideration, be considered devotees of the Lord, nor sincere followers of Shrila Prabhupada. They show by their actions that they are indeed Kamsas and Putanas, and we shudder to think how much more they will destroy in their heinous activities.

Examples of Changes to *Bhagavad-gita As It Is*

A cursory examination of changes to Shrila Prabhupada's original *Bhagavad-gita As It Is* shows the vast majority of them to be unnecessary and even whimsical, adding nothing to the under-standing of the translation, and in dozens, if not hundreds, of cases *change* the meaning of the translation. It must be noted that Shrila Prabhupada personally read from his *Bhagavad-gita* daily – he knew his own book – yet he never asked for such changes to be made.

Omission of significant words

Original, authorized 1972 edition:

> "It is said that the soul is invisible, inconceivable, immutable and **unchangeable**. Knowing this, you should not grieve for the body."

BBT International posthumously edited 1983 edition:

> "It is said that the soul is invisible, inconceivable and immutable. Knowing this, you should not grieve for the body."

Original and authorized 1972 Macmillan edition:

> "**All of them—as they surrender** unto Me—I reward accordingly. Everyone follows My path in all respects, O son of Prtha."

BBT International's posthumously changed 1983 edition:

> "**As all surrender** unto Me, I reward them accordingly. Everyone follows My path in all respects, O son of Prtha."

Changed words with changed meaning

Original, authorized 1972 edition:

> "The great generals who have highly esteemed your name and fame will think that you have left the battlefield out of fear only, and thus they will consider you a *coward*."

BBT International posthumously edited 1983 edition:

"The great generals who have highly esteemed your name and fame will think that you have left the battlefield out of fear only, and thus they will consider you *insignificant*."

Original and authorized 1972 Macmillan edition:

"All the liberated souls in ancient times acted with this understanding *and so attained liberation*. Therefore, as the ancients, you should perform your duty in this divine consciousness."

BBT International posthumously edited 1983 edition:

"All the liberated souls in ancient times acted with this understanding *of My transcendental nature.* Therefore you should perform your duty, following in their footsteps."

Original and authorized 1972 Macmillan edition:

O descendant of Bharata, he who dwells in the body *is eternal and* can never be slain. Therefore you need not grieve for any *creature*.

BBT International posthumously edited 1983 edition:

O descendant of Bharata, he who dwells in the body [omissions] can never be slain. Therefore you need not grieve for any *living being*.

Original and authorized 1972 Macmillan edition:

…Discharging one's specific duty in any field of action in accordance with *varnasrama-dharma* serves to elevate one to a higher status of life.

BBT International posthumously edited 1983 edition:

…Discharging one's specific duty in any field of action in accordance with *the orders of higher authorities* serves to elevate one to a higher status of life.

This change is significant since, as I have commented in several places, the authorities of ISKCON are endeavoring to remove any scent of social reformation from Shrila Prabhupada's teachings, and bring ISKCON in line with the status quo of today's atheistic, materialistic civilization. Any mention of the words 'varnashrama dharma' and its concepts have actively been discouraged.

Original and authorized 1972 Macmillan edition:

> If someone gives up _self-gratificatory pursuits_ and works in Krishna consciousness and then falls down on account of not completing his work, what loss is there on his part?

BBT International posthumously edited 1983 edition:

> If someone gives up _his occupational duties_ and works in Krishna consciousness and then falls down on account of not completing his work, what loss is there on his part?

These two concepts are clearly not the same.

Changes to the Chaitanya-charitamrita

Original 1975 edition of the Chaitanya-charitamrita, Madhya 19.157:

> If one thinks that there are many pseudo devotees or non-devotees in the Krishna Consciousness Society, **one can keep direct company with the spiritual master, and if there is any doubt, one should consult the spiritual master.** However, unless one follows the spiritual master's instructions and the regulative principles governing chanting and hearing the holy name of the Lord, one cannot become a pure devotee.

BBT International posthumously edited 2003 edition:

> **Even** if one thinks that there are many pseudo devotees or non-devotees in the Krishna Consciousness Society, still **one should stick to the Society;** if one thinks the Society's

members are not pure devotees, one can keep direct company with the spiritual master, and if there is any doubt, one should consult the spiritual master. However, unless one follows the spiritual master's instructions concerning the regulative principles and chanting and hearing the holy name of the Lord, one cannot become a pure devotee.

The added word "even" implies that there are NO pseudo devotees! But if you think that there are still you should stick to the society (not the spiritual master). This is a very blatant effort to manipulate innocent devotees to deny their own intelligence.

Changing Shastra to Match Current GBC Deviations

An egregious example of the mentality behind the changes to Shrila Prabhupada's sacred books is the effort to make them conform to, and support, the *current thinking* and practices of a GBC who have deviated from Vaishnava siddhanta.

BBTI editor Dravida Dasa has made a startling change to one of the first slokas of Shrila Prabhupada's *Caitanya-caritamrita*. A paragraph at the beginning of the first chapter, written by Shrila Prabhupada, was initially published as:

> The direct disciple of Shrila Krishnadasa Kaviraja Gosvami was Shrila Narottama dasa Thakura, who accepted Shrila Visvanatha Cakravarti as his servitor. Shrila Visvanatha Cakravarti Thakura accepted Shrila Jagannatha dasa Babaji, who **initiated** Shrila Bhaktivinoda Thakura, who in turn *initiated* Shrila Gaurakisora dasa Babaji, the spiritual master of Om Visnupada Shrila Bhaktisiddhanta Sarasvati Gosvami Maharaja, the divine master of our humble self.

However, in the recent edition of *Caitanya-caritamrta* (a 9-volume edition, not the original 17 volume edition) that same passage was changed to read:

The direct disciple of Shrila Krishnadasa Kaviraja Gosvami was Shrila Narottama dasa Thakura, who accepted Shrila Visvanatha Cakravarti as his servitor. Shrila Visvanatha Cakravarti Thakura accepted Shrila Jagannatha dasa Babaji, the spiritual master of Shrila Bhaktivinoda Thakura [note: the word 'initated' is absent], who in turn *accepted* Shrila Gaurakisora dasa Babaji, the spiritual master of Om Visnupada Shrila Bhaktisiddhanta Sarasvati Gosvami Maharaja, the divine master of our humble self.

This edit drastically changes the understanding of the parampara and how it is continued, which Shrila Prabhupada has explained in several places.

This uproar following this edit forced Dravida Dasa to explain his reasoning:

> On the side of not changing the "initiated" phrases we have the strong bias against changing the books unless absolutely necessary and the fact that Shrila Prabhupada did indeed say that Jagannatha das Babaji initiated Bhaktivinode.

> [However,] Leaving one or both 'initiated's will strongly imply that the use of the phrases 'direct disciple' and even 'accepted [as his disciple]' indicate formal initiation as we know it in ISKCON, which is far from the truth.[2]

Please note that Dravida clearly ADMITS that Shrila Prabhupada DID indeed write that "Jagannatha das Babaji INITIATED Bhaktivinode," and to any sincere disciple this would be the ONLY reason required to NOT tamper with Shrila Prabhupada's writing. But Dravida thinks his reason for changes outweighs what Shrila Prabhupada himself actually wrote and taught. *He states that we must change Shrila Prabhupada's teachings to ensure they conform to what is currently understood and practiced within ISKCON with regard to initiation.*

This is wrong! It is the teachings of the *Acharya* that must inform *us* of the various meanings of initiation! It is the duty of the disciple to adjust his understanding to the teachings of the *Acharya*, rather than changing the teachings of the *Acharya* to support the disciple's faulty understanding. Such reasoning is extremely dangerous, and opens the door to unlimited future changes by materially conditioned fools based on the same faulty reasoning.

Given the history of changes in the society in only forty years since Shrila Prabhupada's passing, and given that the GBC show no willingness to adhere to established Gaudiya Vaishnava siddhanta, we can only imagine what the accepted culture of ISKCON will be in say, 200 or 300 years, and how the books will have been changed to agree with, and support those changes.

Bhaktivedanta "Archives" Removes the Original Books

The Vedabase is an electronic database of all of Shrila Prabhupada's written and transcribed words, and is a project of the Bhaktivedanta Archives, originally created to preserve Shrila Prabhupada's teaching intact. However, it is becoming an archives in name only. In the initial 2003 release of the Vedabase there was a section for Shrila Prabhupada's original books, where 14 volumes were included. Unfortunately, in the 2018 release, that section only includes two volumes of the Macmillan editions of the *Bhagavad-gita As It Is*. The other original, pre-1978 original books are no longer included. Otherwise, the books given in the Contents section are the books containing post-humous adulteration of Shrila Prabhupada's works, and these are updated with new edits with each release of the Vedabase. Thus the purpose of the Archives has been undermined, and is no longer an archive in the truest sense of the word. Intimating that the Archives preserves Shrila Prabhupada's works is thus clearly another extremely disappointing deception from ISKCON's leadership.

Thankfully, sincere and dedicated devotees have created a Vedabase of Shrila Prabhupada's original, un-edited works, available from Krishnapath.org.

The Struggle to Preserve the Books Unchanged

We are fortunate today to have access to Shrila Prabhupada's original books, despite the actions of the GBC and BBT managers efforts to prevent this. It came about as part of the settlement agreement offered to Hansadutta Dasa, the one-and-only bona fide BBT Trustee at the time, in a court case brought against him by ISKCON and the BBTI. It is important that this story be told, and therefore I am including here a statement of that history written by Hansadutta, to offset the fact that the official history is written by the winners, and that the BBTI and GBC present a radically different version of this history. Also because I personally have absolutely no faith nor trust in the GBC nor BBTI authorities to tell the unvarnished truth. On the other hand, I have known Hansadutta personally since 1978, and despite his personal failures and misgivings, believe him to be a sincere servant of Shrila Prabhupada – due to the fact that he fought so hard to print, distribute and preserve Shrila Prabhupada's original books. Hansadutta had to settle the court case brought against him by ISKCON and BBTI due to not having the unlimited funds to match the deep pockets of ISKCON – funds derived from distribution of the changed books to undermine the original books.

Attempt to Eliminate the Original BBT

Hansadutta was named as a Trustee of the BBT by Shrila Prabhupada and was added to the Trust documents as a legal trustee. As such he figures prominently in the all BBT activities. Unfortunately, due to his own personal failures in the early 80s, although a trustee for life, he neglected his BBT duties. Later, the

BBTI and ISKCON of California filed a lawsuit to remove him as a trustee.

The following letter by Hansadutta explains how that lawsuit came about, as well as describing: the original purpose of the Bhaktivedanta Book Trust and how it was intended to function; how the GBC *illegally* transferred the BBT copyrights to another newly created *corporation* BBT International, Inc. that had no legal relationship with the original BBT; the machinations that were engaged in by ISKCON authorities to eliminate Shrila Prabhupada's original BBT, and take the copyrights from Shrila Prabhupada himself and transfer them to the BBT International. This story details some of the cheating and manipulation wrought by so-called ISKCON authorities to bring the BBT totally under their control.[3] Finally, it is Hansadutta Prabhu who we have to thank that Shrila Prabhupada's original, unedited books remain in print – although this legal right is constantly being challenged.

Originally posted by Hansadutta Das on August 1, 2010

> My Dearest Urdhvaga Prabhu,
>
> Obeisances, all glories to Shrila Prabhupada.
>
> Having been appointed by Shrila Prabhupada to act as trustee for life, I owe it to Shrila Prabhupada and to the devotees, to yourself, to clarify what happened with the BBT.
>
> In your post "Copyrights Transferred to the BBTI?," published on the Sampradaya Sun, you've understood correctly that BBTI is not the same as Prabhupada's BBT.[4] BBTI (Bhaktivedanta Book Trust International, Inc.) is a California *corporation* (non-profit) that was registered in 1988, in a deliberate attempt to bypass the legal trust.
>
> Immediately thereafter, ISKCON GBC voted to assign the copyrights from BBT to BBTI. *However, they had no*

legal authority to do so, because Prabhupada gave express instructions in the trust document that ISKCON was to have no jurisdiction over the [BBT] trust. [According to Ramesvara Das, the devotees involved in this – Harikesha Swami, Hridayananda Swami, Tamal Krishna Goswami – although appointed by Shrila Prabhupada to manage the affairs of the BBT, were never added to the trust document as *legal* trustees. Nonetheless they, and Ramesvara, managed BBT affairs both before and after Shrila Prabhupada's passing. In a meeting of these "Trustees" Nov. 30 1986 they voted to create a corporation – the Bhaktivedanta Book Trust, Inc. – and illegally transfer to it the assets of the legal BBT.]

But that's not all… for years Ramesvara operated a shell as if it were the actual BBT – used ISKCON of America and later another ISKCON registered in California for which he applied to use the name "Bhaktivedanta Book Trust" as a DBA ("doing business as"). In other words the Bhaktivedanta Book Trust was no longer an independent legal entity but operated under ISKCON of California. In this way, for so many years he **bypassed Shrila Prabhupada's actual trust and trustees.**

Devotees did not know it, but Ramesvara was never a BBT trustee – he was only ever appointed secretary by Prabhupada. He might have been a trustee of the Indian Bhaktivedanta Book Trust, which was really only a publishing trust and did not hold the copyrights to Prabhupada's books.

So you can see that the term "BBT" has been loosely applied to any one of a few different legal entities, a convenient smoke screen for ISKCON to take over the trust.

First of all, let's stop here and understand what a trust actually is. A legally constituted trust consists of the Settlor, or the person who is making the trust; the property vested in the trust; a beneficiary, or the party who benefits from the trust; and trustee or trustees, who carry out the terms of the trust.

Prabhupada's trust, the Bhaktivedanta Book Trust, is no different. Prabhupada is the Settlor and was, until his departure, one of the trustees. He made ISKCON the beneficiary of the trust.

And he vested all the copyrights to his books in the trust. As for the trustees, he designated that there be no more than three at any time.[a] Initially there were just Shrila Prabhupada, Karandhar and Bali Mardan. Later, when Karandhar resigned, Prabhupada appointed me to replace him.

Prabhupada inserted a provision in the BBT Trust Agreement stating that the BBT existed independently of ISKCON and that the trustees were bound to carry out the duties of the BBT separately from, and independent of, ISKCON's GBC.[b]

But even without such a provision, by law the beneficiary of a trust has no legal right to direct the trustees or to take over the trust assets. So what the ISKCON authorities did was actually *illegal*. ISKCON's so-called authorities bypassed the trustees and took over the operation and property of the BBT.

Let's say a father sets up a trust for his children, and vests all his property in it, and appoints a trustee to look after it in the interests of the children. But somewhere along the line, the children decide they want direct control over the property and so they scheme to get rid of or go around the trustee and seize the assets for themselves. Why is this wrong? After all, they are the beneficiaries, and the trust is supposed to be for them.

But no, the court takes the view that the trust belongs to the Settlor, not the beneficiaries, and although the Settlor may have departed, his expressed wishes live on in the terms of the trust document, and so the court upholds the trust, and finds that the children have attempted to convert the trust resolution illegally. This is exactly what has happened in the case of Prabhupada's BBT.

Or another example to illustrate – which is what I presented to Amarendra. Amarendra asked me, during settlement negotiations, "What does it matter to you if BBT exists or not as long as BBTI carries on the BBT's work? The books are being published, they're being distributed. What's the difference?"

So I asked him, "Suppose I take your wife, I do all those things that you do with her – maybe even better than you do – what does it matter to you?" Poor Amarendra was shocked. **The point is: BBT belongs to Prabhupada, not to ISKCON. Prabhupada set it up to work in a particular way, and ISKCON has no right to interfere or to take over, as they have done.**

Going back to 1988, the time when BBTI was incorporated, devotees may remember that around that time ISKCON began blacklisting devotees who were outspoken against GBC or official ISKCON policies, especially with regard to the policy of forced re-initiation.

Some devotees had gone through four gurus! Many left ISKCON and went back into material life; and the few who

---

[a] Actually the Trust document stipulates no less than three and no more than five trustees at any one time, although according to Ramesvara there were six even when Shrila Prabhupada was present.

[b] See DivineOrDemoniac.com for a copy of the BBT Trust Agreement

tried to go it on their own were subjected to a campaign to extinguish them – they were made unwelcome at ISKCON temples, they were unable to buy Prabhupada's books at wholesale rates for sankirtan, and ISKCON devotees went out of their way to sabotage their preaching efforts.

This is what happened in Singapore to Bhima das, who, with one other brahmachari, had been distributing Prabhupada's books in Malaysia and Singapore, even Philippines, Thailand and Taiwan, at least 1.5 million books from 1978. But from 1988 the regional "BBTs" refused to sell to him, and he was refused even when he approached "BBT" in Australia.

Not only this, but the BBT was letting so many books go out of print, and publishing only Jayadvaita's adulterated books.

In 1990 I approached Tamal Krishna Goswami to buy Chinese Bhagavad Gitas from him, he refused, telling me he would sell them to me only at the retail price. OK, I said I'll buy two copies, thinking enough is enough. So with these we printed *Bhagavad-gita As It Is* in Chinese in 1990. Within a few months, Bhima received a letter from a lawyer alleging copyright infringement.

The lawyer's client was none other than Sundar Gopal in Singapore, then still working under Tamal Krishna Goswami. Shortly afterwards, BBTI brought a lawsuit against Bhima in Singapore, claiming their copyrights had been infringed and asking for damages.

We challenged BBTI to prove ownership, and they came back with a fake, back-dated document signed by Svavasa, supposedly assigning BBT copyrights to BBTI. But we presented the original Trust Agreement for Prabhupada's Bhaktivedanta Book Trust and the resolution bearing Shrila Prabhupada's signature appointing myself as trustee, and demanded that BBTI prove its legal connection with the original BBT. When they couldn't do that, they all at once backed out of the lawsuit.

That's when ISKCON and BBTI sued Hansadutta, myself, in 1997. It was not actually a lawsuit against myself personally. It was a direct attack on Prabhupada's original BBT.

ISKCON and BBTI were seeking a court declaration that Prabhupada's BBT was never a legally valid trust and thus never held the copyrights to his books; or in the event that it was once valid, that it had ceased to be valid; moreover, that Hansadutta, myself, was never a trustee of that trust, or if I was, then I had ceased to be or should be removed and new trustees appointed. (See endnote for Complaint[5]).

Over the course of more than a year and a half, much came to light. For instance, ISKCON claimed that Prabhupada had never owned the copyrights, that they were "works for hire", meaning that Prabhupada was ISKCON's hired worker – they supplied Prabhupada with room and board, dictation machine, paper, pen. . .and whatever he wrote was the property of ISKCON. Download it to see what ISKCON said.[6] [Reading the interrogatories it is very plain how the plaintiffs are being totally disingenuous, and even downright dishonest, avoiding giving straightforward and truthful answers as is expected of any person having personal integrity and moral character, in other words, a person trained as a brahmana. Such behavior is detestable for a person in a position of leadership of a spiritual society, and yet there it is in black and white on a legal document. Such so-called leaders, devoid of integrity, are fit to be abandoned.]

I did not relinquish my position as BBT trustee lightly. It was a grave decision. I understood very well that Prabhupada had appointed me for life to safeguard his books, and I would never have simply thrown it away. But after 17-18 months of litigation, we had no financial resources to continue the legal battle into trial. Our lawyer, Fedorowsky (Gupta das), required us to come up with another $100,000 in advance payment to go to trial.

Contrary to what has been reported by some, I did not leave ISKCON with money, and I have never done business or been gainfully employed, so I had to rely on Krishna to send help in defending Prabhupada's BBT. Bhima had spent more than a million dollars fighting the BBTI court case in Singapore. Then when ISKCON – BBTI changed course and filed legal action against me, again Bhima came to the rescue, but by then he was pretty much tapped out.

He scrambled to put up the money to retain Fedorowsky. Veda Guhya also contributed. But when Fedorowsky called for more money for trial, we just didn't have it, and no one responded to our appeals for help. Everyone just kept silent. No one came forward, and former friends retreated. Talk of betrayal... I felt betrayed at that time, deserted by godbrothers who would not support the defense of Prabhupada's BBT.

Moreover, Fedorowsky advised me that even if we were to proceed to trial and if we should prevail, there was every likelihood that ISKCON and BBTI would appeal and that ISKCON would petition the court to remove me from the trust in any case, and the matter could drag out for years. We didn't know it at the time, but Fedorowsky had already misappropriated money that was to pay his fees for an investment scheme.

Had we known that, we would not have trusted him, but we did trust him, and we had no other option for an attorney

– Fedorowsky knew the ins and outs of ISKCON, he had a grasp of the legal issues, which baffled all other attorneys we consulted, and he had made us an offer impossible to refuse – very discounted fees.

And so it was that 18 months into litigation, I was corralled into accepting a settlement, crafted by Gupta and Amarendra. Fedorowsky promised me that in exchange for stepping down from the BBT trustee position, BBTI and ISKCON would give me an "unfettered" license to publish all of Prabhupada's original pre-1978 books, pretty much worldwide. This turned out to be otherwise, but at the time I trusted Fedorowsky's legal advice.

I had to consider that if we went to trial and lost, BBTI and ISKCON would get away with everything, spelling the end of Prabhupada's original books and depriving many devotees of access to buying books for distribution. And I had to consider that even if we went to trial and won, it would not be the end of it; ISKCON and BBTI would fight on and eventually I would be removed as trustee.

Then too, Fedorowsky spoke of the cost of protecting the copyrights, how if the original BBT did not file legal action for each and every copyright infringement, then the copyrights would be lost to public domain – which might have been done anyway. So thinking to make the best of a bad bargain, I made the decision that I felt would protect the integrity of Prabhupada's original books and enable their publication and make them accessible to the devotees everywhere regardless of their affiliation with ISKCON.

I considered also ISKCON's and BBTI's assurances that the BBT would be left intact. It was for Prabhupada that I did what I did. For Prabhupada and the devotees. In the end,

I could only hope that the settlement would resolve our differences, and so I took a leap of faith to trust our godbrothers at their word, give them a chance to make it possible for us to participate in serving Prabhupada and his mission by printing and distributing his unadulterated books.

I did not do so with personal profit in mind. That was not the case at all. For that reason I did not object when Fedorowsky added his own name to the board of the licensee, Krishna Books, Inc. (KBI).ᶜ

Out of gratitude to him for his services, and desiring to include the persons who had sacrificed money, time and energy to defend Prabhupada's BBT and the purity of Prabhupada's original books, I consented to the naming of Fedorowsky, Veda Guhya, Bhima and his wife all as members of the board. As for the settlement money, it was initially agreed that the money would be used as startup capital for printing Prabhupada's books.

However, Fedorowsky laid claim to it, and a dispute arose. As it turned out, Fedorowsky, with the support of Veda Guhya, Bhagavan and Niscintya, pulled the carpet out from beneath us, and took control of the license, ousting myself, Bhima and his wife Das devi dasi. But I assure you, I did not ever intend to betray Shrila Prabhupada or his Book Trust. I acted in good faith. Fedorowsky and others took advantage of my trust and good will. If you are looking for those who betrayed Prabhupada, look to them, look to ISKCON and BBTI.

As you have pointed out, I have since put ISKCON and BBTI on notice that their failure to pay out the settlement monies as per the terms of the settlement means that the settlement has been breached, and so I have rescinded my resignation as trustee of the BBT. As far as I know, the BBT is intact.

But ISKCON and BBTI continue to produce and distribute counterfeit books, and the BBT court case has been swept underneath the rug.

To check them with legal action is prohibitively costly. But if the devotees rally and demand remediation, that Prabhupada's BBT be restored and that BBTI cease all revisions of Prabhupada's books, then it's possible that one day things will be right again with the movement. This is my stand. And I call for all Prabhupada's faithful disciples to stand with me, to stand by Prabhupada's Bhaktivedanta Book Trust, to stand for Shrila Prabhupada and his books.

Remember the Alamo! But devotees need to do more than talk. Many devotees have strongly protested the changes to the books, but BBTI and ISKCON turn a deaf ear to them and will continue to do so unless and until they are faced with real consequences such as court action. This costs money. So put your money where your mouth is, and let's see who is willing to do for Prabhupada.

I know that I have disappointed you and so many other devotees. I am very sorry for so many things I have done recklessly and for having failed to live up to all our expectations. All I can do is ask again for forgiveness from you and from the devotees everywhere, and for your blessings to be allowed to serve Prabhupada alongside his faithful devotees.

We are meant to follow Prabhupada, all of us as members of his entourage, as his servants, in this life and in the next and the next after that, forever, and this is all I look forward to –

---

[c] As a result of this trial Krishna Books, Inc. was formed and granted an unrestricted license to print all of Shrila Prabhupada's original books, without expiration.

meeting up with Shrila Prabhupada wherever he may be and being counted once again as one of his disciples. Please do not think too badly of me and cast me out from your association.

Your servant, Hansadutta das

GBC and BBTI Continue the Attack

Fast forward to 2017. Jitarati Dasa as an authorized agent of KBI has been printing Shrila Prabhupada's original, unedited books for years. He and his team worked for years to produce a beautiful case-bound set of Shrila Prabhupada's *Srimad Bhagavatams*, printed in India, but before they could be shipped, BBT Bombay and ISKCON filed lawsuit to have the books destroyed, alleging copyright infringement and that the KBI license had expired, although there is no expiration mentioned in the original agreement.

In a letter of amazing hypocrisy, the head of the Indian BBT explained to intermediary Basu Ghosh Prabhu, why he thought the action was necessary. (Bear in mind that the Indian (Bombay) BBT was also established by Shrila Prabhupada and allowed to print books, but the copyrights were all held by the American BBT) :

> I think we need to make one thing clear here, that is Shrila Prabhupada formed a trust called The Bhaktivedant Book Trust. Shrila Prabhupada assigned the rights to his writings in the same trust. So, it should be clear that our Spiritual Master wanted his books printed by the trust. Shrila Prabhupada didn't want even his own temples printing his books what to speak of individuals. So, the trustees of the BBT have a duty to print the books and see that the rights are not infringed upon.
>
> Call whatever name but we still have to perform as trustees because as trustees we are duty bound to Shrila Prabhupada to print.[d]

It is both shocking and ironic that in this letter the author says he has the duty to see that the rights are not infringed upon, when the BBTI is totally infringing on Shrila Prabhupada's original BBT! Why doesn't he make that claim *against BBTI?* The BBTI has infringed on Shrila Prabhupada's original BBT by attempting to eliminate it and transfer its assets (the copyrights) to itself. It is further infringing on Shrila Prabhupada's original BBT by making unlimited, unnecessary posthumous changes to the books.

In response to Basu Ghosh, Jitarati replied:

> I have always been open to real negotiation to alleviate the fear of BBT India that KBI books are ending up in their market. I tried my best to do that but was last told that I should just stop printing and let them do everything. That is not negotiation, but dictating, and worse, trying to take my life and soul service away from me. . . Worse than that is holding a court order over me and saying they want to negotiate. Worse than that, they are holding Prabhupada and Krishna prisoners in Their own books. Holding them hostage for ransom and dictated terms of a so-called negotiated settlement. . . They knew very well that it was a work in progress for years and that I had all legal rights to print with KBI under their license. They lied and cheated their way into the court and have continued to lie and cheat and manipulate the court system. . .

The Bombay BBT kept these beautiful Bhagavatams locked in a warehouse for more than 12 months, finally releasing them only after the judge *ordered* both parties to come to an agreement!

Further pertinent details are added in another letter from Jitarati to Basu Ghosh:

> The famous letter from Shrila Prabhupada that Bhima quotes to prove that I am acting unilaterally is an example of the

misuse of common sense. The letter instructs temples to not print independently of BBT, so [BBT India] says that applies to individuals like me. First of all it is a bold-faced lie that I am printing independently, as explained above. Secondly, Prabhupada was trying to keep BBT strong and fulfil its purpose to support the beneficiary of BBT, namely ISKCON.

In 1990, ISKCON LA and BBTI attempted to extinguish both BBT of California and BBT India. That document is in the court documents from the 1998 case and so the situation of wiping out the two Prabhupada created BBTs was thwarted and a mood of cooperation was established. Why are they trying to wipe that out again?[7]

Tenth and later Cantos Authored by Shrila Prabhupada?

We have learned that the Indian BBT applied for copyright registration in India in 2011 for the entire *Srimad Bhagavatam*, including *all* chapters of the 10th canto and all the 11th and 12th cantos, *claiming that they were all authored by Shrila Prabhupada!* A brief look at items #5, #7 and #9 in the photocopy of the copyright registration below will make this very clear. "General History" is the title of the 11th canto, and this is the application for the second volume. Moreover, this book could not have been published in 1982 because it didn't exist until 1983 or 84, and were first printed in the United States. I know this for a fact since I was the production manager when this book was produced, and I sent it to the printer! This application also goes against Shrila Prabhupada's original arrangement that the copyrights would be held by BBT Los Angeles, with BBT India given only *the right* to print all of Shrila Prabhupada's books.

---

[d] From: ISKCON BBT Bombay to Basu Ghosh Das, Cc: Jitarati Das Tuesday, May 9, 2017

As is the case with the *Bhagavad-gita* As It Isn't, the BBT is attempting to fool everyone into thinking that the books written and changed by conditioned souls were/are Shrila Prabhupada's original books. Again we are forced to wonder what exactly they are doing, or plan to do with such lies! This cheating is totally uncharacteristic of bona fide Vaishnavas, proving them to be unfit to have the positions of trust they occupy. This is a repeat of the changes to the "Bible" – sections written by conditioned souls with the work put forward as "the inspired word of God." Such falsehoods are not protecting Shrila Prabhupada's legacy, but destroying it.

Advocating for the Original *Bhagavad-gita As It Is*

Shrila Prabhupada's disciple Garuda Das earned a Ph.D. and has established himself as a respected and prominent academic in the field of religious studies. He and others have gathered a group of academics to make a serious study of the changes to Shrila Prabhupada's books, and specifically the 1972 Macmillan *Bhagavad-gita As It Is*. In an initial explanation of their efforts Garuda writes:

> Our core group is comprised of four disciples of Shrila Prabhupada. . . We are working in conjunction with a panel of six academic consultants—three scholars who are practicing Vaishnavas and three scholars of Vaishnavism. In addition, the project is assisted by persons in the fields of publishing, law, research, IT, social media and other professional services.

> The purpose of this group is to call for reconsideration of the presumption that Shrila Prabhupada's 1972 Macmillan *Bhagavad-gita As It Is* required extensive editing and revision to comply with academic and publishing standards.

Garuda later issued this interim statement:

> We can also all agree that Shrila Prabhupada never gave any instruction to Jayadvaita Swami, nor to anyone else, that he

wanted an improved and revised edition. On the contrary, Prabhupada repeatedly warned devotees about what he called "the changing disease." It is incontrovertible that Prabhupada rejected the notion of "changing" what he had written. He only approved minimal editing for mistakes and omissions; nothing more. He never requested anyone to go back to earlier drafts and transcriptions for "improving" what he had already personally approved. In my experience in the field of academic writing and publishing, I am certain that if the MAC72 were still a Macmillan publication, the posthumous BBT83 changes would never be accepted, nor even entertained by Macmillan unless it came directly from the author.

Also, please allow me to share a personal, and, admittedly, uncomfortable, thought regarding the problematic nature of this presumption on the part of the editorial team. I cannot [help] but see the replacement of the Macmillan '72 Gita with the BBT's 83 edition as inescapably calling into question Prabhupada's awareness and knowledge of how his writings were published. By direct implication, the placing of previously unpublished words "into Prabhupada's mouth" via BBT83 can be seen as an indictment on Prabhupada's judgment and an assertion of the BBT's superior judgment over his. It matters not if they were drawn from un-finalized drafts, for in the absence of the author's direct approval, such efforts to get us "closer to Prabhupada" may well produce the converse result, namely, the BBT83 that is "further away from Prabhupada." As I understand it, it is precisely this concern that distresses so many devotees.

Garuda and his associates have planned a full academic conference to be held at the Graduate Theological Union in Berkeley, California in February 2020. This conference will bring scholars together to examine how the posthumous editing of leading

Government of India
Copyright Office
Extracts from Register of Copyrights

Dated: 08-03-2011

1	Registration No:	L-37560/2011
2.	Name,address and nationality of the applicant:	THE BHAKTIVEDANTA BOOK TRUST HARE KRISHNA LAND, JUHU, MUMBAI - 400 049, INDIAN
3.	Nature of applicant's interest in the copyright of the work	OWNER
4.	Class and description of the work	LITERARY
5.	Title of the work:	SRIMAD BHAGAVATAM - GENERAL HISTORY (PART - 2)
6.	Language of the work:	ENGLISH
7.	Name, address and nationality of the author and if the author is deceased, date of his decease:	LATE A.C. BHAKTIVEDANTA SWAMI PRABHUPADA ADD : SAME AS IN COL.2 ABOVE INDIAN Nov 14 197 7
8.	Whether the work is published or unpublished:	PUBLISHED
9.	Year and country of the first publication and name, address and nationality of the publisher:	1982 INDIA SAME AS IN COL.2 ABOVE
10.	Years and countries of subsequent publications, if any, and names, addresses and nationalities of the publishers:	LAST PUBLISHED IN 2008
11	Names, addresses and nationalities of the owners of various rights comprising the copyright in the work and the extent of rights held by each, together with particulars of assignments and licences, if any:	SAME AS IN COL.2 ABOVE
12.	Names, addresses and nationalities of other persons, if any, authorised to assign or licence of rights comprising the copyright:	NIL
13.	If the work is an Artistic work, the location of the original work, including name, address and nationality of the person in possession of it. (In the case of an architectural work, the year of completion of the work should also be shown)	N.A.
14	Remarks.	
	Diary No.	3909/2010-CO/L
	Date of Application:	08-04-2010
	Date of Receipt:	08-04-2010

DEPUTY REGISTRAR OF COPYRIGHTS

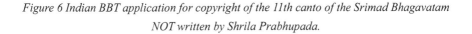

Figure 6 Indian BBT application for copyright of the 11th canto of the Srimad Bhagavatam NOT written by Shrila Prabhupada.

authors within religious communities has been handled and to look at how it could be or should be handled. The extensive posthumous editing of the works of Shrila Prabhupada will be the major focus of this conference.

Given the academic weight that is being assembled it is hoped that the BBT Trustees will be convinced to put aside their adulterated versions and again print *only* the original, unedited editions. Personally I have absolutely no trust in those who, by their actions, show themselves to be Putanas. Even if they agree to revert to the original editions for the time being, what will be done in 100, 200 or 300 years hence? As warned by Shrila Bhaktisiddhanta Sarasvati *"These lexicographical interpreters are employed by Kamsa in putting down the first suspected appearance of any genuine faith in the transcendental."* This is exactly what has happened. We are not fooled by appearances, dress, title, or position of the so-called editors. Based on their actions what can they be except agents of Kali?

As they have demonstrated over many years, neither the "lexicographical interpreters," nor the institutions behind them, care for what anybody thinks, whether academics or sincere devotees, and will work to insure that the transcendental message is destroyed by their damn work, and if not today, then whenever the future allows.

All of Us Must Protect Shrila Prabhupada's Legacy

Every sincere devotee should learn of the ongoing corruption regarding Shrila Prabhupada's books, starting from two sources: 1) the book "Arsha-Prayoga – Preserving Shrila Prabhupada's Legacy," and 2) the website www.bookchanges.com.[8] Much, much more that has been written regarding the changes to Shrila Prabhupada's books can be found with a simple internet search. But these two references examine in minute detail Shrila Prabhupada's instructions, and *how his legacy continues to be destroyed far beyond any excuse for correction by those who are charged to protect it!* **Thus, each and every sincere devotee must understand that, just as the Jewish Vaishnavas endeavored to protect their teachings for posterity, they must do whatever they can individually to preserve Shrila Prabhupada's works for future generations.**

Understanding how the Kamsas and Putanas obliterated and destroyed the teachings of Jesus has prepared you, my reader, to see how the same methods are being employed to destroy the appearance of the Eternal Religion in the 21st century. Both of these groups – the GBC body and the BBTI Officers – *the supposed fiduciaries charged with protecting Shrila Prabhupada's legacy – are the very people destroying it.* By their actions they demonstrate that they cannot dedicated servants of His Divine Grace. THEY MUST BE SEEN FOR WHAT THEY TRULY ARE, AND REJECTED! Just as Shrila Prabhupada condemns the book changers here:

> *Guru-mukha-padma-vakya, cittete koriya aikya.* . . if he makes addition, alteration, *then he is finished.* No addition, alteration. You have to approach guru. Guru means the faithful servant of God, Krishna, and take his word how to serve Him. Then you are successful. If you concoct, 'I am very intelligent than my guru, and I can make addition or alteration,' *then you are finished.* Lecture *Srimad Bhagavatam* July 12, 1975

CHAPTER SEVEN

Destroying the Followers

It is the bounden duty of the chanter of the kirtan of Hari to oppose clearly and frankly any person who tries to deceive and harm himself and other people by misrepresenting the Truth due to malice or bona fide misunderstanding. This will be possible if the chanter of kirtan is always prepared to submit to be trodden by thoughtless people if any discomfort to himself will enable him to do good to his persecutors by chanting the Truth in the most un-ambiguous manner. Shrila Bhaktisiddhanta

The Roman church tolerated no dissent. Those that disagreed with, or challenged the Church's teachings were considered heretics, and could be physically punished or even killed. Thousands were burned alive, which was meant to, and did, have a chilling effect on dissent. Yet, somehow or other, five hundred years ago a German monk's challenges to the selling of indulgences were allowed to pass without consequence. Although condemned as a heretic, only Luther's writing was burned and not he himself.

261

This is because the control mechanism of the population was being shifted from religion and belief to state-issued money. Thus for the first time in some 1,500 years people were allowed to believe as they chose without fear of reprisal from the pontiff, bishops, or priests. In the present day the control mechanism of money is complete. Nobody can live without it, and we are free to have freedom of conscience and believe as we like, without the fear of retribution or death – as long as we live according to the ways prescribed for us by our controllers. Therefore when the Eternal Religion manifest in the form of the Hare Krishna Movement and posed a threat to the established way of life, it was no longer possible to kill the followers in order to eradicate it as was done in earlier centuries. Other methods of controlling its growth and popularity would have to be used.

The methods used were characteristic of Kali – attacks against the weak and defenseless – specifically: 1) the women, 2) the *kanishta* bhaktas, and 3) the innocent children. All of these efforts have been extremely successful. Each of these are extremely emotional issues that has affected the lives of thousands of devotees. Volumes have already been written about each from all sides, and it is impossible to duplicate that here. Rather I present a glimpse of the effect of these tragedies, and demonstrate that they have *not* been due to the accidental indiscretions of young inexperienced disciples, but each has been deliberately carried out by a "leadership" that deliberately ignored Shrila Prabhupada's instructions.

Let us remind ourselves that no serious devotee willfully disobeys the order of the spiritual master, since following the order of the bona fide spiritual master is the secret of success.[1] Since these actions were all instigated by "leaders" who would certainly know better, their motivations and objectives must be questioned. Our guiding principal in looking at this history will continue to be *phalena parichyate* – judging by the result. Since the result was so devastating we must suspect that that was the intention, leading to our conclusion that agents of Kali had infiltrated the society and were behind all of these acts.

Discouragement and Disparagement of the Women

Shrila Prabhupada was an exemplary Vaishnava who saw everyone as a spiritual being, and it was his desire to save everyone – the whole world – as far as possible. As an *Acharya* he understood spiritual principles and the necessity of adjusting them according to time, place and circumstances.

Thus upon his arrival in America upon and surveying the social scene he understood that Krishna Consciousness could not be established in the West in the same way it was practiced in India. The culture was too different. Specifically he saw that men and women mixed freely and that women were accorded nearly the same status as men. Thus he recognized that he must accept women as his students, although this was not traditionally done.

One woman, Janaki, was among his first group of initiates, and within two weeks of her initiation Shrila Prabhupada engaged in another act typically forbidden for *sannyasis* – he married her and her boyfriend, Mukunda Dasa. Soon afterwards he made another adjustment to normal Vaishnava practice by sending this married couple to open temples. First in San Francisco and then to London. Another woman, Janaki's sister Joan, later initiated as Yamuna, would become one of Shrila Prabhupada's most prominent disciples. Other women were attracted to him and his teachings and he accepted all of them, not only without discrimination, but he cared for them as a father would for his daughters, seeing to their needs and protection, while encouraging them to engage in Lord Krishna's service. This concern and care for his female disciples never changed despite the criticism that it drew from his godbrothers. As noted by one writer:

Women who lived in India during the early days of ISKCON told me that Founder-*Acharya* Shrila A.C. Bhaktivedanta Swami Prabhupada always made sure that his women disciples were treated well and that they felt included. He personally took care of details like making sure that they had adequate living quarters, good food and rides to events. When the devotees went places as a group, Shrila Prabhupada invited the women to ride with him in his car to make sure they got there. He set it up so that women could stand at the front in the temples to behold the altars [*darshan*], he also encouraged women to give *Bhagavatam* class and lead *kirtan*. . . [2]

And he taught this to his disciples as well. In an early room conversation in 1968, Shrila Prabhupada instructed:

> Now another thing, the girls should not be taken as inferior. Of course, sometimes scripture we say that 'woman is the cause of bondage.' So that should not be aggravated that "woman is inferior," or something like that. *So the girls who come, we should treat them nicely.* . . anyone who is coming to Krishna consciousness, man or woman, is very fortunate. The idea of addressing "prabhu" means "you are my master." So everyone shall treat others as "my master." This is the Vaishnava understanding. . . So this should be the attitude, that women, *Godsisters, they should be nicely treated* so that they may not feel any. . . After all, they are weaker. That should be our policy."[3] (emphasis added)

In my early days, from joining ISKCON in 1973, and through 1975, this was the mood, as I experienced it. There was an innocent comradery between men and women who worked side-by-side spreading Krishna Consciousness. We were on a war-footing at that time – in a war against Maya – and as in any war the women carried their weight equally with the men. However, this was to change dramatically around 1975, an undoing created by Shrila Prabhupada's increasing number of sannyasa disciples, some of whom engaged in a literal campaign of condemnation of the female devotees. *This was to lead several decades later to the devastating result of undermining Shrila Prabhupada's absolute position and authority as the Acharya of ISKCON, effectively relativizing him as just one authority among other modern mundane thinkers.*

The Condemnation Begins

I clearly remember the day in 1975 that Tamal Krishna Goswami came to our Gainesville, Florida temple initiating his campaign of discrimination against the women. A simple example demonstrates his fanatical stance that has nothing to do with spiritual principles. While giving the *Srimad Bhagavatam* lecture he condemned the word "deve" in Shrila Prabhupada's pranam mantra as unacceptable since it was the feminine form. He insisted that henceforward it must instead be chanted and sung as the masculine "devum."[a] He also demanded that since the women were like fire and men like butter, and thus their presence presented a spiritual danger for the men, they were to stay at the back of the temple room, behind the men, during all temple functions, while prior to this the room was divided lengthwise between the men and women. With this, the earlier innocence and collegiality between the sexes was vanquished, and bodily consciousness began to replace transcendental Krishna Consciousness.

To fuel their campaign against the women, the single men, themselves still very much neophyte and in the bodily conception of life, found support by misinterpreting Shrila Prabhupada's purports about women as being less intelligent, lusty, personification

---

[a] This despite the fact that Shrila Prabhupada himself stated that either version was acceptable, but that deve should be used.

of Maya, and so on. In their classes they condemned sex, and women along with it. Women routinely faced disparaging and demeaning public lectures by *sannyasis* and other men, in which their intelligence, motives and capabilities were criticized or dismissed.

Many women were given second-class status, and marginalized in ISKCON'S culture. Whatever freedoms they might have earlier enjoyed as partners with the men in the mission of their spiritual master, were lost. Belittled in such a way many women lost confidence in themselves and in their material and spiritual abilities, and accepted the part that was expected of them, being brainless, ignorant, and unproductive.[3] Naturally they became discouraged upon finding that ISKCON temples, instead of reflecting the teachings of Shrila Prabhupada that initially attracted them, had instead become a society that emphasized the bodily conception of life, in some places going to extremes:

> I wasn't allowed, ever, to look up from the floor if there was a man around. (laughter) In fact we [women] lived on the fourth floor. If there was a man going up the stairs and I was going down, I had to go all the way back up to the fourth floor. I couldn't be anywhere near the stairs if there was a man on the stairs. And if a man walked near me, I'd put my face in a corner until they walked past. I'd face the wall and go like this (covering her face with her sari), in the corner (laughter).

> Man: Having lived as a brahmacari in the same temple at that time, I would say you're not at all exaggerating.[5]

> What happened to me was that all I thought about was men and saris. 'There's a man. Is my sari on right? Is it the right color? Do I have any hair showing in the front [coming out from where the sari is wrapped around the head]?' And that was all I thought about. I stopped thinking about Krishna and Prabhupada.[6]

I've never so much regretted being born in a woman's body since I joined the ISKCON movement. I've never been so much criticized, abused, slandered, misunderstood, or chastised because I have this woman's body. It makes it very difficult to do my service and/or assist others with their service if they are always thinking about these bodily designations instead of the constructive things I could do or say to help them in their service and to help this movement go forward.[7]

[I] was insulted, resentful and outraged when his male students interpreted Krishna Consciousness as sexism, with their imperious attitude toward women. That made my hackles rise and made me bristle with indignation. The behavior of these men damaged me. Each undermining act, each belittling comment piled up on the others to create a scar within me.[8]

Such negative attitudes against the women also filtered down to the gurukula where the girls were taught to be ashamed of their bodies. One girl growing up under such conditions drew an image of her shame as a black hole in the center of a beautiful multi-faceted diamond.[9]

This influence and change did not take place everywhere and all at once. For years Shrila Prabhupada had been receiving complaints about mistreatment and abuse from his female disciples. He received one such letter from Ekayani Dasi as early as November 1972. She was disturbed by new policies against the women in the New York temple restricting them from the temple at certain times, giving the men priority. Shrila Prabhupada was quite upset to learn that his students were not following his instructions, but taking it upon themselves to institute widespread changes in the society at their own whim:

I do not know why these inventions are going on. That is our only business, to invent some new program? We have already got our Vaishnava standard. That is sufficient for MadhvAcharya, and RamanujAcharya. It was sufficient for Lord Chaitanya, the six Goswamis, for Bhaktivinoda Thakur, for my Guru Maharaja Bhaktisiddhanta Sarasvati, for me, for all big saints and Acharyas in our line – why it shall be inadequate for my disciples so they must manufacture something? That is not possible.

Who has introduced these things, that women cannot have chanting of japa in the temple, they cannot perform arati, and so many things? If they become agitated, then let the brahmacaris go to the forest. *I have never introduced these things.* If the brahmacaris cannot remain in the presence of women in the temple, then they may go to the forest, not remaining in New York City, because in New York there are so many women, so how they can avoid seeing? Best thing is to go to the forest for not seeing any women if they become so easily agitated. But then no one will see them either and how our preaching work will go on?[10]

This letter demonstrates that such demeaning attitudes toward women did not originate from Shrila Prabhupada, but from the *sannyasis* and other men, and this fact is widely recognized. However, Shrila Prabhupada was unable to correct the situation, since, on some issues, his leaders, and many of the followers, simply would not follow his instructions. Our opinion is that this abuse was the specific agenda of many of these men, seeking to undermine the Hare Krishna Movement.

This condemnation and criticism of women lasted for decades. It is impossible to know how many, but likely hundreds of women left ISKCON in disgust, while perhaps thousands more, who might otherwise have taken up Krishna Consciousness, stayed away. Resentment and anger brewed among those that stayed.

Not surprisingly undercurrents developed that sparked a backlash and rebellion from the women in the early 90s, fueled significantly by revelations that their children were being abused in the society's boarding schools, the gurukulas.

Undoubtedly the most tragic result of this abuse was the destruction of Shrila Prabhupada's position as the absolute authority of ISKCON, *effectively relativizing him as just one authority among other modern mundane thinkers.* I shall say more about this in the last chapter of this section.

A survey of ISKCON's membership conducted for Shrila Prabhupada's 1996 Centennial showed the degree to which women in ISKCON had been adversely affected by such treatment. Almost one-third (31%) of the 137 female respondents *strongly agreed* with the statement "as a woman, I sometimes encounter a degree of sexism in our movement that is a barrier to my spiritual advancement," while an almost two-thirds majority (61%) agreed. In addition, more than a third (37%) *strongly agreed* that "many women devotees suffer from low self-esteem largely because they feel mistreated by devotee men," with more than half in agreement. The negative treatment of the women was not lost on the men, who, recognizing the mistreatment of women were two-thirds (68%) in agreement.[11]

In his book *Hare Krishna Transformed* ISKCON's sociologist and friend, Professor Burke Rochford, notes how the women found the courage to seek redress:

Far more important however, was Prabhupada's personal example in dealings with his earliest women disciples. It was in these encounters between Prabhupada and his early women disciples that pro-change women unearthed the critical ingredients to construct a viable collective action frame... Not only did these stories portray Prabhupada's respectful attitude and behavior toward his women disciples, but they also indirectly revealed how ISKCON'S leadership had misinterpreted or otherwise misused their guru's instructions and teachings. In hearing these anecdotal accounts, women came to realize that their rights and interests as women and devotees had been sacrificed to further the religious and political agenda of ISKCON'S renunciate leadership.[12]

The reason attributed by Rochford is very kind on his part, and perhaps the most benign interpretation of those dealings. My opinion is that the women were not sacrificed to achieve another higher agenda, but their sacrifice *was* the agenda.

Driving away the Loyal Followers

At the Annual General Meeting of the GBC in Mayapur in 1978, one of the first acts of the GBC body, now freed from any correction and restraint by Shrila Prabhupada, was to arrogate to themselves authority above long-established siddhanta given by the Gaudiya *Acharya*'s. After all, they were now "the Ultimate Managing Authority,"[b] and they began to act the part. Why should they follow the previous *Acharyas*? They had been empowered! And as they had already done a number of times even in Shrila Prabhupada's presence (for which they were severely admonished), took it upon themselves to make ISKCON into what they thought it should be, either forgetting Shrila Prabhupada's instructions as well as Gaudiya siddhanta, or simply ignoring both.

They declared that 11 of their own members would be the exclusive channels through which Shrila Prabhupada's mercy would

---

[b] Such a descriptor was not given by Shrila Prabhupada, but written by Tamal Krishna, although signed off by Shrila Prabhupada. Were Shrila Prabhupada himself to have written this he may well have chosen different words, giving a very different understanding of their authority.

flow. They, and none of the other equally, or perhaps more spiritually qualified godbrothers, would have the authority to initiate new members of ISKCON. On what basis? None, in fact. The only statement found in the resolutions of their meeting regarding gurus was: "for 1978, no new Spiritual Masters shall be appointed other than the 11 selected by Shrila Prabhupada." *However, the truth is that Shrila Prabhupada never selected, nor appointed, any spiritual masters.*

This lie was perpetrated by a deliberate misinterpretation of the July 9th, 1977 letter listing 11 ritvik representatives to perform initiation on Shrila Prabhupada's behalf.[c] There is *nothing* in this letter that can even remotely be construed as instructions by Shrila Prabhupada that these persons should be gurus of ISKCON, especially *exclusive* gurus, after his departure. Tamal Krishna confessed to this in a conversation recorded at Topanga Canyon in late 1980, stating that he and the others had done the greatest disservice to the society by perpetrating this falsehood.Indeed. Although he promptly forgot that fact after the GBC removed the restrictions they had placed on him.[d]

---

[c] These 11 were selected by Shrila Prabhupada in a room conversation July 7, 1977. It is obvious that this conversation refers to initiations while Shrila Prabhupada was with us, as he states *"India I am here."* Further, the genesis of this list is from the earlier recorded conversation of May 28 when select GBC men approached Shrila Prabhupada about initiations *"after he was no longer with us."* That the May 28th query *did not* clearly answer the question of how initiations would be carried out *after* his departure is obvious due to this contradictory response.

[d] At the time Tamal and Hansadutta had been suspended as ISKCON gurus by the GBC. Given his vindictive nature, if Tamal couldn't be guru then he would bring down the whole show, and nobody would be guru. Not long after this confession he was reinstated and discussion of there being no appointments was never heard from him again.

After the Mayapur meeting it was summarily announced to the society that these 11 were the spiritual inheritors of Shrila Prabhupada's legacy and that they would be the only gurus in the society. Almost immediately in-fighting and turf wars developed between these "maha-bhagavats" and quickly each of them became the only guru allowed to initiate within their assigned GBC geographic zone. Unfortunately for the yet-to-be-initiated devotees, again contrary to Gaudiya siddhanta, they were given no choice in the matter. If they wanted a connection with Shrila Prabhupada and the parampara they were forced to accept the local guru, often proving to be a disaster for their spiritual lives, or to pick up and relocate to the "zone" of the guru they preferred. Thus the "Zonal *Acharyas*" became just the first train-wreck of the Ultimate Managing Authorities regarding guru-tattva.

Needless to say this news was greeted with great alarm and protest by many Shrila Prabhupada's disciples who clearly understood the philosophy. Many senior men wrote lengthy papers, copied and widely circulated, objecting and predicting that this would destroy the society. They were received with great appreciation by the rank and file devotees, but either ignored or condemned by the GBC leadership.

The newer devotees accepted the GBC's declarations that the status of the 11 was conferred on them by Shrila Prabhupada and innocently received them as pure devotees and successors to Shrila Prabhupada. Many, if not most, of Shrila Prabhupada's disciples on the other hand, were distraught with what they saw as an usurpation of the society by unqualified men posing as pure devotees. They had been working side-by-side with them over the years and, knowing them intimately, knew that they lacked the qualifications of guru given in shastra. In those early years after 1977 there were many heated and very emotional discussions about what became known as "the guru issue." Despite being presented with many sound philosophical and practical arguments by knowledgeable and loyal devotees, predicting that this decision would be disastrous for the society, the GBC ignored them.

As predicted, an exodus began as dismayed and broken-hearted devotees realized they were powerless to rectify the situation. That exodus only increased over the coming years as the devotees were shocked and alarmed to see that *those very persons who had taken control of the society, and who were charged with protecting it, were in fact bringing about its destruction.*

Many gurus demanded that godbrothers and sisters worship them as they had Shrila Prabhupada, and if they would not they were rejected from the society. The new gurus, having the support of the many adoring disciples became the predominant political force, and Shrila Prabhupada's disciples, although senior and experienced, were the odd-man out. Insubordination was dealt a heavy-hand. The policy everywhere was not one of love and co-operation, or even live and let live, but my-way-or-the-highway. A hierarchy immediately developed in which godbrothers and sisters who subordinated themselves to the 11 were offered perks, while dissenters were shown the door. The horror show was just beginning.

Then in 1983 a heavily edited version of Shrila Prabhupada's *Bhagavad-gita As It Is* was printed and greeted by many with shock and dismay that their spiritual master's precious words were tampered with. Not long after that the mass distribution of Back to Godhead Magazine, which Shrila Prabhupada described as the "backbone of the Movement," and whose monthly circulation had reached *one million copies*, was stopped with no satisfactory reason offered. Instead it was to become a subscription magazine when at its peak even 30 years later, hardly achieved 1% of those numbers. Then in the early 80s, not even a few years after the declaration that the chosen 11 were pure devotees qualified to be guru, they began to fall down into drugs and illicit sexual affairs that revealed them to be ordinary fallen, conditioned souls. At the same time many sannyasa leaders of the society began falling, one after another. Those who had held the rank of GBC and guru demonstrated that they were far from fit to lead the society, being unable to maintain their vows of renunciation, which is the hallmark of spiritually advanced persons. Although they had the form, they lacked the substance. Recognizing this charade for what it was, the exodus became a torrent. The preaching stopped, since the devotees could not wholeheartedly, and without reservation, bring new people into what had become a corrupt society. The protestations reached a crescendo in 1985 when the second tier of leaders – dedicated *sannyasis*, temple presidents and other leading men – formed a "50-Man Committee" that could not be ignored, demanding rectification.

Moreover, it was not just Shrila Prabhupada's disciples who could see through the charade. Within several years, the rose-colored glasses fell off even the new initiates who began to see, sometimes literally, that the emperor had no clothes. They too began to defect in large numbers. Within ten years the temples that were once bustling havens of enthusiastic transcendentalists were empty, and in places the deities outnumbered the devotees. Such was the devastation of the society under the mis-leadership of the Ultimate Managing Authority.

Based on the contents of this book it is my thesis that this result did not come about by accidental misfortune and innocent mistakes, but was the intended goal, *for if our enemies had the opportunity to destroy us, they could not have done a better job. Phalena parichyate.*

We have seen that the rank and file devotees as well as many of the women were discouraged and driven away. We now need to look at another category of innocents whose faith was intentionally destroyed – the children of Krishna.

Destroying The Second Generation

Shrila Prabhupada had a vision for widespread social transformation. Understanding the cause of suffering in the world to be lack of genuine spiritual sustenance, and ultimately separation from Krishna, he wanted to establish Krishna Consciousness as the panacea for the ills of *Kali-yuga*. His plan for doing so was to re-establish the authentic Vedic culture in his society. This would be done through his books, and the widespread distribution of them; by training his young disciples in the principles of spiritual life; by establishing Deity worship in temples around the globe; by establishing schools to train children in the spiritual values of life instead of the indoctrination of sense gratification; and by establishing the varnashrama culture that would give shelter for everyone in their pursuit of the spiritual values of life.

To say that this was an ambitious agenda is a huge understatement, especially given the fact that he began his mission alone at the advanced age of 70. Even the attempt to establish a spiritual culture in this material world is a formidable task, but he was hoping to at least lay the foundation for others to build upon.

The plan for doing so had already been given in the Vedic shastra and histories. Shrila Prabhupada wasn't attempting to invent anything new, but simply to again establish the wonderful culture of earlier ages, doing so on the spiritual strength of the Lord Himself in the form of the maha-mantra.

A critical part of his endeavors depended not only on the training of his young followers, but on their purity of purpose as well. Shrila Prabhupada was quite aware of their inadequacies and foibles, but he had a long-range vision. Rome wasn't established in a day, and neither would this *Kali-yuga* be transformed overnight. The success would be determined by who would take up the work, and, of course, who Sri Krishna would bless with success.

Shrila Prabhupada had great hope that if young boys were properly trained from the beginning of life that, upon maturity, and freed from the indoctrination of sense gratification and the lower modes of nature, they would be fit to do great good for the world. Thus early on, as his followers children became school age, he established schools of spiritual training known as the *gurukula*. The precedence for this was established by the Supreme Lord Himself. In all of His incarnations, as Rama, Krishna, Rishabdeva, etc., although the knower of all, the Lord attended the school of the spiritual master to give the proper example to all citizens.

Regarding the Gurukula Shrila Prabhupada wrote:

I am very much anxious to open schools for educating children of responsible leaders in our Krishna Consciousness way of life, especially also in India. If these leaders simply become a little convinced about the real purpose of human life, there is tremendous potency for improving the world. . . The old system of gurukula should be revived as the perfect example of a system designed to produce great men, sober and responsible leaders, who know what is the real welfare of the citizens. Letter to Satsvarupa 21 November 1971

Now I very much appreciate your activities for conducting our school to the highest standard of Krishna Consciousness behavior, and I consider your work the most important in the society because you are shaping the future generation of our Krishna Consciousness preachers, and this is not any small thing. So I am depending very much upon you all to assist Lord Caitanya in fulfilling His mission for saving the human kind from very quickly gliding into hell. Letter to Rupa Vilasa, et. al., Los Angeles 20 June 1972

Gurukula is our most important project. If the children are given a Krishna Conscious education from early childhood then there is great hope for the future of the world. . . So if you go to Gurukula, try to help develop things there and make it the model educational institution in the world. Letter to Dayananda, Nandarani 27 January 1973

It is clear from these letters that Shrila Prabhupada placed great hope in these teachers, as well as handing them great responsibility. Having faith in Shrila Prabhupada and wanting to assist him in his effort to create a spiritual revolution in the world, his followers dutifully sent their very young children to the gurukulas. In many cases this was with done with great anxiety and concern for the welfare of their precious children, hoping that by doing so these children would indeed become the guiding lights for the world as Shrila Prabhupada indicated. Everyone hoped for the best, not even knowing at that time how significant this effort was to the future success of the Movement.

Professor of sociology and comparative religion, Rodney Stark, has stated that the integration of the second generation within the fold is key to the success or failure of new religious movements. He even goes so far as to say that "no new religion has been successful without the participation of their second generation." The truth of this fact has made the children an important target for those wishing to impede the establishment of the Eternal Religion in the 21st century.

During the early centuries of Christendom the followers of the Eternal Religion were eliminated simply by killing them, all in the name of protecting "the true religion" of course. Since killing people for what they believe is no longer possible, today's followers must be eliminated by other means, and a significant aspect of this would be the discouragement of the second generation. The fact that ISKCON's children were separated from their parents in boarding schools made them easy targets for Kali's agents. And targeted they were.

278 | DIVINE OR DEMONIAC?

As the children of the gurukulas came to adulthood they began to reveal the horrors they had been put through at the hands of their "caregivers." Despite the fact that Shrila Prabhupada *repeatedly instructed and emphasized* to school authorities that the children must not be punished, "cruel and unusual punishments" were going on almost from the beginning. For example, children were kept in trash bins and locked in closets for extended periods, and if they wet the bed as very young children often do, they were sometimes made to wear their soiled underwear on their heads! And more. Much more. And this was widely known. By 1978 I had heard enough horror stories of the Dallas school that there was no way that I was going to send my then 4-year old son there.

The abuse was pervasive throughout the Western as well as the Indian schools. Burke Rochford notes:

> Over the years any number of estimates have been offered ranging from 20% of all students who attended an ashram-gurukula suffering some form of abuse, to as many as 75% of the boys enrolled at the Vrindavana, India, gurukula having been sexually molested during the late 1970s and early 1980s. Whatever the actual incidence of child abuse, it remains clear that abuse directly and indirectly influenced the lives of a sizable number of children.[e]

It is now almost fifty years since the first gurukula in Dallas opened its doors, and over those decades thousands of ISKCON's children were abused, many egregiously so. If this was deliberately carried out, and we will present evidence that it has been, it has been extremely effective in destroying the faith of the second generation. Their participation in ISKCON after their gurukula experience is almost nil, and for many their belief in God instead of blossoming, was destroyed:

---

[e] Rochford, E., Child Abuse in the Hare Krishna Movement 1971-1986

To me God does not exist at all. I prayed to him every single day, 'Please take me away from all this [his suffering in the gurukula]. Please give me a pain-free life. I just want to be happy. Please, Lord. Please, Krishna, help me.' And what happened? Nothing. Everything just got worse. I'm starting to get angry now – but not at God, since he does not exist for me.[f]

I have so much pain in my heart. . . So much pain and tears. . . If you could just see what you have done to me, to us. . . All in the name of worshiping Krishna. . . Well now [. . .] can kiss my suicidal ass! Cause that's all I think about is just ENDING my miserable life. . . Everyday I have to find a reason why I should stay. I have nothing but you and all your tortures that keep me crazy. . . I sit here remembering all that [. . .] has said, all that ISKCON has done to me. I just want to die.[g]

One teacher reports on the abysmal results of the gurukula schools:

These kids were growing up and seriously leaving [ISKCON]. Not a little bit leaving. Not leaving and being favorable, still chanting and living outside. Nothing like that. They were leaving. And suddenly it was like 'What happened?' And then then it started to be revealed that the kids were molested.[h]

The feelings expressed for one teacher give some indication why:

As a gurukuli growing up under her regime...I always thought the worst of this despicable being.[i]

---

[f] Lutz, Daniel. My Karma My Fault, Kindle edition. Locations 447–450.
[g] https://krishna.org/iskcon-destroys-a-whole-generation-of-devotees-lives-updated/
[h] Long-time ISKCON teacher, interview 1990. Rochford, E.. Hare Krishna Transformed, p. 74. Kindle Edition.

And a mother of three children, all of whom were abused in the gurukula, reports:

> They now want nothing to do with ISKCON, what to speak of Krishna Consciousness.[j]

Gurukula veterans began going public with their stories in the late 80s and continued doing so through the 90s, revealing the tragedies that they had to live through in the gurukula. If you haven't heard their stories, then to understand something of the depth of this tragedy you *must* read their accounts in books such as Daniel Lutz's (Devavrata Dasa) *My Karma, My Fault*; Ragunatha Anudasa's *Children of the Ashrama*;[k] the website Krishnachildren.com that presents the official CPO case files and other relevant documents; read also *surrealist.org/gurukula* where a great deal of the history and abuses have been catalogued. Read the books and articles of Burke Rochford,[l] the sociologist who studies ISKCON and documents its history. He provides much history and examples of child abuse. Read the articles of Dhira Govinda Prabhu,[m] the first CPO director, such as "A Festival of Red Flags,"[n] his 2004 CPO Annual Report,[o] and his article published in The Journal of Religion and Abuse;[p] read also the article by Yudhisthira Das, son of ISKCON leader Ravindra Svarupa,[q] looking back at his gurukula experience.

---

[i] https://www.facebook.com/gopinath.dasa.1/posts/2075025002771805
[j] Wolf, David, Child Abuse and the Hare Krishnas, The Hare Krishna Movement, The Postcharismatic Fate
of a Religious Transplant, Edwin Bryant and Maria Ekstrand, eds. p. 337
[k] http://surrealist.org/gurukula/timeline/children.html
[l] Hare Krishna Transformed, Rochford, E. Burke,
[m] The Hare Krishna movement : the postcharismatic fate of a religious transplant / edited by Edwin F. Bryant and Maria L. Ekstrand, Columbia University Press. 2004 p. 321; Report on the Bhaktivedanta Gurukula Village, 1999 at http://krishnachildren.com/h-references.php;

Visit and read the website praylikeprahlada.wordpress.com. Read the many articles on child abuse posted on the Sampradaya Sun website. And for more recent information (2016) watch the *Cost of Silence* video and *Cost of Silence II.*[r]

As you read about the many, many horrors and tragedies be prepared for an emotional meltdown as you realize the extent of the abuse and that each instance devastated an innocent and helpless child who had no protection, destroying their faith in Krishna consciousness and God, debilitating their functional adult lives to one degree or another, necessitating years of counseling and therapy, and leading some two dozen to suicide.

The horrors of this abuse did not affect just the children, but presented yet *another huge crisis* that the devoted members of ISKCON had to somehow accommodate, piled on top of all of the earlier crises of the 80s of undermining the preaching with paraphernalia selling, fallen leaders and gurus and unauthorized book changes. What to speak of the lifelong burden of guilt and shame the parents of the abused children have been saddled with. ISKCON members that have been paying attention have been horrified to hear the details as they began to come out, many openly crying in shame and sadness hoping, that it wasn't true and their ears were lying to them. Not only did the abused children run from ISKCON, but many of their parents and other devotees, who had finally had enough, left with them in disgust:

---

[n] http://www.harekrsna.com/sun/editorials/05–10/editorials6083.htm

[o] http://www.harekrsna.com/sun/editorials/01–10/editorials5650.htm

[p] https://www.tandfonline.com/doi/abs/10.1300/J154v07n03_05

[q] The Hare Krishna movement, Bryant and Ekstrand, ibid., p. 345

[r] https://www.youtube.com/watch?v=UvlRAyM3p4Q and https://www.youtube.com/watch?v=wX1BiRhSpig&t=5s

282 | DIVINE OR DEMONIAC?

Three of Chatterton's children told him about a Hare Krishna man that had abused them. Chatterton, a former temple president, asked Kalakantha, then temple president, to ban the man from the premises, but his request was refused for 'lack of evidence.' [*three* children's testimony apparently was apparently not evidence enough!] Two years later, Harivilas, the regional director, asked the man to leave, but by then Chatterton had left the movement. 'I took all my faith and dumped it,' he says.[s]

Studies have shown that child abuse perpetrated by clergy has effects on victims are particularly devastating:

Children molested by religious authorities often suffer from depression, suicidal ideation, and affective disorders. Moreover, it is not uncommon for those sexually abused by clergy to change religions, or more likely still, to repudiate religion altogether. *Such an outcome appears even more likely when clergy sexual misconduct is hidden or otherwise covered-up by the church hierarchy.*[s]

Abuses by religious authorities not only leave long-lasting psychological effects that generally profoundly damages the spirituality of the victims, but their families and other community members as well. But even more devastating and troubling than learning that such things happened, is *learning that this abuse was knowingly allowed, covered-up, and even deliberately fostered and perpetuated by the top leadership*, and evidence for this will constitute the remainder of this chapter.

We must point out that not every adult involved in the gurukula was abusive. There were many sincere, dedicated and hard-working ashrama and academic teachers and administrators who often

---

[s] Julia Lieblich, Young Victims of Krishna Consciousness, LA Times, June 13, 1999

were simply overwhelmed with what they were tasked to do. One ashrama teacher for example, had 50 children to care for, many as young as 3 or 4 years of age![u]

GBC Foster Child Abuse – and Look the Other Way

In 1983 parents of children attending the day-care center at the Los Angeles ISKCON temple learned that their children were being abused, but after the parents alerted *the local GBC of the fact he resisted dealing with the situation.* The parents then directly confronted the abuser who fled the state forcing the closure of the school. The perpetrator was later caught and charged with endangering and molesting four children. The father of another, who left ISKCON as a result, described his 7-year-old boy as "a tormented, anguished child," who had been diagnosed as severely emotionally disturbed, suffering from sleeping disorders and hyperactivity. Police said the perpetrator used 'considerable force' in molesting the youngsters while he operated the day care center from November 1982 until September 1983. He was convicted and given the maximum 50 years imprisonment.[v]

These two instances, that made the newspapers in each city, clearly reveal that these two GBC men knew that sexual and physical abuse was going on at least by the early 80s and covered it up instead of acting to properly deal with the situation. Knowing that abuse was going on in the N. American schools responsible authorities would have alerted all ISKCON schools, and brought the matter to the GBC body for emergency action. But they deliberately avoided doing so allowing the abuse to continue on their watch.

---

[u] http://surrealist.org/gurukula/timeline/fromateacher1.html

[v] http://articles.latimes.com/1986-06-06/local/me-8975_1_molestations; also statements to this author by an involved parent.

However, when another GBC member did raise the issue with the GBC body even in the late 1980s, he was told that it was a grihastha issue that did not actively concern the GBC.[14] By 1989 the distraught clamor from parents could no longer be ignored, and the child abuse issue was finally discussed at the GBC's Annual General Meeting (AGM). Was it because it was considered a grihastha issue that the GBC were not spurred to action? Could they somehow have *not* realized that the future of the movement was in jeopardy, and take immediate action to stop to it and remove the perpetrators? We rather suspect that the abuses were intentionally allowed, evidenced in part by the action taken to foster it, the reluctance or refusal to address it, the slow start to correct it, as well as the other evidence presented here.

In that first meeting the GBC mandated that all incidents of child molestation in ISKCON be reported to government agencies for civil or criminal action. The Board of Education (BOE) was directed to compile and maintain a record of children abused in ISKCON schools, to arrange for professional help for parents and children, and also to keep detailed records of the ongoing progress of each child and report their status each year to the GBC body. However, inexplicably, nothing proactive was slated to deal with the problem, such as finding out the perpetrators and removing them. That took yet another year.

In 1990, although the GBC passed a resolution to establish a system of investigating, reporting, and preventing incidents of child abuse, the resolution supplied no practical means to enforce its elements.[15] The BOE introduced a more detailed policy for dealing with child abuse with specific actions to be taken, and consequences for the perpetrators, but amazingly allowed abusers to continue to stay on ISKCON properties and projects, supposedly separated from children, with the consent of 75% of the parents. In communities where devotees are trained to trust their authorities, especially if that authority is their guru, it would not be too difficult to convince them to agree. Although it stipulated that any confirmed child abuser may never again serve in association with children in any ISKCON project, and that the BOE would make the names of abusers available to all ISKCON projects, this rule would be ignored again and again, and at times even openly and strongly objected to by various ISKCON authorities.[w]

CPO Established

Despite this early action, the abuses continued, and more and more horror stories were revealed by the kulis. Finally, in reaction to rising unrest and anger about the revelations of child mistreatment in ISKCON, the GBC formed the ISKCON Child Protection Task Force in 1997. That Task Force issued a report, which recommended the establishment of an ISKCON Central Office of Child Protection. Early in 1998 the GBC established that office, which became known as the Association for the Protection of Vaishnava Children (APVC). The APVC officially opened in April, 1998.

Dr. Maria Ekstrand, Ph.D. in Psychology, aka Madhusudani Radha Devi Dasi, was involved in the review of the very first draft of the CPO manual. She assembled a team of devotees with relevant experience, none of whom was financially dependent on ISKCON and therefore free to speak their mind without fear of loss. She reports about their work:

> We read the draft carefully and made multiple recommendations
> for changing the proposed process. We strongly urged the
> GBC to set up internal consequences for various crimes

[w] See for example, Dhira Govinda's 2004 Annual CPO Report, and his article "Chile Abuse and the Hare Krishnas" in The Hare Krishna movement: The Postcharismatic Fate of a Religious Transplant, Bryant and Ekstrand, and the quote of Bhaktin Miriam below.

against children including when perpetrators should not be allowed to be around children, not allowed to have leadership positions, not allowed to maintain sannyasa status etc. We thought these consequences should be decided in advance by the GBC. However, we also felt strongly that the GBC should stay out of both investigations and applying the consequences. Instead, we suggested that all investigations be conducted by outside professionals, paid for by ISKCON, because they have received years of training and there is no need for ISKCON to replicate that. Finally, we recommended that the CPO simply be in charge of issuing the judgment, using the conclusions of the outside investigators and applying the rules previously decided by the GBC (which they should have put in writing *before* the whole process started). The GBC thus would have no role whatsoever in deciding on sentences and we also removed the stupid rule that 3/4 of the GBC could overturn any conviction [because] they are biased, especially when the accused is one of their friends. . .

So, what happened to our recommendations? Absolutely nothing! They were completely ignored.[16]

It's telling that although the GBC sought the input of professionals to review the CPO manual, they inexplicably chose to ignore their suggestions, hampering its potential effectiveness. One is forced to wonder why? That question is answered however, by observing the callous actions of the leadership regarding this delicate issue over the coming years. *Phalena parichyate.*

CPO aka APVC

The main functions of the APVC are explained by Dhira Govinda Dasa:

[The APVC] as outlined in the task force report, are to investigate and adjudicate cases of alleged child abuse in ISKCON, both past and present; to establish a grant program specifically for people who suffered mistreatment when they were children under the care of ISKCON representatives; and to assist ISKCON schools and temples in developing child protection programs.[17]

The original task force report estimated that the APVC would need to investigate and adjudicate about one or two dozen cases, but the APVC received accusations against more than 300 people connected in some way with ISKCON, with only a small number of the alleged incidents occurring after the association was established in 1998.[x]

It took ten years from the time the child abuse issue was first raised at the GBC meetings for the Child Protection Office (CPO) to finally be established, but it finally began it's somewhat hampered life with a serious and professional devotee director – Dhira Govinda Prabhu, who had a Ph.D. in Social Work and years of practical experience in fields such as foster care, children and family counseling, crisis intervention, and medical social work. He worked diligently for more than six years and accomplished a great deal in setting up the office, putting practices in place, setting up

[x] Dhira Govinda wrote to this author in private correspondence: "To give some perspective I'll also say that many of the alleged incidents really had no connection with the schools. In some instances they practically had no connection with the ISKCON temples. For example, there were cases of alleged child sexual maltreatment against an adult congregation member who occasionally attended a Sunday feast program. Such alleged incidents may not have taken place on temple property, or at an ISKCON educational institution, but the neighbor was a congregation member who sometimes attended morning programs, and some parents weren't comfortable with him hanging around the temple."

training programs, and arranging interviews of many ISKCON children and gurukulis about their abuse. The results of his investigation indicated that child abuse within ISKCON was extremely widespread.

Even before the CPO was established, an investigation was made into the abuse at the Mayapur gurukula due to the many tales of abuse, and a report issued on July 11, 1991. *That report however, was not made widely available, and likely few parents saw or read it. The report reveals a prejudice against the investigators by school staff*:

> The staff of the school cooperated with the investigation. However, the general attitude of the staff towards the investigation was disturbing. Many seemed to be downplaying its importance. Many have, as yet, failed to accept that they were neglectful in not preventing the occurrences. Many have failed to demonstrate that they have honest feelings of sympathy for the abused small children.[18]

Following up that report, Dhira Govinda representing the APVC, continued investigating alleged cases of abuse in the late 1990s and 2000. He interviewed many of the school's teachers and others about their knowledge of the abuse. In his report on the Bhaktivedanta Village Gurukula, Dhira Govinda states that *all of them* maintained that incidents of forced sexual abuse occurred regularly in the school throughout the year, and over a period of many years. However, in his interview with the schools director, Bhaktividya Purna Swami (BVPM), Dhira Govinda was told by the Maharaja that the report spoke of only a limited number of incidents and that all occurred within a few months of that investigation, and were incidents of sexual exploration (i.e., consensual, not forced) between boys of essentially the same age. However, in his report Dhira Govinda writes:

In the July 11 report there are many statements clearly indicating that there was extensive child sexual abuse perpetrated by older students on younger students, and that this sexual abuse involved force, coercion, intimidation and fear. Some these of statements include: 'Repeated incidents of homosexual attack of many boys of different ages.' 'Threatened many boys,' 'Abused several younger boys, threatened many boys,' 'Several younger boys reported that he (16 years old) abused them,' [etc.]"[19]

Dhira Govinda was incredulous at BVPM's ignorance of the actual facts of the situation. Was Maharaja ignorant, disingenuous, or was he lying? Or did he not bother to read the report? Dhira Govinda however said that if you actually read that report carefully "it is not something that you will forget in this lifetime!" In either case, for years the Maharaja was criminally negligent with the children under his care. The CPO investigation in 2000, following the standards of CPO adjudication, concluded: "Bhakti Vidya Purna Maharaja won't serve in any capacity that is directly connected with children until January 1, 2002. After that time he may serve in a non-managerial and non-administrative capacity connected with children if the ISKCON Education Ministry agrees that he may do so. Bhakti Vidya Purna Maharaja *may not at any time assume a managerial or administrative role in ISKCON, and especially not in connection with children.*"[20]

However, disregarding the CPOs decision on the matter, BVPM was again involved with the management as early as 2002.

Bhakti Vidya Purna Maharaja became a prominent figure of attack by the children who had been abused both by him, and others, at the Mayapur school. An internet search will bring up a number of documents detailing the abuse, the many efforts to have the situation dealt with in a responsible way, and the repeated frustration of those involved in seeking justice.

During his work with the CPO Dhira Govinda was frustrated by *repeatedly* observing that discovered perpetrators *after removal from one school would soon be found working at other schools, sometimes within months*. His frustration with trying to stop the perpetration and abuse is palpable in the Cost of Silence video, where he states:

> Besides dealing with all of the allegations, abuse and perpetrators, perhaps the most disturbing part [of doing this service] was *the corruption around these areas amongst many in the ISKCON leadership.* I don't want to paint with a broad brush here. There were many dedicated and concerned leaders. . . *But there was also a very dark side.* In my annual report of 2004 I had a section titled Culture of Accountability, which actually means *the lack of a culture of accountability.* And in saying that there are even minimally effective systems. . . it's just a sham. . . *Some of the leadership, to a large extent,* wanted to be able to say that they had an international child protection office, *but they didn't want the office to actually do its service, and do it effectively.*
>
> In places like Mayapur, where the most egregious abuse took place, *the abuses were covered up again and again.* There is a culture there of cover-up. Even in the past few days [in 2015!] I've gotten reports from Mayapur.

Dhira Govinda resigned from his position as the director of the CPO in 2004. The following comments are excerpts from Dhira Govinda's 2004 Annual Report of the ISKCON Central Office of Child Protection:

> In addressing cases of neglect of supervision by gurukula headmasters in schools where abuse was extensive, *the CPO met with impassioned resistance from GBCs and other leaders* who have worked closely with the headmasters, or former headmasters, under investigation. In a first world justice system

acting within a society holding contemporary views toward child protection, cases of the supervisors of the managers would likely be processed. Considering the extent of child suffering and maltreatment in some ISKCON locations, *a secular court would very possibly find criminal neglect on the part of the overseers of the administrators. To date, the CPO has not substantially investigated or in any way adjudicated the cases of upper-level leadership.*

As per standard CPO procedure in cases such as this [referring to one case of a temple president's sexual abuse of a 13-year old girl], the CPO informed leaders, including several members of the GBC body, in the locality and on the continent where the alleged abuser was serving, in the capacity of temple president, that an investigation was being conducted. This also included standard CPO precautionary recommendations that during the process of investigation the accused not have service connected with children and not assume a position of leadership.

The advocate for the defense questioned these recommendations, and *the local and continental leaders declined for a substantial time period to follow the recommendation of removing the accused from a leadership position. . . The CPO was repeatedly challenged by ISKCON leaders about the reasoning and impartiality of such recommendations,* and the CPO wrote several letters of explanation. . .

In the particular case under discussion, various ISKCON leaders have grasped for ways and means *to extricate the accused from CPO investigation* and *restriction.* This discussion is not about the contents of this case itself, but rather it is *about the dynamics amongst the leadership,* especially in regards to a culture of accountability in child protection issues.

Lacking legitimate, rational agency for accomplishing their goals, the leaders simply disregarded their own policies, and allowed, even facilitated, the accused to flagrantly violate the constraints of the CPO decision. Such transgressions were flaunted, as in articles on popular Vaishnava websites proclaiming the accused leading kirtana at ISKCON functions.

For years, the CPO Director has regularly spoken to several members of the GBC body about the apparent lack of integrity, responsibility and propriety about this case, and the likely damage to the credibility and image of Shrila Prabhupada's movement, what to speak of the possible risk to children and youth. Frequently this was met with assurances of remedial action, *with no action, or at least no results, actually ensuing.*

This case illustrates that, although individuals within the system may act at various times responsibly and prudently in child protection matters, *the system lacks a culture of accountability.* This lack, when combined with fears and needs inherent in the group dynamic, for acceptance, approval, and maintenance of position, prevents rational decision-making in regards to child protection. *The machinations described in this case are quite typical.* In many instances where ISKCON leadership has a vested interest in the confirmed or alleged child abuse perpetrator, *the intrigues, inconsistencies and paucity of reasonableness are considerably more involved and severe than in this case.*[y] (all emphasis added)

The very high profile case referred to here was ongoing after Dhira Govinda's resignation. It led to a uproar among the body of rank and file devotees, many of whom were frustrated in their efforts to get ISKCON leaders to fulfill their promised statements of support for abused children, and who protested vociferously

---

[y] Report on the Status of the ISKCON Child Protection Office June 30,2004

online. We shall return to this shortly below. What Dhira Govinda writes above is a mere sampling of what was going on. The full extent of it all cannot be grasped without extensive reading of the material recommended above.

The seriousness, rather the lack thereof, of the GBC's commitment to the children of ISKCON can also be judged by their financial support for the CPO. For approximately the first two years of its operation CPO annual funding was about US$160,000, most of which came from individual members of ISKCON leadership. For the next two years funding dropped to about US$120,000 per year, and for the next two years the funding was substantially below that.[z] Claiming that their budget simply cannot provide more, by 2008 the amount budgeted by the GBC plummeted to US$7,500.[aa]

A "Company Man" Becomes Director of the CPO

It is often seen that a person is appointed to a position because of their willingness to do the bidding of the establishment. They give themselves away by the nature of their irresponsible oversights, mistakes and failures that somehow always seem to benefit the establishment parties at the expense of the individual. Of course by this point in time (2004), corporate ISKCON had developed a power structure typical of all secular establishments. The leaders control the assets and wield the perks. *Prakrita bhaktas* who are bewildered by form and have a material conception of spiritual life often think that the institution itself represents God (in our case Shrila Prabhupada and/or Lord Krishna) and must therefore be protected at all costs. They also think that climbing the institutional ladder and acquiring titles and authority is a marker of

---

[z] See Dhira Govinda's report of 2004 (cit. 33); See also the Resolutions of the GBC Annual General Meeting http://gbc.iskcon.org/gbc-resolutions/; from 2013 on the budgeted amount was approximately US$10,000
[aa] See GBC Resolutions 2008.

spiritual progress. With such a mindset they are all too willing to do whatever pleases the authorities of the institution.

Understanding this, we can see a significant difference between the first and second directors of the CPO. The first being dedicated to helping the victims of abuse and preventing further abuse, as intended by the office. The second and later directors have apparently been more dedicated to working with the leadership to merely give the impression of child protection without actually doing so. There were several high-profile cases handled so badly during the second director's tenure that the very purpose of the office was brought into question. The last example above is one.

CPO Has No Teeth

In that case a senior male temple president was discovered to have had repeated sexual intercourse over the course of about a year with a girl, child really, of just 13 years of age. Supposedly the sex was "consensual," however by law a 13-year old is considered a child and incapable of giving consent. Each act was therefore one count of statutory rape, a felony of the first degree, aggravated sexual assault, punishable in a criminal court from no less than five years to life imprisonment, and a fine not to exceed 50,000 dollars. By secular legal standards this is criminal behavior because the act is considered to greatly harm the victim.

The CPO guidelines for child abuse state that the devotee that committed the abuse must apologize in writing to his victim and provide a minimum restitution of $3,000. The CPO report for this case states that he should not be allowed to give classes, lead kirtans or hold managerial positions, and if the individual failed to follow these guidelines they would be forever banned from ISKCON. However, although in this case the abuser *did not* follow the CPO guidelines, *did not* make a written apology, *did not* make restitution, and *did* indeed lead kirtans and give classes – even with GBC members present – yet he was not banned from ISKCON.

Concerned devotees made repeated inquiries to the director of the CPO but the director simply stonewalled without giving any reply. The previous Child Protection Office Director, Dhira Govinda Prabhu, also brought the failure of enforcing CPO adjudication to the GBC's attention with no result. Tellingly, this was not the only instance. Another concerns a Maharaja who had been allowed to continue managing a school and teaching despite the fact that he holds the record for the longest and oldest CPO case file of anyone. *Phalena parichyate.*

The perpetrator of the 13-year old rape filed an appeal and the appeals panel upheld the original CPO decision on this child abuser. Yet, inexplicably, with no additional evidence the appeal panel reduced the time that the abuser was required to follow the CPO's injunctions from five years to three years. One outraged devotee wrote of it: "Every justification the panel gave for reducing the sentence was false. It appeared that the conclusion was pre-determined, and they had to find some reasons to base it upon, and didn't really care about their validity."[21]

Numerous devotees protested vehemently online about the failure of the leadership to enforce their own standards, raising questions about why ISKCON's leadership allowed this person to abuse the CPO recommendations with impunity. Those questions were simply ignored by a leadership displaying an elitist mentality. One of the loudest of the voices was that of one Bhaktin Miriam. To give you a sense of her angst and frustration I'll quote at length her letter to the second CPO director:

So, prabhu, given these facts, which no one contests, how is it that [. . .] gets reduced terms on his injunctions? Why are we rewarding [. . .] for his defiance of the CPO's resolutions and thereby making a mockery of the whole process? In ISKCON culture we have a lot of trouble with facts, Prabhu. In fact, in ISKCON we have a lot of trouble with honest language. And honest language, along with a willingness to confront truth, is a necessary tool against obfuscation and propaganda. I am quite sure many devotees who are in denial about child abuse in ISKCON would rather all this was discussed in Sanskrit, for example.

Another instance of thought control, is our fixation on proper tone, etiquette, offenses, etc., etc., all tried and true Vaishnava tactics to discourage critical thinking and rational analysis by an authoritarian culture with no accountability standards and not accustomed to being challenged on any issue. Only, on this matter of child abuse, I will not play along.

Prabhu, you say that you provided as many facts as you could. How unfortunate that you feel that way. The questions that I asked and to which you did not reply were very legitimate. I think all devotees have a right to know these things. We have not only a right, but also a duty to ask how this could happen. You say that you cannot comment on the appeals panel's motivations, discussions and deliberations. But, Prabhu, I never asked you those things. What I asked is if the victim also had a lawyer. You didn't answer that. I also asked if the sexual abuser sent a letter of apology and gave restitution to the victim. You didn't answer that either. I also asked what the justification was (which has to be in the report) for reducing the sexual abuser's "sentence" after he had defied most of the injunctions and has not shown one iota of remorse or concern for the victim. You didn't answer that either. You never even sent me the appeals report as you promised.

Sorry for rubbing this in on you yet again, but Prabhu, please try to see things from my perspective and that of the victims of child abuse. I was asking legitimate questions and my letters were not responded to. I felt very, very frustrated being ignored like that. Prabhu, please try to see that things cannot be done behind closed doors. I can understand the issue of confidentiality. But my questions were not the sort of things that have to be kept secret. Devotees have the right to be kept informed about how such an important decision could be so flawed – even after a 9.5 million-dollar child abuse lawsuit. Transparency, Prabhu.

It's a fact [. . .] did not follow the injunctions on numerous occasions. You know this is true, and there is plenty of documentation about these facts because he never took the trouble to hide his defiance. I also found out that not long ago he gave a lecture in India. Prabhu, your assertion that there was only "one" instance when [. . .] did not follow the injunctions is simply not an accurate statement at best. At worst, its yet another misrepresentation of the facts that are readily available to anyone willing to make a few phone calls.

I ask, what is the use of the GBC writing a letter saying that the injunctions should be followed *if they themselves saw him breaking the injunctions with their own eyes and did nothing to stop it?* What is the use of the GBC letter if to this day they know fully well that [. . .] was breaking the injunctions stipulated by the CPO? That letter had the net effect of just one more public relations stunt because [. . .] recently broke the injunction yet again by leading kirtan and giving lectures in Gita Nagari. *And all this just begs another question: what exactly does the CPO do? What is its purpose if it cannot even enforce even the most elemental of injunctions and then even rewards the perpetrator for not following them?*[22]

Miriam later protested in an online editorial:

Someone has got to speak up concerning the persistent child abuse problem in ISKCON. This is not a thing of the past, it's happening right now. *Seeking help from ISKCON's upper management and leaders has not helped because they are the ones causing the problem by deliberately covering up for and protecting child abuse perpetrators whom they favor.*

According to CPO requirements if an abuser does not follow the injunctions, the only alternative is for them to be banned from ISKCON. But far from being banned this person's (and others) kirtans and lectures were even promoted. Such behavior on the part of ISKCON authorities, in just the two instances cited above, allows their pledge to prevent child abuse to be seen for what it is – a public relations smokescreen meant to give the impression that they care about the children, while their actions reveal that child abuse will continue to be allowed and even abetted.

The Children of Krishna Sue ISKCON

In 2000 a lawsuit was filed by about 40 abused and frustrated gurulukis who had finally had enough of the demonstrated neglect on the part of ISKCON's leadership. Desiring to force the leadership to acknowledge and realize the scope of the problem they retained Wendell Turley, the lawyer that successfully sued the Catholic Church over child abuse by church priests.

ISKCON's leadership stalled and did the best they could to avoid the suit, but when they realized that they were cornered they changed their tactic to invite as many of the abused children (now adults) to participate. They presented this as a good will gesture on their part – a symbol that they realized that all of the children should be compensated for their suffering in ISKCON's schools. So invited, some 350 former students of gurukula became additional plaintiffs.

The case never went to trial but was settled in 2006 for $9.5 million. In an effort to save the existing assets of the society the N.

American temples filed for Chapter 11 bankruptcy protection, and created a fund for the payout.

Although the GBC wanted to *appear* benevolent and concerned, the actual facts of the situation are otherwise, as told by Yadunandana Dasa, who was present while the "leadership" were brainstorming their response:

> You can quote me and I am willing to testify in court if this ever goes to trial again in any manner. I sat as the secretary (taking notes) for the North American GBC (2003) then involved in the Turley case. When they saw that there was no way to win the case and that ISKCON was going to have to pay all the claimants millions of dollars, an evil (possibly a crime) was pursued.
>
> Their tactic within that one meeting became a malignant "punishment" to the then original 150 claimants. Headed by Gopal Bhatta Das and the other members of the group called the SSPT. The topic came up of "what to do with these claimants who are attacking Prabhupada by taking this case to court."
>
> It was no longer than a few minutes before the entire room came to agreement that "the best way to get them back is to make sure that they each don't get any large amount of settlement by inviting as many possible claimants worldwide to join in the distribution of the funds." This was an idea spearheaded by Gopal Bhatta dasa, Badrinarayana dasa, and Ramabhadra Dasa.
>
> It was put to a vote and decided by the members of the SSPT/North American GBC. A campaign immediately was launched worldwide asking for anyone who had any kind of claim to come forward, and be supported by the ISKCON authorities. They set a stage for anyone within ISKCON or

affiliated in any manner to be able to sue ISKCON with the support of ISKCON. It was more than encouragement; it became a campaign. This they said, "will teach those original claimants a lesson and it will make us look like we are trying to be forthcoming and deliver justice."

The following are the members who conspired in these meetings on this issue: Gopal Bhatta das, Romapada Swami, Badrinarayana dasa, Jayadvaita Swami, Ramabhadra Dasa, Bir Krishna Swami, Rabindra Svaraup Dasa, Malati Dasi. There were three others whose names I will not mention because they were against this unethical, possibly illegal approach.

I resigned in protest. You have my written permission to share this viral. And I hereby swear on the all Holy Scriptures that this is precisely the way it went down.[23]

It seems incredibly strange to me that anyone could think of the lawsuit as an attack on Shrila Prabhupada instead of what it is – an attack on the defendants named in the lawsuit. Strange as it may seem however, displacement is a common psychological response – "it's not about us, it can't be us, therefore it's an attack on Shrila Prabhupada!" But it was *those named in the lawsuit, not Shrila Prabhupada*, who were directly or indirectly involved in the abuses that were going on for *decades*. Perhaps their displacement of the focus of the suit explains why even after agreeing to pay millions the abuses continued, and were not dealt with according to the CPO guidelines and GBC resolutions – which *if applied* are intended to have the effect of reducing, if not eliminating, the abuse. *Could it be that the guidelines are not followed because abuses are the intended and desired result?* Indeed, there are some (many?) that hold such an opinion. *Phalena parichyate.*

How did the children of ISKCON view the offer of settlement?

Many thought the offer was disingenuous – not an attempt to actually recognize the problem and actually help them heal the past. One kuli who has been very involved with the mishandling of child abuse cases by the CPO, Sanaka Rsi, wrote an opinion that is shared by many who have long ago become cynical about anything the leadership does: "ISKCON authorities as a whole did not really start to take child abuse seriously until it cost them money, and sadly many still don't. ISKCON paid because it was forced to, because it did not have a choice in the matter, and for no other reason. It is at best deceptive for ISKCON and/or its representatives to somehow try and take credit for this payout."[24]

Many of them took the money with indifference in order to, once and for all, close that chapter of their lives. They simply wanted their entire connection with ISKCON and Krishna to be over and done with, put behind them, so that they could move on with their lives. Most of them do not want to talk about their past experiences as it simply opens their psychological wounds yet again. The parent of an abused child told me that his son experiences twitching and other physical nervous reactions simply by hearing the word "Krishna" even though he is now well into middle age.

Abuse Continues Despite the Lawsuit

Although the Turley lawsuit was devastating to ISKCON, both in terms of image as well as financially, it seems that lessons were not learned. The CPO, under the leadership of director #2, who also was a member of the GBC and therefore had blatantly compromised interests, as well as the GBC body, continued to disregard their guidelines regarding the penalties for abusers, especially those who had friends on the GBC, similar to the cases cited above.

Sanaka Rsi was abused while in the Vrindavana gurukula and became involved as a representative of the other students when his abuser's case was investigated by the CPO. He had numerous frustrating dealings with both CPO directors 2 and 3, in an effort to get answers as to why CPO guidelines were not enforced and justice was not being served. He expressed his frustration in a number of articles posted on the Sampradaya Sun, a website that agrees to publish articles not allowed on the "ISKCON-friendly" (no bad news) dandavats.com. In 2009 he wrote:

> My experience with the CPO brings me to believe that the primary purpose of the people that control the CPO today is first and foremost the protection of what they perceive as being the best interest and welfare of the institution.

> The interests of the children and of the devotees are secondary and are often taken into consideration only if and when they do not conflict with the interests of the institution. What I see as the real problem is that ultimately to the CPO does not seem to value truth as much as practicality, convenience and good PR.[25]

Finally by 2015, the lies and lack of response by the CPO directors finally convinced him that to get performance he would have to publicly embarrass them, and ISKCON, by bringing wide attention to the hypocrisy and neglect with video. He then produced the *Cost of Silence* video, released the next year, in which he detailed many of the issues he had unsuccessfully been pressing for attention and resolution for years.[26]

The video showcases aspects of gurukula abuse, and CPO neglect, including:

- *Refusal by school authorities* to accept, and respond to, students' complaints of abuse
- *Blatant ignorance of school authorities* to know, or acknowledge, the many abuses taking place right under their nose
- *Demonstration of several instances how CPO sanctions*

against those convicted are continually ignored by those with friends in high places (GBC), and even sometimes encouraged by the Ministry of Education

- Efforts of the GBC *to apologize to, and placate those investigated for grievously abusing students, or allowing them to be abused while under their care.*
- *GBC allowance, even support, of convicted abusers to violate CPO sanctions*
- How persons with *no relevant experience* are placed in positions of authority in ISKCON schools
- Local GBC's *refusal* to oversee and correct careless school management regarding child protection
- Teachers being told to "mind their own business" when reporting the presence of known child molesters on school premises
- Teachers being asked to leave the school for reporting child abuse
- The efforts to keep known instances of abuse "within the family," rather than reporting them to legal authorities as GBC resolutions and CPO guidelines stipulate
- Known child molesters being allowed in the school environment because "they are very well connected and know a lot of very, very big people" (i.e., ISKCON donors)
- CPO investigators being removed from school premises while making an investigation, and the suspected abuser reinstated without further inquiry
- The fact that school Principals sometimes live very far away from the school

Even before producing the video Sanaka Rsi expressed his bewilderment regarding the behavior of ISKCON authorities: "It is baffling for me to see how time and again, the GBC just doesn't seem to want to acknowledge that if we do not care for, protect, nurture, guide and inspire the children of ISKCON, the very survival of ISKCON comes under great peril."[27]

Indeed. Many, many devotees are similarly baffled and frustrated by the recalcitrant leadership. However, we ourselves are not bewildered. Our conclusion, judging from the results of five decades, is that the ongoing abuse is exactly what is intended regardless of lip-service paid to the contrary – and for exactly the same reason stated by Saunaka Rsi – the threat to the survival of ISKCON. This must be the intended result because they are doing everything they can to bring that about.

There is a dark side to the leadership, at least on the part of some who have an inordinate amount of influence, who are using their authority to destroy the lives of many devotees as well as Shrila Prabhupada's mission. After almost fifty years of the same thing we can understand that this cannot going on by chance, or benign neglect.

CHAPTER EIGHT

How Far Would They Go?

The spiritual master is to be honored as much as the Supreme Lord, because he is the most confidential servitor of the Lord. This is acknowledged in all revealed scriptures and followed by all authorities. Therefore I offer my respectful obeisances unto the lotus feet of such a spiritual master, who is a bona fide representative of Sri Hari. By the mercy of the spiritual master one receives the benediction of Krishna. Without the grace of the spiritual master, one cannot make any spiritual advancement. Therefore, I should always remember and praise the spiritual master. At least three times a day I should offer my respectful obeisances unto the lotus feet of my spiritual master.

Shrila Prabhupada instructed his disciples to sing these words every morning. We do so in Sanskrit - *saksad-dharitvena samasta-sastrair* – and in many temples the devotees also recite the translation. The principles expressed in the verses of Sri Sri Guruvastaka quickly become well-known to every devotee, and are accepted as the key to progress in spiritual life. That being the case, how could any devotee even think of attempting to kill the *Acharya*, what to

305

speak of carrying it out? The thought is absurd. For this reason many devotees are of the opinion that the mere thought that Shrila Prabhupada was poisoned is ludicrous, and the proponents of such ideas can only be great offenders.

Absurd as the notion of poisoning appears, a great deal of evidence, initially surfacing in 1997, suggests that it did happen, sufficient to convince any person of discrimination who bothers to seriously investigate. When the historical evidence is combined with the reality that the Kamsas and Putanas of this world do not hesitate to carry out such acts, the possibility becomes even more real. When that is combined with an acceptance that the contest between the *asura*s and devas has continued throughout history, and continues to this very day, the possibility becomes even more real. Combining that with Shrila Prabhupada's statements that demonic *rakshasas* currently control this world, it becomes easier yet to accept that this could have happened. And if you add to that, the fact that Shrila Prabhupada said that they might try to kill him, and the fact that Shrila Prabhupada himself said that he was being poisoned, we must finally come face-to-face with a reality too terrible to contemplate.

Acknowledging this truth forces us to deal with the tragedy and horror that immediately spring to mind, as we quickly begin to connect the dots of ISKCON's sad history. Well, if that happened, then that explains . . . and then this makes sense. . . and that must be why. . . etc., etc.

Doubts automatically arise that cannot be ignored: Krishna would not allow His pure devotee to be poisoned! He promises that His devotee is never vanquished! Surely Shrila Prabhupada would have known what was going on and stopped it. All he would have to do was tell Brahmananda. How could those who were closest to Shrila Prabhupada do such a thing? Everyone could see the devotion that was displayed by those in his inner circle, etc., etc., etc.

The doubts which spring to mind can be resolved by evidence and facts. The actual evidence is there – if we can summon the courage to look at it. Can we accept the evidence of background whispers? Shrila Prabhupada's own statements that he was poisoned? Can we accept the evidence of Shrila Prabhupada's hair analysis showing poison had been in his body for an extensive period of time, matching his physical symptoms and his debilitating health? Will we read about, and recognize, the extensive efforts made to try to control Shrila Prabhupada and prevent him from making Govardhana parikrama, and the bizarre behavior of those present when Shrila Prabhupada said he was poisoned? Have we bothered ourselves to read the evidence presented in his room conversations? Or do we rely on sentiment, ignoring the evidence in the belief that such a horrific thing could never occur, and something we should not even contemplate? Cognitive dissonance, refusal to accept a truth that overturns ones firmly held beliefs, is a well-known feature of human psychology. Many simply cannot accept the idea that Shrila Prabhupada was poisoned, regardless of the great amount of evidence to the contrary. The very thought is too threatening to their tightly held concepts of reality.

However, those who accept the evidence as real are also forced to accept that members of Shrila Prabhupada's inner circle were infiltrators – agents of Kali, there to put an end to Shrila Prabhupada and his spiritual movement, or "useful saints" who cannot see, or cannot begin to suspect, what is taking place. Acceptance of this fact allows us to then make much more sense of ISKCON's dismal history both before and after Shrila Prabhupada's departure. All of the dots then begin to connect and a clear picture emerges.

If Shrila Prabhupada had been poisoned all of this history begins to make sense in a way it never had before. And Krishna's revealing it after years of crushing disappointments *by the very persons who were supposed to be leading and protecting the society*, finally allows us to recognize the unmistakable truth that our "leaders" are in fact agents of Kali. As he desired, Shrila Prabhupada died on the battlefield, and by doing so he has informed us that *the enemy is within our own camp.*

All of this is somewhat easier to comprehend for those who joined Shrila Prabhupada's movement in the 60s, 70s and early 80s, especially in Australia, Western Europe and the United States, because they have personally witnessed how the once wonderful and powerful ISKCON was reduced to a mere shadow of its former glory. Those who had experienced actual transcendence and the spiritual energy flowing through them, also experienced how the mercy has gradually dwindled to nothing. Those who came to Krishna Consciousness in the 90s and beyond, especially in India and the former Soviet Union, who do not have the benefit of experience of the early history, are more inclined to accept the GBC cover story because it preserves the integrity of the ISKCON that they know. One of the greatest problems for any devotee to deal with is to admit that the ISKCON they thought portrayed what they read in Shrila Prabhupada's books, the one they have so completely given their heart to, does not, in fact, serve Shrila Prabhupada's instructions.

There is an ongoing battle between the forces of light and darkness in the world today. It is not merely some theoretical contest taking place only in the pages of the Bhagavatam, but is eternally played out in the material realm we live in. It is very much a part of our reality, right here and now, and although it may take place in ways that are not immediately apparent, it is *always* going on.

An important part of strategy in war is to take out the leader of the opposing army, leaving the foot soldiers bewildered and confused. This was done with Jesus and James, and however painful it is to admit, it was also done with Shrila Prabhupada. Those who were closest to him maliciously poisoned him over an extended period of time with the intention of killing him, endeavoring to make it look like the ravages of old age and inexplicable disease.

I want to state unequivocally that I do not accept that Shrila Prabhupada's was killed by poison. Life and death are controlled by Krishna, especially in the case of His pure devotee. Reading Shrila Prabhupada's health history it is observed that at times Shrila Prabhupada appeared quite ill and would then have an immediate and almost miraculous turn-around and his health would improve. Perhaps by Krishna's grace the effects of poison were removed, as was the case with Prahlad Maharaja. Nonetheless, the poisoners were convinced they could remove him with their poisons, and acted in that way. Shrila Prabhupada said that Krishna left it up to him whether he would stay in this world or not. It is clear to me that Shrila Prabhupada decided to leave when, after unequivocally stating that he was being poisoned on November 10, 1977, everything continued as before without any change. Under the circumstances, if Krishna has given him the choice, why would he stay?

The poisoning of Shrila Prabhupada is not some work of fiction, it is not some fairy tale cooked up by a handful of malcontents, or the creation of "ritvik envy." Thousands of devotees accept as fact that Shrila Prabhupada was poisoned, most of them leaving the institution controlled by a GBC who, rather than earnestly seeking the truth to what can only be the most important event in ISKCON's history, rubberstamped a cover-up crafted by none other than a sishya disciple of the main suspect.

The GBC Decree

In 2017 the smoking gun was revealed: analysis of hair samples delivered by *the GBC* to forensic labs showing an astounding level of cadmium – *225 times the amount normally found in hair!* Cadmium is a heavy metal, and an extremely toxic substance. Moreover, the hair tests confirm that poison had been administered over an extended period of time – since Shrila Prabhupada began suffering unexplained health problems.

Shortly after Nityananda Dasa released irrefutable, conclusive, forensic analysis with the cadmium findings, the GBC issued an intimidating letter totally ignoring the evidence, warning that merely looking at it would damage one's spiritual life. Note the unnerving adjectives intended to frighten the reader:

> The new accusations raise *pseudo-scientific* arguments that actual science rejects. Therefore, to protect innocent devotees from *devastating* offenses, the GBC is preparing a detailed response to the latest *accusations*, which are themselves *the actual poison* in this case.

> The GBC requests ISKCON devotees to focus their attention on serving Prabhupada's mission and to avoid hearing these *monstrous* accusations, until the GBC presents a response to the latest *poisonous theories*. (emphasis added)

As of this date, *twenty-three months later*, they have yet to deliver their response. If the results are so pseudo-scientific why does it take so long to write a rebuttal?

This letter was signed by *every* GBC member, clearly demonstrating that at least 9 of them (about one-fourth of the GBC body) to be *devoid of integrity*. I write that because I asked them face-to-face whether they did *anything at all* to investigate the allegations and NOT ONE OF THEM DID *ANYTHING* TO INVESTIGATE THESE ALLEGATIONS! There could not be a greater dereliction of duty, since nothing could be more significant than the poisoning of their spiritual master! Yet they wouldn't bother to lift a finger to investigate the matter on the simple presumption that such a thing is impossible. Such irresponsibility is beyond comprehension.

This reflects the behavior of the GBC quoted earlier from Ramesvara Dasa: "No one back then did their job or acted with full responsibility for what they were endorsing."

Thus what we have is a decree from the GBC:

HEAR YE! HEAR YE!

WE DECLARE THAT Shrila PRABHUPADA WAS NEVER POISONED!

Nonsense.

As if, like the Roman Popes, they can just decree the "truth" and everyone is to accept it without question. "Don't look at these 'monstrous accusations' or *you will lose your soul!*" Mere Dogma. A bogeyman meant to scare the neophytes. Actually, anyone that bothers to investigate, to even the slightest degree, they cannot help but come to the conclusion that Shrila Prabhupada was indeed poisoned, the primary evidence being that he said so himself! The fact that the GBC is covering it up rather than making a real investigation, indicates that they themselves are guilty, or are protecting the guilty!

Why do the GBC ignore the direct evidence as well as the great amount of anecdotal evidence? Because with one notable exception, the perpetrators of this horrendous crime are still at the helm of the institution, and they don't want anybody to realize the fact. So don't ask any questions! It is forbidden!

---

[a] This group was founded by Naveen Krishna Dasa after he resigned his GBC post due to the neglectful manner in which the GBC pursued the allegations of Shrila Prabhupada being poisoned. The Nov. 14th Commission included ten devotees besides Naveen Krishna.

Truthful Investigations

Doing what the entire GBC body could not do, Nityananda Dasa made a very thorough investigation, as did the members of the November 14th Commission,[a] and the evidence was collected and presented in several books: *Someone has Poisoned Me, Judge for Yourself,* and *Kill Guru, Become Guru.* As distasteful as it is, any person that wants to know the truth of the matter for themselves must read these books. Don't throw away your discrimination based on the GBC's red herring of ritvikism, and threats of maha-aparadha. Those are merely their efforts to discredit the truth.

Unfortunately, due to cognitive dissonance, or perhaps simply blindly following their mis-leaders, many ISKCON devotees willfully ignore the facts. For those with such weakness of heart we remind them of the consequences of blind following:

> Leaders who have fallen into ignorance and who mislead people by directing them to the path of destruction are, in effect, boarding a stone boat, and so too are those who blindly follow them. A stone boat would be unable to float and would sink in the water with its passengers. *Similarly, those who mislead people go to hell, and their followers go with them.* SB 6.7.14

While all of the GBC may not be guilty, their complicity supports the *kali-chelas* misdirecting the society. Sadly, naïve GBC members have been manipulated to sign their names to a document based on nothing more than sentiment. They think they are defending ISKCON, but in fact are defending the *kali-chelas* destroying the ISKCON they are pledged to protect! Wake Up!

In this chapter I put forward a sampling of the evidence demonstrating that Shrila Prabhupada's closest men poisoned him with the intention to kill him. There is evidence that they had help from the Kamsas who will do anything to maintain their control of this world. Remember Shrila Bhaktisiddhanta's alarm:

King Kamsa is ever on the lookout for the appearance of the Truth for the purpose of suppressing Him before He has time to develop. It is necessary to put down the transcendental heresy the instant it appears.

Shrila Prabhupada's Own Statements are the Strongest Proof

Shrila Prabhupada's own statements provide the most significant evidence of this fact. Will the sincere followers who are willing to accept *anything* Shrila Prabhupada said or wrote as the Absolute Truth, *also accept the three times he said he was poisoned?*

I will not duplicate the entire conversation here. It can be read in the books cited that thoroughly investigate the issue. The transcripts of room conversations are available from the Bhaktivedanta Archives. Get it while it is available, for it will likely disappear sometime in the future. However, a sampling provides irrefutable evidence that Shrila Prabhupada, *and others in his presence*, absolutely understood that he was being maliciously poisoned. *The big question is: why was it business as usual after that?*

Shrila Prabhupada had asked the Kaviraj to invite a mutual acquaintance, Balarama Misra, to visit him. During his visit on November 9th Shrila Prabhupada put aside all preliminary niceties that usually accompany seeing an old friend after a long time. Immediately he disclosed this dark information to an outsider – not his inner circle – indicating that perhaps he was not sure who he could trust:

SP: (Bengali) Someone says that I have been poisoned... it's possible.

Balarama Misra: Hmm?

Kaviraja: (Hindi) What are you saying?

SP: (Hindi) Someone says that, somebody has given me

poison.

Kaviraja: Kisko? / To whom?

SP: Mujhko. / To me.

Kaviraja: (Hindi) This thing Maharaja. You know how you said today that someone said somebody gave you poison? Did you get some indication or feeling about this, or what?

SP: (Hindi) No. Someone said that, when given poison, this happens... Maybe it's written in some book.

Kaviraja: (Hindi) That happens from some foods. Raw mercury makes it happen. And there are other things with which it can happen. I mean, who would do that to you? My understanding is that anyone who thinks about doing this to a saint is a *rakshasa*.

Kaviraja: (Hindi) Who is saying?

SP: (Hindi) All these friends.[b]

We have heard that the gossip in Vrindavana at that time was Shrila Prabhupada's being poisoned, and it is possible that his friend Krishna Dasa, who visited earlier, is the person referred to as "all these friends." The subject came up again the very next day on November 10th:

Bhavananda: Prabhupada was complaining of mental distress this morning

Bhakti-caru: Shrila Prabhupada?

Prabhupada: Hm?

Bhakti-caru: (Bengali) ...mental distress?

---

[b] My Bengali-speaking friends listening to this conversation say that Shrila Prabhupada is unmistakably saying that he is being poisoned.

Prabhupada: Hm, hm.

Kaviraja: (Hindi)

Prabhupada: (Hindi -- mentions word "poison")

Kaviraja: (Hindi)

Devotee: Someone gave him poison here.

Kaviraja: (Hindi long explanation)

Tamala Krishna: Prabhupada was thinking that someone had poisoned him.

Adri-dharana: Yes.

Tamala Krishna: That was the mental distress?

Adri-dharana: Yes.

Kaviraja: (Hindi)

Tamala Krishna: What did Kaviraja just say?

Bhakti-caru: He said that when Shrila Prabhupada was saying that, there must be some truth behind it.

Kaviraj: Caru Swami…

Bhakticharu: Yes.

Kaviraj: … (Hindi) Listen, this is the understanding – that some demon has given (poison). ..some demon has given (poison). This can happen. It's not impossible.

In these conversations Shrila Prabhupada states multiple times that he was poisoned, and this is repeated by the others present. *Yet where is the cry of alarm?!* Can you imagine if you were there and you heard Shrila Prabhupada saying that he was being poisoned? Immediately, you would have taken action and changed everything about Shrila Prabhupada's care to protect him, yet *nothing changed* in terms of persons surrounding Shrila Prabhupada, the way his food was prepared, etc. NOTHING WAS CHANGED DESPITE Shrila PRABHUPADA SAYING HE WAS BEING POISONED! This is incomprehensible, unless of course he was deliberately being poisoned. Inexplicably and shockingly, instead of finding the possible perpetrator(s) the focus of the conversation shifts from Shrila Prabhupada being poisoned to Shrila Bhaktisiddhanta having been poisoned. What?!

Read the transcripts of the room conversations in Shrila Prabhupada's last days. This simple act will clearly reveal that something very strange was taking place. Indeed. The poisoning of the Lord's pure devotee. Let's not be lethargic or lazy. This is no ordinary person – it is our spiritual master and *Acharya*! Read the transcripts!

Whispers of the Conspirators

Isha Dasa had been Satsvarupa Maharaj's secretary in Dallas in late 1977. When Satsvarupa Maharaj returned from Vrindavana just after Shrila Prabhupada's departure, Isha was given 20 tapes with instructions to make 10 sets of copies to send to various ISKCON leaders before forwarding the original tapes to the BBT Archives in Los Angeles. He did this, and made an extra set for himself. After 20 years of being in storage he dug them out and made copies, giving one set to Mahabuddhi as a birthday present.

Mahabuddhi, former temple president, and founder of the Florida Vedic College, listened to the tapes with his son:

We listened to Shrila Prabhupada's tape of November 10-11. When I was out of the room, my son Mahasimha heard a whisper, so he called me back and we played this whisper again. We enhanced it and listened to it, and it really sounded strange. We became a little bit shocked, because we thought we had heard something like: DID YOU PUT POISON IN

THE MILK?, and the more we heard it, the more we listened to it, about 100 times that night, the more it sounded that way.

Mahabuddhi alerted his friend Isha and together they continued to listen, finding yet *more* alarming whispers. On November 30, 1997 Isha posted the audio files of whispers he had found on those tapes on the Vaishnava News Network (VNN) website:

1. "Put poison in the milk"
2. "poison ishvarya rasa…get ready to go"
3. "the poison's going down, the poison's going down"
4. "put poison in different containers"

The shocking news traveled the entire globe in an instant. Continuing to listen to the tape recordings of Shrila Prabhupada's final days, more whispers were found and posted on VNN on December 5th:

1. As Shrila Prabhupada is drinking milk the whisper: *"Push real hard, it's going down him..(giggle) the poison's going down."*
2. After Jayapataka says, "follow the same treatment," a whisper: *"Is the poison in the milk? Followed by a confirming "Um hum," followed by (imagine!) a snickered giggle.*
3. After Shrila Prabhupada says, "Daytime we expose...," we hear the whisper, *"Do it now."* Then Shrila Prabhupada drinks something.
4. The whispers, *"will you serve Shrila Prabhupada poison?"* then several negative responses followed by *"Nette, nette."*
5. After Jayapataka says, "Should there be kirtana?" we hear a Bengali phrase, and then the whisper "Poison ishvarya rasa." Srila Prabhupada says weakly and very surprised, "Me?", then we hear, "Take it easy, get ready to go," then a few seconds later, "The poison's in you Srila Prabhupada." Then, "He's going under... He's going under." Then Hansadutta's kirtan began.

6. On side A of the "poison tape," November 11, 1977, the following whispers were found: *"Going down" "Did it hurt?" "He's gonna die" "Listen, he's saying…. Going to die" "Yes, heart attack time"*

Without revealing any of the details about the tapes Mahabuddhi sent them to a professional forensic analyst for examination. After a week, Jack Mitchell, the sound engineer, called Mahabuddhi and advised that he should be arranging for legal counsel as it appeared that what he was analyzing was a poison conspiracy. Jack Mitchell had another acoustic engineer, Helen McCaffrey, independently analyze the tapes. She confirmed his findings. Copies of the documents stating their findings can be found in Nityananda's book, and on our website.[1]

Another analyst, Mr. Tom Owen of OWL Investigations, Inc. was also consulted. After examining the tapes he gave this opinion: "Based on my training and experience, the word poison is clearly audible and intelligible in several instances." And this conclusion: "There is conversation about poison and the use of it. In my opinion there is certainly a basis for further investigation. . . A forensic toxicologist and homicide investigator should be consulted."

Manufactured Controversy?

Controversy surrounded the whispers because, although so many devotees *could* hear the whispers, ISKCON's leadership *unanimously* claimed they *could not*. Three GBC members making their own analysis declared that the word "poison" was never spoken. Yet one honest GBC member, Naveen Krishna, went to a local sound studio and had the recordings cleaned up to make them as high-quality as possible. He then brought dozens of devotees to the studio to listen to the enhanced recordings. After listening carefully a few times most agreed about what is being said, and they were left with no doubt that *Shrila Prabhupada was being poisoned by his closest "disciples."*

What became known as the "poison" tape was analyzed by *five* audio forensic laboratories, and their impartial analysis unanimously confirmed that the word 'poison' was repeatedly spoken. However, ISKCON authorities content to hear what they wanted to hear, based on their own unprofessional and subjective analysis, felt no need for independent, impartial professional analysis – *rejecting the results of the five analyses already performed.* That lack of action, in and of itself, makes their motivations suspect. The rest of their so-called investigation and analysis is just as shoddy. When their official investigator, Balavanta Prabhu, asked for $6,000 to analyze Shrila Prabhupada's hair clippings, the GBC considered the sum too great, and would not advance the money! Their "investigations" were efforts to avoid the truth, rather than discover it.[2]

A very detailed history of the tapes, their analysis, and the results, are given in Nityananda's book "Kill Guru Become Guru." [3] Anyone who wants the full facts must read it. The tapes and whispers can be found on the DivineOrDemoniac.com website and elsewhere online as of 2019, and I encourage everyone to listen to them and draw their own conclusions.[4]

Damage Control

When the whispers came to light ISKCON leadership tried to dismiss them with ridicule as an absurd waste of time that didn't merit any response other than denial. However, behind the scenes Tamal Krishna Goswami was busy with his friends doing everything they could to belittle the idea. Tamal's leaked emails tell of a well-orchestrated covert propaganda campaign to squash any concerns about the "poison issue."

Why was he doing this when *he was personally present and heard*

Shrila Prabhupada saying that he was being poisoned? Further, if the allegations of Shrila Prabhupada being poisoned and the whispers were such a non-issue, then why undertake such extensive efforts behind the scenes to discredit the matter? His actions demonstrate the duplicity of one who was, and is, the main suspect, as he strictly controlled everything surrounding Shrila Prabhupada in his last year.[c] Here are some segments of Tamal's emails from various dates:[5]

> Tamal Krishna: I am of the opinion that we would benefit by two websites. . . Chakra's mission statement is becoming clarified. Its mood is feisty and confident and clearly partisan. But I would recommend a second website more news oriented and apparently neutral [this is the origin of the Dandavats. com website], something like VNN. Is this too ambitious a project? . . . [VNN was simply publishing the news regardless of content. In other words, the truth.]

> Tamal Krishna: There is urgent need for an evaluation of Bhagavat's statement and its bearing on seeing Prabhupada as a martyr. Who will do it? I also feel that someone must write a comment on Bhagavat's statement where he indicates that he is not strictly following. In other words, what is the real proof of loving Prabhupada? Persons who have been strictly following are accused of hating Prabhupada, poisoning His Divine Grace, and subverting his movement by those who don't strictly follow but who truly love him. Does it sound right? Who will write it? . . . [efforts to discredit anyone who

---

[c] Bhaktisiddhanta das was posted as a security guard by Shrila Prabhupada's garden door, and remembers that nothing happened without the sanction of Tamal: *"A security cordon was set up by Tamal around Shrila Prabhupada. As security men we were instructed not to let anyone in without Tamal's OK first."*

accepts the allegations as true]

Vipramukhya Swami: We need to prioritize our work of attack. We also need to increase our team of writers. I also would appreciate help to do some of the work behind the scenes.[6]

Tamal Krishna: . . .I don't think that this counterattack is going to get us very far. I appreciate that this may have to be done by some, to win the "war of words," but I doubt that I should be one of those who do it. . . Before the appearance of CHAKRA, *our side* [!?] was not scoring very well at all. . . What we really need is to convince the 'middle,' the vast number of uncommitted. If we cannot convince the 'middle' then we are lost.

Having earlier heard Shrila Prabhupada saying he was poisoned as the cause of his mental distress, why he is now asking others to propagate the "Not That I am Poisoned" idea? The above texts are not those of one searching for truth, but a guilty party endeavoring to evade the truth.

Shrila Prabhupada's Startling Comments

In addition to his statement of being poisoned, there are other statements made by Shrila Prabhupada, which are inconceivable under normal circumstances, indicating suspicion that his disciples were trying to kill him! For example, in a room conversation October 22, 1977 Shrila Prabhupada makes the following statement:

Prabhupada: Don't move me to hospital. *Better kill me here.*
Swarupa Damodar: We won't Shrila Prabhupada
Bhavananda: Never
Prabhupada: But if you are disgusted, that is another thing.[7]

And on November 3, 1977 he makes another shocking statement:

> This is my only request, that at the last stage *don't torture me and put me to death.*[8]

About a week later Shrila Prabhupada requested to go on parikrama around Govardhana Hill, insisting that if he did so his health would improve. Rather than follow the spiritual master's order without hesitation, Tamal Krishna, Bhavananda, Bhakti Caru, and other suspects in his poisoning strenuously opposed him, feigning that the journey would be too arduous and would kill him. Reading the transcript of that November 10th room conversation it is unmistakable that they were trying to manipulate him and keep him in his rooms. Shrila Prabhupada then stated in no uncertain terms why he wanted to go:

> Jagadisa: Shrila Prabhupada, can you tell us why you want to go on the parikrama?
>
> Tamala Krishna: This seems like suicide, Shrila Prabhupada, this program. It seems to some of us like it's suicidal.
>
> Prabhupada: And *this is also suicidal.*
>
> Tamala Krishna: Hm. Prabhupada said, "And this is also suicide." Now you have to choose which suicide.
>
> Prabhupada: *Ravana will kill and Rama will kill. Better to be killed by Rama.* Eh? That Marica – if he does not go to mislead Sita, he'll be killed by Ravana; and if he goes he'll be killed by Rama, that is better.

Could it be clearer than that? Shrila Prabhupada is unequivocally stating that a Ravana (demon) was killing him. Yet, despite this revelation nobody was startled, and his request was denied. Such behavior is completely out of character for innocents, and indicates that he was, in fact, surrounded by Ravanas.

These statements are inconceivable from anyone surrounded by loving friends and well-wishers. They directly and unmistakably indicate that he knew his disciples were killing him. Shrila Prabhupada made statements over the years that the demonic forces of this world might try to kill him, and excepting that the deed was being carried out by his own "disciples" this would not surprise him:

> So as Krishna was attempted to be killed, [and] eight years before His birth the mother was to be attempted to be killed. So there may be attempt like that. And Lord Jesus Christ was killed. *So they may kill me also.* Conversation Honolulu 5March76

> As soon as you speak of God, this opposition will come. Jesus Christ was crucified. They are so kind they have not yet crucified me or [by!] my men. But *you have to expect all these things.* Conversation Bombay 9Jan77

Shrila Prabhupada Requested What?!

Incredulously, within days of Shrila Prabhupada's Samadhi, Satsvarupa Goswami recorded Tamal Krishna telling him that Shrila Prabhupada asked to be given some "medicine" to cause him to "disappear"!

> Tamal: "A number of times he (Shrila Prabhupada) would say: 'Can you give me medicine. Please give me medicine that will allow me to disappear now. . .' And other times: 'I want most now to disappear. . . I want to die peacefully . . . let me die peacefully.'

> "Now on one hand we could take it and give him that medicine or let him stop eating and fast until death, we could have done that. And yet it seemed. . . of course we could not. . . do that out of love for him and he seemed to respond beautifully to

that, our loving requests that he would not leave, that he, he stay with us longer."[9]

You can listen to the recording and hear Tamal say this on our website DivineOrDemoniac.com. Our opinion is that Tamal said this is an excuse to fall back on, or a possible insurance policy, should the truth ever come to light.

Regardless of what Tamal has said, this was no mercy killing. Analysis of Shrila Prabhupada's hair cuttings, taken over an extended period of time, prove that the poisoning was going on for more than six months, and his health symptoms indicate that it was ongoing for more than a year.

Physical Symptoms Tell the Truth

Dr. Mehta, a practicing Ayurvedic physician since 1948, was shown several photographs of Shrila Prabhupada during His last days, and he also observed the video documentary of Shrila Prabhupada's last months entitled "The Final Lesson." His summary comments are:

> The expression and symptoms of the face, the eyes and the manner of speaking indicate to me that Shrila Prabhupada was poisoned, most probably by arsenic or mercury. He Himself said that He was poisoned, confirmed by dullness of the face and how the natural color of the body is gone. This is very hard for the average person to understand; only the experienced eye can tell.

The symptoms of arsenic poisoning are numerous but include many of the health problems plaguing Shrila Prabhupada for the last year of his time with us. Patients exposed to arsenic report progressive weakness, anorexia and nausea, and Shrila Prabhupada had nausea and gastro-intestinal problems from June 1976 onward. Dark glasses and swollen hands are clearly seen in the below photo of Shrila Prabhupada, taken in 1977. The swelling of extremities, a condition known as edema or dropsy, is one of the symptoms of arsenic poisoning. Likewise arsenic causes the eyes to become very sensitive to light. Hence Shrila Prabhupada wearing dark glasses in this picture, something that he was never previously known to do.

Nityananda's research into possible mercury and arsenic poisoning of Shrila Prabhupada is extensive. Over more than 150 pages of "Someone Has Poisoned Me" he examines Shrila Prabhupada's health history through the entire year of 1977, comparing his

Figure 7 Shrila Prabhupada exhibits symptoms of arsenic poisoning: swollen hands and light sensitive eyes

symptoms with those of several cases of known arsenic poisoning. Almost all of Shrila Prabhupada's health problems are found in these comparative health histories, allowing him to conclude: "All these symptoms of arsenic poisoning very closely resemble the physical symptoms Shrila Prabhupada exhibited during His 1977 'illness.'"

Hair Analysis Provides Proof Positive

The body excretes wastes through various means, one of which is the hair, so hair analysis is one method of looking into the health history of the body. Shrila Prabhupada's hair was regularly cut and many devotees had precious keepsakes of his hair. Nityananda and others endeavored to obtain his hair samples for analysis.

One method of hair analysis is "neutron activation," and it provides a full reading of *all* elements present using only a very small sample which is left intact afterwards.

Balavanta Prabhu, the devotee deputed by the GBC to make the official investigation, obtained hair from clippers that only Shrila Prabhupada used. ***Not understanding the full capability of the testing equipment, he had the first of the samples tested only for arsenic by Dr. J. Stephen Morris*** at the Nuclear Analysis Program, University of Missouri. His equipment produces the very best accuracy with the smallest of samples. Upon analysis Dr. Morris reported:

> The arsenic concentration found was 2.6 micrograms arsenic per gram of hair (or 2.6 parts per million i.e. 2.6 ppm). **The concentration is approximately 20 times higher than what I would consider a normal average for unexposed individuals living in the United States.**

The normal range of arsenic in the general public is from less than 0.05 parts of arsenic per million up to perhaps 0.1 to 0.2 parts per million, depending on exposure to environmental contaminants. Farmers and others regularly working with pesticides might temporarily attain as much as 1.0ppm. However, the level of 2.6ppm is actually from 13 to 50 times what is normally expected, Dr. Morris giving a more conservative estimate. This extremely

Sample ID	Mass (g)	Analysis start date	As (PPM) [95% CI]	Cd (PPM) [95% CI]	Sb (PPM) [95% CI]	Hg (PPM) [95% CI]
"D"	0.00072	March 4, 2002	0.640 [0.064]	19.9 [2.0]	0.661 [0.066]	3.72 [0.56]
"A"	0.00064	April 15, 2002	0.200 [0.020]	12.4 [1.2]	0.186 [0.019]	5.16 [0.77]
"J" (77-3)	0.00085	May 15, 2002	0.082 [0.021]	<2.3	0.080 [0.020]	1.62 [0.41]
"ND-2"	0.00310	June 11, 2002	0.141 [0.021]	0.206 [0.052]	0.013 [0.007]	1.85 [0.46]
"M"	0.00077	November 6, 2002	0.357 [0.036]	<1.45 [0.22]	0.100 [0.010]	5.37 [0.81]
Q-2*	0.00012	July 19, 2005	0.85 [0.49]	14.9 [3.8]	not measured	

*Sample Q-2 was recovered from electric hair clippers and included a few clippings approximately 2 mm in length with a combined mass of 0.00012 grams.

Figure 8: Dr. Morris' results from testing Shrila Prabhupada's hair

high level cannot be accounted for by any accidental means. It must have occurred through either accidental or intentional ingestion.

Five samples of Shrila Prabhupada's hair were tested by this method, the one obtained by Balavanta Prabhu, two provided by the GBC, and the other two obtained by Nityananda Dasa, who arranged for all four of the other tests. The lengthy history of how these samples were obtained can be read in Nityanada's book, which I will not duplicate here, but they were undoubtedly Shrila Prabhupada's hair.

At Dr. Morris' suggestion the other four tests analyzed for the elements cadmium, antimony, arsenic and mercury. The test results summary are found on the previous page and our website.

Dr. Morris reported "Checking some of the other elemental contents in sample D, I checked the calculations several times to make very sure, there is a most unusual and strikingly high amount of cadmium… It has 23.6 parts per million of cadmium." He later double checked the results to make sure they were accurate and not the result of contamination, and adjusted the result to 19.9.

The average normal levels of hair cadmium in human society is about *0.065 ppm*. Thus samples D, A, and Q-2 were 306, 190, and 230 times over normal cadmium levels.

The average of A, D, and Q-2 is 15.73 ppm, or 242 times normal levels, and, based on the dates the hair was cut, is roughly the hair cadmium level throughout the last 6 to 12 months of Shrila Prabhupada's physical presence. This entire report can be viewed on our website www.DivineOrDemoniac.com.

When asked what such high levels of cadmium would mean, Dr. Morris explained in detail that cadmium is *an extremely toxic element in the same family with arsenic, mercury, lead and thallium.* Cadmium's effects are most well understood by its causing kidney disease, which appeared to be Shrila Prabhupada's primary health problem.

Nityananda did a lot of work to get expert opinions regarding this level of cadmium in a person's hair – gathering nine expert opinions, among them:

1. Dr. Anil Aggarwal specializing in Forensic Toxicology. A Professor of Forensic Medicine: *"Cadmium 20 ppm in hair is prima facie evidence of poisoning with malicious intent."*

2. Dr. Dipankar Chakraborti, Director of Environmental

Studies, Jadavpur University, India. Asked what he thought would be the significance of a person having a hair level of 20 ppm cadmium. His reply was: *"He will be finished. He can't survive more than three, four days."*

3. Analytical Research Labs president Kenneth P. Eck, whose lab performs 35,000 hair analysis tests annually, rarely sees cadmium levels over 1 ppm, with the usual range 0.02 – 0.10 ppm. *Mr. Eck remarked that 19.9 ppm was "off the chart."*

4. Dr. Page Hudson, Jr., M.D. A forensic pathologist: *"One ppm is considered a rather hefty load of cadmium. About 20 ppm is distinctly abnormal. Wasting, kidney disease, and the spillage of sugar are certainly consistent with cadmium toxicity, but unfortunately are common with many other conditions and diseases* [thus making it difficult to detect and suspect]*."*

Further asked who would be knowledgeable about cadmium as a poison, Dr. Morris replied: *"Someone with a very good knowledge of chemistry and poisons."* This rules out amateurs who generally use ant or rat poison. This likely also rules out those in Shrila Prabhupada's immediate circle who would not likely be knowledgeable about such things. It does suggest however, the participation of, or collaboration with, professional assassins. Immediately the mysterious Chandra Swami [d] comes to mind, along with Adi Keshava and his father's CIA connections. These findings further fit well with our already expressed suspicion that the powers-that-be

---

[d] This person is said to have connections with intelligence agencies and to have been involved with the assassination of Indira Ghandi. He traveled several times to New York to see Adi Kesava Swami for some reason, and also supplied the makharadhvaja 'medicine' for Shrila Prabhupada at no charge. After taking it only once Shrila Prabhupada said that it was 'poison' and took no more. For more background information about the so-called Chandra Swami, see chapter 76 of *Kill Guru, Become Guru*.

wanted to eliminate Shrila Prabhupada and his movement in order to maintain their tight grip over this material world.

Anyone interested in seeing what an honest and thorough investigation into Shrila Prabhupada's passing looks like must consult the books of Nityananda Prabhu. He has examined every possible angle in great detail, *including those that would rule out malicious poisoning*. Comparing the work of Nityananda to the rebuttal of the GBC in their book "Not That I am Poisoned," shows it to be an unmistakable cover-up, meant to cloud the issue and confuse the innocent devotees who submissively defer to them.

The evidence from every possible angle is quite clear, and leaves no conclusion other than the unfortunate truth that Shrila Prabhupada was intentionally poisoned by those who were closest to him.

Summary Conclusion

I'll close with a summary of the most important points: [10]

Aural Evidence:

- Shrila Prabhupada said very clearly on November 9 and 10, 1977 "Someone has poisoned me," and all his caretakers clearly acknowledged that Shrila Prabhupada was speaking of an actual homicidal poisoning, and not some "bad" medicine as is nowadays claimed by the ISKCON leadership. Yet without alarm everything continued as usual.

- The three poison whispers are "The poison's going down, the poison's going down," "Is poison in the milk?" and "Poisoning for a (long time)." The word "poison" is confirmed to be spoken by numerous expert audio forensic laboratories.

- The whispers are about poisoning, and there is no innocent explanation for this word in the given context. *Why are they whispering about poisoning Shrila Prabhupada three days before his departure? How is it that Shrila Prabhupada left this world only several days after he raised the issue of being poisoned? Was it because they were revealed and had to finish the job quickly?*

- A type of lie detector test called Voice Stress Analysis (VSA) has determined that there was considerable amounts of deceit in key sections of spoken conversation by leading disciples of Shrila Prabhupada during late 1977.

- Aural evidence, certified by 5 independent labs, concludes that Shrila Prabhupada's caretakers were discussing poisoning him.

Hair Tests Reveal Arsenic and Cadmium

- A 1999 test of Shrila Prabhupada's hair (Q-1) extracted from his hair clippers contained 2.6 ppm of arsenic, a level 20 times the normal average of 0.13 ppm. Chronic arsenic poisoning with 1 to 5 ppm in hair will cause serious health deterioration.

- Shrila Prabhupada's arsenic level is synonymous with chronic arsenic poisoning levels and would be expected to be a considerable contributing factor to his demise, as stated by experts.

- The GBC sent samples of Shrila Prabhupada's hair to a lab in 1999 but abandoned them without testing them. They were located in 2001 and properly tested, and they were found to have about 250 times the normal level of cadmium, a heavy metal more toxic than arsenic.

- A third test in 2005 again confirmed the same extremely high levels of cadmium in Shrila Prabhupada's hair.

- There is no plausible explanation for these super-high cadmium levels found in multiple, differently sourced hair samples, other than homicidal malice. These cadmium levels are unprecedented and not found even in those who have major environmental or occupational exposure.

- The hair tests establish massive cadmium poisoning from at least as early as February 1977 until Shrila Prabhupada's departure November 14, 1977. Cadmium is thus determined to be the primary poison, arsenic secondary.

Evidence of Witnesses

- Shrila Prabhupada stated that he heard others speaking about his poisoning.

- Bhakta Vatsala das, a gurukula student in 1977, overheard a group of senior devotees discussing the poisoning of Shrila Prabhupada.

- Several respectable Vrindavana residents have privately testified to knowledge of Shrila Prabhupada's poisoning, as ascertained by analysis of his urine by Ayurvedic doctors.

Medical Evidence

- Shrila Prabhupada's health history reveals a list of physical symptoms which are identical to those of chronic cadmium and arsenic poisoning. Many of these symptoms are in conflict with other explanations, such as diabetes, dropsy, kidney disease, etc. Chronic heavy metal poisoning causes and exacerbates diabetes and kidney failure. Prior to mid-1976 Shrila Prabhupada's health was quite good, and his diabetes was mild and non-insulin dependent.

- Throughout 1977 Tamal Krishna aggressively discouraged the services or involvement of competent doctors to diagnose or treat Shrila Prabhupada. Although Shrila Prabhupada himself was not keen on doctors and preferred to rely on Krishna, his disciples strangely declined non-invasive and simple "home" medical tests. There was a perplexing parade of doctors, and of changing and discrediting both Ayurvedic and allopathic doctors, regardless of their qualification and willingness to cooperate with Shrila Prabhupada's every wish.

- At least one of Shrila Prabhupada's medicines, which he himself described as poison, was donated by the shadowy and notorious Chandra Swami. What was the intention behind this sinister gift?

Political Evidence

- The GBC's steadfast denials, shoddy investigation, and mounting evidence constitute a dishonest cover-up. The GBC endorsed book *Not That I Am Poisoned*, produced by the suspects themselves in their own defense, is a gross misrepresentation of facts and devious manipulation of the evidence.

- ISKCON authorities blindly endorse a cover-up by disciples of the chief suspects as the "final" resolution of the issue.

- The GBC's failure to properly fund their official investigator and to respond to his recommendation that further investigation is required.

- The irrational, persistent and hardline GBC refusal to conduct an impartial, honest and independent investigation, in itself supports the conclusion that Shrila Prabhupada was poisoned.

- The steadfast condemnation of Nityananda's motives and his investigation, which, by any impartial observer, is far, far superior to theirs.

- The GBC's steadfast rejection and unwillingness to hear the opinions and conclusions of dozens of senior devotees that challenge their official conclusion.

Other Evidence

- Shortly after Shrila Prabhupada's departure, Tamal made extremely suspicious statements that appear to be groundwork for a "mercy killing" defense.

- Motive itself is typically considered as supporting evidence to a crime, and there was more than sufficient motive to poison Shrila Prabhupada. Such evidence is presented in the foregoing chapter of this book regarding the powers-that-be. Additionally the leading disciples involved stood to gain imme*asura*ble material benefits by stepping into his place as successor gurus, which is exactly what they did.

GBC Whitewash and Cover Up

- The GBC did not deny the existence of the poison whispers, instead resorting to diversion and fabrication in their book.

- The GBC failed to identify the arsenic levels found in Shrila Prabhupada's 1977 hair, deceitfully quoting only three dubious scientific references while ignoring the broader selection of scientific materials. What they left out is more important than what they included.

- They erroneously claimed average "normal" arsenic in hair

can be anything under 10 ppm, while in actuality it is 75 times less, namely about 0.13 ppm.

- The GBC attempt to twist Shrila Prabhupada's statements about being poisoned into a claim of his denial of being poisoned. Any honest person that reads the transcript knows that this is deceitful.

We are indebted to Nityananda Prabhu, Naveen Krishna Prabhu, and other devotees who have spent much time and money to find the truth. Sadly, but not surprisingly, the GBC – both individually and collectively – have failed to make even a fraction of this effort.

Would Krishna Allow This to Happen to His Pure Devotee?

Finally, I want to address the doubt that most commonly arises: Sri Krishna would never allow His most dear servant to suffer in this way. And why would He allow it to come to light only so many years later?

Those who express such doubts should read the *Srimad Bhagavatam* more carefully. It is full of examples of Krishna's very close devotees being put into extremely difficult circumstances. These challenges demonstrate the devotee's full surrender and unlimited devotion to Krishna. The trying circumstances, perpetrated by demons are the eternal struggle between the godly and godless. This same struggle continues today, despite the benign appearance of our modern world.

The truth of Shrila Prabhupada's passing being revealed twenty years later, has allowed us to understand the true nature of the "leaders," and thus understand that all of the tragedy both before and after Shrila Prabhupada's departure was not simply the result of bungling, but dedicated servants, as we are led to believe.

By learning that Shrila Prabhupada was poisoned we now know of the actual character of some of those closest to him. Who but demonic agents of Kali, literal demons, would poison Shrila Prabhupada? We also learn of Shrila Prabhupada's great magnanimity by engaging these wretches in Krishna's devotional service. We learn of their nefarious intent to remove him and to destroy what he created. And why do we want to learn this? Because with a few exceptions they still (mis)lead the society! Sincere followers must protect his legacy against enemies from within and without, and against present and *future* deception by Kali's agents, just as the Ebionites were intent to protect against future heresy by preserving their documents for posterity in the sands of Nag Hammadi and the caves of the Dead Sea.

Shrila Prabhupada spoke the truth about this world and his passing many times. How many times do we have to hear it before we will accept it?

> *So there are these snake-like persons. They are envious about our movement*, and they are opposing. That is the nature. Prahlada Maharaja also was opposed by his father, what to speak of others. *These things will happen. . .he was also served with poison.* Lecture Mayapur 28Feb77

> So as Krishna was attempted to be killed... And Lord Jesus Christ was killed. *So they may kill me also.* Conversation 3May76,

> There are many instances. Just like Prahlada Maharaja. His father is being killed before him. This is sinful. *Can you tolerate? Suppose if somebody comes to kill me, and you will see and laugh? Will you do that? Why? That is sinful.* Lecture 1.3.28 3Oct72

Woe is reserved to those who know the truth of Shrila Prabhupada's passing but say nothing. Kashyapa Muni states the result of keeping silence in the Mahabharata:

> If one knows the truth but does not disclose it upon being

questioned, or, if out of anger, fear, or some other motive, one gives a false reply, then he is bound up by 1,000 nooses of Varuna. . . If someone commits a sinful act in an assembly, then it is the duty of all those who are present to chastise the wrong doer. If they fail to do so, then the perpetrator of the sin receives one-fourth of the reaction, the leader of the assembly has to accept one-half, and all others present suffer one-fourth. A witness is one who has seen, heard of, or otherwise understood a thing, and he should always tell the truth, for in that way his pious merit will never suffer diminution.

Disclaimer

I want to make it absolutely clear that I have come to these conclusions by my own thorough and impartial study of the available evidence. Although I cite the work of Nityananda Dasa and Naveen Krishna Dasa, I have not taken this position due to my relationship with them. Further, I am not a subscriber of ritvik-vada, or a proponent of it. This is not an issue of "ritvik envy" as the guilty parties claim.

CHAPTER NINE

Varnashrama Dharma –
The Fifty-Percent Threat

Those who serve the Truth, at all time by means of all of their faculties, have no hankering for the trivialities of this world and are always necessarily free from malice born of competing worldliness. They are, therefore, fit to admonish those who are actively engaged in harming themselves and others by opposing or misrepresenting the Truth. Shrila Bhaktisiddhanta Sarasvati

In an emaciated condition, literally rising from his death bed, Shrila Prabhupada left India at the end of August 1977 with the intention of teaching his followers at the Gita Nagari farm in Pennsylvania the socio-economic system of Varnashrama Dharma. I was residing at the Gita Nagari farm at the time, and all of the devotees there were eagerly anticipating his arrival and instruction on this next phase of the Hare Krishna Movement. However his health took another inexplicable and mysterious turn for the worse while in London, forcing his return to Vrindavana. He told Avirama Prabhu and Bhakti Charu Swami that his only disappointment was that he had not established Varnashrama Dharma, and because of this he thus considered fifty-percent of his mission incomplete.

This is The Point

Now we have arrived at the reason for all of the foregoing: why known pedophiles were kept in positions in the gurukulas, why the women were dealt with so harshly and exploited rather than protected, why the books have been changed and only changed books are printed by the BBT, why mass distribution of Back-to-Godhead magazine was stopped, why a limited number of gurus in the zonal *Acharya* system was contrived and forced on the devotees, why the GBC's system subordinates the gurus against shastric injunction, why the GBC controls who can initiate and be initiated, why *kali-chelas* are promoted as "saints" to be honored and revered for all posterity, and why they conspired to end Shrila Prabhupada's life by poisoning him over an extended period of time – because *this movement, along with the Vedic worldview and philosophy, are an existential threat to the control of the demonic powers of this world.* It is the same reason that the Roman powers eradicated the Jewish Vaishnavas, and followers of the Eternal Religion for hundreds of years.

This is also why the "leaders" of ISKCON have not lifted a finger in forty years to even begin to understand what Shrila Prabhupada considered 50% of his mission – the independent living and high thinking of Varnashrama Dharma. Those infiltrators-cum-leaders have been put in place to thwart this very thing from happening. This is why, although Shrila Prabhupada instructed us to develop farms, they have been neglected, sold and lost, with those remaining sitting empty and idle – farms in name only.

This is why ISKCON has been led to conform to mainstream status quo, the revolutionary fervor of the early days of ISKCON now lost. Instead of continuing the war against Maya devotees are told to stay in school, get university degrees, and a job, and live according to the ways of modern society where they cannot help but be influenced by the lower modes of rajas and tamo-guna. Have a job and give money to the local temple and visit on weekends. *This is the 'churchianity' of the status quo* – not the revolutionary mission of Shrila Prabhupada.

Sattva-guna is the Preliminary Goal

However, it seems that the devotees, and especially the leaders, intentionally or not, have failed to understand that the modern way of life is extremely antithetical to developing Krishna Consciousness, which requires gradually lifting oneself from the lower modes of nature, passion and ignorance, to the platform of sattva-guna, and from there to transcendental pure goodness, suddha-sattva:

> . . . one has to rise to the platform of the mode of goodness (sattva) so that one can be eligible for the devotional service of the Lord. Srimad Bhagavatam 1.2.24 Purport

> We have to conquer over the quality, the infection of quality of rajas-tamah, and then we have to situate ourself in sattva-guna. Then we are in the safe position. And if we do not allow to be infected again by the rajo-guna and tamo-guna, if we keep ourselves purely in sattva-guna, that is called suddha-sattva, purified sattva-guna. Then we will be able to understand what is Krishna, what is God. Lecture Srimad Bhagavatam 3.25.24 24Nov74 Bombay

> *Unless one comes to the platform of sattva-guna, there is no question of perfection.* Nobody can understand, nobody can achieve perfection on the platform of rajo-guna and tamo-

guna. Lecture Cc. Madhya 6.149 13Feb71

There are many such instructions about the gradual process of lifting oneself from the lower modes of nature in order to attain the stage of liberation. This *is* the process of *bhakti-yoga*, but apparently this understanding has been lost since devotees continue living a modern lifestyle that insidiously infects one with rajas and tamo-guna.

Shrila Prabhupada rejected the modern way of life because it conditions us to the lower qualities of passion and ignorance, and encouraged the simple living of village life which is conducive of sattva:

> Varnasrama-dharma, therefore, is essential, for it can bring people to sattva-guna. Tada rajas-tamo-bhavah kama-lobhadayas ca ye (SB 1.2.19). Tamo-guna and rajo-guna increase lust and greed, which implicate a living entity in such a way that he must exist in this material world in many, many forms. *That is very dangerous. One should therefore be brought to sattva-guna by the establishment of Varnashrama Dharma and should develop the brahminical qualifications of being very neat and clean. . . In this way, one should stay in sattva-guna, and then one cannot be influenced by tamo-guna and rajo-guna.* Srimad Bhagavatam 10.13.53 Purport

> The idea which I am giving, you can start anywhere, anywhere, any part of the world. It doesn't matter. Locally you produce your own food. You get your own cloth. Have sufficient milk, vegetables. Then what you want more? And chant Hare Krishna. This is Vedic civilization: plain living, high thinking. And poor thinking, poor in thought, poor in behavior, and living with motorcar and this, that, nonsense. It is all nonsense civilization. . . *gradually we shall develop a society that all these unnecessary rubbish things should be rejected. That is*

the idea. Conversation 5Oct75 Mauritius

The global controllers know that they cannot exploit people who derive their sustenance independently from the land, and therefore they fight it everywhere in the world, and quash any threat, regardless of how remote, as soon as it appears. In the case of ISKCON, the great threat once posed by the development of the alternative culture of Varnashrama Dharma has been defused by the "leaders" who ignore our *Acharya*'s desire to establish Varnashrama Dharma, and instruct devotees to remain "congregational members," living in the passion and ignorance of the cities.

There is no doubt that the establishment of Varnashrama Dharma will be enormously challenging, but it is needed today more than ever. There is no doubt that Varnashrama Dharma is the panacea for all of the ills of modern society, and there is no doubt that one day it will be realized. Just as he successfully predicted the rise of a great temple across the Jalangi River from his kutir in Mayapura, Shrila Bhaktivinoda Thakur has also predicted that "some person imbued with the power of God will again establish the true Varnashrama Dharma in accordance with the Divine Dispensation." That opportunity remains open for any determined person to fulfill – despite the efforts of the Kamsas and their *kali-chela* minions.

CHAPTER TEN

The Enemy Within

Persons who are always planning to do harm to other living entities are not eligible to understand Krishna consciousness and cannot enter into the realm of transcendental loving service to the Lord. Also, there are so-called disciples who become submissive to a spiritual master most artificially, with an ulterior motive. Srimad Bhagavatam 3.32.40 Purport

Those who are opposing Krishna consciousness movement, we have to fight with them to our best capacity. Never mind if we are defeated. That is also service. Krishna sees the service. Defeated or victorious, depend on Krishna. But fighting must be there. Lecture Mayapur 1Mar77

The legitimate criticisms, complaints and critiques of GBC actions over the years fills a library. Those voices of deep concern selected for the chapters of this book are chosen because they mirror the attacks of the Kamsas and Putanas on the Jewish Vaishnavas several thousand years ago. History is being repeated.

The preceding chapters regarding the changes to Shrila Prabhupada's books, the destruction of the second generation and other followers, the failure to follow Shrila Prabhupada's desire to create an alternative spiritual culture (Varnashrama Dharma), and the poisoning of Shrila Prabhupada, *are all symptoms of the problem,* not the actual problem. We need to understand the source of the problems and deal with them, not be distracted by the symptoms. *All of these symptoms point to the "leadership" as the source of the problems.*

In this chapter we are going to take a direct look at the GBC and demonstrate that they have stepped far beyond the boundaries of their legitimate authority, thereby demonstrating that they are fit to be abandoned as leaders of Shrila Prabhupada's society.

GBC Never Fulfilled Their Duty

Let us be very clear that ISKCON was created by Shrila Prabupada himself. He established the GBC *to assist him as his representatives and do as he was doing.* As stated in the Direction of Management, wherein he created the GBC, "The purpose of the Governing Body Commission is to *act as the instrument for the execution of the Will of His Divine Grace.*" Again and again Shrila Prabhupada repeated these instructions to the GBC in letters to them:

> I want that the GBC men should leave the management of the individual centers to the local presidents and concentrate themselves upon preaching work. *They should be constantly traveling from one center to another center to see how the students are learning and to give whatever advice is necessary for improving the temple standards.* Letter to Madhudvisa 12Jun72

> You will not be too much involved with local temple management, but for management which will require the larger interests, that will be your responsibility as GBC. . . Your first job should be to make sure that every one of the

devotees in your zone of management is reading regularly our literatures and discussing the subject matter seriously from different angles of seeing, and that they are somehow or other absorbing the knowledge of Krishna Consciousness philosophy. Letter to Satsvarupa 16Jun72

There are dozens of such letters, to practically every GBC man, as well as to temple presidents. Thus the duty of the GBC man cannot be misunderstood. Shrila Prabhupada never gave instructions contrary to these cited above.

However, almost from the outset those appointed to the rank of GBC misinterpreted, or willfully ignored these simple instructions, interpreting their role as being controllers of the society:

GBC *members are simply to see that things are going on.* Other centers have got president, secretary, etc. and they are managing separately. That is the formula. So how is it that the GBC are the final authority? They are simply to examine that things are going on nicely, *that is all.* Letter to Umapati 9Jul71

Sometime there are complaints against the GBC which is not very favorable. I set up the GBC with hope that I shall get relief from administration of the mission but on the contrary I have become the center of receiving so many complaints. So it is not a relief for me, rather it is becoming troublesome. Letter to Tamala Krishna 14Aug71

There are many more letters such as these.[1] These problems never ended. Shrila Prabhupada was not relieved from management of the society by appointing these secretaries, but as he indicated, the problems increased.

GBC's Absolute Position Enshrined in ISKCON Laws

Despite Shrila Prabhupada's instructions that the GBC are not meant to exercise absolute control, they have done exactly that.

In fact they have enshrined their control in laws to which all ISKCON members must conform. ISKCON Law requires oaths of all ISKCON devotees, not only to Shrila Prabhupada, but *to the GBC themselves*, requiring everyone to submit to GBC dictates or risk censure, up to excommunication (rejection) from the society.

The Romans tried to control the Jewish Vaishnavas by saying that since God had given the Romans their power it was against God's will to resist them. Similarly, the GBC argue that since Shrila Prabhupada established them as ISKCON's "ultimate managing authority" (an expression that did not come from Shrila Prabhupada, but was coined by one many consider the main usurper of ISKCON, Tamal Krishna Goswami) they can determine what is correct for all devotees, and amazingly claim that to challenge them is to challenge Shrila Prabhupada himself!

The GBC have compiled 165 pages of laws, of which the most recent version available to devotees is more than 20 years old. In 2010 an updated version was promised within a year, but that had not materialized by the time of this writing, April 2019. Perhaps this is because, as one of the GBC Secretaries put it "...it is not advised to spread it [GBC Law Book] around as it is meant *only for internal use* of the GBC Secretariat."[2] Hmm. According to him the members are not allowed to see the laws that they are supposedly governed by!?

The contents of the law book say a great deal about the people who put it together. In it, the GBC repeatedly equate "ISKCON" with the GBC, and loyalty to ISKCON meaning solely, loyalty to the GBC, although Shrila Prabhupada never, ever, indicated such a thing. Recall the earlier quotation of Shrila Prabhupada that anyone chanting Hare Krishna is a member of ISKCON. The law book seems to be an attempt to control who can be a member of ISKCON while also limiting their thinking and understanding, and engendering complete submission.

Hridayananda Das Goswami (HDG), a current member of the GBC body as of this writing, analyzed ISKCON's Law Book in 2016.[3] A significant part of his analysis demonstrates that the GBC place themselves above all other devotees, and exempts them from the many requirements or restraints that they impose on ISKCON's gurus, institutional leaders and followers. The GBC's position, established by themselves, and never sanctioned by Shrila Prabhupada, gives them total control of the entire institution and all members, including ISKCON's gurus. To understand the significance of this sleight of hand and how it deviates from Gaudiya siddhanta we must first understand the position of the *bona fide* guru.

The Bona Fide Guru

Throughout his writing and in his lectures, when referencing the guru, Shrila Prabhupada takes pains to almost always preface the word guru with the qualifier "bona fide." Because of this emphasis we must understand the definition of a bona fide guru, of which Shrila Prabhupada gives the following requirements:

1. The bona fide bona fide guru must come in a line of disciplic succession from Lord Krishna. (Purport Bg. 11.43)
2. The bona fide guru must have studied the Vedic scriptures and, having realized their conclusion, is able to convince others of the same. (Purport SB 4.29.55)
3. The bona fide guru must be in contact with the Supersoul, for Whom he acts as the external manifestation, or transparent medium, to the neophyte disciple. (Purport SB 3.28.2)

In order to give proper guidance to the neophyte how to progress along the path of bhakti, these requirements are absolutely necessary, otherwise the guru is not able to fulfill his function as Krishna's external representative. In addition, the guru must be qualified, as expressed in the first verse of the Upadeshamrita, *The*

Nectar of Instruction: "A sober person who can tolerate the urge to speak, the mind's demands, the actions of anger and the urges of the tongue, belly and genitals is qualified to make disciples all over the world." This is Gaudiya siddhanta.

Curious to know what was being taught, I took the "ISKCON Guru Course," and was quite dismayed that these qualifications were not even mentioned, what to speak of stressed. Since the leadership does not require such qualifications, it is not surprising that they have no problem subordinating the guru to their control. For their absolute control they contravene siddhanta that gives the bona fide guru total freedom as the external representative of the Supersoul, Who, of course, cannot be limited in any way. How then can the gurus of ISKCON be faithful to the Supersoul whose instruction might contradict any of the GBC's sometimes apa-siddhantic limitations? Are the GBC more omniscient than the Supersoul? And can any ISKCON guru, who allows himself to be politically appointed and submits himself to such control, actually be a bona fide guru? Such violations of Vaishnava siddhanta destroy the position of the bona fide guru, and with it, the clear path Back to Godhead. Although the GBC imagine themselves as absolute authorities, they most certainly are not. They, and every serious Vaishnava, must conform to the standards established by guru, shastra and *sadhu*.

GBC – Above the Guru and Free From Restraint

HDG's analysis of ISKCON Law (posted in it's entirety on our website) includes the following summary of the ways in which the guru is limited by, and subordinated to, the GBC, of whom no similar qualifications are demanded.

Although the following are required for ISKCON's diksha gurus, *there are no corresponding requirements for GBC members*:

1. twice-initiated for at least ten years.
2. be in good standing in ISKCON [read: submissive to controlling authorities].
3. have substantial knowledge and realization of sastra, including a Bhakti-sastri degree.
4. must preach according to Shrila Prabhupada's teachings.
5. must work cooperatively with local authorities.
6. must have no loyalties that compete with or compromise one's loyalty to Shrila Prabhupada, to his teachings, and to ISKCON [read: the GBC].
7. Spiritual degrees strongly recommended—Bhakti Sastri, etc. for no objection status to serve as a guru in ISKCON.

Additional requirements for gurus with *no corresponding requirement for GBC*:

1. Endorsement by an Area Council. E*ight* sections of GBC law stress the need for local community support for a would-be guru.[4]
2. Required to have local evaluation
3. Required to have "No Objection" letters

It's inexplicable that the GBC established a system that *requires prospective gurus* to be sanctioned by those perhaps significantly junior to them!

There are nine general standards of guru conduct—plus three standards in relation to the GBC body, three standards in relation to GBC Zonal Secretaries, eight standards in relation to ISKCON spiritual authorities, four standards in relation to a temple – *a total of twenty-seven required standards for gurus.*

In comparison, GBC members have only three standards to meet: they must practice Krishna consciousness, do not permit or perform illicit or illegal activity, and they must not publicly criticize other GBC members.

Discipline of Diksa-gurus

1. Nine kinds of Misconduct and Failure to Follow Religious Principles or "Higher Spiritual Authority" (should be the Supersoul, but we suspect they intend that to mean the GBC)
2. Two kinds of Improper Discharge and Neglect of Duty
3. Four kinds of Spiritual Discrepancy
4. Five ways to censure a diksa-guru
5. Two ways to place on probation, suspend, or rescind the power to initiate, of a diksa-guru
6. A statement that none of the above limits the power of "any Regional Governing Body, Divisional Council, National Council, or other local authority to withhold permission for a...diksa-guru to [initiate] within their jurisdiction."
7. Definitions of Censure and Probation
8. Details of Suspension Pending Investigation
9. Details of Suspension
10. Details of Rescindment
11. Five ways to restrict a Guru under suspension
12. Five circumstances in which one rejects a fallen guru.

The GBC are obviously above the law as *there are NO specific GBC laws to discipline a GBC member or censure the GBC body. Neither are there any circumstances permissible in which one may reject a GBC member's order.*

Amazingly, despite the greater requirements and restrictions for gurus than the GBC, the gurus are required to subordinate themselves to GBC control.

Laws for the GBC are Minimal and Unenforced

There is a law requiring every GBC to follow the regulative principles, give regular classes, participate in festivals and *Harinam*

Sankirtan, live in or near a temple community, and associate with devotees. But it is well-known throughout the world that this "law" is frequently neglected. For example, the long-suffering devotees of Australia have complained and written extensively on-line about the deviations of their local GBC, all to no avail.

Further, this unenforced rule says nothing about the charac-ter of a GBC, nor how the GBC treats other Vaiṣṇavas, although ISKCON's Gurus and Temple Presidents have specific rules that regulate their exercise of power and their treatment of other devotees.

In reading this we cannot help but think of the Popes and how they established their absolute position, and although devoid of any standard of morality could not be censured. It seems that the GBC through their "Laws" are attempting to recreate the Roman church!

ISKCON – A Society of *Sudras*?

Shrila Prabhupada wanted to establish the brahminical class of men capable of guiding society. The GBC on the other hand, by demanding submission in all respects are creating a society of *su-dras*. Whereas persons of a *sudra* nature, in exchange for shelter and security do as they are told, the higher-class of men, the dvijas, are independent by nature. They do not need, *and will not have,* somebody telling them what to do. The businessman, for example, is the boss, and he takes the trouble to create a business and run it because that is the type of man he is. He will not have anyone telling him what to do. The same for those of a *kshatriya* nature, and especially so for the brahminical types who are so indepen-dent-minded that they traditionally will not accept support from anyone, preferring to depend directly on the Supreme Lord in all situations.

Shrila Prabhupada of course understood, and in his letters to them, attempted to teach his GBC, the proper understanding of human nature:

> *Sudra*s are meant for working under somebody, not brahmanas. If you do not know this principle, you should know it now. All our men living in the temple are basically brahmanas. [meaning that they are not meant for working under anybody] Otherwise, why they are offered sacred thread? [5]

> Krishna Consciousness Movement is for training men to be independently thoughtful and competent in all types of departments of knowledge and action.[6]

> This propaganda is meant for creating some brahmanas all over the world because the brahmana element is lacking, *so one who seriously comes to us, he has to become a brahmana. So he has to adopt the occupation of a brahmana, and he has to give up the occupation of a kshatriya or a sudra.*[7]

> So the problem is that if we keep men fourth-class or increase only fourth-class men, so these things [crime] are automatic, the resultant action. Therefore, *in the western countries especially, everywhere, all over the world, the attempt should be how to create first-class, second-class. At least these two classes required*: good politicians, administrators, and good advisors. So this program we are placing before the world. This is Krishna consciousness movement.[8]

Shrila Prabhupada was able to attract very capable men because he challenged them and gave them the freedom and independence to meet those challenges. Intelligently working with such capable men, he was able to establish Krishna Consciousness throughout the entire world in eleven short years. Most unfortunately the GBC have not understand this very basic principle. If they continue with their extensive control, they will be unable to fulfill Shrila Prabhupada's desire to establish ISKCON as the leaders of society. Perhaps that is the intended result. *Phalena parichyate.*

Gatekeepers to Vaikuntha

It is readily seen that the great churches of today have established their representatives as the gatekeepers to heaven, indoctrinating their followers that they cannot be "saved" without their baptism, confirmation, blessings, etc. Thus they intercede between man and God.

The Vaishnava doctrine also requires an intercessor – the spiritual master – by whose grace the aspirant can connect to the Lord and perfect his life. However, in their role as the "ultimate managers," the GBC, against Vaishnava siddhanta, insert themselves as a third party into the guru–disciple relationship, requiring total allegiance and submission from both the guru and the disciple. *There is no basis for this anywhere in Gaudiya siddhanta or Shrila Prabhupada's teachings.* It has been concocted under the plea of cooperation in service to Shrila Prabhupada, giving the GBC total and absolute control over everyone in the society. How do they overlook the fact that control of others is actually a demonic propensity and an anathema to spiritual freedom? In Part 3 of this book we will discuss how complete cooperation can be realized without the need of controlling anyone. Next, let's look at how the GBC have indoctrinated all of ISKCON's gurus and disciples into obsequious compliance.

ISKCON's Diksa Process

It is not easy getting initiated in today's ISKCON. Sincere persons inspired by Shrila Prabhupada's books and desiring initiation are institutionally indoctrinated by the initiation process. The first restriction in this process is that the candidate may not directly approach the person they desire to receive initiation from, but must go through the local ISKCON leader. He is the first gatekeeper. Only if that person approves of the candidate (and they may not be approved for political reasons as some have experienced) is the prospective guru informed of the candidate's desire for initiation.

If the guru agrees, the candidate is then required to pass the "ISKCON Disciple Course." We note that from the very beginning of his devotional service the aspiring disciple is indoctrinated into the understanding that s/he is an *ISKCON disciple,* an identity that is reinforced again and again throughout the course.

Following the course, a rather elementary test is given. In some yatras the course and test is administered by only one person, but whether one or more this person is the second gatekeeper. Obviously this person has a great deal of power.

The test can be passed by anyone who has read Shrila Prabhupada's books and has a decent grasp of the philosophy. However, subservience and allegiance to the GBC is further reinforced by the test with questions such as: "What is the position of the GBC Body?" "What is ISKCON?" and "Why should one remain in ISKCON?" Of course anyone not giving the politically correct answer runs the risk of failing the test. Or if they happen to challenge the power structure. I've heard of qualified candidates being failed for political reasons. I've seen test answers meriting a passing grade failed, likely due to fact that this bhakta was challenging the known illegal activities of their GBC. But how could mere bhaktas challenge that their GBC's actions are against the law? They obviously do not understand how the parampara works!

Candidates are informed that they may take initiation only from an "ISKCON approved" (GBC compliant) guru, a real gamble considering that a third of them have fallen from from the post. Of the 104 ISKCON gurus approved between 1977 and 2004, 34 were relieved of their positions, and an additional

14 were sanctioned by the GBC for misbehavior.[9] Perhaps this is because they are approved due to becoming an obsequious sycophant rather than being bona fide? The approved gurus are required to take an annual oath of allegiance to the GBC before Shrila Prabhupada's murti, and to send a signed copy of such vows to the GBC's Corresponding Secretary. Those vows reiterate no less than five times that as an ISKCON guru he is subordinate to the GBC, and that he must instruct his disciples in the same way.

Finally, during the initiation ceremony the candidate, besides making an oath to take the spiritual master's order as his/her life and soul, is required to also make *two* oaths to the GBC: the first to remain faithful to the order and teachings of Shrila Prabhupada (after it has been thoroughly drilled into him/her that Shrila Prabhupada established the GBC as the "ultimate managing authority" of ISKCON and thus they represent him); the second "to remain faithful to Shrila Prabhupada's order *by maintaining loyalty to ISKCON and its ultimate managing authority, the GBC.*"

Obviously young impressionable devotees take this oath very seriously and as such are convinced that in order to remain a devotee faithful to Shrila Prabhupada they must also forever abide by the decisions of the GBC, fearing if they reject the GBC due to its deviation from proper Gaudiya siddhanta, they are breaking their initation vows. Thus the GBC has them forever. This is identical to the practices of the Roman church that seek political power through their vast number of followers indoctrinated since birth. Since any experienced devotee knows that such concepts violate Gaudiya siddhanta we can only wonder why our Godbrother gurus go along with all of this(!?), although the GBC's purpose in demanding absolute allegiance is no mystery at all – absolute control of the society.

The GBC's Golden Rule

Over the decades devotees have witnessed all manners of fall downs, failures and misbehaviors of GBC, gurus, *sannyasis* and other leaders, with the GBC typically showing unlimited tolerance for their misgivings. However, there is one thing they will not tolerate, the one rule that is inviolable and draws an immediate and harsh reaction – any challenge to their authority. This rule is inviolable. Anyone that publicly challenges their authority is immediately attacked, and there are numerous examples that can be pointed out.

Kundali Prabhu is one. He was called on the carpet after his well-intentioned book "Our Mission" was published. Although it warned that ISKCON was getting off-track, it could hardly be considered harsh criticism, yet the GBC took exception to his "delivery." Kundali explains the reaction in his second volume:

> . . .*the first volume of Our Mission brought the full weight of the GBC to bear on me.* The. . .most vocal members, did not like that I dared to publish a book giving honest critical feedback and analysis of the dynamics in our society, and to some extent, unavoidably, casting them in an unflattering light. This they did not articulate openly. They complained about "the delivery." The code for "not enough homage, praise, and flattery."

> I met with a GBC sub-committee for four hours to discuss the book, but we never got around to doing so. My attempts to focus on the subject matter of the book were ignored. Meanwhile, no one specified what was wrong with the delivery. . . Worse, they attempted to punish the author. . . In light of these considerations, and the GBC's failure to specify what was wrong with the delivery, reading between the lines I had to conclude that delivery was not the issue at all, but the *truth* of the analysis.

ISKCON's Non-Existent Constitution

Almost 50 years ago, in his "Direction of Management" document, where Shrila Prabhupada officially established the GBC, he also wrote that an "ad hoc committee be set up to form the constitution" for the society. To this day there is no constitution, although it is said to be "just now coming" as the most recent committee has been "seriously at work" on it – for more than fifteen years?!

The official GBC website references the constitution stating "The current draft, which has now been through five reviews with the GBC body, is presented along with the background and rationale of each component. The focus is on answering questions and receiving participants [sic] feedback on the Committee's work."

A constitution is not so difficult to construct. It would contain elements already drafted by Shrila Prabhupada and referred to in his letters such as this:

> GBC does not mean to control a center. GBC means to see that the activities of a center go on nicely. . . The GBC men *cannot impose anything on the men of a center without consulting all of the GBC members first. A GBC member cannot go beyond the jurisdiction of his power. . .the next meeting of the GBC members they should form a constitution how the GBC members manage the whole affair. But it is a fact that the local president is not under the control of the GBC.* Letter to Giriraja 12Aug71

The GBC were clearly missing the point from the very beginning when these letters were written – or they deliberately ignored these direct instructions of Shrila Prabhupada as to how his society should function, as they pursued their own agenda. If one decade would be considered negligent, what should we think of a *fifty year* delay?

In 2002, at the GBC's AGM in Mayapura, a resolution [607] passed that a constitution be "formulated," and approved some

360 | DIVINE OR DEMONIAC?

"Organizational Principles" as a preliminary step to guide its development. There are 11 so-called principles listed each of which is preceded by the statement "We *believe* that. . ."

Why is it necessary to believe anything? Shrila Prabhupada clearly indicated the specific *items* that were to be included in the constitution – such as spelled out in the Direction of Management, and the fact that the GBC is *not* meant to control a center and exert absolute authority. Instead of taking serious action on his instruction the GBC continue to feign loyalty to Shrila Prabhupada saying what they *believe* Shrila Prabhupada wanted, which amazingly, does not include what Shrila Prabhupada actually wanted. It sounds so nice and even submissive, coming from "the pseudo-teachers of religion, the Putanas, whose congenial function is to stifle the theistic disposition at the very moment of its suspected appearance," but it lacks the known guidelines regarding how Shrila Prabhupada wanted *his* ISKCON society to function.

Hridayanada Goswami made a critique of the most recent draft of ISKCON's constitution (not available to the general mass of devotees) and wrote that it "is well-intentioned, and wise on some points, but it ultimately fails to inspire, mandate, or explain justice in ISKCON. Thus it does not fulfill its stated purpose – to protect our rights, and establish a constitutional foundation for a rational, just ISKCON."[10]

Development of a Huge Bureaucracy

We have already cited several attempts by the GBC to centralize management and create bureaucracy that were dismantled by Shrila Prabhupada. The following exchange indicates that Shrila Prabhupada saw no reason to create standing committees that increase bureaucracy:

> Jayatirtha: So then the next thing, besides having a zonal responsibility, a GBC man may have a functional responsibility,

like we've already discussed.

Prabhupada: Functional, *main functional responsibility is to go and see that the temple regular work is going on, the president is doing nicely, to check in this way.* You can sit down in the class and see how things are going on. That's it. . . [this was repeatedly stressed by Shrila Prabhupada]

Jayatirtha: For example, one committee that I would propose is in the United States, since we share so many similar problems and so many problems overlap...

Prabhupada: No, the GBC is already there. But that is... Committee is there, the whole committee. But for any *special purpose*, if committee is required...

Jayatirtha: Another example of a kind of committee would be some projects. Say...

Prabhupada: Project will be decided by the GBC.

Jayatirtha: Say, the Gurukula, for example...

Prabhupada: [here giving an acceptable example] Now I have elected this committee in Europe because the German trouble is going on. *When the German trouble is over, there is no need of committee. It is only for this particular purpose* because there we have to defend court, we have to see... So two, three heads, not one head. One head may be puzzled. *Committee means for special purposes. Otherwise, the standing committee, GBC, is already there.*

Prabhupada: Just like I appointed the committee to investigate... So that committee is not standing. Yet similarly, a committee may be formed for some special circumstances, but otherwise the GBC committee is sufficient. . . Not unnecessarily spending. That is the duty of the GBC.[11]

Despite the fact that Shrila Prabhupada's warned "once there is bureaucracy the whole thing will be spoiled," the GBC carry on creating a huge institutional bureaucracy with layer upon layer of officials who are only required to manage the bureaucracy!

Shrila Prabhupada's org chart had three levels: himself, his 12 assistants (GBC), and the temple presidents, expecting that once he had departed only two levels would remain. As of this writing, 2018, the following layers of bureaucrats are working to oversee the institution:

1. GBC Executive Director
2. GBC Divisional Directors (8)
3. GBC members (40)
4. Assistant GBCs
5. GBC candidates
6. GBC deputies (22)
7. GBC Corresponding Secretary
8. GBC Nominations Committee
9. Global Duty Officers
10. Zonal supervisors
11. ISKCON Central Secretariat
12. ISKCON Disciple Course Secretariat
13. The SABHA (Spiritual Advisors Bhagavata Assembly)
14. Office for prevention of leader misconduct
15. Twenty-two (*standing*) Committees
16. Child Protection Office and the ISKCON Property Office

Young, inexperienced devotees are recruited to fill up the bureaucracy and thus are indoctrinated to an institutional hierarchy as the real ISKCON, blindly following authorities and never troubling themselves to understand what Shrila Prabhupada wanted. In this way an institutional religion is created and propagated in the name of Shrila Prabhupada, that will prove to be impotent for self-realization, but exceptionally good for limiting and controlling spiritual understanding. As Shrila Bhaktisiddhanta Prabhupada has indicated in his article Putana:

> The idea of an organized church in an intelligible form, indeed, marks the close of the living spiritual movement. The great ecclesiastical establishments are the dikes and the dams to retain the current that cannot be held by any such contrivances. They, [the great ecclesiastical institutions] indeed, *indicate a desire on the part of the masses to exploit a spiritual movement for their own purpose. They also unmistakably indicate the end of the absolute and unconventional guidance of the bona fide spiritual teacher.* The people of this world understand preventive systems, although they have no idea at all of the un-prevented positive eternal life.

Next we'll look at how the GBC, by their actions and inactions, thwarted the purpose that ISKCON was meant for, and could have fulfilled.

ISKCON has Lost the Ideological Battle

The top leadership of every organization must see that the purpose of the organization is being fulfilled. They are the ones directing the entire enterprise and they are the ones charged with keeping everything on track. In the case of ISKCON the GBC body is at the helm. They should have the broad vision of what ISKCON is meant to be. While it might be said that this is being done, we challenge that it is their own vision for ISKCON they are fulfilling, not Shrila Prabhupada's.

Throughout his books and teachings Shrila Prabhupada clearly establishes a theistic and personal worldview and ideology that he exhorted his followers to adopt and follow, and he indicated that ISKCON could create a cultural conquest of the world. However, the Vaishnava ideology is clearly in conflict with that of the atheistic, materialistic culture that dominates all of modern society. In the very early days of the society, and early members of ISKCON for the most part rejected the values of modern society in favor of the transcendental culture of Krishna Consciousness. They actively and determinedly sought to establish an alternative spiritual culture in city temples and farms. Indeed, this Cultural Revolution was one of the most attractive features of Krishna Consciousness for many, given the social scene and ideological conflicts being played out in America and Western Europe at the time.

However, as devotees married and began to have families, the financial demands of raising children began to interfere with the rejection of mainstream society. Many devotees found themselves struggling spiritually as they straddled two very different cultures. Shrila Prabhupada anticipated this, and instructed his followers to purchase farms so that devotees could live simply, producing their own necessities from the land. Although many attempted to follow that path it was fraught with difficulties due to lack of capital and experience, but mostly due to a lack of vision of how that life would be conducted. Many mistakes and minor disasters on ISKCON's farms proved that it was not at all simple to establish a culture of simple living.

Long-time ISKCON observer and well-wisher Dr. Thomas J. Hopkins anticipated this cultural clash, and in 2007 predicted a pending ideological battle between the two cultures was about to begin in order to settle questions of authority and identity for members of the society. He wrote:

> There are still many problems to be faced, however, not the least of which is defining ISKCON's identity more clearly in terms of both its past history and its future goals. This is not primarily an organizational [sic] issue to be solved by management decisions, but rather a basic theological concern

that can only be resolved by intensive intellectual effort and spiritual insight over a period of time. At stake are ISKCON's fundamental values and basic commitments, the core identity or self-identity that must be understood and accepted by all of its members before the central mission can be properly carried out.[12]

The question Dr. Hopkins is raising is whether ISKCON's members will continue to maintain a cohesive group identity and doctrinal ideology that is in many ways diametrically opposed to the materialistic values of its host culture. In a very well-supported rebuttal, ISKCON observer and commentator Krishna Kirti Dasa, has written that ISKCON's struggle to establish its self-identity and ideological foundation, has already been lost:

> If ISKCON's internal conflicts have been fundamentally ideological, then victory means that one of the warring ideologies has finally come to predominate over the others. . . there is presently more reason to believe that the ideological battle has already been won. *The ideological victor is Western culture, with its attendant ideologies, and the reasons to believe this are to be found in ISKCON's present state of cultural alignment* and in statements made by intellectuals who have the ear of ISKCON's management.[13]

In other words, for the most part, ISKCON members, without understanding the significance, nor the far-reaching consequences of their actions, have embraced the values of the dominant materialistic culture. This is a matter of group dynamics, and happens when expansion is too rapid and the culture brought by incoming members dominates the group, rather than the group being dominated by experienced, senior members. Looking back we can understand that this is why in 1972 Shrila Prabhupada cautioned against fast expansion, and instead instructed the leaders to "boil the milk," meaning making sure the existing members became fixed in their understanding and practice of Krishna Consciousness.

Another cause of this was the leadership themselves embracing the values of the dominant culture, such as many gurus and other leaders pursuing Ph.D.'s and Post-doc education.

Krishna Kirti offered five significant, and by then (2008) already existing, facts about ISKCON's culture as proof of its ideological defeat:

1. *The proliferation and widespread use of modern psychology within ISKCON*
2. *The high value ISKCON by then was placing on post-doctoral education*
3. *ISKCON's lack of its own internal economy*
4. *ISKCON's social and political commitment to gender equality*
5. *An increased emphasis on worldly activities*

I'll comment in some detail on two of these, but a reading of the entire paper is recommended, and can be found on my website DivineOrDemoniac.com.

The Lack of an Internal Economy

In its early days, following Shrila Prabhupada's example and instructions, ISKCON as a spiritual society practiced a form of spiritual economics – a gift economy based on *giving* Krishna, and Krishna Consciousness, to others. There was little thought of *getting* money, and by and large devotees were free from the demands that money imposed on society in general. Seeing the kirtan party chanting on the streets people would sometimes yell "get a job!" Shrila Prabhupada retorted that we are working, but working in a joyful way, and he invited the entire world to join us. Support predominantly came from book distribution providing the simple necessities of life, and afforded the devotees time for a full morning sadhana. However, being young and inexperienced we did not anticipate the coming challenges nor could we understand what would be required to sustain the cultural challenge we were involved in. As is the case with many young people we thought little about the future, happily pursuing the present effort of making the world Krishna Conscious.

The cultural clash and financial challenges began when devotees married and began to have children. Some of the sannyasis campaigned against their hard work supporting the children – the products of others' "sex enjoyment," – as they expressed it (it would seem they thought they were doing fruitive work and not devotional service). The sannyasis wanted the householders, who were all doing devotional service in some form or another, to get jobs to support themselves and their families. Although this was traditionally done in India, ISKCON up to that point was not following the Indian model, and it was conceivably possible that the entire society could have continued mutually supporting each other as they had been doing, as everyone continued to push on the mission and their own spiritual development.

That could have happened but didn't. The *sannyasis* were successful in driving the grihasta's out of the temples and back into the culture they abandoned to join Shrila Prabhupada's movement. However, having a job meant living predominantly in the dominant culture with its attendant time demands. Caught in between the two cultures, the Krishna culture gradually subsided, mostly because the other one that provided material necessities could not be given up. Thus sadhana became weak, and with that, zeal for Krishna Consciousness. Moreover, there was a push that the grihastas should become "congregational members," and ISKCON thus became similar to any other church, its members visiting the temple and seeing the Deities mainly on Sundays. Thus the ideological threat that ISKCON once posed to the dominant culture was successfully quelled.

Destruction of Shrila Prabhupada's Absolute Position

In an earlier chapter we discussed how the women who were attracted to ISKCON were discouraged and driven away by the fanatic behavior of the *sannyasis* and other men. The results of this issue have gone far, far beyond the treatment of women however, destroying one of the pillars of Vaishnava siddhanta within ISKCON – the Absolute position of the founder-*Acharya* – and this destruction has been carried out by none other than the so-called ultimate managers themselves, the GBC.

For the women who carried on despite the abuse, resentment and anger gradually built up, creating a backlash. Through those years women in the dominant culture were taking a stand against exploitation, and the women of ISKCON did likewise, employing similar language and tactics. What became known as the "women's issue" came to a head in the 1990s, and the GBC responded to the pressure, not by dealing with the problem – the abuses by the men – but with the symptoms of the problem – the complaints of the women. They dealt with the problem in a way that could not even address it, but could be interpreted such – increasing the bureaucracy by creating the International Women's Ministry in 1996. In the year 2000 the GBC passed a resolution that all devotees must be allowed equal and full service opportunities regardless of gender, allowing the women to do everything the men did. In one sense this was no different than what Shrila Prabhupada allowed in his personal presence, but the underlying factors had now changed everything.

After the GBC granted women equal privileges with ISKCON's men, and even elected a woman to the GBC, a backlash erupted with some men under the name GHQ, challenging the GBC's decisions on the matter, sensing this decision as having the potential to dangerously undermine Shrila Prabhupada's teachings. And they were right.

Soon Shrila Prabhupada himself began to be criticized – *within ISKCON, and by the leaders of ISKCON* – over his statements about women. This feminization of ISKCON rallied. Burke Rochford, in his book *Hare Krishna Transformed*, writes extensively about the women's issue and its aftermath as one of the major influences bringing ISKCON in line with the dominant culture. Rochford:

> *As one GBC member acknowledged,* Prabhupada's statements are "under currently established norms of business, government, and academics, labeled 'sexist,' and regarded as on the same moral level as anti-Semitic or racist utterances" (com 2000a). Another suggested that the leaders, though 'not wanting to talk about Prabhupada's mistakes,' also found it important to

> > 'distinguish between what Prabhupada says about the tradition and what he said about contemporary issues. 'To say that Prabhupada is a pure devotee, which I believe he is, *doesn't mean that he is materially omniscient. What Prabhupada said about World War II or women's intelligence, he himself didn't represent as absolute truth. He had a human side; he gave his opinions that go beyond quoting and commenting on the scripture itself. We have to place these opinions in a different box from his commentaries directly addressing matters of scripture. . .* Let's face it, twenty years ago what the GHQ is saying was accepted. It was the way we thought. But there has been a gradual, steady, historical transformation. There has been a gradual and peaceful shift in ISKCON, in the Prabhupada hermeneutic. Given the extreme sensitivity of some of these issues, I think the GBC is relieved that this shift has occurred.' (interview October 2005) [14]

The campaign of criticizing and condemning female devotees in the 1970s led several decades later to *the devastating result of undermining Shrila Prabhupada's absolute position and authority as the Acharya of ISKCON, effectively relativizing Shrila Prabhupada as just one authority among other modern mundane thinkers.* **Rochford recognized this fact although it seemed to have escaped the understanding of the GBC:**

> The politics surrounding women's place in ISKCON clearly point to the ways that the Krishna movement has edged ever closer to American mainstream culture. The GHQ's failed attempt to turn back gender equality only reinforced this shift. Although inequalities continue to exist, as they also do in mainstream societies, ISKCON's organizational policy now fully endorses equal and full opportunities for men and women devotees alike. Such a cultural turn is significant because *it signals the ways in which traditionalism no longer serves as the foundation of ISKCON's religious culture. In embracing gender equality, ISKCON's leaders aligned the organization with a defining feature of modern liberal culture* (Chaves 1997:51).

> The conflict over gender equality, incited by the GHQ's determined effort to assert traditional Vedic conceptions of dharma, opened a Pandora's Box that may forever remain open. *The debate about women's roles and place in ISKCON led to critical questioning of Prabhupada's scriptural commentaries, as well as to his overall authority as Krishna's pure representative.* **The fact that the leadership failed to act decisively on Prabhupada's behalf was an acknowledgment that his authority no longer was absolute.** Given ISKCON's increasingly pluralistic membership, it was perhaps inevitable that Prabhupada's teachings would be questioned, especially in light of their past misuse resulting in the abuse of devotee women and children. **Yet as these teachings become reframed as guides for thought and action, in place of being "absolute truths," traditionalism will continue its**

march to the margins of ISKCON. As it does, the goal of creating a viable cultural alternative to mainstream American culture will cease to exist.[15]

Allowing Shrila Prabhupada's Absolute authority to be undermined is perhaps the greatest failure of the GBC, and have thus proven themselves unfit for leadership of *his* society. Having taken an honest look at the GBC's efforts over almost 50 years there is enough evidence to judge by the result – *phalena parichyate* – whether they have understood what Shrila Prabhupada wanted from them and carried it out. Here are their grades:

The GBC's Report Card	Grade
Protection of Shrila Prabhupada's authority as Absolute	**FAILED**
Protection of Shrila Prabhupada's legacy in the form of his books	**FAILED**
Following Shrila Prabhupada's instructions in his initial constitution, the Direction of Management (DOM)	**FAILED**
The GBC having no jurisdiction over the BBT (stealing the copyrights)	**FAILED**
Protecting and promulgating unadulterated Vaishnava siddhanta	**FAILED**
GBC's obligation to act as Shrila Prabhupada's representatives	**FAILED**
Protection of ISKCON's women and children	**FAILED**
Creating a society of independently-thinking brahmanas who can lead the world	**FAILED**
Seriously investigating the alleged poisoning of Shrila Prabhupada (engineered a cover-up instead)	**FAILED**

Promoting and establishing simple living alternative lifestyle, with cow/bull protection, Vedic culture of Varnashrama Dharma and 50% of Shrila Prabhupada's mission	**FAILED**
Following Shrila Prabhupada's instructions for the GBC and ISKCON	**FAILED**
Protecting the transcendental ISKCON society from encroachment by the values of the atheistic, materialistic, dominant culture	**FAILED**

The GBC's Authority is Hereby Rejected

The GBC have failed in every respect to carry out Shrila Prabhupada's instructions to themselves and for his mission. They have taken charge of Shrila Prabhupada's ISKCON as if it were their own to do with what they please, rather than acting as fiduciaries carefully protecting what Shrila Prabhupada had entrusted to them, and in fact are acting in opposition to Shrila Prabhupada's direct instructions. Therefore, using the guideline of *phalena parichyate* – judging by the result – we must conclude that they are unfit for their role. Given the problems generated by them for decades we are forced to ask:

How far must the GBC deviate from Shrila Prabhupada's instructions before they no longer represent him?

At what point do we reject a "leadership" that is clearly misrepresenting Shrila Prabhupada and the Gaudiya sampradaya they claim to represent?

In fact, this threshold was crossed long, long ago, and thus the GBC have shown themselves fit to be rejected by any devotee claiming to be a follower of Shrila Prabhupada.

It is time to stop submissively giving our energy to their wayward mis-leadership, walk away from them, and work to establish the ISKCON as Shrila Prabhupada intended. It is time to Start the Hare Krishna Movement Again!

To reject an errant GBC is NOT to reject ISKCON (Shrila Prabhupada's ISKCON), nor Krishna Consciousness, and especially is not a rejection of Shrila Prabhupada (though they will make that claim). Rather, it is the way of embracing Shrila Prabhupada and his actual instructions, and proper Gaudiya siddhanta. Blind following is condemned by our *Acharyas*, and every devotee who rises to the Madhyama stage must develop proper discrimination regarding their association. One must examine the character of others and determine who is fit to associate with and who must be neglected.

> *A mundane person in the dress of a Vaishnava should not be respected but rejected. This is enjoined in the shastra (upeksha). The word upeksha means neglect. One should neglect an envious person. .. There are many jealous people in the dress of Vaishnavas in this Krishna consciousness movement, and they should be completely neglected. There is no need to serve a jealous person who is in the dress of a Vaishnava.* Cc. Madhya 1.218 Purport

In the next section of this book we will discuss Starting the Hare Krishna Movement Again, in the manner that Shrila Prabhupada intended.

Epilogue to Part Two

Are *All* the GBC Criminal?

The question will naturally be raised as to whether *all* of the GBC are guilty of the above claims. To make it absolutely clear, I explicitly state that *I do not make such a claim.* But that is not the issue. In this analysis we are not looking at individual GBC members malfeasance (which others have documented in books and online over many decades) – but the result of their collective actions as a body.

I've stated repeatedly that our conclusion is to be based on the principle of *phalena parichyate* – judging by the result – and that conclusion is, the GBC body has collectively shown themselves unfit for leadership and should be abandoned. No wasting any more energy trying to correct them, criticizing them, calling them ill-names, publicly shaming them, etc., all of which has brought little or no result. Why continue?

Devotees feel powerless because they have given their power to the GBC, but we are not powerless! All we need do is take back our power and follow Shrila Prabhupada directly, redirecting our energies to the positive end of preaching to the innocent public. Forget the wayward leadership. Let them do what they want. They are of no interest to those who are focused on serving Shrila Prabhupada and the Supreme Lord.

There are good lessons for us in this regard in the first canto of *Srimad Bhagavatam.* While touring his kingdom Maharaja

Pariksit came across the personality of Kali cutting the legs of the bull Dharma. Inquiring from Dharma who had hurt him, Dharma refuses to identify Kali as the wrong-doer. Shrila Prabhupada's comments offer us an important lesson:

> Although the bull, or the personality of religion, and the cow, the personality of the earth, knew perfectly well that the personality of Kali was the direct cause of their sufferings, still, as devotees of the Lord, they knew well also that without the sanction of the Lord no one could inflict trouble upon them. According to the Padma Purana, our present trouble is due to the fructifying of seedling sins, but even those seedling sins also gradually fade away by execution of pure devotional service. Thus even if the devotees see the mischief-mongers, they do not accuse them for the sufferings inflicted. They take it for granted that the mischief-monger is made to act by some indirect cause, and therefore they tolerate the sufferings, thinking them to be God-given in small doses, for otherwise the sufferings should have been greater.

> Maharaja Pariksit wanted to get a statement of accusation against the direct mischief-monger, but they declined to give it on the above-mentioned grounds. Speculative philosophers, however, do not recognize the sanction of the Lord; they try to find out the cause of sufferings in their own way, as will be described in the following verses. According to Shrila Jiva Gosvami, such speculators are themselves bewildered, and thus they cannot know that the ultimate cause of all causes is the Supreme Lord, the Personality of Godhead. Srimad Bhagavatam 1.17.18 Purport

We also note that Shrila Prabhupada, when directly asked by Tamal Krishna who was giving him poison, followed this same principle by remaining silent, refusing to identify anyone. In the same way we should forego any further attempts at identifying wrongdoers. Since we clearly know that the GBC have ignored and deviated from Shrila Prabhupada's instructions, our duty to Shrila Prabhupada is to abandon them. Shrila Prabhupada did not want blind followers.[a]

Let us also therefore carefully avoid Vaishnava aparadha and, without making friends or enemies, simply offer respect *from a distance.* What's done is done. Let us let the past go and stop wasting time.

Please do not use this book to condemn anyone, but use it to understand where to direct your energy. Personally I am not going to spend any energy working against the GBC or anyone else, rather, I will be using my energy to follow Shrila Prabhupada as he has instructed us, and encourage everyone to do the same. That said, my hope is that the more innocent among them (the GBC) will read this book and abandon the GBC's ISKCON to humbly serve Shrila Prabhupada's ISKCON.

The Aftermath of Realizing the Truth

Current and former ISKCON devotees will likely be emotionally reeling after having read this section of the book. This is normal, and expected, for anyone realizing that what they love is being destroyed by those they once trusted, and that their trust has been violated. It takes time to adjust to and accept such truths, to assimilate them, and to reconcile the many historical incidents and details. Those who have not previously processed, or fully

---

[a] For example, when devotees innocently followed the instructions of the New York temple president to offer chicken to the temple deities on behalf of his wife, the so-called heiress to the Toyota fortune, he rebuked the temple devotees for blindly following such a wayward authority, insisting that they should have known better and refused his instructions.

processed, this history, will find themselves going through one or more of the stages of grief: denial, anger, bargaining, followed by depression, reconciliation and finally acceptance.[b]

These stages of grief are a natural response to a tragic event or great loss. They can happen in any order and may include additional emotions. Denial is generally the first reaction. It is a defense mechanism that protects against emotional shock – "this can't be right!" Denial is typically followed by anger, during which intense emotions are projected onto others, typically the messenger. For example, the anger may be directed at the doctor who diagnosed a loved one's terminal illness.

During the next stage, bargaining, feelings of helplessness are accompanied by regret. One might have thoughts such as, "We should have noticed the signs earlier," or "We should have taken action earlier to prevent this!"

Fearing that their own inadequacies have contributed to the outcome, devotees may bargain with the Lord for a successful outcome, such as "I will strictly follow all of the principles if it will help Shrila Prabhupada's movement to be saved." Depression follows bargaining. During this stage, feelings of loss, deep sadness and regret take hold.

The final stages are acceptance and reconciliation. During the stage of reconciliation one examines past events in light of the new information to reevaluate and make sense of history. Depending on the length of their emotional involvement in this history, this can take some time. One weighs the new information against against

---

[b] I've added the stage of reconciliation which is not normally listed as one of the primary stages. I've done this because for some there is much history that didn't seem right, or make sense, that they have to sort through. Events and experiences that were inexplicable in the past may begin to make sense, triggering a new round of anger, etc.

the old to come to a new and adjusted understanding.

Devotional service is simple for the simple, and serious devotees can understand and follow the purpose of ISKCON – Shrila Prabhupada's ISKCON – by the study of his books and letters wherein his instructions for us are perfectly clear.

Let's now look further into how Shrila Prabhupada intended his mission to function and how his sincere followers can establish that today – protected from unwanted, demonic influences.

Part Three

Start the Hare Krishna Movement Again!

Foreword to Part Three

Tushta Krishna Swami was preaching independently from ISKCON but came to meet with Shrila Prabhupada who spoke to him very openly, saying: 'If you want to start your own spiritual movement, then you have my permission.'

Tushta Krishna replied 'No, Prabhupada. That's not my desire.' To which Shrila Prabhupada returned 'There's no harm. Unless a tree has many branches it is not beautiful.'

He then paused and spoke gravely. 'But the taste of the fruit must be the same. The branch must bear the same fruit as the branch it has grown from.' From: *My Glorious Master*, by Bhurijana Das

Because ISKCON is apparently thriving, at least in several parts of the world, questions will be raised about my motives and intentions in the proclamation to Start the Hare Krishna Movement Again! The fact, however, is that in the United States and Western Europe, Hare Krishna, which was once a household word, is now completely unknown. In the U.S. the large numbers of Indian diaspora keep some of the temples functioning, but the ethos, culture, and especially the enthusiasm for total surrender – giving up all fruitive activity and the endeavor for creating an alternative to materialistic society, so characteristic of ISKCON in its early days – no longer exists. And while the Indians may follow even to a high standard, the fact is, they unfortunately do not preach to the people of the host country, as Shrila Prabhupada wanted. His temples are filled with Indian diaspora with hardly a Westerner to be seen. Thus the objection to the "Hinduization" of ISKCON that has been expressed over the years. In Western Europe, where there is no Indian diaspora, the Hare Krishna Movement hangs on by the efforts of a few determined members. The fact is that in these parts of the world ISKCON is hardly a shadow of its former glory and potency, and hence there is a great need to Start the Hare Krishna Movement Again!

When I say "Start the Hare Krishna Movement Again!" I mean to again establish it as Shrila Prabhupada established it and intended it to function. Great detail regarding Shrila Prabhupada's vision for ISKCON, and his instructions to his leaders, was given in Part 2 of this book, and it is not necessary to repeat that here. Rather, in this section I will focus on other aspects of organization, some of which Shrila Prabhupada did not write or even speak about, such as his management methods. Shrila Prabhupada wanted his leaders, especially his GBC men, to simply do as he was doing, and as he constantly showed by his example. For some reason or other they could not, or would not, but in any case, they did not. Perhaps this was because of our (all of us, not just the GBC) cultural indoctrination and conditioning, or because as I have earlier suggested, they had another agenda. But Shrila Prabhupada gave us everything, and all we need do really, is simply to understand his instructions and intentions clearly, and follow them.

Shrila Prabhupada meant for ISKCON to be more than books, temples and congregation members who continue living according to the ways of a demonic culture. He intended that his Hare Krishna Movement would make a thorough overhaul of the demonic culture we now live in. So in explaining what I mean when I say "Start the Hare Krishna Movement Again!" I will also elaborate on the full scope of the cultural revolution Shrila Prabhupada desired to create. Many do not see, and thus cannot understand, this bigger picture, the 'forest,' due to focusing on the 'trees.' But the big picture needs to be understood because all of us are strands in that tapestry, and it is helpful to know how the part we are playing contributes to the whole. Shrila Prabhupada explained all of this, but due to our youth and inexperience, in both life and Krishna Consciousness, his broad vision and especially the profound implications of what he intended for ISKCON, were quite beyond our grasp. Thus, in starting the Hare Krishna Movement again it is necessary that we understand, and act, to fulfill his vision.

This third part of the book is also an answer to questions that have been asked by many, and succinctly stated by a relatively new, but intelligent and observant devotee, one "Bhaktin Rachel." In 2012 she posted a paper online asking "Who Will Clean Up This Mess?" where she states and asks:

> . . . I scoured the internet and found out more and more about the ISKCON society some of it good and some of it bad. I was happy at least there was open dialogue with devotees discussing the problems of the society in websites such as this one but I could not help but feel that there is something overall wrong with the ISKCON society. . .

> It seems to me that should I continue on my path to serve Shrila Prabhupada and Krishna the way I understand it to be then I will have to set myself against the bulk of the devotees in ISKCON. I am not sure that I want to do this. I want Shrila Prabhupada and Krishna but at what cost will this be to me? Will I be shouted at or run from the temple by the very devotees who I have known for nearly four years? Will I be thought of as their enemy?

> I know from reading it must have been hard for you all [Shrila Prabhupada's disciples] but why didn't you stand up against these 11 gurus that are mentioned in the many articles around

the internet? Because you didn't, it will be up to every new devotee who joins and does not want to take a cheap guru, to fight against the institution if they want to be part of a temple, which I don't think is very fair at all.

You see I didn't allow this to happen – the older devotees did. So how is it my fight? How is it my problem to fight off the Temple devotees who are attached to their fake gurus?

This is my problem – I want to be a devotee, and sure, I want it easy. I gave up so many thing to come this far, and now that I am smitten by this I can see that the real problems I have to face are inside the very society I want to join! This is the legacy of the older devotees who were present in Shrila Prabhupada's time and took initiation from him. I want that they are the ones who fight for us. We will help but it is not our fight – it is your fight – a fight for your guru, Shrila Prabhupada.

So without meaning to be offensive, if Shrila Prabhupada is your guru too, then before you die I beg you to please correct the wrongs that your god brothers and god sisters have done in the name of Shrila Prabhupada, to make it easier for us and future generations to join.

I wanted to add that I don't want to join any group affiliated with ISKCON – I want to be in Shrila Prabhupada's ISKCON so please don't, as others have, suggest I join their ISKCON society. I want this society sorted out so I can join what Shrila Prabhupada started. Thank you. [a]

---

[a] Posted on prabhupadavision.com, May 12, 2012

We Will Clean Up This Mess

Bhaktin Rachel echoes the statements and sentiments so many devotees have expressed over the years. I thank her for her clear observations, candid remarks, and challenge to "clean up this mess." By writing this she demonstrates that even a newcomer who has studied Shrila Prabhupada's books can understand the deviations of the GBC more clearly than the GBC or ISKCON's gurus!

In Part 2 of this book I have explained why what she calls "Shrila Prabhupada's society" cannot be sorted out. It has proven impossible to correct leaders, who have demonstrated for more than 40 years, that *they do not want to be corrected, and will not be corrected.* There is a great deal of history of devotees attempting to "clean up the mess," beginning almost immediately after Shrila Prabhupada's departure, only to be shown the door as a result of their efforts. Bhaktin Rachel is obviously unaware of this long history, but it is not true that nobody has tried.

This is why these conflicting issues are not openly discussed in the temples, and devotees only speak about such things under their breath. Rachel has astutely understood the consequences of speaking forthrightly and openly – fearing that she will also be criticized and shown the door. Those who want to continue to have access to Shrila Prabhupada's temples, prasadam, kirtans and deities, have to bite their tongue. And when no longer able to violate their conscience they vote with their feet. It is time for a mass exodus, for many to vote with their feet and recreate "Shrila Prabhupada's ISKCON" As It Was, As It Should Be, and As It Can Be. It is time to Start the Hare Krishna Movement Again! and I hope that you, and the thousands of others who clearly see the mess the GBC have made, will join us.

In the coming pages I will offer some thoughts about how "Shrila Prabhupada's ISKCON" can be established.

CHAPTER ONE

Institutions and Their Influence in Our Lives

Shastra instructs us to neglect those who are envious, and in the last chapter we concluded that the GBC should be neglected due to their deviations from, and failure to protect, Shrila Prabhupada's mission. The question then naturally arises as to how Shrila Prabhupada's sincere followers should proceed. The answer is simple: follow Shrila Prabhupada's instructions as he has given in his books, lectures and letters: "We have our standard so everything must be conducted on the basis of Krishna Consciousness as I have taught it."[1]

The organizational structure Shrila Prabhupada used, *and wanted*, can be described as *non-institutional*, as he repeatedly railed against centralization, standing committees, etc. Many will object to this on the basis that Shrila Prabhupada himself created the institution of ISKCON. Yes, but we must understand that while Shrila Prabhupada did *incorporate* the society, he took strong measures to prevent the hierarchical command-control organization typical of most institutions. The first time the GBC attempted to centralize ISKCON and create a bureaucracy he suspended them.

The second time he again disbanded the effort writing a lengthy and strongly-worded letter to Karandhara warning that such an arrangement would ruin everything. Both incidents have been detailed in Part 2.

In order to properly establish Shrila Prabhupada's intentions for his organization we must carefully understand the characteristics of institutional organization. That will help us appreciate how his method of non-institutional organization was different, and why he insisted on it. In this chapter I will first discuss institutional organization, and then why institutional organization not only does not serve, but actually undermines, spiritual pursuit. In the following chapters we will look at methods of *non-institutional* organization, and how they are better suited to quickly spreading Krishna Consciousness.

Institutional Organization

The vast majority of institutions employ a hierarchical command-control structure that has permitted the creation of huge enterprises – large government bureaucracies, as well as global corporations with great resources and influence. Such arrangements allow one person, or a small group of people to control the activities of large numbers of people. This arrangement, coupled with a money economy, forces employees to directly serve the interests of others, while serving their own interests only indirectly – doing their job to get the money to get the things that they actually want.

This arrangement of serving our interests indirectly seems natural to us only because we are so conditioned to this way of life, but the fact is that most people resent it. They don't go to their job because they like to, but because they *have* to. The bills must be paid, the family sheltered and fed, and the only way to do that in this world is through the agency of money. People hanker to have both the time *and* money for a few weeks of freedom (vacation), after which they get back in their hamster wheels, continuing to run while going nowhere. Slang phrases such as – "TGIF," (Thank God it's Friday), and "Hump day," (Wednesday after which there are only two days of slavery before the weekend) – indicate how people really feel. It is a life of *tyaga* and *bhoga* – austerities followed by a little freedom, and hopefully enough money for some sense gratification.

The fact is however that the jiva desires full freedom and independence, as Shrila Prabhupada writes: "The need of the spirit soul is that he wants to get out of the limited sphere of material bondage and fulfill his desire for complete freedom." [2] However, this world is controlled by the demonic whose natural tendency is to control and exploit others, epitomized by the demon Hiranyakasipu:

> While performing austerities the great demon was thinking: 'By dint of my severe austerities, *I shall reverse the results of pious and impious activities. I shall overturn all the established practices within this world*'. . . Asking for benedictions from Lord Brahma he said: 'Grant me that I may have no rival. *Give me sole lordship over all the living entities and presiding deities*, and all the glories obtained by that position.'. . . Being situated on the throne of King Indra, Hiranyakasipu *controlled the inhabitants of all planets*. The demigods were forced to bow down to Hiranyakasipu and *personally serve him*. SB 7.3.9, 37; 7.4.10

Hiranyakasipu wanted total control of everyone and everything. Our present culture, created by the demoniac for similar purposes, has arranged that control by establishing institutions in every aspect of our lives, so much so that we unconsciously accept them as "normal." Perfectly natural and just the way things ought to be. Because this is typically our only experience of organization, even devotees unconsciously use hierarchical methods of organization. Shrila Prabhupada, however, did not.

Our Institutional Indoctrination Began in Childhood

Early in life each child is his or her own person, doing as they are naturally inclined to do with adult guidance and encouragement. Learning is not forced since children are naturally inquisitive and drawn to explore and understand the world around them as their mind and intelligence develop.

When we enter the government school however, we quickly learn to conform our behavior to various authority figures who are tasked with teaching us. Lessons are put before us that do not arise out of spontaneous inquiry, so we must learn to force ourselves through a process that was previously naturally inspired. We learn to conform our behavior to the commands of an authority figure and are judged according to our ability to respond appropriately. So seriously do we take compliance with authority that we now force compliant behavior in about 20% of our children with drugs (Ritalin, etc.).

This childhood indoctrination conditions us to accept similar arrangements everywhere in life, especially for work. We have already learned to arrive on time, follow the Monday to Friday schedule, do as we are instructed, and please authorities with superior rank and title while suppressing our natural impulses. This Pavlov conditioning is repeated at every stage of life, and in every area of life – school, church, doctor, workplace – making the majority easily controlled by the minority.

Through this process we become "outer directed" and too often lose connection with our own selves and the Supersoul within. In place of knowing ourselves we pursue additional layers of false ego – title and rank – and are rewarded as we do so. Achieving higher rank we consider ourselves superior to others, and enjoying the perks that go with our improved status, we enter further into the world of envy. All of the indoctrination, conditioning and rewards are applied to make us forget and forego our own interests while serving the interests and goals of others, and those who excel at that are well rewarded. For these and other reasons Shrila Prabhupada called modern schools "slaughterhouses," and decried modern society as "a soul-killing civilization."

The Nature of Modern Institutions

Institutions are relatively modern creations, with the first legally established commercial institution being the 17ᵗʰ century East India Company. Today's institutions are almost always legal corporations. A corporation is a *fictional* (mental) *construct* that exists *only* in law, and which continues *in perpetuity* (forever). Corporations have no tangible existence. You cannot point to one or touch it. Similarly, you cannot point to Google, the French government, or MIT University. Their offices are not the corporation, any more than your house is you. The corporation itself is a fiction. This legal form places ownership and control of assets in the hands of a real person allowing them to profit from the activities of many people working under their direction, while shielding them from any and all liability for their actions.

Institutions were unknown in Vedic culture. We do not read in the pages of the *Srimad Bhagavatam* about any type of institution be it educational, political, or religious. Vedic culture places authority directly in persons qualified by dint of their demonstrated ability, as well as their understanding of, and dedication to, the principles of dharma. By contrast, most modern institutions caring nothing for dharma, place authority in a seat, or position, to be filled by someone whose most important qualification is not necessarily their ability, but their demonstrated willingness to do as they are told, right or wrong.

Institutional leadership is bestowed upon those who have not only demonstrated their allegiance and obedience, but who also agree to reflect the institutional point of view. Those who will not are weeded out, and even those who reach the top of the organizational pyramid will be removed should they cease to adhere to, and promote, the institutional perspective. In recent years we have witnessed several ISKCON gurus openly challenging the GBC's doctrines, only to be heavily censured and threatened with excommunication. One of them wrote to me in private correspondence of his despair: "I am shell-shocked, punch-drunk, and hopeless about effecting any major change."

Institutional organizations almost inevitably develop an identity and purposes of their own that are *separate from, and superior to,* those of the individuals who make them up. They also develop a leadership that is distinct from the members. Individual and group interests therefore can, and often do, become divided. The leaders, identifying themselves as representatives of the institution, regard as one of their major functions the control of the members, forcing them to submit to institutional identities and behaviors. In so doing, they induce, reward, promote, and coerce, or even manipulate and threaten group members into subordinating their personal interests, and understanding, to "superior" and "more important" organizational purposes.

Our Definition of Institution

For the remainder of this discussion I will use a very specific definition when referring to institutions and "institutional organization(s)," especially in regard to the GBC's ISKCON, which is:

> any permanent social organization with purposes of its own, having formalized and structured rules and methods for pursuing those purposes, and making and enforcing rules of conduct in order to control those within it. An institution is an

independent, self-justifying, self-perpetuating organization *that, for all practical purposes, is not accountable to, nor under the control of, its members.*[3]

Although Shrila Prabhupada did not want this to happen to his organization, the GBC's ISKCON can now accurately be described in this way. The GBC has boldly discarded Shrila Prabhupada's admonitions on this matter, and the consequences are painfully obvious even to newcomers to Krishna Consciousness such as Bhaktin Rachel.

This explains why Shrila Prabhupada did not want his organization to develop into a centralized, hierarchical institutional structure, warning that by doing so "the whole thing will be spoiled." Reading the memoirs of ISKCON's first devotees it is apparent that very early on there was no alternative purpose, no hierarchy of positions and perks, and nobody trying to control others. Repeatedly we hear how all of the devotees felt as if they were one family, and that was also my experience in my early years. Gradually however, it has been transformed into an institutional beast. Author Butler Schaffer explains how insidiously the transition takes place:

> The changes that transform a member-oriented group into an organizationally-centered institution are gradual. To see it one needs to become aware of the significance of subtle and gradual transformations: to learn to read between the lines of resolutions and memos; to note the increase in organizational rules and their impact upon one's autonomy and purposes, as well the emergence of organizational hierarchies and the increased importance of the organizational entity itself. One must learn to observe the increasing distinctions between the roles and authority of organizational leaders and others within the group, with decision making increasingly centralized; and to be sensitive to the increased importance attached to obedience, protocol, bureaucratic procedures, and the "greater good" of the group.[4]

This transformation can be seen in ISKCON with even a cursory study of its history.

As difficult as it might be to appreciate since we are so conditioned by institutional ways of thinking, the culture institutions evoke is demonic, in that, rather than uplifting and serving the members of society as Vedic culture does, institutional hierarchies add layers of ego and legitimize using people to serve the wishes of others.

Under Shrila Prabhupada's direction ISKCON was to be an *informal organization* that was to function according to the principles he had laid down. *Temple presidents were to be independent,* and *the GBC were to be advisors without command authority* using only moral suasion. However, upon Shrila Prabhupada's departure the GBC transformed ISKCON into a hierarchical command-control institution, complete with layers of bureaucracy similar to any corporate organization. More than a corporation however, they have created the impression of being an unassailable imperial institution with a voluminous book of laws that are trotted out whenever the need suits them, even though the GBC themselves cannot remember most of them, and in many cases do not follow them.

Institutions Have No Place in Spiritual Pursuit

If we consider the above points in relationship to individuals and spiritual organizations, including ISKCON, it will be seen that spiritual *institutions* (as defined above), rather than facilitating our spiritual development and freedom put additional stumbling blocks in front of us, and this is especially true for neophyte devotees. Here we identify and explain some of them.

Position and Title Add Additional Layers of False Ego

Titles and corresponding command of others create additional false ego designations, fanning the *rajarsic* flames of "I and mine" and *tamasic* influences of controlling others. Under such influences, especially with the adulation of fawning neophytes, devotees who prematurely accept high positions prior to the stage of *anarta-nivriti*, will water the weeds of *pratishta* instead of their bhakti creeper, eventually bringing about their downfall. This has happened to dozens of ISKCON *sannyasis* and gurus. Title, position, followers and attendant perks can also feed envy and unhealthy competition within immature devotees. Desires to be more influential and more important than others develop – conceptions that are contrary to the das das anudas consciousness of genuine spiritual culture. Institutional positions are unnecessary, and are even shunned by devotees who are pure in heart, as we have pointed out in the earlier chapter "Who is A Devotee?"

We pursue self-realization in the effort to free ourselves from designations, but a command-control organization is counterproductive because of adding *additional* designations that take over from where the old ones left off. If I leave my job as an "engineer" to move into the temple as a "brahmacari," have I really freed myself from any ego-imposed boundaries? It certainly is possible that our new "spiritual" designations may bind us more tightly than the material ones ever did, possibly because some spiritual ego layers provide more sense gratification than the material ones could. As a "*sannyasi*" or "guru" I may become very attached to the service and adoration of others that I would never receive as a mere engineer. In this way it is possible that those adopting spiritual and institutional titles become even more attached to a material identity than before beginning their spiritual journey.

This is why Lord Chaitanya teaches: "*I am not a Brahmin. I am not a kshatriya. I am not a vaisya. I am not a sudra. I am not a sannyasi. I am not a grhastha. I am not a brahmacari.*" Self-realization means to replace all of our materially-imposed designations with the one true identity: "*Gopi-bhartur pada-kamalayor dasa-dasanudasa* – I am the servant of the servant of the servant of the servant of Krishna, the maintainer of the gopis."[5] And Shrila Prabhupada admonishes us: "unless you come to this stage, free from all designations, you cannot serve Krishna."[6]

Mistaking Position and Title for Spiritual Progress

Titles and authority often create a misleading understanding that achieving a higher position within the organization equates to spiritual progress. This is simply not true. This misunderstanding can happen to the one with the title or position, the supposedly "advanced devotee," as well as their followers, who intrinsically equate the two. Neophyte devotees have little understanding by which to discriminate between who is advanced and who is not, and are thus inclined to accept title or position as indicators of spiritual advancement. If the person with position and title falls from grace it can have a devastating effect on those neophytes, who have placed so much faith in them, causing them to abandon either all discriminating intelligence to remain "faithful," or their own personal spiritual pursuit.

Acting through False Ego with Religious Conviction –

Those with high position, if not completely pure in heart, mix their own polluted consciousness with their religious institutional identity and authority. Since they are *empowered* to "act for God" it is not surprising to see them do things they otherwise would not, and justify themselves in so doing. Impure men acting on the basis of this ego-extension gives rise to the observation of Blaise Pascal that "Men never do evil so completely and cheerfully as when they do it from religious conviction."

Institutional Norms Undermine Spiritual Freedom

Instructions of spiritual authorities are meant to assist the neophyte in their spiritual progress, but eventually every devotee is meant to achieve direct contact with the Lord in the heart and surrender directly to Him: *sarva dharman parityajnya.* However, who is to be followed when an institutional authority gives conflicting instructions? Spiritual life means complete freedom of choice and action, and every individual must have the freedom to follow their heart. Yet even gurus, who are supposed to be in direct contact with the Supersoul, are required to submit to the GBC. Incredibly this imposition is mandated by the "ultimate managing authority," who have replaced Shrila Prabhupada with themselves as ISKCON's highest authority. Their externally imposed authority demonstrates either their lack of understanding of the spiritual process, and/or their contempt for it, since they interfere so willingly and dramatically with it.

Who Serves Who?

Shrila Prabhupada set the perfect example of service. From the very first day of ISKCON he was dedicated in service to all – cooking, cleaning, teaching by example, etc. The Vedic culture is that everyone engages in service to others, but modern institutions turn this idea on its head by requiring members to serve the institution. This mentality has also developed in ISKCON, where devotees eagerness to engage in voluntary devotional service somehow becomes turned into an obligation where the members are pressured to serve, even to the point where they cannot take care of their own legitimate needs. Too much of such "service" (exploitation) has caused many to leave Shrila Prabhupada's shelter.

The fact is that people always serve their own interests. They come to ISKCON because of their perception that doing so serves their interests, and they leave ISKCON when they perceive that staying no longer serves their interests.

Institutional False Ego

To one degree or another, all of us are steeped in institutional conditioning and unconsciously act in that way. From the days of our school experience we unquestioningly continue the same behavior throughout life. As the tree is bent, so it grows. The consequence of this is to remove us from an understanding of our own selves. In the process of learning to please institutional authorities, and serve them, we become attached to them and learn to feel secure and protected in the institutional sanctuary, despite the fact that doing so may interfere with our ability to know ourselves as individual beings. As a result of submitting ourselves to institutional authorities everywhere, we become outer-directed and self-alienated, immersing ourselves in the *nirvishesha-sunnyavadi* – voidism and impersonalism – Srila Prabhupada is trying to save us from!

In order to maintain our place within the institutional social order we learn to conform to the expectations of others, repress any conflicting ideas, while extolling the virtues of institutional duty and personal sacrifice.

To relieve stress that might arise from conflicting interests between ourselves and the leaders of the institution we identify with, we must conform to the institution and its leadership, giving up our own individual understanding of truth in the process. Even Bhaktin Rachel recognized and objected to this fact. By conforming against our will we become the institution, not collectively, but quite personally. We create or adopt a role and personality within the group – our new group oriented identity – which, even in, or especially in, religious or spiritual organizations, does not free us from false ego, but becomes an additional ego layer.

Institutions train us to be irresponsibly submissive, with the consequence that when problems arise we cannot help but see others as the cause – "*they* made me do this," or, "*they* did this to me." There are hundreds of examples of such finger-pointing at institutional authorities and castigating them for our problems. We've heard so much about how "ISKCON" has done this or that, but remember – ISKCON is actually a fiction. It is only real people acting in the name of ISKCON that do things. But because we have been made powerless in order to conform we blame our problems on the institution and its authorities.

If we wish to understand how institutions have affected our lives, we must begin by understanding how our attitudes have been influenced by *our own voluntary involvement* with them. We must be willing to stand back and observe what we have become, while resisting the temptation to do what we have been trained to do: look to others (our "superiors") for answers. Only when we become aware of our role in our dependence will we be in a position to understand the consequences in our own lives and spiritual progress. This is not to say that we should not be submissive to seniors who teach and guide us. However, we must guard against becoming unthinking, blind followers and institutional sycophants.

The solution to the problem of institutional identification and conformance lies in the act of freeing ourselves from such institutional constraints. Liberation does not consist of reforming or destroying institutional prisons or their commanders, but simply by letting go of our self-imposed dependence. We do not have to reform others, or somehow force them to do the right thing, or get them out of our way. It is simply a matter of getting (our self-imposed dependence and unquestioning compliance) out of our own way.

Self-realization will never be achieved by following someone's instructions, nor is it a matter of simply boarding the Good Ship

ISKCON and kicking back to enjoy the ride Back to Godhead. Nothing will happen without our active and determined participation. Letting go of institutional constraints does not mean abandoning our relationships to our *shiksha* and *diksha* gurus, or others that guide and nurture our spiritual development. Naturally those relationships are very important, but to be most effective we need to be free from institutional constraints that artificially, and impersonally, control us.

Now let's have a detailed look at Shrila Prabhupada's non-institutional ISKCON and his management methods.

CHAPTER TWO

Shrila Prabhupada's Methods of Organization

The bona fide teacher of religion is neither any product of nor the favorer of, any mechanical system. In his hands no system has likewise, the chance of degenerating into a lifeless arrangement. The mere pursuit of fixed doctrines and fixed liturgies cannot hold a person to the true spirit of doctrine or liturgy. Shrila Bhaktisiddhanta, Putana

Institutional v. Non-institutional Organization

The distinction between institutional and non-institutional forms of organization is the difference in the relationship between the organization per se and those who comprise it.

In non-institutional systems, the organization is little more than a convenience, an informal tool that serves and assists its members, each of whom further their individual interests through participation in the group. Such organizations have no independent identity or purposes of their own separate from that of the members. They represent only the composite of the personal objectives of the members.

A good example of this would be any marriage or family, wherein the couple join together to further their mutual interests of emotional security and love. When marrying the couple does not create a separate organization called "the marriage" or "the family" whose interests supersede the interests of individual family members (although this might be the case in certain "aristocratic families" or families of "royalty"). Another non-institutional organization would be a club, such as a bowling league, or card club, whose members meet weekly to socialize while sharing a common interest. However, these groups have no independent existence and cease to exist without participation of the members.

The non-institutional organization, having no formal identity apart from the members cannot have any division of purpose – and thus no conflict – between personal and group purposes. Thus no attempt is made to control the members of non-institutional organizations. The group is simply a reflection of the interests of those within it. If the group has any leadership, it tends to be temporary and informal. The leaders would not set themselves or their purposes apart from the others, or perceive their functions as being policymakers or supervisors over the rest of the group. Such leaders function more as "player coaches," rather than controlling authorities. Shrila Prabhupada was one such leader, and early ISKCON functioned as a non-institutional group. But to fully appreciate the importance and impact of Shrila Prabhupada's non-institutional style, it is necessary to understand the context of those times.

The Fertile Environment of the 1960s

In the mid-1960s America was an extremely conservative society where not only proper behavior, but appearance, was expected and even required. The Beatles shocked the world by sporting hair to their ears, when such a haircut could cost a young man his job. The Cold War with the Soviet Union was constantly hyped, and nightly news programs displayed the awesome terror of atomic bomb tests. We were conditioned as children to live in fear of nuclear holocaust, to "duck and cover" under our school desks should atomic bombs start raining from the skies.[a] The terror continued in our teen years as the death and horror of the Vietnam War was graphically displayed on every living room on the new color TV, provoking strong emotional reactions, causing millions to take to the streets in protest.

To compound the confusion, thousands marched in the streets in other challenges to the status quo: Black leaders protested racial discrimination, women wanted "liberation," as did "gay rights" activists, and additional thousands alarmed by Rachel Carson's "Silent Spring" marched for environmental protection. Practically anybody that felt restricted or threatened by conventional and conservative American society was in the street demanding change.

However, the chilling consequences of challenging the power structure were made starkly real by the shocking assassinations of America's most beloved heroes and promising leaders – President John Kennedy, his brother Robert, and black leaders Dr. Martin Luther King, Jr., and Malcom X, shattering many American's dreams for a different future.

---

[a] A brief anecdote to illustrate this point. My parent's house was on the flight path to Detroit Metropolitan Airport and in those days the jet engines were very loud. Sometimes after I lay down to sleep, the planes would roar overhead, and I would think "Oh no! The Russians are coming to drop The Bomb!" I'd pull the blankets over my head and hold my breath waiting for the inevitable explosion that never materialized, breathing a sigh of relief after the plane had passed.

406 | DIVINE OR DEMONIAC?

In short, it was a time of great confusion, tension, turmoil and violence. A time when tens-of-millions were searching for Truth instead of hypocrisy, for peace instead of war, for freedom instead of restriction. The shallowness and hypocrisy of modern living, the manipulation, artificial values, and outer-directed lives of the times, whereby they were directed to live according to someone else's standards of right and wrong, and die in a senseless war, were poignantly felt by the youth. They were looking for anything other than a status quo they felt was strangling their inner call for freedom. The youth could see through the manipulation and rejected it, preferring to live on the streets as penniless hippies. They wanted to change the world into something very different but they lacked any understanding of how to do so.

This was the scene that Bhaktivedanta Swami entered in the fall of 1965. Swamiji, as he was first referred to, was strikingly original and genuine, and he gave American youth that something different – different haircuts, different clothing, different vocabulary, different ways of living, and above all, a different understanding of life! His followers were eager to adopt these changes – not only as a rejection of society's shallow values – but because he was showing them how to bring genuine change to the world – by lifting everyone up through God consciousness. Shrila Prabhupada offered real liberation – liberation from the material values of life, and it was exhilarating.

Shrila Prabhupada's Management Style

Shrila Prabhupada's society reflected the rebelliousness of the times. ISKCON was not only transcendental – it also had a revolutionary spirit – and the devotees, many former hippies, seriously believed they had now found the means by which to bring dramatic and lasting change to the world.

A significant aspect of Swamiji's appeal was his easy-going, non-institutional method of organization – a perfect fit for youth who were rebelling against institutions of every kind. The temples provided a new way of living, reflected not only by the dramatic appearance and activities of the devotees, but also in the freedom with which they were organized.

Being completely pure of heart, Shrila Prabhupada's desire was simply to serve his followers and help them become fixed on the spiritual path of Krishna conscious. He had no desire to control, or even restrict anyone against their will. He explained the principles and the eternal benefit of following them, and gave listeners the freedom to do as they wished, never demanding anything. He commanded respect and inspired obedience by doing himself exactly as he encouraged his followers.

Inspired by his revelations and vision, young and inexperienced followers wanted to assist him, and whatever they lacked in terms of experience, or training, was made up for by determination and zeal. Whether it was in publishing Back to Godhead magazine, painting transcendental pictures, printing and selling books, or opening temples, their only thought was pleasing Shrila Prabhupada, and by Krishna's unlimited grace they accomplished miracles. The devotees embarked upon things totally new to them, and developed the necessary skills to master them in short time. We are blessed to now have many books recounting those early adventures, and misadventures.[1] Lots of mistakes were made, but they were overlooked because everyone was focused on the goal, not the journey. Working together they experienced the joy and comradery of teamwork committed to undertaking difficult tasks. Shrila Prabhupada had given them the moral equivalent of war.[b]

---

[a] In the early 20th century opinion-makers everywhere were speaking against a European war. But William James in a now famous article opined that there would be war until the time when there was a "moral equivalent of war." His arguments were based on the fact that the threat of annihilation brought out wonderful qualities that people longed to experience – heroism, great

Needless to say, there was a great deal of chaos, but there was also order, based on central shared principles he had established. Devotees were eager and enthusiastic to broadcast the spiritual wisdom given by Shrila Prabhupada, a wisdom previously unheard of in their world, offering complete liberation from the shackles of ignorance and bondage. It was revolutionary and something to shout about!^c And shout they did, for hours on *harinam sankirtan* and book distribution. Because every center was newly established, any and all help was welcomed, and every eager newcomer had the opportunity to contribute according to their ability and desire.

By giving his followers freedom in action, while at the same time requiring adherence to stated principles, Shrila Prabhupada unleashed within his followers such exuberant energy and enthusiasm that the devotees worked day and night, expressing amazing creativity and ingenuity in their service. The excitement of attempting the unknown, which they often did, was pervasive, and they were often happily surprised by their success. Shrila Prabhupada continually encouraged them to try for the seemingly impossible – "shoot for the rhinoceros" – saying "Krishna will give you the intelligence of what to do," and He did.

Combining Chaos and Order

Shrila Prabhupada gave his inexperienced followers freedom in their efforts to preach, and naturally this invited a certain amount of chaos. But his guidance gave the order that was necessary to

---

determination, putting aside of petty squabbles, sacrifice for others, etc. Shrila Prabhupada did indeed give his followers the moral equivalent of war, and it was wonderful!

^c Nobody at that time (and even today) was offering such profound and clear spiritual truths, saying unequivocally "you are not that body," and explaining the science of God.

achieve global success. Interestingly, the same methods Shrila Prabhupada was using to successfully spreading Krishna consciousness around the globe were also being used by another person to achieve amazing results at the same time. Dee Hock threw out traditional hierarchical command to give his team the freedom to develop an entirely new, and at the time, impossible, business – the VISA credit card. His method allowed for the development of a "transcendent" (his word) organization that brought together in wholly new ways, an unimaginable complex of diverse countries, institutions and individuals, to develop the first truly global credit card.

Hock emphasized freedom and accepted the chaos that would inevitably come with it. He went on to champion the combination of chaos and order, which he dubbed "Chaordic," to express what he thought would become the business model for the twenty-first century.

VISA grew at a minimum of 20% and as much as 50%, compounded annually for three decades. Within 30 years VISA had 22,000 owner-merchants, was accepted at 15 million merchant locations in hundreds of languages, in more than 200 countries. Three-quarters of a billion people were using VISA to make more than 14 billion transactions annually, processing more than $1.25 trillion of business. This stratospheric business expansion remains unrivaled to this day.

Under Hock's management, nobody at VISA had a job title, nor was there any hierarchy of management, yet the organization was able to accomplish greater growth than any other organization in history. This growth was based on the principle that people can manage themselves and do what needs to be done if the "leaders" will simply stay out of their way. Time and time again the VISA organization demonstrated Hock's axiom: "the truth that given the right conditions, from no more than dreams, determination, and liberty to try, quite ordinary people consistently do extra-ordinary things." In describing the transformation of ordinary people who, when unrestrained and free to contribute wherever they could, he writes:

> Leaders spontaneously emerged and reemerged, none in control, but all in order. Ingenuity exploded. Individuality and diversity flourished. People astonished themselves at what they could accomplish and were amazed at the suppressed talents that emerged in others.

> Position became meaningless. Power over others became meaningless. Time became meaningless. Excitement about doing the impossible increased, and a community based on purpose, principle and people arose. Individuality, self-worth, ingenuity, and creativity flourished; and as they did, so did the sense of belonging to something larger than self, something beyond immediate gain and monetary gratification.

> The effort was fueled by a spontaneous expansion of nonmonetary exchange of value – things done for one another without measurement or prescribed return – the heart and soul of all community. People discovered that any receiving worthy of the name is an inexorable product of giving. They gave of themselves without expectation and received in ways beyond calculation.

> In the process our perception began to change. It was as though we could now see with different eyes. Even more with a different mind. Even beyond that *with a different consciousness, and it was incredibly exciting.* (emphasis in the original)[2]

What the devotees experienced and felt during the early days of ISKCON and the "Hare Krishna Explosion" (as Hayagriva Dasa put it) could not be better stated, for exactly the same reasons – leaders spontaneously emerged, ingenuity exploded, diversity flourished, and things were done for one another without measurement or prescribed return, etc. Except in our case the effort *was* transcendental, fueled by the desire to serve the Supreme Lord Sri Krishna and His pure devotee.

Vidura Dasa, former temple president of Mombasa, tells how non-institutional methods created amazing results in Kenya during the 1980s:

I introduced the spinning of cotton to local villagers and the result was incredible. Previously they sold their raw cotton to the international buyers who came from Europe and Japan. I bought a simple spinning device, made from an old bicycle wheel, from the Gandhi Institute in Vrindavana and brought it back to Kenya. I had a local mechanic make a couple of dozen copies of the wheel, and gave them out in the village. The villagers couldn't believe how much yarn they could produce from their raw cotton. I couldn't believe it either! What to do with all the yarn? We got an old loom from somewhere and they started weaving. Amazing cloth, simply beautiful. When I went back to see them they were all lined up on the road, men, women and children, with their produce as a kind of an honor guard.

I helped them market the cloth to some tourist outlets and sales took off, bringing much needed income that provided medicine, school books, cooking oil, salt and other basic things the people could not previously afford. The head teacher of the local school had been a student in the same school. He told me that of the approximately 800 students, not a single student had sat for the national primary exam for the previous ten years, or more, in that school. There were simply no books to teach with, and no desks to sit at. The children had to bring a cement block to school at the beginning of term which acted as their desk. The year after the cotton spinning began every student in the final year sat for the end of primary exam and every student passed. It was the first time in their history that every child went on to higher education. The infant mortality rate dropped from over 35% to less than 5% in a short time. Every person in the village could spin. Blind, disabled, pol*io, old, young, ill, healthy, men, women. There was no limit and no targets. If you had a few minutes you did a little. There was a queue in the family to see who could have the next turn on the spinning wheel. The activity of spinning transformed the village.*

Either the Round Table Club or the Lions Club provided funding to bring ladies from India to teach the initial lessons. The UN, Oxfam, Save the Children, UNICEF and all these organizations had been in that district for decades with no results. I gave a little input, tiny, with no resources, nothing, and the result was massive. The Ministry for Health in Nairobi, hundreds of miles away, sent a delegation to find out why the children were not dying anymore. The previous hundreds of infant deaths were just a statistic they recorded for their ledger books over decades – but nothing was done to prevent the catastrophe. However, when the statistics changed for the better, they couldn't understand why and sent a delegation to find out. Of course the politicians wanted to jump on the bandwagon after the fact, and claim the credit. But it was the people themselves who did everything. I just provided the kernel of an idea and they ran with it.

Chaordic is Krishna's Method of Organization

Shrila Prabhupada did not speak or write *directly about* his method of organization. It was just natural for him. Free from the need or desire to control others he gave his followers father-like guidance along with the freedom to apply what he taught them. He expected them to do as he asked, but if they sometimes could not, or would not, with seemingly unlimited patience, he repeatedly corrected them.

Thinking only briefly about this world, we can realize that this is Sri Krishna's method, by which this entire material world functions. Humans are given complete freedom and unlimited lifetimes to learn higher principles and to demonstrate that learning. Hock observed Chaordic principles in nature, and that nothing in nature has any similarity to institutions that limit and control behavior:

> There's no principal blackbird pecking at the rest of the flock. There's no Super frog telling the others how to croak. There's no teacher tree lining up all the saplings and telling them how to grow. . .
>
> Life is uncertainty, surprise, wonder, speculation, love, joy, pity, pain mystery, beauty, and a thousand other things we can't yet imagine. Life is not about controlling. It's not about getting. It's not about having. Life is eternal, perpetually becoming, or it is nothing.[3]

I've included this cameo on VISA to demonstrate that Shrila Prabhupada's management method was also used by others to achieve similar amazing results. But beyond VISA there are other stellar examples of the growth and complexity that can be achieved when there is no limiting authority. The internet is an amazing example that provides unlimited information to anyone in the world.[4] The very different Alcoholics Anonymous (AA) is another. AA has spread all over the earth with no organization whatsoever because it effectively meets real needs!

Shrila Prabhupada's Principles of Organization

Shrila Prabhupada's organizational principles facilitated the spreading of Krishna Consciousness over the entire world in just 11 short years. Let's take a detailed look at just what those principles were. After this we will take a deeper look at non-institutional organization and get really clear about what that means. Armed with an explicit understanding of non-institutional organization we will be ready to discuss their application to Start the Hare Krishna Movement Again!

1. Principle-centered, based on clearly shared principles and purpose
2. Self-organizing and self-governing in whole and in part
3. Primary purpose is to enable and serve the constituent parts
4. Powered from the periphery with responsibility distributed through every node, and unified at the core
5. Operate not through hierarchies of authority, but through networks of equals
6. No centralized command, no obvious headquarters, and no glittering center of power
7. Not owned by anyone
8. Harmonious combination of cooperation and competition
9. Durable in purpose and principle, malleable in form and function
10. Learn, adapt and innovate in ever expanding cycles
11. Compatible with the human spirit and the biosphere
12. Natural expansion due to meeting real needs very effectively

Shrila Prabhupada applied these principles in his management methods as follows:

Principle-centered, Shared Purpose and Principles

Shrila Prabhupada created ISKCON as a vehicle to educate people in the spiritual values of life with the goal being the escape from bondage in this material world, and as *Acharya* adjusted the principles for people of the modern age. This is promoted throughout Shastra and is a key principle of Vaishnava siddhanta:

> Krishna will accept a devotee who strictly follows the regulative principles and the method prescribed in the various books and literatures published by the authorities. *The Acharya gives the*

suitable method for crossing the ocean of nescience by accepting the boat of the Lord's lotus feet, *and if this method is strictly followed, the followers will ultimately reach the destination, by the grace of the Lord. . . One must accept the Acharya-sampradaya, otherwise one's endeavor will be futile.*

Practically, it is in your hands now to manage things, so I can translate and write books. This routine program is the backbone of our Movement, and we stand solid on such program such as chanting, speaking, arati, reading scriptures, prasadam, like that. These things are sufficient for us. Any sane man will be attracted to such program. And if we perform everything nicely and always seize every opportunity to preach about Krishna, that is our formula for success. [5]

The first quote emphasizes that the *Acharya* establishes the principles, the second quote our shared purpose and principles. There are many, many such statements from both Shastra and Shrila Prabhupada emphasizing these points.

Self-organizing and Self-governing

Shrila Prabhupada was not a micro-manager. He frequently gave responsibility and freedom to relatively inexperienced young devotees. He gave direct instructions to do so to some, but others took the initiative on themselves out of enthusiasm. Every center was expected to follow the principles and practices he had established, and to ensure this he himself constantly traveled from temple to temple. Shrila Prabhupada wanted his GBC to follow his example.

He established that each center be independent and self-governing, but his leaders several times went beyond their authority in the attempt to centralize management and create a hierarchical bureaucracy, for which they were chastised. In a now famous letter to Karandhara, Shrila Prabhupada wrote:

> I have heard from Jayatirtha you want to make big plan for centralization of management. . . I do not at all approve of such plan. *Do not centralize anything. Each temple must remain independent and self-sufficient. That was my plan from the very beginning*, why you are thinking otherwise? Once before you wanted to do something centralizing with your GBC meeting, and if I did not interfere the whole thing would have been killed. . . *Management, everything, should be done locally by local men. Accounts must be kept, things must be in order and lawfully done, but that should be each temple's concern*, not yours. *Krishna Consciousness Movement is for training men to be independently thoughtful and competent in all types of departments of knowledge and action*, not for making bureaucracy. *Once there is bureaucracy the whole thing will be spoiled.* 22Dec72

Exist to Enable Their Constituent Parts

The "constituent parts" referred to here are the end users. In the case of Krishna Consciousness it means those newly introduced and beginning to learn about the Absolute Truth. To "enable the constituent parts" means that the purpose of the organization is to serve the individual, as opposed to institutions where members are expected to serve the organization. The chaord of the internet is to serve the individual users, and the chaord of Alcoholics Anonymous (AA) exists to assist members' freedom from alcohol addiction. AA members are not there to serve the AA organization, and internet users do not go online serve some supra-entity called "The Internet."

ISKCON was created by Shrila Prabhupada for the same purpose – to *give* Krishna Consciousness to those ignorant of spiritual reality, and teach them how to come closer to God, Krishna, and develop love for Him. He served the newcomers and taught his followers to do likewise. ISKCON was thus meant for *enabling* everyone to come closer to Krishna. Shrila Prabhupada did not teach, nor expect, his followers to serve the notion of an institution called "ISKCON." The point of the service was always to give Krishna Consciousness to the "consitutent parts" – the people of the world – and that is what he did – GIVE. He *gave* spiritual knowledge, he *gave* prasadam, he *gave* kirtan, he *gave* understanding and truth – without requiring anything in return, and ISKCON was built into an international organization by those who, out of gratitude, reciprocated by giving him what they had – their energy in the form of money and service.

The GBC have made the institution the prominent focus of every aspect of the society, and all aspects of Krishna Consciousness are expressed specifically in relationship to the institution. For example, the "ISKCON Disciples Course" is required for initiation, despite the fact that NO shastric injunction has ever stated that one should become a disciple of an institution. The course, required by the GBC for all initiates, repeatedly emphasizes the relationship with the institution, as in this promotion:

> This *ISKCON Disciples* Course is a training program which is meant to help you deepen your understanding of guru-tattva and gurupadashraya *within the multiple guru culture of ISKCON*. This is a mandatory course for all devotees preparing to *take initiation in ISKCON*. *This ISKCON Disciple* Course is based on the teachings of Shrila Prabhupada and current *ISKCON Law* and gives reference to the writings from the broader Gaudiya Vaishnava tradition.[6]

There is also the "ISKCON Guru Seminar" for those aspiring to become "ISKCON gurus." Note that they are not simply gurus, but "ISKCON gurus," that is, institutional gurus. Those actually qualified to be guru would never participate in this apasiddhanta, designed to control both guru and disciple.

Shrila Prabhupada never mentioned the idea of "ISKCON gurus" or "ISKCON disciples." He, as well as his guru, taught that the bona fide guru is a transcendental autocrat, not an institutional sycophant. Shrila Prabhupada emphasized that the proper role of the corporation of ISKCON was as a tool for spreading Krishna Consciousness, not an instrument for controlling members.

We must Start the Hare Krishna Movement Again as a non-institutional organization and eradicate the idea of a controlling corporate institution in spiritual affairs. We must establish Shrila Prabhupada's ISKCON as an organization that serves its members by teaching them how to use their free will to serve Sri Krishna according to the principles established by our *Acharyas*.

Powered from the Periphery, Unified at the Core

This means that power is not reserved for those at the top, but purposefully distributed to those at the periphery of the organization, who may not even be ready to properly use it. Yes this sounds counterintuitive, but this is exactly what Shrila Prabhupada did. He authorized very new devotees to act even beyond their capacity, and to make decisions necessary to getting the job done, but he was always there to guide them and answer their questions. The "core," or center of the Krishna Consciousness Movement in early ISKCON was – and should always be – Shrila Prabhupada. Authority extends from him and his teaching, to the devotees at the periphery, whether then or now. This can be established once again simply by understanding the principles Shrila Prabhupada set in place and adhering to them.

Operate through networks of equals

In Shrila Prabhupada's ISKCON there were two layers of management: himself and the temple presidents. He never functioned as a manager but rather as a guide. He wanted the temple presidents to use their own individual initiative and innovation to present Krishna Consciousness in their local area. The GBC were created to take Shrila Prabhupada's place so that he could focus on writing, and he expected them to do as he was doing: traveling from center to center, seeing that the devotees were chanting japa and following the principles, give classes on Krishna conscious philosophy, enthuse the devotees, and deal with any problems. He never wanted the GBC to create additional layers of management or to centralize anything, as they are doing now.

No centralized command, and no glittering center of power

Shrila Prabhupada's ISKCON was *not* a for-profit organization meant to project a powerful product, image or brand around the world. It is meant to teach the principles of Krishna Consciousness, and provide places where devotees could gather to share their interest in Krishna Consciousness. Each temple was autonomous, and meant to function within the guidelines established by His Divine Grace, thus there was no need of a central headquarters directing their activities. Neither did Shrila Prabhupada establish a hierarchical body of management that generally occupies such headquarters. Power, meaning the power to make decisions and take initiative, rested with each individual temple president. Thus there is no need within Shrila Prabhupada's ISKCON for any headquarters or "center of power." Temples are meant to attract people, but they are not necessarily for the devotees:

> As preachers, we do not require elaborate temples for our work. No, we are content to live under a tree. So, as long as your preaching work is going on, never mind there is no temple. Of course, in your western countries people must have a comfortable place to sit down or they will not come for

chanting. So as soon as possible you may get a nice place and invite the general public by making it very attractive. Letter to Locanananda 8Dec71

Not owned by anyone

Shrila Prabhupada incorporated ISKCON as a New York charitable not-for-profit religious organization that would not be owned by any person or group of persons, whose profits are not allowed to accrue to any person but meant to further the aims of the organization, in ISKCON's case, to spread of Krishna Consciousness. He wanted each center to be incorporated independently following the New York model. Legal separation of the temples is important to prevent a lawsuit of one temple from taking the assets of all.

Combine Cooperation and Competition

Shrila Prabhupada was very pleased when temples would combine their resources and manpower to put on large-scale festivals such as Rathayatra. He was also pleased to see the devotees compete with each other to see who could distribute the most books. Shrila Prabhupada's ISKCON accommodated both cooperation and competition through a network of equals.

Durable in Principle, Malleable in Form and Function

The Chaordic Permaculture Institute is a group created to share information about permaculture design principles around the world. They offer a good example of a group applying Chaordic principles, because although *the principles are the same everywhere*, they *must be uniquely applied according to local conditions*. The principles and purpose of permaculture are durable – to create natural and sustainable agriculture, but malleable in how they are applied in each unique situation.

Similarly, the principles and purposes of Krishna Consciousness are eternal – but are malleable in application according to time, place and circumstances. As the *Acharya*, Shrila Prabhupada, made necessary adjustments. His explanation of this is given in the purport to this verse from Chaitanya-charitamrita, Adi 7.38:

Sri Chaitanya Mahaprabhu appeared in order to deliver all the fallen souls. Therefore He devised many methods to liberate them from the clutches of Maya.

Purport: It is the concern of the *Acharya* to show mercy to the fallen souls. In this connection, *desa-kala-patra* (the place, the time and the object) should be taken into consideration. Since the European and American boys and girls in our Krishna consciousness movement preach together, less intelligent men criticize that they are mingling without restriction. In Europe and America boys and girls mingle unrestrictedly and have equal rights; therefore it is not possible to completely separate the men from the women. However, we are thoroughly instructing both men and women how to preach, and actually they are preaching wonderfully. . . The results of this are wonderful. Both men and women are preaching the gospel of Lord Chaitanya Mahaprabhu and Lord Krishna with redoubled strength. In this verse the words *saba nistarite kare caturi apara* indicate that Sri Chaitanya Mahaprabhu wanted to deliver one and all. Therefore it is a principle that a preacher must strictly follow the rules and regulations laid down in shastra yet at the same time devise a means by which the preaching work to reclaim the fallen may go on with full force.

Learn, Adapt and Innovate

How the devotees learned to spread Krishna Consciousness and adapted to their local culture and customs are recounted in many memoirs. Stories about how the devotees first distributed

Back to Godhead Magazine, and then the KRSNA Book, and then big books are told again and again, because they demonstrate how they took unusual risks with determined effort to do something that had not been done before. The story of the six devotees meeting the Beatles and establishing the London temple is one of surrendered commitment, courage and audacity. Likewise, getting the permit for New York Rathayatra to parade down 5th Avenue, Manhattan's biggest thoroughfare, was inconceivable, but with the ingenuity and daring risk of Toshan Krishna, Krishna made it possible. ISKCON's devotees have thousands of such stories from every country, and there is no reason that they should ever stop. All that is necessary is an earnest desire to please Krishna and His pure devotees.

Compatible with the Human Spirit

Practically speaking, nothing in the world is more compatible with the human spirit and proper living on this earth than Krishna Consciousness. Shrila Prabhupada's ISKCON allows devotees to be free to follow their inspiration, and their heart, in service to guru and Krishna – in choosing their guru, in the service they perform, and how they apply their inspiration in their service. Krishna Consciousness is in a literal sense an art, an expression of love, and art requires freedom of expression.

Natural expansion due to meeting real needs very effectively

The VISA bankcard fulfills a universal need for easy payment, and Alcoholics Anonymous fulfills a sadly universal need for those suffering from addiction. These organizations are not the result of creating unnecessary necessities by clever advertising, but are called into service by already existing need and demand.

Similarly, understanding our existential condition is a perennial need for which people search for answers. Also, in our time people are everywhere becoming aware of problems not just in their backyard, but all over the world – from plastic-filled oceans, mass animal die-offs, electro-smog pollution, poisoned land, water and skies – and they hope and long for leadership that can solve these problems. Shrila Prabhupada's mission is meant for this. His mission is meant for more than our own individual salvation. It is meant for more than temples, kirtan and books. It is meant to create an entire culture based on Dharma, providing for a revolution in the lives of a world's misdirected civilization.

Shrila Prabhupada's ISKCON is non-institutional by his design but the GBC having totally missed the point, are taking the mission in a completely different direction. Therefore we say that it is necessary to Start the Hare Krishna Movement Again! The GBC can do whatever they like, but Shrila Prabhupada's ISKCON must be continued for the benefit of the entire world. The next chapter will provide some detail to doing just that – as Shrila Prabhupada intended.

CHAPTER THREE

Establishing a Non-institutional ISKCON

At the present moment practically the entire world is afraid of rogues and non-devotees; therefore this Krishna consciousness movement is started to save the world from irreligious principles. . . The main business of human society is to think of the Supreme Personality of Godhead at all times, to become His devotees, to worship the Supreme Lord and to bow down before Him. The Acharya, the authorized representative of the Supreme Lord, establishes these principles, but when he disappears, things once again become disordered. The perfect disciples of the Acharya try to relieve the situation by sincerely following the instructions of the spiritual master. SB 4.28.48

Creating Shrila Prabhupada's Non-institutional ISKCON

In starting the Hare Krishna Movement again we need to be very conscious about how we are organizing to protect against past failures. Due to our institutional conditioning and the tendency to unconsciously revert to it, we must clearly understand the nature of non-institutional organizations and how they apply to our needs, which will be the focus of this chapter.

Non-institutional organization does not mean anarchy. Any organization of people, institutional or non-institutional, requires rules and guidelines, otherwise there is no meaning to organization. Shrila Prabhupada's non-institutional ISKCON is based on three rather simple points: 1) the principles of Gaudiya Vaishnava siddhanta, established in Shrila Prabhupada's books, 2) freedom of association, and 3) freedom in action.

Books are the Basis, Purity is the Principle

The method of formally establishing Shrila Prabhupada's non-institutional ISKCON is simply to teach, learn, share, and assist each other in following the teachings and practices that have been given us, not creating anything new:

> Any path you follow, you have to follow the regulative principles as they are enacted by authorities. So in our disciplic succession, previous Acaryas, they have advised that you should have your dress like this, you should have your head like this, you... So we have to follow that. Our principle is to follow the footprints of authorities. So these things are not unauthorized. These are being followed from time immemorial. . . We are not introducing anything new. We are simply following the footprints of our predecessors. *That's all.* Lecture 14Jan69

Not only is there nothing to be gained by creating something new, but the very real possibility exists that the essential principles will be overshadowed and lost. This is the entire point of Starting the Hare Krishna Movement Again – the mission has been lost by the introduction of new ideas not supported by Vaishnava siddhanta.

Freedom of Association

Freedom of association means just that – the group does not have to accept everybody, and has the right to reject whoever they like. This helps prevent infiltrators misleading them or creating destructive conflict. This may be a closed group requiring a vote to admit new members. Or, in a less formal manner, the group may decide to reject the participation of any person creating disunity. Of course the group may have open events, but an inner circle of committed members would admit others conditional to their agreeing to the goals of the group, which would generally be their mutual progressive development in devotional service. The members commit to hold each other accountable and assist each other in spiritual progress. The group not only has the right, *but the obligation*, to correct *any* member of the group that deviates from the principles. It is both the steadfast adherence to the principles and the closed nature of the group allows the group to protect itself from uncommitted, ill-motivated, wayward, or otherwise irresponsible association.

Naturally the group will have a leader, and most likely this will be person who takes the initiative to begin. However, with the non-institutional arrangement, the group may elect to operate in any manner they choose. Leaders should be knowledgeable and experienced both in practical life and spiritual realization, and lead by example. A deviant leader should be corrected, but if he proves to be incorrigible the group is obligated to reject him. Assuming the group has not devolved into sycophants who have lost sight of the principles, they are protected from deviant leaders who have fallen victim to Maya.

Adherence to foundational principles protects the group from deviation, since it is the members, *not the leaders*, who insure the group stays on track. In one sense the followers lead by choosing who they follow. They understand that they come together to serve their mutual interest of Krishna Consciousness as taught by Shrila Prabhupada, and have the responsibility to reject anyone from their group who abandons that goal, especially a wayward leader. Had such principles been in place at New Vrindavana years ago, Kirtanananda's attempts to change the dress, devotional songs, etc., would have failed. Similarly, the GBC body would never have been able to create the bogus zonal-*Acharya* system, nor their bogus system for *diksa*, nor carry-out their unauthorized empire building. Following these principles the wayward GBC could be brought back in line, if they would agree, or else be totally rejected from the society of devotees, and the society could have been protected from their deviations.

The Advisory Body Commission

Regarding leadership, the question of the GBC will come up since Shrila Prabhupada created that body. The first thing to point out was the circumstances of the time when ISKCON was rapidly expanding and Shrila Prabhupada desperately needed help. Even though his senior men were at most 4 years in Krishna Consciousness, they were all he had to work with. All of them knew first-hand how Shrila Prabhupada operated since they all had personal association with him. He asked them to simply do as he was doing. As we have already seen, that instruction was followed only to a limited degree.

The situation today is far different than in 1970. Now, almost 50 years later, there are many mature, capable, and advanced devotees who understand the entire process of devotional service who may be candidates for such positions – provided they understand and accept the concept of a non-institutional ISKCON based solely on Shrila Prabhupada's teachings.

As Shrila Prabhupada's ISKCON develops and the need is felt, a group of guides can be established. But rather than having the title of Governing Body Commission, a more appropriate title would be the Advisory Body Commission (ABC). The purpose and function is exactly the same, except it is explicitly understood that the GBC/ABC is not a controlling body, but are instead advisors and counselors.

As each temple group is established, the group can elect a senior devotee of their choosing to provide guidance as needed. In a non-institutional organization the ABC will have only moral suasion, which means that they offer suggestions based on scriptural evidence, Shrila Prabhupada's teachings, and their own experience. The temple group is under no obligation to accept such advice. As with any relationship either party may choose to end the relationship, without the need for justifying the change to any third party. No GBC/ABC can be imposed on them against their wishes. The point is that everyone is responsible for their own spiritual life, and must therefore develop responsibility and discrimination about who they associate with and who they follow, and live with the consequences of their decisions.

Freedom and Independence in Action

Creating a non-institutional organization is quite simple: experienced and enthusiastic devotees invite people over for a Nama Hatta type gathering and share philosophy, kirtan and prasadam. Those who are so inspired may create a formal center with deities. Or one can simply spread a blanket on the ground, display Shrila Prabhupada's books, and invite people to sit to chat and chant. However it is done, the purpose is simply to create space and a place for people to learn about Krishna Consciousness.

No permission is needed, and there is nobody who can say "No!" The order is already given by Sri Chaitanya Mahaprabhu himself: *yare dekha, tare kaha 'Krishna'-upadesa amara ajnaya guru hana tara' ei desa* – Instruct everyone to follow the orders of Lord Sri Krishna as they are given in the *Bhagavad-gita* and *Srimad Bhagavatam*. In this way become a spiritual master and try to liberate everyone in this land. Madhya 7.128

The main features of non-institutional organization are freedom and independence. Freedom of activity, and freedom to direct oneself on the spiritual path, learning from mistakes and being guided by one's own realizations and the voice of the Supersoul within.

Freedom does not mean freedom for neophytes to think and do as they might whimsically desire. Just as a child requires the protection of parents until s/he matures, neophyte devotees require the guidance of seniors, be they a GBC/ABC, and/or *shiksha* and/or *diksa* guru, otherwise they become a disturbance to the social order. Nonetheless, the neophyte must have the freedom to follow or not. Self-realization can never be made compulsory! Love cannot be forced. Freedom of thought and action must be allowed, and are critical to the development of spiritual responsibility wherein the *sadaka* demonstrates their desire to serve guru and Krishna voluntarily.

You Represent ONLY Yourself

One of the significant features of Shrila Prabhupada's non-institutional ISKCON is freedom of personal expression, in that everybody can be who they are. There is room for personal expression, without the requirement to conform to some uniform institutional image. In a non-institutional setting nobody represents anything or anyone else. Everyone is their own person.

That does not mean that there are no standards, or that any kind of behavior is acceptable. Anyone who presents themselves as a preacher is in one sense a representative of the entire *parampara* and should behave as such. If their personal behavior is not up to the standard then the members should encourage them to make the needed adjustments, and each party always has the freedom to reject undesirable association. This is how free relationships naturally work – we accept and reject personal association as it suits us. Nobody is under any obligation to accept the association of another.

The intention here is that there is no pressure to conform to an institutional image. There is also no cover-up to avoid group embarrassment over one individual's wayward behavior. If someone falls down it is only *their* problem and does not shame anybody else. At the same time nobody can ride presumptuously Shrila Prabhupada's coattails to glory simply by being given a title or position. This diminishes the tempting *pratishtha* that representatives of a large organization are often subjected to, not infrequently to an unhappy end. Actually advanced devotees have no interest in self-aggrandizement. Their only desire is to serve.

The Dvijas

Freedom is also a *prerequisite* for men of ability. Men of ability are the higher orders of the social body (dvijas) who, by their very nature, do not require – *and will not have* – someone telling them what to do (although they will have advisors). They have sufficient discriminating intelligence to know what to do and what not to do. That is the very meaning of higher order. These are the type of men that run the world – political leaders, businessmen, analysts and thinkers in today's world; *kshatriyas*, vaisyas and brahmanas in Vedic culture. Unfortunately, the GBC insist on controlling everyone, and because "independence" has become a bad word in their institution, self-respecting men of ability cannot find their place, and will not stay. The capable men that Shrila Prabhupada attracted, who took Krishna Consciousness all around the world, have, except for a handful of fairly independent *sannyasis* and gurus, left the society.

Thus, instead of creating a society of men who are "independently thoughtful" as Shrila Prabhupada desired, the GBC are creating a society of *sudras* or sycophants who need and want the security of someone telling them what to do every step of the way. *This is exactly what Shrila Prabhupada did not want.*

Tragically the innocents who come to the GBC's ISKCON in pursuit of spiritual growth are placed under the guidance of such incapable "authorities" of a *sudra* nature, whose main qualification is their demonstrated submissiveness to follow orders, and in turn demand the same from others. Such "leaders," unable to think outside of the institutional box, perpetuate institutional decrees that limit free inquiry and expression, driving away any who question too much or will not submit to such conditions – the dvijas – the very people that are needed to lead society.

Shrila Bhaktisiddhanta Sarasvati elaborated so much on the need for freedom in spiritual life. In an article from The Harmonist he wrote:

> The Scriptures . . . never favour [sic] the creation of sect or dogma in their ordinary worldly sense. They want to set us free from the fetters of all worldly creed and dogma. They never prescribe any mechanical course to any individual. *The formulation of general rules which are intended to be binding on the members of a community is the sorry device of our bankrupt rationalism for contriving the destruction of free individual functioning.* . . The Church of Lord Nityananda is open to all souls who really desire to function on the plane that is absolutely free from all limitations.[1]

Goals and Purpose

Although Shrila Prabhupada desired to see the day that the entire world would be Krishna conscious, he knew that that could only come when the message of Godhead was properly presented. To that end he wanted his followers to be well-trained in Krishna Consciousness:

> Now I want that we shall concentrate on making our devotees Krishna conscious and ourselves becoming Krishna conscious, *and not be so much concerned with expanding ourselves widely but without any spiritual content.* Just like boiling the milk, it becomes thicker and sweeter. Now do like that, boil the milk. Letter to Rupanuga 9May72

In starting the Hare Krishna Movement again, focus should be where Shrila Prabhupada wanted it: on creating quality devotees who free themselves from the shackles of Maya and develop love for Krishna. The primary purpose of Shrila Prabhupada's ISKCON is to teach people about the principles of spiritual life and guide them in their spiritual development – *without any thought of controlling them, or exploiting them, in any way.*

Organizational Methods

The question will be asked as to how non-institutional organizations manage their affairs. The answer, as might be expected, is with non-hierarchical, non-command-control methods. Such methods, sometimes referred to as "spontaneous order," have been developed. Chaordic is one example of spontaneous order, as are the organizational systems of Sociocracy and Holacracy. This is not just theory. These systems are being implemented in many forward thinking companies such as the clothing company Zappos, and video gaming company Valve. Like Hock's Chaordic system, *at Valve there* **are no bosses, no delegation, no commands, and no attempt by anyone to tell someone what to do.** These methods can easily and immediately be adopted to simpler

434 | DIVINE OR DEMONIAC?

temple organization, and even the GBC's ISKCON, if they would ever be willing to let go of control. Links for more information are provided in the endnotes.[2]

These organizational methods eliminate hierarchical decision-making, pushing authority and responsibility to all levels of the organization. They make the organization much more efficient by giving authority and decision-making power to the person doing the work. This requires responsibility from everyone, eliminates bottle-necks, removes pressure from the top, and allows the organization to function in the most expedient way. There are of course rules by which such decisions are made, but rather than restricting behavior, the rules unleash initiative, just as right-of-way rules improve the flow of traffic. That said, the group has full freedom to arrange their affairs as they like.

Learning new methods of behavior is kind of like learning to ride a bike. It's a bit wobbly at first and takes some practice, but soon enough it becomes automatic.

Conclusion

Start the Hare Krishna Movement Again!

Living Philosophy

There was a time not so long ago, when people's lives were guided by philosophical and religious beliefs. No more. In today's world neither philosophy, nor beliefs have a role in shaping how we live. We live instead, according to the dictates of a monetary system, philosophy subsumed to demands of "paying our way," or "making the ends meet." Man has become the only species that must earn the right to survive, and anything not profitable, regardless of how noble, often struggles to exist. This artificial way of living has been deliberately created by the demonic, allowing them to suck the energy of everyone without their slightest understanding of the fact, all to enhance their deluded sense of "I and mine" and, like Hiranyakasipu, to own the entire world.

For the common man, the demands of this way of life distort the finer values and sentiments taught by family and church. While we may harbor the values of peace, love and goodwill to all men, we are nonetheless *forced* to live as money dictates. We thus become cultural schizophrenics, professing one thing while doing something entirely different. Kali is thus the age of hypocrisy.

I would shock many devotees on this point as I lectured throughout my travels (30 countries and many, many destinations). Holding up the Bhagavad-gita, I challenged that although we claim it is our scripture, and profess to believe everything stated within, we do not live as Sri Krishna admonishes. We attend temple worship, and read and study the slokas over and over again, but we live in ways antithetical to the Gita, ways given to us by the atheistic, materialistic host culture – yet hardly one devotee in a hundred realizes this fact.

For example, Sri Krishna states in the second chapter of the *Bhagavad-gita* (2.47) "You have a right to perform your prescribed duty, but the fruits of your work do not belong to you." But most devotees have jobs and work for a paycheck which is the fruit of their action, which they use as if it were "theirs." Is there a contradiction here? I suggest there is, and that it goes unobserved due to our cultural indoctrination and conditioning. Strangely, I've heard one respected Godbrother who, noting this discrepancy, suggest that we cannot follow this instruction of the Gita today – as though the *Bhagavad-gita* were some sort of anachronism, only applicable at particular times and places.

Another example is the Isavasyam principle – everything animate and inanimate within the universe is controlled and owned by the Lord. The culture modern devotees *live in and live by*, however, is *founded* on the principle of ownership of unlimited personal private property. Under such influence every person, including devotees, are forced to think in terms of, "my house, my bank balance, my car, etc.," to the exclusion of everyone else. The values of this money culture create such damnable situations as in Ireland where there are now as many empty houses as there are homeless families, and globally where a mere 8 people own as much wealth as the poorest *half* of humanity.[1] It's not that the current economic system doesn't work; in truth it's doing exactly what it is designed to do – transfer wealth from the many to the few.

Our Vaishnava values can be followed, but the context of our host culture, arranged as it is for the purposes of the demons, makes doing so very difficult.

Reviving the Sattvic Cultures of the Past

If we look into history prior to global colonization, the indigenous cultures of the world were sattvic, by-and-large, and their spiritual principles were fully integrated into every aspect of their lives. In many societies God was accepted as the owner of everything – not just in theory, but in fact. Land was jointly-owned by the group, work was done as a group, and the results of work were distributed to the group. In many of those cultures there was no extreme disparity between social classes, and people were satisfied with only what was needed.[2] These are the characteristics of sattva-guna. The profit motive, exploitation of land and people, and intentional accumulation of wealth are demoniac values the Europeans imposed on those they colonized. However, with the passage of time this way of life has become the way of life the world over, and is now considered normal – normal, that is, to those overcome by rajo-guna and tamo-guna.

The point I am making is that every aspect of our lives is meant to be integrated with our spiritual principles – that Sri Krishna is the supreme proprietor, the supreme enjoyer of all work and sacrifice, and the dear most friend of everyone. The fundamental principle of *Bhakti-yoga* is that all actions are to be done as an offering of love for the enjoyment of the Supreme Lord first – not the tax man first, with left-overs for Sri Krishna.

This is the full extent of Shrila Prabhupada's vision for his ISKCON society – he desired that ISKCON would develop into a fully integrated spiritual culture, such that after several generations, Krishna Consciousness would be the most natural thing in the world:

> Our position is different. We are trying to implement Krishna consciousness in everything. Our duty is that we shall arrange the external affairs so nicely that one day they will come to the spiritual platform very easily, paving the way. Room conversation 14Feb77 Mayapura

Start the Hare Krishna Movement Again!

When I advocate starting the Hare Krishna Movement again, I advocate for this – the development of the complete Krishna culture of Sanatana Dharma, such that, anyone who is raised in the culture learns only devotional service as a way of life, and where the concept of fruitive work for personal gain would be looked upon with sympathy and pity. Of course this won't be achieved quickly or easily, and will require knowledgeable, capable and determined devotees, who have this goal – to eventually become free of the values and practices of the present demonic dominant culture.

We must find a way to establish a culture in which the philosophy of Krishna Consciousness is reflected in our understanding of life and every act in it. Beginning with the Isavasyam principle, the ownership of everything by the Lord, with nothing that we would even think to claim as our own, for personal profit. Everything – all work and action – would be performed in the spirit of devotional service, with Krishna as the benefactor and enjoyer of all work, the results of which would then be distributed as His prasadam.

The economic system of the Krishna culture is not the cheating money system, using so-called laxmi of worthless paper (maya-laxmi), but agriculture, which is in fact the only true method of economic growth. One seed planted becomes 10, or 100, or even 1000 – a 1,000, 10,000, or 100,000 percent return on investment! A return *given* by Sri Krishna out of love. Recognizing His gifts we reciprocate by offering those transformed gifts back to Him – an exchange of love that continues as He then returns the same to us as His prasadam.

The cow and bull are a central requirement of the Krishna culture. Not in terms of maintaining goshallas of dozens or hundreds of animals, but as household members of each family. The many benefits that they provide – fertile dung for the gardens and field, the traction power of the bull, milk for health and tasty dishes, have great value and cannot be obtained in any artificial way that does not harm the environment. However, the most important gift of these animals is they *force* us to live in sattva-guna.

One of the preliminary goals of *bhakti-yoga* is to become free from the lower modes of nature and become situated in sattva-guna, because from there, pure unalloyed goodness, suddha-sattva can be achieved. And the opulence of the economics of agriculture allows time for spiritual pursuit. This is the great value of the village life Shrila Prabhupada wanted for his followers.

When I say "Start the Hare Krishna Movement Again!" I am advocating that we pursue the *complete* Krishna culture that Shrila Prabhupada wanted to give us – a way of life Sri Krishna intended for human beings in this world. A way of life that naturally prepares us to enter into Sri Krishna's Vraj lila.

This simple life also offers the wonderful benefit of solving almost all of the world's problems without extraneous endeavor. Varnashrama culture truly is the panacea for all of the ills of *Kali-yuga*, eliminating the pollution problems, the hunger problems, the stress problems, the economic problems, etc., all of which result from living under the influence of passion and ignorance. By adopting the sattvic Krishna conscious way of living, the earth can be healed and *everyone* can become happy, and everyone can make their human life successful. Daiva-varnashrama is the ultimate win-win-win solution for human beings, the animals and Mother Earth.

The Bigger Picture

The over-arching theme of this book goes far beyond the subversion of religion, Jesus and James, ISKCON, abuse of the Kulis, the butchery of Shrila Prabhupada's books, the infiltration and misgivings of the GBC, etc. All of these are, in fact, symptoms of the much bigger, underlying problem – the reality of the demoniac elements and their control this world.

While the forces of evil vie with each other on the global chessboard for ultimate control, they also carry out a stealthy plan to subjugate the populace. It is a silent war carried out with all manner of deceit and subtlety, always tightening their noose of control while justifying their actions as necessary to fight terrorism that they create, disease they create, environmental problems they create, or some other real or imaginary enemy.

Is it not obvious by now that literal *demons* with immense power are literally engaged in unbeneficial horrible works meant to destroy this world? If you are not aware of this fact, I suggest that you invest some time researching the dangers of the coming ubiquitous 5G radiation, directed energy weapons, intentionally debilitating infants with poisoned vaccinations, chemtrails, Agenda 21 and Agenda 2030, terminator seeds, architects and engineers for 911 truth, glyphosate and its effects on health, genetically modified plants and life forms, eugenics and depopulation, Project for a New American Century, and on and on. And beyond all of that, and whatever other terrible things they might do, these demons will continue to do whatever they can to eradicate the Eternal Religion. Take the red pill and wake up to the realities of modern life, then join the Spiritual R-Evolution to save this world.

What has been, and is, happening to the Hare Krishna Movement can, in one sense, be considered a minor skirmish in the aggression of the demonic powers who think nothing of killing and otherwise destroying millions to achieve their goals. They are almost unlimitedly powerful. They control governments, the economy, the militaries, the media, the courts and the schools. There is no possible way to defeat them materially. But they can be "defeated" spiritually. After all, we have the Supreme Personality of Godhead Sri Krishna on our side, or rather, we are on His side. But we need to call Him and ask for His help – just as the devas have done when facing the overwhelming power of their demoniac adversaries.

In this age the Supreme Personality of Godhead manifests in sound, in His holy names, and by vibrating that sound the devotees not only call for the Lord's protection, but also purify the contaminations of this world, lifting the consciousness of everyone – including the demonic. It can all be accomplished with the Spiritual Revolution of the Hare Krishna Movement, *Harinam* Sankirtan, the widespread chanting of the holy names.

The Hare Krishna Movement is meant to save the entire world – and it is the only thing that can! ISKCON was never meant to save just a few thousand lucky souls. Lord Chaitanya commanded us: "para upakara" – do good for others. The Hare Krishna Movement is created for this purpose. That's our job – our wonderful opportunity to be engaged in the service of the Supreme Lord in this epic battle. Lord Chaitanya will inundate this world with love of God, and He mercifully gives us the opportunity to be used as instruments for His purpose.

This book is about freedom. Your freedom and the freedom of those generations that will follow you. Specifically, freedom to live in the way of your choosing, to understand and believe in a reality according to your highest understanding, and the truths connected with it. That wonderful future depends on what *you* do, and specifically on always chanting:

Hare Krishna, Hare Krishna
Krishna Krishna, Hare Hare
Hare Rama, Hare Rama
Rama Rama, Hare Hare

and encouraging everyone you meet to do the same.

It is not the business of devotees to live in this world – our business here is to serve Sri Krishna, the Supreme Personality of Godhead, and His pure devotee Shrila Prabhupada. We are here to create a revolution in the impious lives of a world's misdirected civilization with the mercy of the Holy Names.

There is no other way, *there is no other way,*
there is no other way!

One Last Word

It should never be said that I am against ISKCON – I love ISKCON – Shrila Prabhupada's ISKCON. ISKCON has been my life. I am eternally indebted to Shrila Prabhupada and all of his followers, with whom I've had the honor and fortune to work with and serve. My prayer is that they will bless this endeavor, and by it realize that we all share in the grave responsibility of protecting Shrila Prabhupada's legacy for future generations.

It is not possible to write a book such as this without some finding offense in its contents. To such persons I beg their tolerance and forgiveness. I pray that with time they will give the book a more just appraisal, and appreciate that its purpose is to provide future generations with the same wonderful experience of Krishna Consciousness that we have been blessed with.

To the demonic elements, who have endeavored to destroy Shrila Prabhupada's mission, I pray that you also will one day receive the mercy of Lord Chaitanya and become happy in the Lord's transcendental loving service.

About the Author

Born in Detroit in 1948, he was baptized in the Catholic Church as Don Armand Rousse. Don went to Catholic school through the eighth grade and served as an Altar Boy in the church. Troubled by the philosophical inconsistencies and church dogma, Don distanced himself from the church as a young adult.

In 1972, while in graduate school studying materials science, and nuclear engineering he began to ponder life's existential questions, and soon obtained Shrila Prabhupada's *KRISHNA Book*, which began his real spiritual education, continuing with *Bhagavad-gita As It Is*. Smitten by Krishna's words Don dedicated his Master's Thesis to "Lord Sri Krishna, the knower of all, and object of all knowledge." Upon graduation he came into contact with Shrila Prabhupada's followers and soon joined the local temple. He became a dedicated follower and was initiated as Dhanesvara Das in 1974.

Over the course of the next 45 years Dhanesvara served Shrila Prabhupada's mission in every capacity: as pujari, book distributor, temple treasurer, temple commander, and temple president. He worked with Spiritual Sky Incense Company, and was the production manager for the Bhaktivedanta Book Trust in the early 80s. As a senior member of the society he traveled to some 30 countries from 2005 through 2015, preaching and teaching in ISKCON temples. Petitioning ISKCON's leadership for initiation into the renounced order of Sannyasa in 2009, he was given the green light provided he submit to the GBC's political requirements for the post. Dismayed that the GBC would politicize the ashrama, Dhanesvara withdrew his bid, although he nonetheless continues to live a life of simple renunciation.

He is the author of *Lessons in Spiritual Economics from the Bhagavad-gita, Change the Karma,* and *When a Man is Poisoned It Is Said Like That.* He continues serving Shrila Prabhupada and his mission by writing books and teaching the science of devotional service.

Jewish Christian Glossary

Abraham—Old Testament – the first of the patriarchs, the father of Isaac and the founder of the Hebrew people; Jewish Vaishnavas considered him one of their *Acharyas*.

Acts, Book of—a New Testament book describing the development of the early church; Acts of the Apostles.

Albigensian Crusade—a 20-year military campaign initiated by Pope Innocent III to eliminate Catharism in Languedoc, in the south of France. The Crusade was prosecuted primarily by the French crown.

Alexandria—an Ancient Egyptian town. It became an important center of the Hellenistic civilization and remained the capital of Hellenistic and Roman and Byzantine Egypt for almost 1000 years until the Muslim conquest of Egypt.

Aeon—(in Gnosticism) a divine power or nature (spirits) emanating from the Supreme Being and playing various roles in the operation of the universe, for example, as intermediaries between earth and heaven.

Ananas—the wicked temple priest.

Antichrist—in Christian belief, a person who is evil incarnate, opposes God, and endeavors to lead people away from God. The lord of this world according to the Jewish-Christians who would be defeated by the forces of goodness.

Apocryphal—of questionable authenticity.

Arians—a 4th-century sect of Gnostics who denied Jesus' divinity.

Barnabas—original name Joseph. A Cypriot who became a follower of Paul.

Bible by Symmachus—the Greek version of the Old Testament prepared by Symmachus, who, according to patristic testimony, was an Ebionite.

Bogomils—dualists or Gnostics (people of knowledge) in that they believed in a world within the body and a world outside the body. They did not use the Christian cross, nor build churches, as they revered their gifted form and considered their body to be the temple.

Much of their literature has been lost or destroyed by the contemporary Christian Churches. Bogomilism is best known in Western Europe as Catharism.

Caesarea—capital of Roman Palestine; founded by Herod the Great.

Canon—books of the Bible officially accepted as Holy Scripture. An ecclesiastical law or code of laws established by a church council.

Carpocratians—a Gnostic sect. The Carpocratians believed that men had formerly been united with the Absolute, had been corrupted, and would, by despising creation, be saved in this life or else later through successive incarnations. Jesus, they held, was but one of several wise men who had achieved deliverance.

Cathars—the Cathars were devout, chaste, tolerant "Christians" who loathed the material excesses of the medieval church. Beliefs similar to theirs can be found in the Gnostic gospels, and Essene teachings discovered at Qumran. Also known as Albigensians.

Celsus—2nd century Greek opposed to the developing Pauline Christianity.

Constantine—Emperor of Rome who gathered the Council of Nicea to establish the catholic (universal) doctrine and canon of the Bible. He also made Christianity the official religion of the Roman Empire.

Clement of Alexandria—Christian theologian, original name of Titus Flavius Clemens; not to be confused with Titus Flavius, emperor of Rome from 79-81.

Damascus Document—one of the Dead Sea Scrolls; the only Qumran work known before the discovery of the Dead Sea Scrolls. It is a composite text edited together from different sections of a larger source. A number of the fragments matched documents found later in Qumran.

Dead Sea Scrolls—a collection texts discovered between 1946 and 1956 in eleven caves (Qumran Caves) in the immediate vicinity of the Dead Sea. The scrolls are identified as the writing of an ancient Jewish sect called the Essenes.

Druze—a monotheistic religious community living primarily in Syria, Israel, and Lebanon stemming from ancient times. They call themselves, the Muwahidoon, a word that translates exactly to "followers of the Eternal Religion."

Ebed—servant of God

Ebionites—a Judaistic Christian Gnostic sect of the 1st and 2nd centuries, especially partial observation of the Law, and rejection of St. Paul and gentile Christianity.

Ebionite "Acts of the Apostles"—texts claiming to be documents deriving from the physical descendants of Jewish Christians belonging to the original church in Jerusalem. The pertinent material is provided by those parts of Recognitions 1 which Schoeps has attributed to the Ebionite "Acts of the Apostles," a writing to which Epiphanius witnessed but which, unfortunately, is no longer extant.

Eleazar—leader of the last group of Essenes holding out against Roman troops at the Masada fortress at the end of the 7 Years War. Explaining the eternal nature of the soul he exhorted them to suicide rather than be humiliated by the Romans.

Epiphanius, Bishop of Constantia—Catholic Bishop Epiphanius of Constantia in Cyprus, who was an authority on Jewish sects. He tells us that the Nazoreans differed from other Jews in that they did not sacrifice animals, nor eat flesh thereof. See endnote 21 of Chap 1

Eschatology—the branch of theology that is concerned with such final things as death and judgment; heaven and hell; the end of the world

Essenes—members of an ascetic sect that flourished in Palestine from the second century B.C. to the second century ad, living in strictly organized communities

Eusebius—Christian bishop of Caesarea in Palestine; a church historian and a leading early Christian exegete.

Exegesis—an explanation or critical interpretation of, especially of the Bible.

Exegete—a person that studies and interprets texts, especially religious writings. Also called exegetist; pl. exegetes.

Ezra—a Jewish priest and scribe of the 5th century B.C. sent by the Persian king to restore Jewish law and worship in Jerusalem.

Gnosis/Gnostic/Gnosticism—revealed knowledge of various spiritual truths possessed by people of ancient Judea and surrounding area. Knowledge of spiritual matters; mystical knowledge.

Gnostics—advocates of Gnosticism

Hellenic Christianity—Christianity as understood and promulgated in ancient Greece and the Mediterranean by Paul and his followers

Hellenistic world—the culture, ideals, and pattern of life of ancient Greece in classical times. It usually means primarily the culture of Athens

Heresiologists—church fathers involved in determining heresy and dogma

Herod/Herod Antipas—King of Judea (40 B.C.- 4 A.D.)

Irenaeus—Bishop of Lyon, was attacking Gnosticism as a heresy, wrote vehement polemical works

James—brother of Jesus whom was made the leader of the Ebionite/ Essene community after the crucifixion

Jethro—Jethro was the father-in-law of Moses, and the major preceptor of the Druze.

Jewish Christians/Jewish Vaishnavas—the group or movement associated with James' name and teachings in Jerusalem; also referred to as the Jerusalem Church, or Palestinian Christianity.

Jewish Christian Gospels—modern research has generally differentiated between an Aramaic Gospel of the Nazoreans and a Greek Gospel of the Ebionites. Both originated in the first half of the second century, are inclined to paraphrase like the Targums, and are greatly dependent upon the canonical Matthew, which probably derived from Jewish Christian circles in the Great Church.

Josephus—official historian of the Roman Empire (37-100 A.D.)

Kenites—inhabitants of south Palestine up to the time of David. Moses' father-in-law was a Kenite.

Kergymata Petrou—literally "the preaching of Peter;" lectures on doctrine delivered by the biblical Peter; the Jewish Christian parts of the Pseudo-Clementines.

Lacunae—A blank space or missing part.

Law of Moses—the ancient law of the Hebrews, ascribed to Moses and contained in the Pentateuch.

Logion—attributed saying of Jesus Christ: a saying attributed to Jesus Christ that is not in the New Testament.

Mani—Persian prophet and founder of Manichaeism. His religious movement, a rival to early Christianity, professed that the world is always plagued by the opposing forces of good and evil.

Manicheans—followers of Mani.

Messiah—literally, "the anointed one;" all kings were anointed with oil.

Mithraic traditions—ancient religion popular among Romans during first three centuries A.D., held a strong belief in a supernatural power or powers that control human destiny.

Moses—Hebrew prophet and lawgiver, considered as an *Acharya* by the Jewish-Christians.

Nag Hammadi Texts—a collection of ancient works written on papyrus scrolls, dating from early 2nd century to the 4th century; found in sealed earthen jars near the desert town of Nag Hammadi, Egypt.

Nazoreans—one group of the Jewish Christians among others comprised of Zealots, Sacarii, Essenes, Ebionites, etc.

Nicaea, Council of—a council convened in the city of Nicaea by Roman Emperor Constantine I in AD 325. This first council was an effort to attain consensus in the universal (catholic) Christian doctrine, called the Nicene Creed; an effort to eliminate the teachings of Jesus and the Jewish Vaishnavas from Christian canon.

Origen—Greek scholar, ascetic, 2nd-3rd century Christian polemicist.

Patristic—of, or relating to, the writings of the early Christian "fathers"

Paul (Saul)—an agent of the Roman powers who became an infiltrator of the Jewish-Christians/Jewish Vaishnavas; never knew Jesus, and taught doctrines opposed to what Jesus taught. Instead of following Jesus he created a "religion" in Jesus' name, supposedly based on of Jesus' teachings that we subservient to the Roman powers, and

JEWISH-CHRISITAN GLOSSARY | 453

called it "Christianity." Referred to as "the Enemy," "the Liar," and "Sower of False Things" by the apostles of Jesus.

Pauline Christianity—the main concepts of Christianity came from Paul, and the books of the Bible are written from his perspective. Normative Christianity of today, esp. Protestants.

Pentateuch—the first five books of the Old Testament; same meaning as the Torah.

Pericopes—an extract from a book, especially a passage from the Bible selected for reading during a gathering. The Jewish-Christians believed that the Torah had been falsified and contained many false pericopes that Jesus was to correct.

Peter—one of the original disciples, and staunch follower of Jesus; according to the Nag Hammadi Texts was not the person who Jesus put in charge after his crucifixion.

Pharisees—originally the legitimate incumbents of the seat of Moses and true experts in the Law, who possessed the knowledge (gnosis) with which to distinguish between the true and the false in the Scriptures. However, they betrayed their calling allowing the Law to become increasingly obscured through errors, by their negligence. Accommodating Roman interference in temple affairs they became the establishment party in opposition to James and the Jewish-Christians.

Presbyter—a member of early church administration; in early Christianity, an administrative official of a local church.

Pseudepigrapha— books written under a false pen-name that do not represent the purported author. Spurious writings, especially writings falsely attributed to biblical characters or times.

Psilanthropism—the position that Jesus is human and not God

Pseudo-Clementines—writings originating in the third or fourth century associated with the Ebionites.

Psuedistoria—false narrative(s)

Qumran community—a monastic order and sect of Judaism located near the Dead Sea, who were known to hold all possessions in common and required their members to renounce private property. This group referred to themselves as "the Keepers of the Law," or "the way." "work," or "works." The community can be known as the "early Church" or as other groups generally deemed to be separate — the "Zadokites," the Zealots, and the Sicarii.

Redactor—editor; someone who prepares text for publication

Saul/Saulus—see "Paul."

Septuagint—the pre-Christian Greek version of the Old Testament

Sicarii—a militant branch of the Qumran community.

Sol Invictus—the sun god.

Soteriological—the Christian doctrine that salvation has been brought about by Jesus Christ

Synoptic—presenting or taking the same point of view; used especially of the first three gospels of the New Testament

Taurus—a city in Greece; birthplace of Saul/Paul

Theodicy—branch of theology concerned with the defense of God's goodness despite the existence of evil

Torah—the first five books of the Old Testament; same meaning as the Pentateuch.

Transmogrify—change completely the nature of something

Valentinus—influential early Gnostic teacher, had been considered for election as the Bishop of Rome

Yahweh—the angry, vengeful God of the Old Testament, thought by the Essenes to have substituted a kind, loving God, originally in the Torah.

Zealots—an appellation applied to some members of the Qumran community who were zealous for following the Law.

Glossary of Sanskrit Words and Hare Krishna Expressions

Acharya—a revered spiritual master who is considered the embodiment of religious principles, and who teaches spiritual principles by example. There are many *Acharyas* over the years

Acintyabedabeda tattva—simultaneous oneness, and difference. Refers to the individual the individual living being and God being the same spiritual energy, but different in terms of potency.

Adhikar—spiritual qualification and understanding

Aparadha—an spiritual offense to persons, scripture, etc.

Aryan—a person who follows Vedic culture. Anyone who understands spiritual advancement as the goal of life.

Ashrama—living place where spiritual principles are practiced. There are four ashramas in the social scheme of Varnashrama Dharma: brahmacari ashrama (single students), grihasta ashrama for married couples, vanaprastha ashrama of seniors devoting themselves to spiritual pursuit, and sannyasa ashrama of men who have given up all connection with material life, especially women.

Asura—demon. One who is opposed to the supremacy of God. *Asuras* are atheistic and materialistic.

Avaduta—a person oblivious to social decorum due to being completely free from materialistic conception of life.

Avaishnava—a person who is not a Vaishnava

Avatar—literally "one who descends." A person who is either partially or fully empowered by the Lord for a particular function, or mission, and who has descended to the material universe.

Bhaktisiddhanta Saraswati—(1874-1937) the highly revered spiritual master of Shrila Prabhupada.

Bhaktivedanta Swami—the founder of ISKCON and the present acarya for followers of Vedic dharma in the modern world

Bhagavad-gita—Literally, Song of God; essential spiritual truths spoken by the Supreme Lord Himself to his friend and disciple Arjuna, while on this earth some 5,000 years ago.

Bagawan Rajneesh—a self-styled guru of the 20th century, considered a cheating guru for those that wanted to be cheated by the Vaishnavas.

Bhaktivedanta purports—explanations and commentaries given by Shrila Prabhupada to elucidate scriptural verses.

Bhavishya Mahapurana—an extant scripture of Kashmir wherein Jesus' preaching in the Middle East is mentioned.

Brahma—the first created living being, and secondary creator of the material world. He is the predominating deity of, rajo-guna, or the material quality of passion. He is the head of all the demigods.

Brahmana—one of the four varnas or occupational activities, a member of the intellectual, priestly order of society; a person educated in Vedic knowledge, fixed in goodness.

Chaitanya Mahaprabhu, Sri—An avatar of Krishna Who lived in Bengal and Puri, India in the 15th century. He gave the religion for the age of Kali – the chanting of the Hare Krishna maha-mantra. Considered by Vaishnavas to be non-different from Krishna.

Daityas—a class of demonic persons, descendants of Diti.

Daksha—one of the demigods responsible for increasing population

Darshan—association with a saintly person.

Demigod(s)—empowered beings who control the material elements such as wind, rain, sun, karma, etc. Not to be confused with the Supreme Lord. The demigods live in the heavenly realms.

SANSKRIT GLOSSARY | 457

Demonic/demoniac—those opposed to the rule of the Supreme Lord and religious principles. Demonic persons prefer to follow the dictates of their senses and please themselves regardless of the cost to anyone else. Envious of God, they desire to become God themselves. Lord Krishna explains the nature of the demons in the sixteenth chapter of the *Bhagavad-gita*. The material world is eternally characterized by a struggle between the demonic and spiritual elements.

Demons—persons of a demonic character who are opposed to the Supreme Lord.

Diti—a wife of Kasyapa Muni, and the mother of the demonic lineage beginning with Hiranyaksha and Hiranyakashipu

Demigods—empowered personalities who manage every aspect of the material world, such as the sun, wind, rain, vegetation, karma, etc. They are considered (demi) gods as they have power that is beyond comprehension of ordinary human beings.

Devas/Devata—demigods; empowered beings who control the material elements such as sun, rain, wind, etc.

Dhruva—a great and powerful king of yore who at a very young age successfully completed the yoga process to realize God.

Duryodhana—the antagonist of the Battle at Kurukshetra and nemesis of the Pandavas. He was the leader of the demonic forces plaguing the earth for which Bhumi, the earth personified, cried for relief.

Duskritina—a class of demonic persons

Dvapara-yuga—one of the four yugas or Vedic ages. The Yugas follow each other as do spring, summer, fall and winter, in the order of Satya, Treta, Dvapara and Kali. Dvapara-yuga preceded the current age of Kali and ended some 5,000 years ago.

Eternal Religion—religious principles that are true for everyone in all times and places, i.e., we are all spiritual beings eternally related to

God, Krishna, is one aspect of the Eternal Religion. The Absolute Truth.

Gaudiaya Math—the organization created by Shrila Bhaktisiddhanta Sarasvati to propagate Krishna Consciousness all over India. During his life 64 branches were opened.

Guna / Gunas—the three qualities of material nature that influence the consciousness of the living beings, namely goodness (satva), passion (rajas), or ignorance (tamas). Satva-guna is uplifting, while tamo-guna degrades the consciousness. Every part of material nature has its relative influence as a blend of the three, just as every color is a blend of the three primary colors.

Harinam/Harinam **Sankirtan**—Street chanting

Hiranyakasipu—one of the first demons, son of Diti, the mother of the race of demons. He was notable in his efforts to become deathless. He conquered and controlled the entire creation thinking that by doing so he had become God.

Horse sacrifice—a sacrifice performed in ancient Vedic rituals in which a horse was offered, and rejuvenated

Iksvaku—son of the sun god Vivasvan

ISKCON—International Society for Krishna Consciousness; the organization founded by A. C. Bhaktivedanta Swami in 1965

Kali-yuga—the present age. The age of Kali is typified by quarrel and hypocrisy, during which human beings become increasingly degraded under the influence of tamo-guna.

Kalpa—one day of Brahma, lasting for 4,320,000,000 years.

Kamsa—Kamsa was a powerful but demonic king who was inimical to the Lord and His purposes. In Krishna's earthly lila, or pastimes, Kamsa is Krishna's demonic uncle. King Kamsa imprisoned Krishna's parents Vasudeva and Devaki, and killed their first seven offspring. Krishna appeared as the eighth child.

Krishna—The original and supreme Lord as understood in the Judeo-Christian concept. The Absolute Truth, and origin of all. The cause of all causes. The speaker of *Bhagavad-gita*.

Kshatriya—one of the four varnas or social orders; the kingly order who organize and protect society.

Kunti—Mother of the five Pandava brothers, the cousins of Krishna in His earthly lila or pastimes. She had a difficult life raising her five sons after her husband has passed away, but she prayed to the Lord to continue the trials for they afforded her an opportunity to pray continually for the Lord's help and grace.

Kurukshetra, battle of—a great battle of hundreds of millions that took place at the end of the Dvapara-yuga, some 5,000 years ago. In this battle the demonic forces that were a burden to the earth were vanquished, but due to Lord Krishna's presence at the scene, all those killed achieved spiritual liberation.

Kurus—Sons of Dhritarastra, and a branch of the family that had been rulers of the world for generations. They were the antagonists and cousins of the Pandavas, the protagonists of India's great epic Mahabharta.

Manu—a demigod considered to be the father of mankind, and in charge of human affairs; his instructions for civilized human life is called the Manu Samhita

Markandeya—a great saint, Rishi and spiritual teacher; author of one of the histories of the world, the Puranas.

Mayavadi(s)—philosophers who opine that everything in this world is ultimately illusion, and ultimately everything is one. Monists.

Mlecchas—persons who do not follow Vedic dharma; considered degraded and unclean persons. Similar to the concept of Islam's infidel, or Christianity's heathen.

Naisthika-brahmacari—a lifelong celibate without any connection to women.

Pandavas—the five hero brothers of the epic Mahabharata: Yudhisthira, Arjuna, Bhimasena, Nakula and Sahadeva; all cousins and personal friends of Krishna, who were born as the sons of the demigods. As *kshatriya*s they were warriors who aided Krishna in ridding the earth of the demonic burden during the battle at Kurukshetra.

Paramahamsa—a spiritually

Parampara—disciplic succession stemming from Lord Krishna

Pashanda—atheism

Pashandi—atheist

Prabhu—"master." Vaishnavas use the word "Prabhu" to address each other, ostensibly as an acknowledgement that others are our master or teacher. Unfortunately, it is sometimes used in a more familiar way, sometimes sarcastically, or even derogatorily.

Prabhupada—one at whose feet other masters sit; the topmost spiritual master; a title of honor and affection for the current *Acharya* of ISKCON A. C. Bhaktivedanta Swami; generally preceded by the honorific title "Shrila."

Prajapatis—the progenitors of life in the material world.

Pratishtha—the desire for fame, reputation and recognition, esp. as being superior to others.

Putana—the demoness in Krishna's earthly lila who attempted to kill him; a demonic raksashi, she was able to assume the outward form of a beautiful woman, and she attempted to kill Krishna by putting poison on her nipples and nursing the infant Krishna. Krishna demonstrated His omnipotence as an infant, sucking the life out of the demoness and killing her. His grace is absolute however, and since Putana approached Him as a mother, offering her breast,

Krishna awarded her liberation from material existence. In this work, Putana is an icon of those who attempt to destroy the Truth.

Radha—the feminine aspect of the Absolute Truth.

Radha and Krishna—the Supreme Lord maninfest as a Loving Couple in Whom the purest love is eternally exchanged.

Raja-guna—the qualitative mode of passion; one of the three gunas, or modes of material nature. By the influence of Raja-guna people are restless and stimulated to creation, development, growth, improvement and activity for results.

Rakshasha (rakshashi – fem.)—a class of ungodly beings; the demonic who are opposed to any concept of a Supreme Lord. Their desire is to become God themselves. They are always opposed to God's will. *Rakshasha*s eat human flesh and blood. They have grotesque forms but are able to shape-shift to look human.

Rathayatra—a highly celebrated festival during which the Deity of the Lord is carried through the streets on a great cart.

Ravana—a great demon, the villain and adversary of Lord Ramachandra in the great epic *Ramayana*

Sadhana—spiritual practices and worship Vaishnavas perform daily

Sadhaka—spiritual practitioner striving for perfection

Sadhu—a genuinely spiritually advanced person

Sankirtan—the congregational chanting of the Lord's names

Sannyasi—a person who has officially renounced all connection with the material world to focus on spiritual pursuit. Equivalent to a Catholic Bishop and highly respected in spiritual society.

Satsanga—godly or saintly association or gathering;

Sattva-guna—the mode of goodness, one of the three qualitative modes of material nature; Maintenance is enacted by the influence of sattva-guna. In this state people are peaceful and contented, and are fit to enter heaven when they die.

Satya-yuga—the first of the four yugas or ages, and influenced predominantly by sattva-guna. During Satya-yuga the earth is like a heavenly planet; people are peaceful and strive for self-realization by the recommended process of yogic meditation. During this age people live for very long periods of time, upwards of 100,000 years.

Shaktyavesh avatar—a living being who is empowered (given shakti or potency) by the Lord for a particular function. Avatar means 'one who descends' or comes down to the earth from a higher place, heaven or the spiritual realms.

Shiva, Lord—one of the three principal deities of the material world. As the controller of the material influence of ignorance, tamo-guna, Lord Shiva is in charge of destruction.

Siddhanta—Philosophical conclusions of a spiritual line, as in Vaishnava siddhanta

Srimad Bhagavatam—The Beautiful Story of the Personality of Godhead; also known as the Bhagavat Purana; translated into English by Shrila Prabhupada it is the post-graduate study of spiritual life, and the main scripture of the Hare Krishna Movement.

Sudra—one of the four varnas or social orders; compared to the legs and feet of the social body. *Sudra*s are not generally too interested in spiritual life, and are happiest assisting society by carrying out manual labor.

Svamsa—refers to God. Technically one of two categories of living beings, svamsa is God, the counterpart, vibhinamsa, are all the living beings

Tamo-guna—the mode of ignorance; one of the three qualitative modes of material nature; under the influence of tamo-guna people act destructively; typified and inculcated by activities of intoxication, meat-eating, illicit sex and gambling. It is the predominant influence during this age of Kali.

Treta-yuga—the second of the four yugas or ages, and influenced by sattva-guna and raja-guna. Humans live for upwards of 10,000 years during Treta-yuga.

Ugra-karma—materialistic civilization and activities

Vaisya or Vaishya—one of the four varnas or social orders; compared to the belly of the social body. Vaishyas are the organizers of society for productive activity; they are producers such as farmers and business people. One of the three orders in Vedic society who are encouraged in spiritual pursuits.

Vaishnava—a theist who is a worshiper of Vishnu as the Supreme God; one who understands the purport of the Vedas; not limited to a social class, anyone may become a Vaishnava by agreeing to the conclusions of the Vedas and strictly following them.

Vedas—The system of eternal wisdom compiled by Shrila Vyasadeva, the literary incarnation of the Supreme Lord, for the gradual upliftment of all mankind from the state of bondage to the state of liberation. The word veda literally means "knowledge", and thus in a wider sense it refers to the whole body of Sanskrit religious literature that is in harmony with the philosophical conclusions found in the original four Vedic Samhitas and Upanishads. The message of the transcendence that has come down to this phenomenal world through the medium of sound is known as the Veda. Being the very words of the Lord Himself, the Vedas have existed from eternity. Lord Krishna originally revealed the Vedas to Brahma, the original living being in the realm of physical nature, and by him they were subsequently made available to others by means of disciplic succession.

Venu—a demonic king of yore killed by the sages because of his failure to rule according to religious principles.

Vibhinamsa—refers to the living beings such as humans, animals, etc. Technically one of two categories of living beings, svamsa is God, the counterpart, vibhinamsa, are all the living beings

Vishayee—a materialistic person

Vishnu—the deity in charge of sattva-guna, or the material mode of goodness. Vishnu is an expansion of the Supreme Lord Krishna, Who maintains the material world.

Vivasvan—the sun god

Vyasa or Vyasadeva—also Krishna Dvaipayana—a shaktavesa avatar (empowered incarnation) whose purpose was to make Vedic wisdom understandable for the people in *Kali-yuga*; he is considered to be the literary incarnation of God, and the greatest philosopher of ancient times. He divided the original Veda into four parts, and compiled the eighteen Puranas, the Vedanta-sūtra, the Mahabharata, and the Upanishads. He is still living in this world.

Yuga Dharma—the religion for the age, which changes in each of the great epochs of Satya, Dvapara, Treta and Kali yugas

Yaksas—a class of demonic beings who control the earth

Yuga—Literally, age, or grand division of time of the universe according to the Vedic conception; the Yugas are cyclical following each other as do spring, summer, fall and winter, in the order of Satya, Treta, Dvapara and Kali. A complete cycle is called a divya-yuga, and 1,000 divya-yugas constitutes Brahma's one twelve-hour day, or a kalpa.

Selected Bibliography

Antony Sutton, *Wall Sreet and the Bolshevik Revolution,* Clairview Books; Reprint 2012

Anudasa, Ragunatha, *Children of the Ashrama,* *w*ww.surrealist.org/gurukula/index.html, 2018

Arsa Prayoga – Preserving Shrila Prabhupada's Legacy

Atwill, J., *Caesar's Messiah: The Roman Conspiracy to Invent Jesus,* NLightning WorkZ, 3rd ed. 2011

Baigent, M. *The Dead Sea Scroll Deception,* Summit Press, NY 1991

Baigent, M., Leigh, R., Lincoln, H., *Holy Blood, Holy Grail,* 1983 Dell Publishing, NY

Berry, R., *Food for the Gods,* Pythagorean Publishers, NY 1998

Bhaktisiddhanta, Shrila, *Humble as a Blade of Grass,* The Harmonist,

Bhaktisiddhanta, Shrila, *Putana,* The Harmonist, Vol. 29, No. 7, January 1932

Bhaktisiddhanta, Shrila, *Shree Chaitanya in South India,* The Harmonist, Vol. XXIX, No. 11 May 1932

Bhaktivedanta Investigation Force, Judge for Yourself

Bhaktivedanta Swami, A. C., *Bhagavad-gita As It Is,* Bhaktivedanta Book Trust, 1972

Bhaktivedanta Swami, A. C., *Srimad Bhagavatam,* Bhaktivedanta Book Trust, 1972

Bloom, Harold, *The American Religion*

Bryant E. F., Ekstrand, M. L., The Hare Krishna Movement: the postcharismatic fate of a religious transplant, Columbia University Press, 2004

Chossudovsky, M., The Globalization of Poverty and the New World Order, Global Research Publishers, 2003

Christopher, A., *Pandora's Box,* Pandor's Box Pub., 2007

Das, Dhanesvara, Lessons in Spiritual Economics from the *Bhagavad-gita,* Understanding and Solving the Economic Problem, 2010, Amazon.com

Dasa, Achyutananda, *Blazing Sadhus,*

Dasa, Dhira Govinda 2004 Annual CPO Report

Dasa, Dhira Govinda Das, Report on the Bhaktivedanta Gurukula Village, 1999

Dasa, Dhira Govinda, A Festival of Red Flags

Dasa, Dhira Govinda, *Krishna, Israel, and the Druze – An Interreligious Odessey,* Torchlight Publishing, 2002

Dasa, Dhira Govinda, Report on the Status of the ISKCON Child Protection Office June 30,2004

Dasa, Krishna Kirti, A Brief Exploration of the History of ISKCON's Social and Ideological Conflicts and their Significance for ISKCON's Emerging Constitution

Dasa, Kundali, Our Mission Series, 2000, 2007

Dasa, Nityananda Dasa, Kill Guru, Become Guru, killgurubecomeguru.org

Dasa, Nityananda, Someone has Poisoned Me

Dasa, Shyamasundar, *Chasing Rhinos with the Swami,* 2016

Dasi, Visakha, Five Years, Eleven Months, Our Spiritual Journey Press, 2017

Deadwyler, Gabriel (Yudhishthira Das) Fifteen Years Later: A Critique of *GURUKULA* Personal Story II, The Hare Krishna movement : the postcharismatic fate of a religious transplant, 2004

Dinatarini D. D., Yamuma Devi, A Life of Devotion, Unalloyed Inc, 2014

Dupont-Sommer, A., *The Essene Writings From Qumran*

Dwyer, G., Cole, R. J., eds., ISKCON's Search for Self-Identity, The Hare Krishna Movement: Forty Years of Chant and Change, I.B.Tauris, 2007

Eisenman, R., *James the Just in the Habakkuk Pesher,* Grave Distractions, 2nd ed., 2013

Eisenman, Robert, James, Brother of Jesus, Viking Penguin, 1996

Eisenman, Robert, *Maccabbees, Zadokites, Christians and Qumran,*

Eisenman, Robert, *The Dead Sea Scrolls and the First Christians,* Element Books, 1996

Eisler, Robert *The Messiah Jesus and John the Baptist* London, Methuen 1976

Ferrier, J. T. *On Behalf of the Creatures,* The Order of the Cross, London, 1983

Filoramo, Giovanni *A History of Gnosticism,* Oxford, 1990

Gardner, L., *Bloodline of the Holy Grail,* Barnes and Noble, 2003

Goswami, Tamal Krishna, TKG's Diary, Pundits Press, 1998

Hock, D., Birth of the Chaordic Age, Berrett-Koehler Publishers, 1999

Hopkins, T. J., ISKCON's Search for Self-Identity, The Hare Krishna Movement: Forty Years of Chant and Change, Dwyer, G., Cole, R. J., eds. I.B.Tauris 2007

Howard, R. W., The Vanishing Land, Villard Books, 1985

Icke, David *The Biggest Secret,* Free download: http://ebookscart.com/the-biggest-secret-by-david-icke-pdf-download/

ISKCON GBC, Not That I am Poisoned, publication, 2001

Knapp, Stephen, *Proof of Vedic Culture's Global Existence*

Lieblich, J., Young Victims of Krishna Consciousness, LA Times, June 13,1999

Lutz, D. (Devavrata Dasa) *My Karma, My Fault*; ebook

Muster, N., Life as a Woman on Watseka Avenue: Personal Story I, The Hare Krishna Movement: the postcharismatic fate of a religious transplant, 2004

Mutwa, C., Icke, D., *The Reptilian Agenda,* DVD video

O'Brien, Cathy, *Trance Formation of America,* Reality Marketing Inc; 1995

Owens, L. S. *An Introduction to Gnosticism and the Nag Hammadi Library*

Pagels, Elaine, The Gnostic Gospels, Random House; 1st edition (1979

Picknett and Prince, *The Templar Revelation,* Touchstone, 1997

Radhakrishnan, Dr. S., *Pracya Mattu Paschatya Sanskriti*

Robertson, B. J., Holocracy, Holt and Company, 2015

Rochford, E., Child Abuse in the Hare Krishna Movement 1971-1986

Rochford, E.. Hare Krishna Transformed, NYU Press, 2007

Schoeps, Hans-Joachim *Jewish Christianity: Factional Disputes in the Early Church,* trans., D.R.A. Hare, Philadelphia: Fortress Press, 1969

Schoeps, Hans-Joachim, *Theologie,* (German) Verlag J.C.B. Mohr, Tubingen, 1949

Scrivener, Dr. F. H. *Introduction to the Criticism of the New Testament,* 1883, download from https://bibletranslation.ws/tag/scrivener/

Seldes, G., Great Thoughts That Have Shaped the World, Ballantine Books, 2011

Shaffer, B., *Calculated Chaos – Institutional Threats to Peace and Human Survival,* Alchemy Books, San Francisco, 1985

Sitchin, Z., *The Wars of Gods and Men,* Book 3, Harpercollins, Reprint 2008

Smith, H., *Why Religion Matters—The Fate of the Human Spirit in an*

Age of Disbelief, Hapercollins, 2001

Smith, M., *The Secret Gospel,* Dawn Horse Press; 3rd ed., 2005

Smith, Morton *Palestinan Parties and Politics That Shaped the Old Testament*

Solzhenitsyn, Aleksandr, The Gulag Archipelago, Vintage UK, 2002

Thompson, H. S., *Fear and Loathing in Las Vegas,* Flamingo, 1998

Van Buitenen, J. A. B., *Mahabharata*, translated and edited by, Univ. of Chicago Press 1973

Viola, L., ed., *The War Against the Peasantry, 1927–1930; The Tragedy of the Soviet Countryside*, Yale University Press

Williamson, G.A., *The Jewish War (trans. of Josephus' The Jewish War)*

Wolf, David, Child Abuse and the Hare Krishnas, The Hare Krishna Movement, The Postcharismatic Fate of a Religious Transplant, Columbia University Press, 2017

Wolf, David, **2004 CPO Annual Report**

Notes

Introduction
[1] Only the first video required. Parts 2 and 3 add nothing to the concept.

Chapter One – The Eternal Religion in First Century Palestine
[1] The four characteristics are from An Introduction to Gnosticism and the Nag Hammadi Library written by Lance S. Owens (http://gnosis.org/naghamm/nhlintro.html). These four characteristics are of-fered with this caveat: "The complexities of Gnosticism are legion, making any generalizations wisely suspect. While several systems for defining and catego-rizing Gnosticism have been proposed over the years, none has yet gained any general acceptance.

[2] Elaine Pagels, quoted in An Introduction to Gnosticism and the Nag Hammadi Library

[3] Harold Bloom, The American Religion, p. 49 as cited by Owens

[4] http://gnosis.org/naghamm/nhlintro.html

[5] Bhagavad-gita 5.16

[6] Giovanni Filoramo, A History of Gnosticism (Oxford, 1990), p. 5.

[7] The polemical works against gnosis can be found at: http://www.webcom.com/~gnosis/library/polem.htm

[8] A summary of the Gnostic worldview can be found at: http://www.webcom.com/~gnosis/gnintro.htm; Apocryphal texts can be found at: http://www.webcom.com/~gnosis/library/cac.htm.

[9] Maccabbees, Zadokites, Christians and Qumran, Robert Eisenman, from The Dead Sea Scrolls and the First Christians, p. 5.

[10] The Dead Sea Scroll Deception, by Baigent & Leigh, Summit Press, NY 1991, p. 199

[11] Pliny, Natural History, V, xv.

[12] Biblical Archeological Review, July/August 1989, p. 18

[13] Maccabbees, Zadokites, Christians and Qumran, pgs. 6 & 108, fr. The Dead Sea Scroll Deception, p.172

[14] Epiphanius of Constantia, Adversus octoginta haereses, I, I, Haeres xx, from The Dead Sea Scroll Deception, p.172

15 The Dead Sea Scroll Deception, p. 173

16 Maccabbees, Zadokites, Christians and Qumran, p. 21-2, and footnote 30. See also Schoeps, p. 118, and his Theologie, p. 86

17 Eisenman, Robert, The Dead Sea Scrolls and the First Christians, p. xvii

18 Quoted by Dupont-Sommer, The Essene Writings From Qumran, p. 13

19 Glenn Allen Koch, "A Critical Investigation of Epiphanius's Knowledge of the Ebionites: A Translation and Critical Discussion of 'Panarion' 30," Unpublished Dissertation, University of Pennsylvania, 1976, p. 198. Food for the Gods, Rynn Berry, Pythagorean Publishers, NY 1998, p. 193

20 Smith, Morton Palestinan Parties and Politics That Shaped the Old Testament (New York: Columhia Universtiy Press, 1971), p. 30.

21 Clement of Alexandria, "On Sacrifices," Book VII, cited in J. Todd Ferrier, On Behalf of the Creatures (London: The Order of the Cross, 1983), p. 19.

22 Schoeps, Hans-Joachim Jewish Christianity: Factional Disputes in the Early Church, trans., D.R.A. Hare (Philadelphia: Fortress Press, 1969). p. 14.

23 Schoeps, p. 16

24 Schoeps p. 115

25 Schoeps p. 103-4

26 Schoeps, p. 105

27 Schoeps, p. 23

28 Schoeps, p. 99-100

29 Eisenman, James, p. 833;

30 Schoeps p. 111. This was especially the case concerning oral traditions in a mostly illiterate world.

31 Schoeps, p. 85

32 Schoeps, p. 93, 122

33 Schoeps, p. 64; this is identical to the Vaishnava perspective presented in the next Chapter.

34 Schoeps, p. 99

35 Schoeps, p. 8, 62

36 Stephen Knapp, Proof of Vedic Culture's Global Existence, p. 206

37 Robert Eisler The Messiah Jesus and John the Baptist (London, Methuen 1976), p. 427, from Holy Blood Holy Grail, p. 377

38 Knapp, Proof of Vedic Culture's Global Existence, pgs. 138-140

39 Knapp, Proof of Vedic Culture's Global Existence, pgs. 138-140

Chapter Two – Conquest of the Earth

[1] Mahabharata, translated and edited by J.A.B. van Buitenen, Univ. of Chicago Press 1973

[2] See Purport Srimad Bhagavatam 2.4.18 for a detailed description of the descendants of the *kshatriyas* who fled India who included: Greeks (Pulindas), Germans (Hunas), Arabs (Abhira), Turks (Yavanas).

[3] Purport Srimad Bhagavatam 7.3.13

[4] Lecture on Bhagavad-gita 9.11-14 New York, November 27, 1966

[5] Purport Srimad Bhagavatam 7.1.9

[6] Bhagavad-gita As It Is, Chapter16, texts 4, 9-15

[7] The Biggest Secret, David Icke, especially pgs. 29-40,

[8] The Wars of Gods and Men, Book 3, Zacharia Sitchin, p. 4

[9] The Wars of Gods and Men, Book 3, by Zacharia Sitchin, p. 5 descriptions tak-en from clay tablets,

[10] Srimad Bhagavatam, Purport 9.15.15

[11] Smith, Huston, Why Religion Matters—The Fate of the Human Spirit in an Age of Disbelief

[12] Vol. 29, No. 7, January 1932

Chapter Three – Jesus and James

[1] Eisenman, Robert, James Brother of Jesus, see for example: pgs. xviii, xxvi, 99, 143, 198-9. There are virtually dozens of such confusions with practically every personality of the New Testament. Eisenman's conclusion is that these are nei-ther accidental nor benign mistakes. In Schoeps see p. 38-9.

[2] Eisenman, James the Brother of Jesus, p. xxii

[3] Schoeps, Jewish Christianity p. 1-2

[4] Eisenman, James, p. xxiii

[5] Holy Blood, Holy Grail, p.324, Michael Baigent, Richard Leigh, Henry Lincoln, 1983 Dell Publishing, NY

[6] From the Dead Sea "War Scroll", Eisenman, James the Brother of Jesus, p. xxi, 417

[7] The Dead Sea Scroll Deception, p. 200

[8] For example, "Lord Jesus Christ, he is shaktyavesha-avatar" lecture on Srimad Bhagavatam 5.5.3 Vrindavana, October 25, 1976. There are others.

[9] Hom. 2.10, Schoeps, p. 88

[10] Schoeps, p. 76

[11] Srimad Bhagavatam 1.3.43

[12] Schoeps, p. 95, also p. 91: "Prophets who see falsehood and prophesy de-ceit" shall be excluded from the register of the house of Israel, in accordance with Ezekiel 13:9.

[13] Schoeps, p. 114

[14] Eisenman, James the Brother of Jesus, p. xvii

[15] Matthew 13.55

[16] Eisenman, James the Brother of Jesus, p. xviii

[17] Schoeps, p. 39

[18] Homilies (11.35) Schoeps, p. 56

[19] Eisenman, James, the Brother of Jesus, p. 258

[20] Ibid., p. 307, 310-13.

[21] Eisenman, James the Just in the Habakkuk Pesher, p. 112-3, MZCQ, p. 7, and elsewhere.

[22] Eisenman, James, p. xix

[23] Eusebius, The History of the Church, 2,23

[24] Eisenman, James, p. 963

[25] Eisenman, James, p. xxxi and xxxiii

Chapter Four – The Enemy, Liar, Sower of False Things

[1] Eisenman, James, the Brother of Jesus, p. 588-590

[2] Eisenman, James, the Brother of Jesus, p. 584-9; fr. Syriac version of Recogntions Ch. 1.

[3] James, p. 57, 586

[4] James, p. 590-591

[5] The Dead Sea Scroll Deception, p. 177

[6] Schoeps, p. 51. Kerygmata Petrou is a part of the Psuedo-Clementines, as is Recognitions (Rec.)

[7] Schoeps, p. 55-6

[8] Romans 16.11

[9] Eisenman, James, p. 46

[10] For more information regarding Saul/Paul's Herodian connections see Eisenman, James, p. 524-29; The Dead Sea Scrolls and the First Christians, p. 226-246.

[11] Recognitions 1.70-71; also Acts of the Apostles, Ch. 9

[12] The Dead Sea Scroll Deception, p. 180

[13] The Dead Sea Scroll Deception, p. 188

[14] Schoeps, p. 49

[15] Acts, 1:21-2

[16] Schoeps, p. 51-2

[17] Letter to Galatians, 1:15-6, see also Eisenman, James, p. 257

[18] Schoeps, p. 257

[19] Eisenman, James, p. xxxii

[20] Book of Habakkuk, 2.4

[21] The Habakkuk Commentary, VIII, (ii,4b). Vermes, p. 239

[22] Galatians, 3:28

[23] Eisenman, James, p. 284

[24] Eisenman, James, p. 734

[25] I Corinthians, 11:23-32

[26] I Corinthians, 11:29

[27] At the Fourth Lateran Council commenced by Innocent III

[28] Eisenman, James, p. 274

[29] Eisenman, James, p. 735

[30] See for example, James, p. 725-750

Chapter Five – Putanas, Scribes and Exegetes

[1] Eisenman, James, p. 5-6

[2] James, p. 7

[3] Referring to the Ebionites; see James, the end of the second chapter, item 13 and footnote xxxvii.

[4] Eisenman, James, p. 259

[5] Morton Smith, Secret Gospel, p. 14; and the next quote from p. 15-16

[6] This book was printed in the late 19th century (3rd ed. 1883) but remains a classic reference in print today.

[7] See Origen: Contra Celsus; this is a series of eight polemics directed against Celsus.

[8] See note 17.

[9] Schoeps, p. 12-3

[10] The Bible Library that I use for reference has 23 Bibles, 4 of which are in Latin or Greek. Of the 19 that I can read, twelve make statements to the effect of "three as one."

[11] Holy Blood, Holy Grail p. 362

[12] Food for the Gods, p. 212

[13] Picknett and Prince, The Templar Revelation p. 85 (New York: Touchstone, 1997),

[14] Quoted in: The Great Thoughts; compiled by George Seldes

[15] Lawrence Gardner, Bloodline of the Holy Grail P. 3

[16] The filmed scrolls had been donated to the library by Betty Bechtel who commissioned the filming in 1961; (Bechtel Corporation is a huge engineering firm (and some say Establishment front). The story of the release is recounted in the Postscript to The Dead Sea Scroll Deception, p. 223-5.

[17] The Dead Sea Scrolls and the First Christians, p. xv; JJHP is James the Just in the Habbakuk Pesher

[18] Schoeps p. 57

Chapter Six – Caesar's Messiah and the Creation of Christianity

[1] Josephus, Wars V, ix, 395-96

[2] Romans 13.1-7

[3] For a wonderful explanation of the Druze and how they connected with the modern day Vaishnavas please see Dhira Govinda Dasa's Krsna, Israel, and the Druze – An Interreligious Odessey

[4] Henry Halley, Halley's Bible Handbook

PART TWO

Chapter One - Rise of Sri Chaitanya's Sankirtan Movement

[1] May 3, 1976, in Honolulu

Chapter Two – Shrila Prabhupada – Social Reformer

[1] Spiritual Economics, Dhanesvara Das, 2010, pgs. 102-104

[2] The Vanishing Land, Robert West Howard, Villard Books, 1985

[3] The Gulag Archipelago, Aleksandr Solzhenitsyn; also Antony Sutton, Wall Sreet and the Bolshevik Revolution, and The War Against the Peasantry, 1927–1930 The Tragedy of the Soviet Countryside, edited by Lynne Viola, et. al., Yale University Press

[4] Reported in Cultural Survival Quarterly Magazine, 1989

[5] www.spiritual-economics.com; see especially 'Your Economic Education' un-der the link to 'Material Economics'

Chapter Three – Infiltration of ISKCON

[1] http://whatreallyhappened.com/RANCHO/POLITICS/COINTELPRO/COINTELPRO-FBI.docs.html

[2] http://www.icdc.com/~paulwolf/cointelpro/churchfinalreportIIIa.htm

[3] http://exiledonline.com/provocateur-porn-how-many-spooks-does-it-take-to-infiltrate-a-protest-movement/

[4] http://www.countercurrents.org/zeese150312.htm

[5] See: https://www.youtube.com/watch?v=5kovFsGvrYA; https://www.youtube.com/watch?v=5gnpCqsXE8g, etc.

[6] see https://praylikeprahlada.wordpress.com for more

Chapter Four – Who is a Devotee?

[1] Sajana Toshani 18.2.13-14 (1915)

[2] Shree Chaitanya in South India, Shrila Bhaktisiddhanta Sarasvati Thakur The Harmonist May 1932, Vol XXIX, No. 11

[3] Vaishnava Ninda, Sajjana Tosani, 2 January 2014

[4] Shrila Prabhupada Morning Walk -- July 9, 1975, Chicago

Chapter Five – What is ISKCON?

[1] Achyutananda Dasa Blazing Sadhus, p. 73

[2] Yamuma Devi, A Life of Devotion, by Dinatarini Devi Dasi, Unalloyed, Inc., Kin-dle Edition, Location 1210-1215

Chapter Six – Putting Out the Light of Truth

[1] All quotes from Ramesvara are from Arsa Prayoga – Preserving Shrila Prab-hupada's Legacy, p. 108-111

[2] http://bookchanges.com/why-did-bbt-made-radical-changes-to-page-1-of-caitanya-caritamrta/

³ http://namhatta.com/2013/03/29/what-happened-to-the-bbt/. See more at http://hansadutta.com

⁴ http://harekrsna.com/sun/editorials/01-09/editorials3820.htm

⁵ http://www.hansadutta.com/DOWNLOADS/BBTIvHK.pdf

⁶ http://www.hansadutta.com/DOWNLOADS/BBTIvHK-interr.pdf

⁷ From Jitarati Das To Basu Ghosh Das 14 May 2017. FFI see http://harekrsna.com/sun/editorials/12-09/editorials5481.htm

⁸ Arsha-Prayoga can be downloaded bookchanges.com and from our website: www.DivineOrDemoniac.com/iskcon

Chapter Seven – Destroying the Followers

¹ Srimad-Bhagavatam 2.9.8 purport

² The Hare Krishna Movement – The Postcharismatic Fate of a Religious Trans-plant, p. 315

³ Room Conversation, September 24, 1968, Seattle

⁴ Rochford, E.. Hare Krishna Transformed (New and Alternative Religions) (pp. 119-120). NYU Press reference. Kindle Edition.

⁵ Rochford, E.. Hare Krishna Transformed, p. 56. Kindle Edition.

⁶ Rochford, p. 55

⁷ Rochford, p. 118

⁸ Visakha Dasi, from her memoir Five Years, Eleven Months, end of Chapter 15 (no page numbers in the printed book)

⁹ Bryant and Ekstrand, P. 317

¹⁰ Letter to Ekayani - December 3, 1972

¹¹ Rochford, E. Hare Krishna Transformed, p. 120. Kindle Edition.

¹² Rochford, E.. Hare Krishna Transformed, p. 126-127.

¹³ Statements of Gadadhar Dasa, http://vaishnava-news-network.org/usa/US9811/US06-2464.html

¹⁴ Dhira Govinda, Child Abuse and the Hare Krishnas, Edwin F. Bryant and Maria L. Ekstrand, et. al. 2002, p. 330

¹⁵ See GBC Resolutions of 1990

¹⁶ http://krishnachildren.com/h-references.php

¹⁷ Dhira Govinda, Child Abuse and the Hare Krishnas, Edwin F. Bryant and Maria L. Ekstrand, et. al. 2002, p. 332

¹⁸ Dhira Govinda Das, Report on the Bhaktivedanta Gurukula Village, 1999

[19] Dhira Govinda Das, Report on the Bhaktivedanta Gurukula Village, 1999

[20] ISKCON Central Office of Child Protection, Official Decision on the case of Bhakti Vidya Purna Maharaja, 2000

[21] http://archive.li/Zrdog#selection-363.1037-363.1254

[22] Originally posted on Sampradaya Sun, archived at http://archive.li/Zrdog

[23] http://krishnachildren.com/h-references.php

[24] http://www.harekrsna.com/sun/editorials/07-09/editorials4847.htm

[25] http://www.harekrsna.com/sun/editorials/07-09/editorials4847.htm

[26] https://www.youtube.com/watch?v=UvlRAyM3p4Q

[27] http://harekrsna.com/sun/editorials/05-11/editorials7296.htm

Chapter Eight – How Far Would They Go?

[1] Someone Has Poisoned Me, Appendices 2 and 3, pgs. 295-342; see also on DivineOrDemonic.com

[2] Not That I am Poisoned, published by GBC, p. 318-319

[3] Killgurubecomeguru.org

[4] http://www.harekrsna.org/poison-cd.htm

[5] Judge for Yourself, pgs. 54-56

[6] Vipramukhya Swami, an ISKCON guru, left ISKCON to marry a non-devotee not long after this, giving up Krishna consciousness completely. He became the co-editor of the CHAKRA website

[7] This statement can be found in Shrila Prabhupada's Conversations Book, volume 36, page 46. It is also present in the Room Conversations of the Vedabase as of February 2019. Will it be removed in future edits?

[8] This statement can be found in Shrila Prabhupada's Conversations Book, volume 36, page 282 for November 3, 1977. It is recorded in "TKG's Diary" as an entry of November 4, 1977.

[9] http://www.iskcon-truth.com/poison/prabhupada-suicide.html; and on my website: DivineOrDemoniac.com

[10] This summary is from Nityananda's book Kill Guru, Become Guru

Chapter Ten – The Enemy Within

[1] See also for example, letters to: Satsvarupa, Sydney 10 April, 1972, Satsvarupa Tokyo 2 May, 1972

[2] Email from Lilasuka das, GBC Secretariat, Aug. 22 2005. http://www.harekrsna.com/sun/editorials/10-07/editorials2151.htm

[3] http://hdgoswami.com/essays/iskcons-gbc/

[4] 7.4.1.1; 7.4.1.1.1; 7.4.1.1.2; 7.4.1.1.3; 7.4.1.1.4; 7.4.1.2; 7.4.1.4.3, and 7.4.2

[5] Letter to Hansadutta – London 17 August, 1971

[6] Letter to Karandhara – Bombay 22 December, 1972

[7] Conversation with Professor Kotovsky Moscow 6-22-71

[8] Conversation with the Mayor of Evanston, IL 4-7-75

[9] Rochford, E.. Hare Krishna Transformed, pp. 163-164. NYU Press, Kindle Edi-tion

[10] Hridayananda Goswami, ISKCON's GBC, p. 64

[11] Conversation with the GBC - March 27, 1975, Mayapur

[12] Thomas J. Hopkins, "ISKCON's Search for Self-Identity," The Hare Krishna Movement: Forty Years of Chant and Change, Ed. Graham Dwyer, Richard J. Cole, (London: I.B. Taurus & Co. 2007) 186.

[13] A Brief Exploration of the History of ISKCON's Social and Ideological Conflicts and their Significance for ISKCON's Emerging Constitution, Krishna-kirti Das, 13 February 2008

[14] E. Rochford, Hare Krishna Transformed, p. 157-58

[15] Hare Krishna Transformed, E. Rochford, p. 159-160

PART THREE

Chapter One – Institutions and Their Influence on Our Lives

[1] Letter to: Madhavananda -- Los Angeles 1 January, 1974

[2] Srimad-Bhagavatam 1.2.8, purport

[3] This definition, and other aspects of the discussion of institution is from But-ler Shaffer's Calculated Chaos – Institutional Threats to Peace and Human Sur-vival, Alchemy Books, San Francisco, 1985

[4] Schaffer, Calculate Chaos, p. 11

[5] Cc. Madhya 13.80, puport

[6] Lecture Nectar of Devotion -- October 18, 1972, Vrindavana

Chapter 2 – Shrila Prabhupada's Organizational Method

[1] My personal favorite among the many that I have read is Shyamasundar Prabhu's Chasing Rhinos with the Swami. While reading you feel as if you are part of the adventure over three continents. Very highly recommended!

[2] Birth of the Chaordic Age, Dee Hock, 1999, Berrett-Koehler Publishers, p. 123, 206,207

[3] Birth of the Chaordic Age, Devotee Hock, Berret-Koehler Pulbishers, 1999, p. 24, 38

[4] However, the effectiveness of the internet is losing its effectiveness by companies limiting information due to political pressures.

[5] SB 10.2.31 (emphasis added); see also Adi 7.38, purport, Bg 3.21 Purport; second quote letter to Locanananda 8 December, 1971

[6] http://events.iskcon.org/event/iskcon-dallas-iskcon-disciples-course-jul-2018/ Course given in Dallas, July 2018

Chapter Three – Establishing a Non-institutional ISKCON

[1] Shree Chaitanya in South India, The Harmonist, Vol. XXIX, No. 11 May 1932

[2] See www.sociocracyconsulting.com and www.holocracy.org for more information. See also:

https://steamcdn-a.akamaihd.net/apps/valve/Valve_NewEmployeeHandbook.pdf;

http://blogs.valvesoftware.com/economics/why-valve-or-what-do-we-need-corporations-for-and-how-does-valves-management-structure-fit-into-todays-corporate-world/;

http://www.42projects.org/docs/FreedomBasedManagement.pdf;

do your own search on the expression "spontaneous order"

Conclusion – Start the Hare Krishna Movement Again!

[1] https://d1tn3vj7xz9fdh.cloudfront.net/s3fs-public/file_attachments/bp-economy-for-99-percent-160117-en.pdf

[2] Examples of these can be found in my book Lessons in Spiritual Economics from the Bhagavad-gita. A very good example of sattvic culture can be found in the book and video The Economics of Happiness by Helena Norberg Hodge.

Printed in Great Britain
by Amazon

41247335R00279